Rituals
and
Ceremonies
in
Popular
Culture

Rituals
and
Ceremonies
in
Popular
Culture

**Edited by
Ray B. Browne**

Bowling Green University Popular Press
Bowling Green, Ohio 43403

CONTENTS

Ritual One

Ray B. Browne

American rituals and ceremonies were pretty well set from the beginning of this country because from the earliest stages they reflected the attitudes and filled the needs of society as it developed. To a large extent these rituals were of course inherited from the English, but they were modified and strengthened—or weakened— as various peoples from other countries brought their own to mingle and mix with the dominant ones.

Rituals and ceremonies are codifications and statements of attitudes. Ideas create rituals and rituals spawn ideas. They are codes of and methods for behavior. Rituals are to ceremonies what myths are to mythology, that is ritualism is the mystique that draws forth from deep in the psychology and sociology of a people certain attitudes and potential actions, codifies and forms them and then imposes them on the people in the form of approved forms of behavior with certain mystical (sometimes religious) overtones which tend to make the actions all the more acceptable.

At first deeply based in and strengthened by the religious and quasi-religious attitudes, rituals and ceremonies in America have gradually changed through the years, as America, for various reasons, has changed its lifestyle in many ways and become more secularized. But despite the fact that some of the rituals have lost their base in religion and mysticism (a large number still have these roots) and become what Erik Eriksen in perhaps too fine a distinction calls ritualism because they are empty and meaningless rituals, and although rituals have become modified in intensity and perhaps in the number of true believers, they have perhaps not become any less permeating and influential on individuals and society in general. Rituals stunted and inhibited in one place will surface in other places and in other ways since apparently they are

1

necessary to motivate conscious and unconscious actions of individuals.

In today's increasingly secular society rituals and ceremonies are still important, though in many ways changed from their antecedents as American society's needs and attitudes toward its past have changed. Some of the changes have been evolutionary, some have been revolutionary, some have been "progressive," and because they reflect rather closely a nation's heartbeat and bloodstream, some have undoubtedly become reactionary. These changes have been most obvious since the nineteen sixties, a time of general ferment and change in American society.

Few rituals are so responsive to and revealing of the American nation as transportation. In the big land of America it has always been assumed that people needed transportation and would have it. In the last 40 years the ritual has been to buy a domestic automobile, drive to a gas station or garage when necessary and cover physical distance as one desired. Certain rituals connected with that of vacation were regularized and constant. One got the vehicle ready, selected the spot and the route going and returning, then fulfilled the other requisite rituals.

There rites have now been dramatically changed. America's love affair with the automobile and recreation vehicle if not over is remarkably different. Because of energy shortages and inflation, the average American buys a small (often foreign) car, chooses a different vacation schedule and a different ritual of rationalization and justification for his changed lifestyle.

Another aspect of American culture closely tied in with the automobile has been the shopping mall. Built to tie in with ever-sprawling suburbia the shopping mall has altered the American's shopping habits entirely. Through the years the American has changed from buying an item or two at the general or neighborhood store to purchasing many items at the supermarket, to shopping at the mall. In fact the mall became such a shopper's paradise, a kind of public shrine, that it was no longer used merely for shopping. Instead, the ritual was to visit the mall on an evening or a Sunday afternoon just to see and to be seen, to rendezvous with old friends whom frequently one saw only on these occasions, to "spend a night out." Inflation and energy shortages have caused a drastic alteration in this ritual, and in fact those aspects of life, along with others, have caused a virtual reversal in the concept of the mall in city life.

In the secularization of America many changes in religion and religiosity have come about with resulting changes in rituals and rites. Apparently steadily moving from a religious nation,

Americans have constantly altered and modified their forms of religious practices, at times almost abandoning them. Always, however, the old forms have apparently remained close to the surface. In times of national frustration, anxiety and incertitude, people have found the old forms again. Beginning in the sixties and continuing to the beginning of the eighties various old rituals are resurfacing in the form of great interest in the occult and associated areas and in conventional evangelical religious leaders and movements. Not only are the conventional religious leaders like Billy Graham enjoying a continued success, but rarer individuals like Oral Roberts who has such a following that he can reveal to them that God has told him his soul will be lost if he does not raise $40 million to finish an unneeded medical wing of Oral Roberts University in Tulsa, Oklahoma. More unorthodox religious cults of all kinds and size and purposes, from the broadbased Moonies, say, to strange and paranoid cults whose philosophies and rituals keep them small and obscure pepper the land.

There has been of course a sexual revolt in general but one area in which there has been nothing short of a revolution with shockwaves that are still shaking society is in woman's role in society and the rituals attendant in that role and those designed to keep woman in her conventional role or to free her from it. For over three hundred years in America, women, trapped by the biology of their bodies and forced to preserve a way of life through every ritual known to men from religion, motherhood, patriotism, fashion, preservation of "the good things in life," have in general accepted their role and acted out their part of the ritual. With the general societal uprising of the sixties, however, women began to shake themselves like a sleeping giant and come alive, demanding different roles and rituals.

The battle has not been easy, and is surely far from won. Men have continued to use the old ritualistic arguments—of biology, of "natual" inferiority, that being on the pedestal is better than being in the gutter with men, that it is better to be a saint than a mere human being. But many women have recognized the argument that although they are called the Virgin Mary they really are looked upon as Eve the simpleminded seductress, and are felt to be more emotional, more intuitive, less intellectual and reasonable than men, are being held in and by the rituals of their enslavement.

Many media in popular culture have been the grounds where the battle between men and women for the liberation of the latter has raged. In popular song it has been particularly noticeable. Among the thousands of songs sung by the people through the years, almost all have placed women in emotional, passive roles, as homebuilders, bodies to be loved, inspirations to but tools of men. The stereotype has been almost unbroken. One of the early and clearest examples of this stereotype was the song "Paper Doll," in which a portion of the lyrics talk about the singer wanting to "buy a paper doll" who will be the conventional woman, at home at the end of the day when the man comes home from "masculine" activity "waiting" for him. The other extreme of this attitude—revealing the degree to which that particular ritual in female behavior is unacceptable—is Helen Reddy's *I Am Woman.* She "roars" "in numbers too large to ignore" that "No one's going to keep [her] down again." She is "strong," and "invincible." Such a statement involves rituals far different from those of the "paper doll."

The oldest and a very powerful medium in popular culture for the liberation of women has been of course language. A restructuring of grammar and parts of speech has ensued as women have found that even language through the years has been purposefully sexist.

In print, magazines have fought the rituals battle thousands of times over. Many magazines like *Ladies Home Journal, Red Book* and *Saturday Evening Post,* and hundreds more, have emphasized the old role of women, and have been consoling and useful to women who believed in such values. To a different kind of woman such magazines were anathema.

They turned to other magazines, like *MS, New Woman,* and SELF which have examined such attitudes and modes of behavior and condemned them. Insisting that conventional modes of behavior only perpetuate sexism and bondage these new magazines insist that certain reasonably unimportant biological differences aside, life should be the same for both men and women, that men and women can face and overcome the same kinds of challenges with approximately the same degree of success, should be allowed to and that there should be no artificial barriers and restrictions placed on either sex. Practice seems to be demonstrating this way of seeing things—especially in politics, sports of all kinds, intellecutal and physical activities, as women slowly but surely get into all kinds of activities including the NASA space program.

In popular fiction the battle has raged also. Erica Jong's *Fear of Flying* (1972) demonstrated that women have strong sexual feelings, that they can express these feelings, and that they can effectively state them. There has been a flood of such books since.

In two areas of fiction, the largely formulaic and stereotypical detective and western fiction, the changes have not been so dramatic but they have been remarkable, especially in the so-called hard-boiled school, in which writers have traditionally used women as sex objects and whipping girls. John D. MacDonald, one of the leading authors in this school, in the first 17 McGee novels has through the years had his ace detective, Travis McGee, treat women with real respect. Of some 130 girls and women who have appeared in his novels, all are treated with compassion and sympathy. Although getting the proper woman requires either dissembling or "accepting the involvement, the emotional responsibility, the permanence she must by nature create," as he says in *The Deep BLUE GOOD-BY*, "a woman who does not guard and treasure herself cannot be worth much to anyone else"; "only a woman of pride, complexity, and emotional tension is worth the act of love," he has McGee say.[1] Ross Macdonald, another hard-boiled writer of a somewhat different nature, insists that women have the same rights and obligations in life as men have.

Western fiction, because of the narrowness of its vision and subject matter treating the opening of the west, often has treated women as angels (school marms) or chattel. In the hands of recent authors, however, especially Louis L'Amour, who has spent a lifetime learning about the west and is determined to tell the story of the west as it actually was, women are receiving a more realistic treatment, with all the rites and rituals associated with reality. According to Michael Marsden, perhaps the leading authority on L'Amour, "The ideal L'Amour heroine is expected to possess certain qualities that make her a good woman/wife and a man should seek a woman who will walk beside him; walk with him, not behind him. A good woman/wife is one who can build a home in partnership with her man."[2]

One area in fiction that has been disappointing to women in changing the rituals of their existence has been science fiction. This genre is presumably the most imaginative, the most exploratory, the freest in ideas, the most nearly utopian of all forms of literature. Presumably therefore both "liberated" men and visionary women could use this medium to create all kinds of better or perfect worlds in which men and women could form the "perfect" society. Such, however, has not been the case. Science fiction historically has been a man's form of expression, surveying a man's world filled with dominating men and machismo, making the whole genre somewhat susceptible to the accusation that they were only space operas, filled with highlife cowboys, a genre, paradoxically, less flexible and unsexist than either detective fiction or western fiction. Even the women who read the stories, and there were many, seemed to accept their role and ritual as men decreed them. The last few years have "seen a mini-boom of feminist utopias," which are "concerned with its grossest and simplest forms of injustice."[3] In the latest science fiction a handful of men and few women have wanted to break the mold, for example, Monique Wittig's *Les Guerillieres* (1971), Suzy McKee Charnas' *Motherlines* (1979), Ursula Le Guin's *The Dispossessed* (1974), Joanna Russ' *The Female Man* (1975), Samuel Delany's *Triton* (1976), Marion Zimmer Bradley's *The Shattered Chain* (1976), Marge Piercy's *Woman on the Edge of Time* (1976), Sally Gearhart's *The Wanderground: Stories of the Hill Women* (1976) and a few others.

An important aspect of women's roles and rituals has always been clothes fashions. The rituals associated with selecting, wearing, putting on the proper facial and body make-up to go with the clothes, fulfilling the role rituals that automatically go with the clothes have been staggering. As has long since been recognized by women, although women might in fact have dressed for other women, men have used fashion to keep women in bondage, in their place, to keep them sexually "secure," and to keep them domesticated. These rituals have been broken since the sixties when the democratization of fashions began the shift from the silk to the synthetic. In a revolution that can only be called the jeaning of America (and the world) women have broken the rituals of being clothes horses, have insisted that they dress their bodies as they please, and have made the jean, perhaps the most profoundly democratizing item of clothes of all time, the symbol of this newfound freedom and the clothes in which to exercise the ritual of this freedom.

Two other media—first the movie and then television—have perhaps had even profounder influences on altering styles and rituals than has the printed word. Movies not only developed and spread stereotypes, but through wilful or necessary selection of actors and actresses could provide or keep hidden heroes and heroines to provide role models to break or inspire the following of rituals. Television because of its omnipresence is obviously much more powerful. Like the movies, television has tended to stereotype women—especially in commercials—as beautiful brainless housewives, whose only purpose in life is to greet their husbands in the evening with sinks that are unstopped, bodies with no hemorrhoids and facecream so soft that even the husband won't know his wife is wearing it. In television, however, as in movies, sometimes the obvious is more apparent than real. Not all women on television are ninnies, and not all men, though they may look masculine, are smart. Many of them are ninnies also.

The full extent to which women will immediately change their rituals is not clear, though the long range success cannot be in any doubt. The strongest political instrument now working is the Equal

Rights Amendment. In this women had their female Thomas Jeffersons write their Declaration of Independence, but they have not had their female Tom Paine effect its success. Roles and supporting rituals change slowly, especially in politics because bureaucracies tend to inhibit all motion. Rightly or wrongly politicans believe that more women do not want a new role than do. Obviously a large number of women *are* pleased with their roles and rituals in life. But crusading women have used many ploys to effect what they think is their right, although they have not resorted to that heaviest of all "political" weapons, long ago tried by the Greeks in classical times, denying man's first or second most important ritual, the sexual, with women literally going on a sitdown strike. Extreme causes require extreme measures.

Another respect of changing American rituals has to do with the new concept of what America and an American are. This changing concept is loaded with possibilities or compulsions for change, and probably many of them will shake the nation.

Over the past two decades in the United States there has developed a widespread acceptance of cultural "pluralism" as a philosophic approach to American life, especially in research and scholarship. "Pluralism" is apparently a reversal of the age-old concept of the "melting-pot" as the ideal goal in American culture. Pluralism suggests that the concept of the "melting-pot" was misleading, unfortunate, unreachable and perhaps not even desirable, for its goal was to break down the indivdiual differences existing among the various kinds of people who have come to this country in order to make them uniformly "American." After two or three centuries of trying to reach this goal, the notion now is that melting all people down into a single type of "American," instead of driving toward a goal of unity in diversity tends rather to make everyone a carbon copy of others, to force all people into stereotypes, to deny their differences, to inhibit individual and community growth and through this inhibition to stunt the full desired development of America; in fact, according to this line of reasoning, the "melting-pot" concept might well be culturally un-American.

Instead, pluralism states that differences among Americans are to be respected and appreciated for what they contribute to the nation as a whole. Rather than a "melting-pot" pluralists advocate a "Brunswick Stew" emphasis, which wilfully prevents the undesirable notion of cooking all differences down into a past of indistinguishability labeled "Made in America."

In past studies the ideas of regional and ethnic differences have been subordinated to the national purpose in most studies. In John William Ward's *Andrew Jackson: Symbol for an Age,* for example, there is virtually no treatment of the subject as a regional character as opposed to a national figure. Other studies, for example Louis B. Wright's *The Cultural Life of the American Colonies* and *Culture on the Moving Frontier,* have not lived up to their full potential because of too-narrow definitions of culture.

The new concepts of pluralism give new approaches to culture several thrusts. Two—regionalism and ethnicity—are of paramount importance. Some effort should be made to define the terms.

Regionalism as a concept is perhaps not determined completely, but in general it has to do with land and people, with the various geographical areas of the United States (large and small) and the way of life of the people who live in these various regions, the forces acting on them and subsequently the forces emanating from them. A region can stretch to comprehend such a large geographical area as the South, the Southwest, the Great Plains, or a smaller area, depending on criteria. In general, more regionalists and folklorist/regionalists tend to believe that regionalism should work on a series of concentric circles, radiating from a core out but finally reaching national comprehensiveness. In other words to be effective, regionalism should be comparative or generic. It should not be provincial or parochial except possibly as a starting point.

Ethnicity is another aspect of the current interest in pluralism. It may or may not parallel geographical boundaries or areas. Ethnicity concentrates on ethnic groups—large or small—and their characteristics, their differences and their uniqueness. In other words, studies in ethnicity are interested in what distinguishes a group or racial culture. For example ethnic studies is interested in what makes Chicanos different from other Americans, in the aspects of their lives which are admirable and should be preserved (and theoretcially at least in those aspects which are not admirable and should not be preserved), the impact of general American culture on these qualities of life and the impact of Chicano qualities of life on the dominant American culture. Ethnic studies covers all "ethnic groups" from American Indians to Cubans just off the boats in Florida. Such studies overlap regionalism in certain areas, presumably, in such areas as what does it mean to be a Southerner, or a Mid-Westerner.

Regionalism in its broadest sense turns also on the question of rurality and urbanness. Ethnicity might turn on the question of "nativism" and "foreignness."

Regionalism and ethnicity are both prongs of a driving force in American research and scholarship which have to do with a new interest in the democratic institutions, with concern for everyday people and living, with all aspects of common and mass culture as opposed to elite and exclusive culture. Such concern was undoubtedly the inevitable consequence of widespread education, with shifts in financial security and with the breakdown of all aspects of elite culture.

In general this turn from elite culture is to popular culture. Popular culture is a much larger concept than either regionalism or ethnicity, and tends to include them both. It includes them because the main thrust of popular culture studies is all aspects of a nation's culture. Though much of popular culture studies is concerned with the mass media, though not necessarily the electronic, in general, these scholars are as interested in the popular culture of regions and ethnic groups as in the culture of the nation as a whole. The study of these overridingly important aspects of society are fundamental in understanding a democracy.

Because these concepts of the study of culture are parallel and complementary, as they interface they create new concepts and areas for research and study. Various questons arise. For example,was Crevecoeur too hasty in asserting in his *Letters of an American Farmer* (1780) that simply being in America made a new kind of person different from those in all other countries, and this new person was commendable? Were Frederick Jackson Turner and millions of others wrong in thinking that the American frontier, simply by being there, created a different kind of person out of foreigners and Americans who faced it? Have we all for three hundred years been living and dreaming the impossible dream that it was reasonable to believe that we could take a new land and create in it and by it a new people who will at least work toward the goal of a better people than we have known in the past? Must our old dreams be discarded? Or can they be more completely realized by feeding in and recognizing new ingredients?

Or is it merely a matter of emphasis and labeling? Is the proper way to reach the dream of America the pluralistic rather than the single approach? Is the dream the same but the means of achieving it different? Obviously there are powerful forces at work from both angles.

There are powerful and overriding forces pushing the concept of oneness in America. Some are ideological, some spring from vested interests. Many people insist that it is better to forget the past, and to become "American," to downplay one's ethnic heritage and to rise above one's regional and ethnic origins. To become, in other words, mainstream America. Our language tends to be flattened to the category known as great American, our means of communcation, our fashions, our means of entertainment, most aspects of our culture tell us that we are all finally American. Regionalists and ethnicists, however, tend to insist that we are something else first and American second, or that being Americans does not, should not, downplay that we all are and ought to insist on being hyphenated-Americans; strangely, the old bugbear of the nineteenth and early twentieth century—the hyphenated-American-is now becoming a point of pride, a part of our culture that is to be courted and exploited rather than hidden and forgotten.

The interface of these thrusts opens new areas of research and scholarship which need to be explored because of their inherent value in contributing to our understanding of what precisely it is to be an American in the last quarter of this century. For example there is need for immediate study of the impact of the influx of Cubans, Haitians and other immigrants from Latin America and Asia into the U.S., the impact of their religion, their icons, their fierce nationalism, and their concepts upon America. In a longer range we need more research into the impact of Asiatic immigrants and Americans and Blacks who have migrated to urban areas and the impact of the urban areas on these people, and especially the reverse migration of Blacks to the South, from which they have been fleeing for the last fifty years. Regionally we need to understand why with the rise of the New South there has also been an alarming rebirth of interest in racist fiction such as Onstott's *Mandingo,* (1957), and its many followers written by a whole stable of authors, and what this new thrust portends. With the rise of interest in regional and ethnic museums, as distinguished from regional popular culture collections, we need to understand the differences; in Europe these types overlap; in America do they overlap or conflict, and how can each be served more effectively? These concerns though ethnic and regional in one way are of national importance also.

In another area television touches the lives and interests of us all. Although some people insist that McLuhan's "global village" concept was too grandiose in the first place, television still represents the one medium which can demonstrate and vivify our concept of the one nation indivisible. But others insist that television will destroy the sense of community and family in this country, because it is demonstrable that television tends to isolate individuals as individuals, to separate them from the community and the family, and that, among contemporary television viewers fewer and fewer people are getting married or remarried once they for one reason or another no longer have spouses. The real question is, will the new emphasis on regionalism and ethnicity correct and reverse television's pull, and bring back the sense of ethnicity and regionalism and community which it orginally tended to push out? Another important question: Is television creating a revolution in ethnic groups in this country, as movies and television have tended to do worldwide? In other words, is the new muscle being evidenced by ethnic and regional groups the direct, though perhaps unintended, result of television? These and many other questions need to be confronted and researched.

Another important ritual of American society has been sports of all kinds. Since they threw over the cloud of Puritanism and learned to play, Americans have tended increasingly to be sports lovers. At first sports were mainly participatory—sandlot baseball, school lot football, pond skating in the winter, sidewalk roller skating, bicycling. But in the last twenty years the nature of the ritual has changed from the participatory to the spectator. With the change in the nature of American sports there have come profound changes in attitudes and rituals. Americans are now more inclined to sit in the stands or before the television tube and watch high-priced professionals exercise themselves in golf, baseball, football and soccer (etc.) than to participate. The change in the rituals is obvious. Instead of participating in the rituals of the games, spectators have far more passive ones—such as drinking beer, popping popcorn at home, driving to and from the stadium. Such passive behavior has called forth from the moralists in society certain ritualistic reactions which cry not only shame but also destruction upon a society that is passive instead of active in sports. But a few erroneous conclusions about the function of participation and observation can start a tradition of judgmental rituals which feed upon themselves and are apparently utterly incorrect.[4]

There are numerous other rituals in America everyday that are of the greatest interest and importance; eating (both in elite restaurants and fast food restaurants), cleaning the house, tending the yard, editing a book, etc., etc.,

So the role of rituals in American society is obviously of profound importance. As such rituals should—must—be the object of study of many sets of eyes. For too long a time the study of rituals and ritualism has been left in the hands of those "specialists" who have tended to make it their province. Such people are anthropologists, regionalists, perhaps archaeologists, art historians and the like. They often have been interested in rituals mainly as they applied to distant and exotic lands and peoples, often the more distant, exotic, and relatively unimportant the better— preferably among small groups of primitive peoples in faraway lands. Presumably the study of such peoples and their rituals would have something to say to us in our present-day technological society. But frequently no connection was possible or was attempted. With motivations that in the deepest sense are highly suspect (which probably included chauvinism and racism of the most flagrant sort) anthropologists and other specialists charted exotic practices among primitive peoples (treatment of women, religious rites, hunting preparations and celebrations, etc.) and ended with nothing to say. An excellent example is the recent series on Public Broadcasting Service named *Odyssey* which, although supported by the National Endowment for the Humanities and although beginning with an excellent opener which promised to try to show some relevance, the series really got no further than becoming animated *National Geographic* pictures which had to suffice into themselves.

All well trained and searching eyes turned on rituals and ceremonies need to lead toward a synthesis of sorts. Cultural geographers, for example, are studying the rise and spread of various aspects of culture: music, age groups, art objects, architecture, housing and burial patterns. Contemporary archaeologists and above-ground archaeologists are working with various aspects of artifacts all around us. Oral, urban and old-age anthropologists are studying various patterns of behavior in contemporary rural and urban areas. Folklorists are seeking out the "folk" element in our society. The conclusions reached by these hardy individuals are useful. But the degree to which they abide by their methodologies is the degree to which they probably fail to be inter-methodological or multi-methodological and interdisciplinary, and that is the degree to which their conclusions fall short of the desirable. The popular culture worker is the type which can cross all these barriers, use all the methods, and come up with conclusions that are more valid than the sum of all the parts.

Present day rituals are the ones we must deal in. The others may have historical, antiquarian or anthropological interest but less importance than those *around* us, *of* us. *Our* rituals are numerous, complex, fluid, important. We need to begin with them and work out, as our interests continue, into the other dimensions.

*   *   *

Beginning with present day rituals and working out from them into all kinds of ramifications is precisely what the essays in this book do. They are necessarily samples, as no one book could possibly cover all possible manifestations of rituals in contemporary society. But these essays reveal the richness of the subject and the necessity as well as the rewards in the study of the subject.

They are necessarily samples as no single book could cover them all. But they indicate the richness of the subject in contemporary popular culture and the necessity as well as the rewards for studying them.

In the first essay, "The Contemporary Ritual Milieu," the first of four theoretical studies, Frederick Bird attempts to identify the major characteristisc and functions of ritual codes and, following the line of reasoning of Erik Erikson, to distinguish between live rituals and dead ritualisms. He argues that ritual forms often speak to and for situations of intense and often conflicting emotions and that contemporary Americans, since they must have them, invent and discard rituals as need arises.

To a certain extent this thesis is carried on and illustrated in F.R. Westley's paper, "Purification and Healing Rituals in New Religious Movements." Westley believes that healing and purification rituals represent different and partial solutions to the same social and cultural problem and she tests her theory on a variety of new religious movements.

Bastien and Bromley, in their essay "Metaphor in the Rituals of Restorative and Transformative Groups," have as an assumption that although ritual and ceremony have declined through the years in social importance new rituals are constantly being created because ritual and ceremony are "vital to human societies," and as metaphors "come alive during rituals." These contentions they demonstrate.

On a somewhat different tack, Mann's essay, "Architecture as the Stage for the Enactment of Ritual," could be abstracted in his own words as "Ritual has been described by many anthropologists as a symbolic transformation of beliefs, ideas, myths, ethics and experiences. It is a form of communication which explicitly or implicitly transfers cultural patterns from one person to another or from one group to another. Formal ritual fixes the connection between actions and their meaning while informal ritual reflects changing values and beliefs. Both go hand in hand in a dynamic culture. Architecture is the stage for the enactment of both formal and informal ritual since ritual requires space and artifact for their commemoration. Traditional architecture concretizes formal ritual while popular architecture acts as a window to the future."

In "The Tnevnoc Cult," the beginning of various essays on particular kinds of rituals and ceremonies, Bromley and Shupe play a game of describing a well-known cult under a different name and demonstrating that harsh and violent reactions to strange and exotic cults is not new but probably is unnecessary, not only because they are probably not as dangerous as they seem but because it is the newness and exoticness which make them frightening.

The power of Bromley and Shupe's thesis is demonstrated in the essay by David G. Orr, "Roman Domestic Religion: The Archaeology of Roman Popular Art,"[5] which traces the use of ritual in the everyday kitchen life of ancient Romans. One of Orr's points is that "Roman household worship, as exemplified by these shrines became the vehicle used by Christianity to penetrate into the Mediterranean home.... As Christianity spread throughout Europe, the house cult, now duly converted, went with it.... The needs so wondruously identified by Roman household rituals never have been displaced by the violent patterns of western history."

Bromley and Shupe's thesis is perhaps dramatically illustrated in the essay by James R. Curtis, "Miami's Little Havana: Yard Shrines, Cult Religion and Landscape," which describes contemporary Catholic shrines in the Cuban district of Miami, Florida, and, far more portentous, the activities of the syncretic Afro-Christian cult religion called *Santeria.* As Curtis describes it, "Like other syncretic Afro-Christian folk religions, *Santeria* combines an elaborate ensemble of ritual, magical, medical and theological beliefs to form a total magico-religious word view," which is strengthened and articulated in a highly elaborate and effective ceremony and ritual. Another caution about too violent a reaction is voiced by Michael Marsden in his "Television Viewing as Ritual," in which, taking as a point of non-argument the omnipresence of television he argues that people do not watch television programs, they watch television, as ritual. It is precisely this omnipresence which gives television its awesome power.

Nobody could possibly argue with David Q. Voight in his essay "American Rituals" that sports presents a pervasive and dynamic presence of ritual in American life. Sixty million bowlers use every kind of rite in trying to achieve suitable averages; American football presents a popular tribalizing ritual; and baseball is, in his eyes "the centerpiece of...sporting rituals."

In a different kind of "sport" altogether, the famous scholar of history in art, Alan Gowans, discusses the rituals of pornography. In "Ritual Illustration Functioning as Substitute Imagery: Pornography," Gowans states that "There is a kind of 'static illustration' which essentially functions as didactic substitute imagery.... But converseley there is a kind of substitute imagery which essentially functions as ritual illustration: pornography. Two basic kinds of pornographic illustrations are identifiable: the same figure in a variety of poses going through some action; and illustrations of two or more figures in sexual activity."[5]

Touching on the rich possibilities of studying the various forms of Black entertainment, David N. Lyon in his essay, "The Minstrel Show as Ritual," feels that "this ritual drew its power from the fact that survivals of secular African music appeared arcane and threatening to whites, and the creation of surrogate black music was an imperative element in its efficacy." Thus, as he reads it, black minstrel shows answered "deep psychological and sociological needs" of whites, serving as therapy to a general society.

On a somewhat lighter note in a different kind of entertainment, George Test demonstrates how the American roast, an important kind of entertainment in the democratizing of America, was used to remind the famous and powerful through humor at their expense that they are only human; in this way the American roast is akin to the Roman Saturnalia, the medieval Feast of Fools, and to various other such exercises around the world.

In an altogether different kind of theater, Donald J. Mrozek, in "The Cult and Ritual of Toughness in Cold War America" demonstrates that during the Cold War leaders in government and in the athletic community used sport and physical combat programs in increasingly ritualized forms to generate a "tough," "Combative" and winning attitude. Believing that the results more than justified the means, these leaders came to see actual physical experience as the best and perhaps only teacher; and they showed care in using painful, stressful and even torturous action to create values that they deemed socially beneficial.

As evidence of some of these actions in later theaters of war, William Kelly in his article *Apocalypse Now:* Viet-Nam as Generative Ritual" states that although the movie is flawed, "Coppola's faith in the social power of art is in itself encouraging in this era of private vision and escapist discourse."

Art of a different kind is used to serve an individual's purpose, as outlined by Richard Gid Powers in "Myth, Ritual and the Comic Strip G-Man," the purpose being J. Edgar Hoover's intention to base a comic strip hero on the exploits of the FBI. But this would not work, as Powers points out, for when the image of the real-life Bureau departed from the action detective formula, the Bureau risked losing its popularity, just as the FBI's official comic strip lost its audience when it lost touch with the action detective formula.

Christine Hope demonstrates in her article "American Beauty Rituals" just what a price American women pay to maintain their beauty, in the way of body hair removal, bustline management and dieting. Like similar rituals in more "primitive" cultures, Hope maintains, such American behaviors are useful in distinguishing women from men, although one would think this action not necessary in a society where various other rituals are used to distinguish between the sexes. But they are used, and Hope demonstrates that much can be learned about culture by close examination of these everyday ritual activities.

A different ritualistic use of beauty and the rituals it engenders is demonstrated by Juliette Woodruff in her article "The Prom Queen Turns Pro," in which she demonstrates the still extant custom among many Americans of making a professional bride out of American young women, as much for the joy of the frustrated mother as for the joy of the bride. But in this ritual of turning bride into married person is loaded a whole system and power of society for both youngster and her mother.

As Christine Hope asserts in her essay that we learn a great deal by studying the everyday unconscious aspects of life, Curry and Jiobu demonstrate this thesis exceedingly well in distinguishing between the elite way of dining and the popular way of grabbing food on the run. Sadly or gladly, the former is giving way to the latter as the pressures of daily life bear more and more upon us, with what ultimate result perhaps only time will tell.

C.R. Chandler's essay, "World War II as a Southern Entertainment: The Confederate Air Forces and Warfare Re-Enactment," details an account of a peculiar mixture of infatuation with a certain kind of aircraft, entertainment and general good spirits. The people who recondition and fly the marvelous aircraft of World War II vintage do so as much for the sheer joy of being with the machines as for mixing fun and theatrics with this love. Perhaps, Chandler muses, "it may be ventured that the CAF's commemorative rituals serve, for a considerable number of people, the solidifying functions delineated by Parsons in his discussion of expressive symbolism, and most dramatically stated by Durkheim when he spoke of rites which 'revivify the...collective conscience.'"

Another kind of entertainment which might "revivify the...collective conscience" might be that discussed by Steven L. Del Sesto in "Dancing and Cockfighting at Jay's Lounge and Cockpit: The Preservation of Folk Practices in Cajun Louisiana," in which he outlines a Saturday evening at a Cajun lounge in Louisiana. Del Sesto's conclusion is that these rituals contribute to the maintenance of the larger Cajun sub-culture and are bonafide social institutions those rituals and ceremonies help greatly in the preservation of many practices of the Louisiana Cajuns.

Turning to literary art, C.T. Walters analyzes how Nathaniel Hawthorne's short story "The Artist of the Beautiful," patterning on the cliches of the time characterizes the theme by emphasizing ritual and process. To capture Ideal Beauty, Walters demonstrates, Hawthorne felt that the American artist either relied upon memory or upon the implement of imitation.

Ritualistic in their placement, two essays round out this section of the volume in discussing what some people call the final indignity of life, others welcome as the "final freeing" from bodily restrictions and increasingly most of us are coming to recognize as the final act of living, the rituals of the living upon the death of (presumably) a loved one. Martha Pike's essay "In Memory of: Artifacts Relating to Mourning in Nineteenth Century America" centers on the sometimes "morbid" and sometimes completely understandable rituals associated with death in America in an earlier age. Her conclusion about the study of such practices is: "Studies of past mourning customs may not only help us to evolve more useful patterns of behavior to cope with the grief of death, they should also lead to our greater understanding of earlier societies," especially our own. She sees around us today, "the remnants of Victorian mourning practices. . . seen in an abundance of collected nineteenth century artifacts, and in national mourning for departed leaders."[5]

In a much more up-to-date and less theoretical study Walter Whittaker analyzes the present-day ceremonies and rituals of our contemporary funeral directors and concludes that they are necessary and therapeutic practices which relieve the living of many suspicious and apprehensions. Death without these men and women who act as transitional agents would not be complete for the living.

Two essays which finish the book come back to generalizations about the power of rituals, the way these rituals perhaps subconsciously rule our lives, how difficult yet how necessary it is for us to modify our ritualistic reaction. David E. Wright and Robert E. Snow, in "Consumption as Ritual in the High Technology Society," demonstrate that paradoxes of the high American technological society "offer us freedom of all kinds, yet they impose rigid behaviors and beliefs" which rigidify society, and, they argue that "Either technological fixes will be found so that our primary cultural business can proceed as usual, or we will experience a radical restructuring of American life."

In the final essay, "Ritual and the Humanities 'Intellectual'," Ray Browne argues that the believers in the "Humanities as the one area of intellectual activity which can free us from the ritualized reaction to what the proper function of education and thinking should be ought to reexamine their basic philosophy about what constitutes the "Intellectual" and "intellectual activity." He suggests that a whole new approach to this most cherished of mental exercises is badly needed. He concludes that "It little becomes the 'intellectual' to be victimized by his own process of thinking about ritual while unable to liberate himself from one of its most obvious manifestations."

Ritual Two

[1]For a full study of John D. Macdonald and his philosophy about and treatment of women, see *Clues: A Journal of Detection* 1:1 (Bowling Green University, Ohio: Popular Press, 1980).

[2]*North Dakota Quarterly,* Summer 1978, p. 17.

[3]For the most complete study of this aspect of science fiction, see Marlene Barr, ed. *Future Females* (Bowling Green University, Ohio: Popular Press 1981), especially the essay by Joanna Russ, "Recent Feminist Utopias."

[4]The fullest and most perceptive study of this subject is Allen Guttmann, *From Ritual to Record: The Nature of Modern Sports* (New York: Columbia University Press, 1978).

[5]Reprinted from Fred E.H. Schroeder, ed. *5000 Years of Popular Culture: Popular Culture Before Printing* (Bowling Green University, Ohio: Popular Press, 1980).

[6]This essay will be published as one chapter of the book by Alan Gowans, *Learning to See* (Bowling Green University, Ohio: Popular Press, 1981).

The Contemporary Ritual Milieu

Frederick Bird

TO START WITH it is necessary to set forth a general socio-logical theory about the nature and function of ritual forms, to differentiate among various kinds of rituals in relation to their manifest ritual objectives and latent social functions and to analyze the contemporary shifts in ritual practices from the perspective of these conceptual assumptions.[1]

A. *Phenomenological and Functional Characteristics of Ritual Forms*

Sociologists have often commented disparagingly on ritual activities. Like Merton they have tended to view rituals as meaningless routines, as unthinking habituated activities, or as the overly elaborated ceremonies accompanying certain kinds of political or religious practices. Protestant religious thinkers too have often viewed rituals critically because they sensed that a preoccupation with rites and liturgies detracted attention away either from real, inner religious experiences or from responsible moral action.[2] These criticisms arise in part because of a failure to distinguish between ritual as cultural codes and certain stylized and habituated forms of behavior, which may be acted out in keeping with these codes, and in part because of religious and moral critiques of particular rituals or ritualisms rather than ritual action as such. Rituals are cultural phenomena. As symbolic codes, they regulate human interactions in a wide variety of contexts from religion and etiquette to types of therapies, ceremonies, and intimate exchanges. Without an understanding of the particular nature of ritual actions, we are liable to arrive at quite distorted views of the many activities in which ritual action plays a central part.

Phenomenologically considered rituals[3] may be defined as culturally transmitted symbolic codes which are stylized, regularly repeated, dramatically structured, authoritatively designated and intrinsically valued.[4]

One, rituals are culturally transmitted codes and not particular

19

patterns of behavior. Often the word ritual has been used loosely to refer both to symbolic action as well as to the codes in relation to which this action is performed. Bocock thus refers to rituals as "bodily action in relation to symbols."[5] Similarly with the custom of distinguishing between moral codes as a cultural phenomenon and moral behavior, it is useful and necessary to distinguish between rituals as symbolic codes and ritual actions or ritual processes as forms of behavior, enacted in keeping with these codes. This distinction allows us to recognize that rituals are cultural realities, collective representations in Durkheim's language. That rituals are not merely habituated behavior is illustrated by reference to the celebration of weddings which clearly constitute examples of ritual actions, which are repeated, usually for different persons, but not instances of habituated action. Like other cultural codes, such as language norms, rituals must be learned and a person may adhere to them more or less closely.

Two, ritual codes are like scripts for dramas. The aim of ritual action is to act as closely as possible in ways that approximate these stereotyped scripts. Acting in conformity with the scripts is considered to be intrinsically rewarding. The focus of attention hence is on adhering to the given form rather than on the consequence of these actions. This characteristic aspect of ritual forms contrasts with the discursive forms of ordinary conversation. As viewed from the perspective of participants, the purpose of these ritual scripts is not to provide a collection of gestures and symbols which may be used to communicate personal, idiosyncratic messages for which the scripts themselves retain only incidental, instrumental value and the messages themselves are what are intrinsically valued. Rather, acting in harmony with ritual codes is believed to be intrinsically worthwhile. In the case of religious rituals, these stylized codes have ordinarily been viewed as ordained means for communing with sacred beings. The value attached to the ritual form is evident even in ritual practices like testimonial giving, in which supposedly spontaneous speeches are presented. A close examination of testimonial speech reveals that within given groups they assume quite specific forms in relation to syntax, vocabulary, characteristic message and timing. Even seemingly spontaneous outbursts such as those accompanying glossalia or spirit possession usually take place in stylized patterns specific to particular ritual traditions.[6]

Three, rituals are stylized, highly symbolic codes. The symbolic character of rituals has often been noted as well as the ways in which rituals employ the redundant use of particular symbols which have multiple and fused meanings.[7] It is well to add that rituals are dramatically structured; they have beginnings, which set apart the following actions from what preceded, middles and ends.[8] Ritual users assume that something happens in the process, that a drama of a kind is re-enacted. The dramatic character of rituals is evident in three ways. First, ritual scripts must be acted out and not just spoken. In particular, rituals call for bodily action: participants must stand, sit, gesture or move in particular, prescribed manners. Second, by virtue of the ritual enactment, participants expect something to happen. Ritual action is believed at some levels to have an immediate efficacy. In Leach's terminology, participants assume that the symbolically expressive acts of the ritual will function like natural signals, triggering immediate and effective responses.[9] In many cases ritual participants expect that acting in conformity with ritual codes will release energies and imaginations otherwise inaccessible.[10] Third, as in theatrical drama, participants assume particular valued positions or characters, by virtue of the ritual. These position/characters may be variously designated by terms such as "Child of God," or "Gentleman" or "Lord," or "Servant" or "Disciple" or "Student," or "The one who submits" (the Arabic meaning of Islam). The ritual form enables participants to re-identify themselves in relation to their position/characters, even though at other moments of their life they may think of themselves in quite different terms in relation to specific roles or activities.[11] It is more fitting to argue that ritual participants assume a position/character rather than a special social role because within the ritual the focus of attention is on their sense of identity and on their relation to what counts as reality and not on specific tasks and functions.[12] In acting out many rituals, participants often put on special costumes and masks in order to emphasize this positional and character identification. These costumes may be quite elaborate but are often quite simple, involving the use of changes of clothes, the removal of shoes, or the wearing of hats.

Four, ritual actions are repeated. There are several reasons why rituals call for the repetitive enactment of their scripts. Rituals are repeated because as condensed languages they serve as mnemonic devices to bring to attention and to keep in mind certain thoughts and sentiments.[13] Because they are often associated in memory with particularly moving experiences, the repetition of the ritual serves as means either to re-live those emotions to the extent that they are treasured or to confront and live through these emotions insofar as they are troubling.[14] In this context, the question might be raised about whether and to what extent rituals are re-enacted for the same kind of reasons that persons repeat activities associated with compulsive neuroses. This is a complex issue. However, one difference between ritual action and behavior which is neurotically compulsive is that while the former represents repetitive action in relation to self-acknowledged and public codes the latter represents repetitive action in relation to personally unacknowledged and private codes.

Five, rituals are authoritatively designated usually by custom but also as well by various religious leaders, elders and moral instructors. For this very reason it is often difficult to construct new rituals, not only because the new rituals may seem arbitrary and unfamiliar but because they lack the authority of tradition itself. Rituals gain authority in part through the very process of being repeated. However, rituals may gain authority by means other than tradition. The innovative ritual codes of experimental religious associations, group therapies or even established denominations may achieve an authoritative status by being collectively authorized by participants themselves or commanded by respected leaders. In contrast other new ritual codes merely recommended by committees or only tentatively suggested by officials may possess considerably less authority and are liable to seem more arbitrary.

Religious rituals may be distinguished from other rituals primarily by one feature: they are considered to be a means by which persons establish and maintain their relation to what they consider to be sacred. Sacred realities are here defined as those things which are set apart and revered because they are believed to be extraordinarily powerful and ultimately real. What persons consider to be sacred share a number of family characteristics: people feel awe in their presence, they are protected from trivial exposure, they seem to be the source of natural and moral powers and they are felt to be ultimately true, unchanging and real. Religious rituals are those sets of symbolic codes by which persons seek to affirm, develop and perpetuate their relationships to these sacred realities. Viewed from this perspective, the distinction between religious and non-religious rituals is fluid. Many seemingly secular rites may exhibit religious aspects precisely because they serve as means of re-enacting the relation between persons and some public purposes or personal identities which are held to be sacred.

Magical rituals may be identified as a sub-set of religious rituals. Insofar as they regulate inter-actions with sacred power, they differ from religious rituals in that they are usually acted out instrumentally for purposes of obtaining immediate, worldly benefits, such as health, or power or advice. By their very nature magical rituals tend to be viewed like techniques, but not scientifically verified techniques, since the ultimate authority for these rituals lies not in their claimed empirical results but in their antiquity and/or their authoritative discovery.[15]

Functionally analyzed, ritual codes typically have been utilized to facilitate the following kinds of activities. They regulate human interactions particularly in marginal settings; they serve as means for making transformations in personal and social status and identity; they facilitate the communication of intense and powerful sentiments; and they activate and bring into play otherwise dormant human energies. In particular ways the phenomenological characteristics of ritual codes—their stylized, symbolic, repetitive and authoritative features—render them especially suited for these functions.

1) Ritual codes are often utilized to regulate social behavior at times and places of transition between existing forms of social organization. They are customarily used for marriages, births, deaths, changes in the season, changes in authority, initiations, the beginnings and endings of meetings, the day, or the week.[16] At these times of transition, when persons may have uncertain feelings of identity or feel pulled by contradictory loyalties, ritual codes reduce the sense of uncertainty and conflict by prescribing particular ways of acting, and by re-affirming the identities of persons in relation to given positional and character definitions. Rituals are regularly utilized not only in transitional settings but at times and places when persons seek to re-affirm their fundamental relationships to others. Groups of persons re-affirm their collective identity through communal rites of worships, sacrifice and public ceremonies; individuals may re-affirm their sense of personal identity through rituals of prayer, confession or meditation. Again, what is decisive is that the ritual script prescribes a stylized way of acting that reattaches identities of persons to given character/positions by means of familiar symbols.

2) Dramatic changes in social status and personal identity are often marked, occasioned and brought about by the utilization of ritual codes, which symbolically set forth these changes. Seasonal rites, initiations, life cycle rituals and spiritual exercises are all stylized codes by means of which participants both dramatize and actualize transformations in social relations and personal consciousness. By reciting and re-enacting ritual scripts, participants do not only think about such changes but they also actually relax particular past attachments and affirm and act out new ones.

3) Ritual codes serve also as a means for communicating a wide range of affections and sentiments. What rituals communicate are not new ideas and information or particular, unique feelings. The very repetitive character of rituals means the ritual re-enactment results in a renewing or a re-acknowledging of given thoughts and emotions. The words, rhythms and actions of the ritual invoke

generic identities and sentiments, associated with the characters of the ritual drama and their positions. Rituals facilitate this kind of communication in settings where discursive speech is likely to be more difficult or misleading; that is, in relation to authority, suffering, dramatic transitions from one area of life to another, and intimacy. Rituals have developed in all of these contexts. They provide spoken and embodied vocabularies for communicating and reconfirming intense feelings of respect, awe, sorrow, loyalty, tenderness and attraction, particularly in those situations where the use of discursive vocabularies tend to flatten the depth of feeling and/or stray off into thoughts unrelated to the sentiments themselves.[17] In these settings, rituals provide stereotyped scripts, by means of which persons can acknowledge, handle and express feelings of great intensity. Without these ritual forms, persons often find it difficult to communicate these sentiments not only because they may spend excessive efforts at controlling and limiting their feelings on account of their intensity but also because they may also feel inarticulate at arriving at their own personal expressions. Ironically, ritual codes because of their stylized form seem to facilitate greater articulateness in particularly these kinds of settings.[18]

4) Rituals also function as a means for bringing into play intrapersonal and inter-personal energies and imaginations which otherwise frequently remain suppressed or dormant. Both William James and Emile Durkheim were particularly interested in this function of rituals. James argued that when religious persons acted in keeping with particular rituals—and he focused specially on personal prayers and revivals—they often felt a sudden surge of vitality as they gained access through the ritual to energies which had been previously sub-conscious. There are direct and indirect explanations for this phenomenon. Either the symbolic actions themselves, because they are powerful, put people into contact with otherwise hidden or repressed emotions, or by acting in conformity with the ritual, persons are freed from having to exert controls over the self, thus freeing energies for other purposes. Durkheim argued that collective effervescence often occurred when persons came together in a ritual setting and found in their group existence a contagious attraction and excitement absent when they were isolated from one another. Group rituals bring into life these otherwise dormant inter-personal forces, both because they allow persons to act in concert with one another and their group ideals and because they evoke and channel interpersonal affections.[19] One of the reasons rituals release these unconscious psychic and interpersonal energies is that they provide a structured set of actions in relation to which otherwise contradictory feelings—for

example, the attraction to and jealousies of others—can both be acknowledged, without either one being cancelled or either one dominating the other. Thus, the structured, repeated drama of the ritual provides a form by means of which persons can acknowledge emotions without suppressing contradictory feelings which might otherwise render individuals ambivalent and anxious and apathetic.[20]

B. Rituals, Ritualism and Liturgies

When analyzing rituals it is useful to distinguish rituals which are alive and powerful from dead ritualisms. Erikson coined the latter term in order to describe habituated actions in relation to ritual codes which have become empty, arbitrary and overly formal.[21] Much of the religious and secular criticism of ritual practices may be appropriately viewed as negative evaluations of forms which have developed into ritualisms.

Ritualisms differ from rituals largely because of the attitudes of participants. However, these subjective attitudes frequently have been occasioned by particular characteristics of ritualistic codes. Essentially, ritualisms are symbolic codes which are believed to be neither intrinsically valued nor immediately efficacious. Adhering to a ritualism is like role playing: it means to follow a code which is viewed as being merely a provisional, arbitrary guide, which might well be replaced by another, if one were available or known or could be constructed. Ritualistic codes are viewed as techniques. From the perspective of participants, the dramatic expectation that something happens in the process of the ritual re-enactment is missing. Participants listen, repeat, move, speak because they have done so before, and/or because they may feel it is socially respectable to do so, but not because they feel they will receive an immediate benefit. From the point of view of participants, ritualisms are codes which do not fulfill their expected social and personal functions. They are viewed not so much as means of regulating human interactions but rather as arbitrary routines which may at times obstruct and muffle these exchanges. Rather than being experienced as means for expressing feelings, they are often felt to be empty, formulae that tend to hide or obscure the expression of real sentiments. Most decisively, the performance of ritualism does not seem to be often able to release heretofore latent or unacknowledged psychic or moral energies.

No doubt there is a circular cause and effect relationship between how people view ritual codes and what kinds of experiences they have had as participants. The absence of pragmatic consequences tends to deflate the charisma of religious prophets as well as religious rituals. Participants are led to expect a manifestation of extraordinary power. If the ritual does not yield this power, then belief declines. But without the beliefs and the attendant sense of expectancy and attachment to the ritual forms, it is impossible to experience the ritual as a dramatic process.[22]

Objectively considered, ritualisms arise when ritual forms are too old or too new, too elaborate or too simple or when they lack authority or structural coherence.

Rituals are capable of regulating human interaction and communicating intense sentiments and senses of identity only insofar as their symbols and patterns touch upon and represent vital aspects of participants' lives. With historical changes, there are corresponding shifts in the typical forms of social interaction and identity. Ritual forms which resist change and may thereby in the process lose touch with the evolving forms of social organization, becoming ritualism unattuned to contemporary emotions and life-situations. However innovative ritual codes are also in danger of becoming ritualism because they seem unfamiliar and arbitrary. Repetitive re-enactment is integral to ritual practice. However, the sense of re-enactment is partially obscured when new ritual elements are initially introduced. From the perspective of participants new ritual elements are likely to be dysfunctional for several reasons. Participants may be inclined to turn their attention away from overall ritual drama in order to keep abreast of the details of the ritual; participants may feel awkward if they cannot immediately master and feel at home with the new forms; and the very introduction of new elements seems to imply that ritual elements themselves are arbitrary. The resistance to ritual innovation arises for all these reasons.[23]

If the word ritual is used to describe the overall symbolic form, then the word liturgy may be used to identify the number and richness of symbolic elements within a given ritual. Rituals are liturgically full, when they involve the use of many different actions and symbols or they may be liturgically thin when only a few, simple actions are involved. The Catholic service of the Eucharist is liturgically developed in this sense while the Quaker form of silent meditation is liturgically simple. Both, however, involve the use of highly stereotyped, symbolic speech and action. What makes rituals effective is not whether they are liturgically rich but whether they are authoritatively designated and believed in.[24] Sitting satsang in a Buddhist center, for example, involves few liturgical elements but participants find the experience rewarding to the extent that they adhere to authoritatively given patterns.

Liturgically over-developed and under-developed rituals may give rise to ritualism, partly because in both cases they inadvertently occasion a decline in ritual participation. Because it is often difficult for the lay population to master the details of elaborate liturgy, then increasingly professionals may act out the ritual drama themselves, leaving the laity not as followers and participants but merely as observers. Contrariwise, overly sparse liturgies may also reduce laity to the status of observers precisely because none of the few simple elements deeply engages their emotional responses. As with other kinds of language, ritual codes which are too elaborate or too bare may fail to express and represent particular sentiments and identities either because in their complexity and detail the overall sense of drama is lost to sight or because in their simplicity they fail to touch upon relevant feelings and impressions. In either case from the perspective of participants, ritual forms seem formalistic and arbitrary.

C. Types of Rituals and Their Constructive Functions

Rituals in general function to regulate social interaction particularly in transitional settings. We can now expand upon this analysis by observing that ritual forms serve as means for regulating human interaction by four typical means; they may help to identify and maintain social boundaries, usually through rituals like taboos; they may assert and invoke particular norms and standards and values, as happens ordinarily in life cycle rites and worship; they may foster and re-invigorate attachments to social groupings such as occurs through seasonal rituals; and they may serve as means for augmenting the sense of communal power and status such as happens in public ceremonies.[25] Rituals may also facilitate these same kinds of functions for individuals. In this case rituals function to identify and protect the sense of personal boundary/identity; to re-affirm personal values and standards; to gain a sense of self apart from particular roles and involvements; and to augment the sense of personal power and status. Some ritual forms serve these functions at both the corporate and individual level. In contemporary society, however, there have emerged a number of new religious and para-religious movements which aim in particular at meeting at least some of these functions pre-eminently at the individual level.[26]

Ritual codes themselves may be variously grouped and identified. Durkheim discussed rituals in relation to five categories, identified partly on the basis of their functions, partly on the basis of the attitudes of participants and partly on the basis of typical phenomenological characteristics. In the accompanying table I have listed seven types of ritual forms, identified on the basis of manifest ritual objectives, described from a phenomenological perspective. In several instances these types are further sub-divided to note typical variations in ritual forms. Ostensibly participants enact rituals in order to achieve a wide range of objectives. These same ritual forms may also be analyzed in relation to their characteristic latent social and personal functions. From the perspective of participants, these social functions obviously may neither be acknowledged nor seem important. Still, when analyzing changing patterns of ritual practice, these latent functions must be taken into account. Some types of rituals fulfill various social functions primarily at the group or societal level while others primarily meet social needs of individual practitioners.

Any given religious or cultural tradition may have developed a fairly broad or narrow repertoire of ritual forms and may have developed several forms of the same type. Medieval Christendom incorporated an extremely wide range of ritual practices. One of the consequences of the Reformation and Counter-Reformation was to reduce this range of authorized ritual forms, by eliminating various shamanistic rites, reducing the variety among accepted rituals, and by simplifying liturgical forms in many instances.[27]

D. *Changing Ritual Patterns in Contemporary Society*

As I now briefly depict current development in the utilization of rituals within contemporary North American societies, I will draw upon the preceding observations concerning the nature and function of ritual codes, the differences between rituals and ritualism and the typical ritual forms and their functions. For example, using my initial, fairly broad definition of ritual codes, it is possible to recognize the presence of new and old rituals in a variety of non-religious contexts, associated, for example, with new therapies and public ceremonies. Furthermore, the analytic distinction between rituals and ritualism makes it possible to identify and analyze the widespread ambivalence rather than simple rejection of ritual forms. Finally, the outline of ritual forms and their characteristic functions enables me at a more proximate level to gauge the significance of shifts in prominence of particular kinds of ritual codes. Overall I will identify four major developments in the ritual usage in contemporary North American societies.[28]

First, within the past several decades a number of evangelical Christian groups as well as a number of other Christian and non-Christian congregational groups, like the Charismatics, the Divine Light Mission, Nichirin Shoshu or Jesus People, have either arisen or have been rapidly gaining adherents. In varying degrees these groups have developed ritual repertoires which assign particular force to the following types of rituals: They emphasize certain taboos, which often take the form of prohibitions against alcohol, smoking, in some cases eating meats, and indulging in excessive behavior. They utilize purification rites which in particular serve as

Table One

Types of Ritual Forms:
Identified in Relation to their Manifest Ritual Objectives and Latent Social Functions

Types of Rituals	Manifest Ritual Objectives	Latent Social Functions
1. Taboo	to avoid certain visible things: foods, places, people, objects which are felt to be a source of impurity or contamination	to identify and maintain the boundaries of groups; to maintain a sense of personal boundary
2. Purification Rites: (a) cleansings, exorcisms expulsions (excluding Baptisms)	to clean out or clean off alien, external forces by washings, ex pulsions, exorcisms (This kind of negative ritual often precedes and prepares the way for other positive rituals.)	to detach self from external influences in order, usually to re-attach self to a par- ticular group or in some cases to re-attach self to an inner, real self.
(b) confession	to re-order self in relation to a particular vision or image of self; usually implies some ident- ification of faults in relation to valued standards	to re-assert the importance of particular standards, norms, values
3. Spiritual Exercises: (a) ascetic	to seek unity with some sacred Other by living in accord with a discipline, which requires particular forms of behavior often of a self-denying character	to re-affirm the norms associated with this discipline
(b) mystical	to seek to experience a unity of mind/consciousness as a sacred experience by acting in accord with a discipline which calls for meditation and certain at least minimal moral attributes	to detach self from the larger social forces; to foster a sense of tolerance for others as well as one's self
4. Rites of Passage (a) life-cycle: birth, puberty, marriage, death	to provide ritual forms for these transitional phases of life: (prevalent use of symbolism of birth and death)	to reaffirm social values and norms: associated with being a member of group, being an adult, being a husband/wife
(b) seasonal rites: autumn, spring, winter (also memorial rites for historic events)	these rites occur at particular times of the calendar year when there is a transition from one kind of activity to another	to re-assert group attachments: to re-integrate persons into larger social groupings (May also re-assert group re-assert group values)
(c) initiations: four kinds: inductions ordeals, certifica- tions, ordinations	Different initiations have somewhat different objectives. Ordeals, for example, occur initiates expect to be intro- duced to augmented power (as in shaumanistic rites). Initiation takes persons through various transitions.	Social functions differ with the type of initiation: to group. All initiations help to protect boundaries of the group or status with which they are connected.

5. Worship
(usually implies a primary group service and a secondary individual or family practice; although in some cases, in Brahmin puja is primary)

Worship involves five different elements, which in particular traditions may be given more or less emphasis: these are —
(a) to make offerings and sacrifices to Sacred Other (often sharing portions of offerings with group);
(b) to present readings of sacred texts and prayers on those readings;
(c) to present homilies;
(d) to take part in collective readings, chants, songs;
(e) to allow for personal testimonials and witnessing.

to foster and provide occasions for attachments to group (especially by means of offerings, sacrifices, chants, songs)
to re-assert collective norms (especially by means of homilies, testimonials)

(services of worship call to mind revered paradigmatic events of a sacred past as models for behavior)

6. Shumanistic Rituals:
These may be viewed from two perspectives:
(a) as means for becoming a Shaman, a person with extraordinary powers;
(b) as therapeutic and divinizing rites used by others as a source of health, wisdom, charm, power.

to seek to gain extraordinary sacred power, usually by seeking to have a mystical like experience (usually of an ecstatic character), but also through tutelage to a given shaman.

to call upon extraordinary sacred powers to heal, gain power or gain wisdom.

to augment personal power, status, and/or certitude (in some cases, to gain social status)

to re-attach those who are marginal by virtue of illness, weakness or depression

to augment sense of confidence (group status, power) at times of wars, plantings.

7. Etiquettes

to indicate appropriate forms of behavior and ceremony in relation to particular settings

to regulate interactions between persons in different social positions; to re-assert values of these positions,

---

*Sources for discussion of the distinctions between particular types and sub-types of rituals are as follows: Taboos (see Douglas, 1970; Durkheim, Part III, chp. I); Purification Rites (see Westley, Ricoeur, 1978b; Douglas, 1970); Spiritual Exercises (see Weber, chp. 12; Bird and Reimer; Eliade, chp. 2); Rites of Passage (see Eliade, 1958b), Eliade 1957; Gluckman; Durkheim, Part III, chps. 4, 5); Worship Services (see Durkheim, Part III, chp. II); Shamistic Rites (see Eliade, 1958a, chp. 8; Lewis; Malinowski, chp. one; Skultans; Westley, 1978); Etiquette (Fingarette)

a means of detaching individuals from what they consider to be alien, external ideas and practices. They call upon all the adherents to practice spiritual exercises, usually but not exclusively of a mildly ascetic character, which emphasize abiding by group norms and in some cases witnessing to others. In their worship services they encourage acts of personal offering or sacrifice, by means of altar calls and testimonials and they utilize collective rituals which generate group enthusiasm by chanting and singing. Viewed as a whole, these various ritual forms and practices serve to reinforce a sense of group boundary, to encourage and strengthen attachments within these groups, and to augment the sense of personal status and power by means of participation within these groups. These developments represent a reassertion of traditional sectarian patterns with two modifications: currently a number of non-Christian groups are competing for adherents and in several cases these groups see themselves not as exclusive congregations but as complementary movements, supplementing existing religious bodies.[29]

Second, in the past several decades a number of cultic groups have arisen and been gaining adherents. These cultic groups, broadly identified, include various yoga groups; a number of martial arts groups; assorted Buddhist groups; various human potential movements like Est, Arica, Silva Mind Control, Psychosynthesis and Gurdjieff followers; movements like Transcendental Meditation; as well as diverse palmists, astrologers, mediums and their followers. Taken as a whole these movements assign emphasis in varying degrees to a quite different set of ritual practices: they include purification rites which seek to detach the self from alien forces for the sake of individual autonomy. They encourage adherents to undertake a regime of spiritual exercises, usually of a mystical character, intended at least in part to loosen the attachments of individuals from the thought patterns and mores of the larger society. These same exercises often are viewed like shamanistic rites as a means of gaining greater personal power, health and status by cultivating capacities for healing, divining, physical prowess, and self-possession. Within these movements there is a relative absence of rituals for worship, the life cycle, and seasonal changes all of which would reinforce social norms and group attachments. As an overall pattern, these ritual practices serve as a means both for reducing personal attachments to societal roles, norms and pressures and for augmenting the sense of personal capacity and strength. Adherents of these movements may often continue to participate in other religious or non-religious associations.

Third, viewed from the perspective of North American society as a whole, the last several decades have witnessed both a declining consensus regarding the appropriate ritual forms for puberty and etiquette as well as the emergence of an ever increasing number of new secular rituals and ritualisms. The absence of consensus about puberty rites reflects and expresses societal ambivalences about the relationship between the status of children and adults. There have emerged several trends which tend to de-emphasize these differences by stressing the adult-like character and potentials of children and youth in child-centered, democratically patterned families and in forms of education which foster a democratic milieu within classrooms. In contrast there has been a tendency to delay the actual entrance into adult status, by the creation of a youth/young adult status, which extends over an increasing number of years. The absence of consensus about puberty rites thus indirectly points to ambivalences about these cultural values. There also seems to have been a decline in the utilization of the ceremonial gestures associated with traditional forms of etiquette. Since both puberty rites and ceremonial forms of etiquette function to identify positional differences within society, between adults and children, authorities and non-authorities, in-group and out-groups, and persons of different status, the decline and diffusion of these ritual forms in part reflects the ambivalent feelings about positional differences within a cultural milieu which seems to stress egalitarian values and the importance of personal rather than positional attributes.

However, it is evident that popular attitudes are ambivalent and not simply negative toward such positional and status differences because the many, new, varied and sometimes private or local ritualisms and ritual codes have recently been introduced and developed in the context of these kinds of social exchanges. The passage from childhood to adulthood is now marked by a varied series of ritualized ordeals, of personally-undertaken yet stylized and standardized rites, and of several publicly acknowledged ceremonies. None of these rites themselves authoritatively announce and celebrate this transition but together they still identify and express aspects of transition. Similarly, it is possible to identify within various professional settings and bureaucratically-structured organizations numerous stylized gestures and ceremonial practices, which, even though they lack the sacred authority of tradition and self-conscious public acclaim are still often assiduously followed because in part they serve to identify and protect positional differences.

The proliferation of new, secular and semi-religious rituals and ritualisms has occurred in a number of other settings. The Yule season, which a century ago was celebrated by a few families as religious rites connected with the Christian holiday, has broadened out into a host of festivals, symbolic activities, ceremonial gestures, all of which extend over a several week period and most of which are celebrated by Christians and non-Christians alike. The expansion of therapies and therapy groups has given rise to accompanying ritual forms. Many observers contend that various public athletic contests have come to assume various ritualized trappings, not only as communal festivals of a sort, but in the stylized interactions between participants, the media and audiences. Taken as a whole, these various new rituals and ritualisms function primarily to express and foster interpersonal attachments within families, between friends, among communities of persons rather than, in contrast, to re-assert particular normative standards or group boundaries.

Fourth, the overall contemporary ritual milieu has become increasingly pluralistic. There is both a wider variety of ritual forms than previously but also less consensus about any given ritual codes as compelling and authoritative standards. Various shamanistic and mystical rituals, which often function to foster detachments from social pressures, have increased in number and kinds while at the same time there has probably been a decline in the participation in ritual practices, like worship, confession and ascetic rites, which reinforce common mores and normative standards. North Americans express ambivalence regarding ritual codes such as those for puberty or etiquette, which re-inforce positional differences but have tended to expand upon the number and variety of often secular rituals and ritualisms which serve to foster and celebrate diverse kinds of communal attachments. These various developments have given rise to and reinforced decidedly ambivalent popular feelings about ritual forms, which reflect traditional Protestant criticisms and the sociological biases about rituals as empty gestures and as forms of habituated behavior. In this milieu many persons continue to adhere to traditional ritual practices both in their religious activities and social interchanges. Others have been attracted to new religious and para-religious movements and therapies, in which new rituals play a part. Many others feel disenchanted with what they consider to be ritualistic forms, which seem outdated, contrived or sectarian. They attempt to live rationally and spontaneously without rituals; but they frequently adopt and adhere to some of the newer ritual and ritualisms which may be private, local, or like the Yule season quite public and pervasive.[31]

Notes

¹This paper is based in part upon a research project made possible by a grant from the Quebec Government's Ministry of Education, to study New Religious and Para-Religious Movements in the Montreal area. An earlier version of this paper was delivered as part of the Maurice Manel lectures in Symbolic Interaction at York University under the title, "Symbolic Action in Contemporary Cults." I am endebted to other members of this research project, including Judith Castle, Susan Palmer and Frances Westley.

²See Robert Merton, *Social Theory and Social Structure,* Enlarged Edition (New York: Free Press, 1968), chps. 6, 7; Mary Douglas, *Natural Symbols* (Middlesex, England: Penguin Books, 1973), chp. 1.

³I have made this same argument with regard to the definitions both of religion and of morality: namely, that phenomenological analysis must proceed but also be accompanied by functional analysis. (See Bird, 1979) Paradigms and Parameters in the Comparative Study of Religions. Paper presented at American Academy of Religion, 1979.

⁴The focus of this paper will be on the characteristic forms of ritual codes rather than on their quite varied and elaborate symbols.

⁵See Robert Bocock, *Ritual in Industrial Society: A Sociological Analysis of Rituals in Modern England* (London: Allen and Unwin, 1974), 36; Ruth Benedict, "Ritual," *Encyclopedia of the Social Sciences,* Vols. III and XIV, 396, 397.

⁶Paul Schwartz, "An Analysis of Testimonial Speech in Three Religious Movements," M.A. Thesis, Concordia University, 1976.

⁷Edmund Leach, "Ritualization in Man in Relation to Conceptual and Social Developments." *Reader in Comparative Religion,* Third Ed., eds. William Lessa and Evon Vogt (New York: Harper & Row, 1958, 1965, 1972a).

⁸Edmund Leach, "Two Essays Concerning the Symbolic Representation of Time," *Reader in Comparative Religion, op. cit.;* Johannan Huizinga, *Homo Ludens* (Boston: Beacon, 1950), chp. 1.

⁹Edmund Leach, *Culture and Communication: The Logic By Which Symbols are Connected* (Cambridge: University Press, 1976), 52.

¹⁰Herbert Fingarette, *Confucius: The Secular as Sacred* (New York: Harper & Row, 1972), 3; Emile Durkheim, *The Elementary Forms of the Religious Life,* translated by J.S. Swain (New York: Collier Books, 1961), Part II, chp. 7; William James, *The Varieties of Religious Experience* (New York: American Library, 1958), Conclusion.

¹¹Victor Turner, *The Ritual Process* (New York, 1973).

¹²Douglas, *op. cit.* chp. 2 and 3.

¹³George Herbert Mead, *On Social Psychology,* edited Anselm Strauss (Chicago: Univ. of Chicago Press, 1956), 163, 169.

¹⁴James Bossard and Eleanor Boll, *Ritual in Family Living: A Contemporary Study* (Philadelphia: University Press, 1950), chp. 3.

¹⁵A number of New Religious Movements claim to provide for their participants' knowledge and access to techniques by which they can become healthier, more effective members of society, possessing in some cases extraordinary powers as psychics or persons potentially capable of levitating. While these groups on occasions produce supposedly scientific tests to validate their claims, they rarely openly invite participants to experiment with alternative techniques or produce tests which are genuinely comparative.

¹⁶Max Gluckman, "Les Rites de Passage," *Essays on the Ritual of Social Relations* (Manchester: Manchester Univ. Press, 1962), chp. 1.

¹⁷Douglas, *op. cit.,* 73.

¹⁸The emergence of what has been called psycho-babble reflects the attempt to develop stylized, ritual-like language for intimate and semi-intimate exchanges in the absence of publicly acknowledged and validated ritual forms. What has been noticed about psychobabble is the frequent use of vaguely used psychological terms and impersonal pronouns. What has been missed in the usual analyses of this language is the fact that this language is in fact stylized and stereo-typed like the traditional ceremonial language of etiquette and like this language psychobabble facilitates communication between persons largely in relation to their positions, which in this case, are considered usually to be of common in-group status, rather than in relation to a sense of personal differences. The merit of psychobabble is that it allows a sense of familiarity while still using very vague and indiscriminating terms.

¹⁹James, *op. cit.,* Lectures 9, 10, 19, 20; Durkheim, *op. cit.,* Part II, chps. 5, 6.

[20]Claude Levi-Strauss, "The Structural Study of Myth," *Reader in Comparative Religion,* eds. William Lessa and Evon Vogt, Third Edition, *op. cit.*

[21]Erik Erikson, *Toys and Reason* (New York: Norton, 1975), part Two.

[22]Max Weber, *The Sociology of Religion* (Boston: Beacon, 1963), chp. 1; Douglas, *op. cit.,* 29.

[23]Donald Metz, "The Dysfunctions of Ritual Innovation," Paper presented at the Annual Meeting of the Association for the Sociology of Religion, 1979.

[24]Where rituals are introduced without compelling authority, ritual practices themselves often seem to be less dramatic, powerful and moving. For evidence of this relationship see Peter Slater, *Microcosm* (New York: Wiley & Sons, 1966), 150-166; Darrell Leavitt, "A Study of the Transformation of a Gurdjieff Group," M.A. Thesis Concordia University, 1976; Frances Westley, "Searching for Surrender: A Catholic Charismatic Renewal Group's Attempt to Become Glossalalic." *American Behavioral Scientist,* Vol. 20, No. 6, 1977, 925-940.

[25]The second and third of these four social functions correspond to Mary Douglas' discussions of social interchanges in relation to grid, i.e. regulations, and group, i.e. attachments. (See Douglas, chps. 1-4) The first function corresponds to the utility of taboos and purification rites, which Douglas analyzed in an earlier work (1970).

[26]See Westley, Frances, "The Complex Forms of the Religious Life: A Durkheimian Analysis of New Religious Movements." Ph.D. Thesis, McGill University, 1978; Frederick Bird, "The Pursuit of Innocence: A Comparative Analysis of Religious Movements and Their Influence on Feelings of Moral Accountability," *Sociological Analysis* (Winter, 1979).

[27]Keith Thomas, *Religion and the Decline of Magic* (New York: Scribner's Sons, 1971).

[28]The following observations are based on an overview of social trends since World War II. Many observers have commented on these trends. My purpose is not to document these changes but rather to place these developments within a particular conceptual framework.

[29]Many new religious movements identify themselves not as religions as such but as movements with a religious dimension. In some cases, like the Charismatics or Jesus groups, they view themselves as complements of existing religious traditions, bringing a new vitality to these groups like the early Methodists in 17th century England. In more cases, they view themselves as supplements, making available new wisdom, new practices, ancillary to the religious traditions but capable of augmenting them. This attitude is shared by groups like Silva Mind Control, Spiritualists, even some Yoga groups, Tai Chi and Sufis. Other groups see themselves as being religious without being religious but having nothing more than an accidental relation to existing religious movements.

[30]Frederick Bird, "Paradigms and Parameters in the Comparative Study of Religious and Ideological Ethics," paper delivered to the annual meeting of the Canadian Society for the Study of Religion, 1979.

[31]In her *Natural Symbolism* Mary Douglas argues that ritual patterns can be studied as expressions of moral values and norms. In keeping with Douglas' hypothesis, it is possible to observe several parallels between the contemporary ritual and moral milieux. In both cases there exist an uncoordinated, frequently competitive pluralism among ritual codes and among moral codes. As this moral pluralism and relativism often gives rise to feelings of anomie, so the pluralism and relativism of ritual codes give rise to a sense of the absence of any compelling, culturally shared rituals. As with moral codes, the popular response to this phenomenon often takes the form of ambivalence, in which existing codes are often felt to be arbitrary and empty and in which new, provisional, personal or local codes frequently are being put forward.

Purification and Healing Rituals in New Religious Movements

F.R. Westley

RITUAL HAS BEEN largely ignored in the sociology of religion, having come to be defined largely as an empty form of action, divorced from the internal moods and motivations of the actor. As has been pointed out by social anthropologists, this leaves sociologists with no terminology to deal with symbolic action which correctly expresses the actor's internal state (Douglas, 1973: 20). This inarticulateness is particularly frustrating when attempting to study emerging forms of religious life where the ritual behavior is not only heartfelt by the individual who performs it, but also highly expressive of the group which aids in directing and shaping that behavior. Even when ritual is merely empty conformity, it still presents a problem of the relation of symbols to social life. But when conformity is genuine, ritual offers an arena for exploring the relations between the individual and the group, the group and the symbol system in which it finds expression (Douglas, 1973: 21).

When one anthropological theory, that of Mary Douglas, is applied to the rituals of purification and healing in new religious movements there is gained an insight into the role and significance of particular rituals for particular movements and the beginnning of a vocabulary for dealing with contemporary rituals of all kinds.

I. Body Rituals and Social Structure: Mary Douglas' Theory

Purification and healing rituals have one thing in common: they are both body rituals. Such rituals, oriented to the maintenance and restoration of the physical self of group members, are prevalent in many of the new religious movements despite the 'new spirituality' or 'new consciousness' which many claim to see in these groups.

Such concerns have of course been one of the foci of ritual life throughout history. In her study of primitive tribes, Douglas placed particular emphasis on such rituals. The human body, she suggests, is a 'natural symbol' for the social group, a human whole made up of interlocking parts (1973: 12). In rituals concerning the body,

36

Douglas claims it will be used literally and figuratively to reflect the social body and its concerns. The body has internal and external boundaries and systems; it is a largely closed system which must nevertheless interact with its environment in order to survive. The social body is very similar. When the order and the boundaries of the social body are threatened from without or within, Douglas argues, these threats will be acted out in body rituals (1966).

The ritual correspondence between social and physical body is relatively straightforward. If a social group sees itself as threatened from the outside, body rituals will reflect a preoccupation with external boundaries and the orifices which permit or regulate entrance to the body. If the social boundaries which are threatened are the internal ones (such as those separating clans, families, classes from one another) it will be the internal lines of organ systems, etc., which will receive attention. Two other potential threats to the social body often symbolized in body rituals are danger from between the margins (from socially anomolous or deviant groups which do not occupy a clear place within the social order) and the danger from internal contradictions (which Douglas terms 'the system at war with itself' and which might suggest a social order in the process of breakdown or in the process of civil war) (1966).

The actual social groupings (or organizations) and the norms and values governing the interaction of these groups are seen as interrelated. Social groups have a reality only insofar as they are named as distinct and given a place or role in the complex fabric of social relations. A given society can therefore be threatened both physically and symbolically. Either kind of threat may find expression in a body ritual. The body is used as a natural symbol not only for those boundaries which separate one tribe, one family, one individual from another, but also for the boundaries formed by social norms which are the grid work holding up the social construction of reality.

Take for example the still prevalent body ritual of punishing a child by washing out his mouth with soap and water if he says a 'dirty' word. In our culture, as Leach pointed out, such words are usually those which name human excrement, organs of excrement, sexual acts and/or those which call people by animal names (particularly those domestic animals with which we are in closest contact (1972: 207). What all these words have in common is their expressing points of contact or merging between man and his environment. Those named objects actually physically transcend this barrier and hence blur an important distinction. In an effort to preserve this distinction, the words themselves are made taboo or unmentionable, as if by refusing to recognize verbally the existence of excrement it disappears. Hence, the child who says the forbidden word threatens important social distinctions on two levels: he breaks a social norm (confusing the distinction between the mentionable and the unmentionable) and in speaking the word he renders the physical object named culturally visible, hence threatening the important distinction between man and his environment. The ritual washing out of the mouth resolves the threat on both levels. The physical orifice which produced the offending dirt (the word) is physically washed out. Symbolically the taboo is reasserted (it is the word, after all and not the actual excrement which is washed away) and the distinction between man and environment originally dirtied or blurred is made once again clear.

With this example in mind, let us turn to the kind of body rituals which are prevalent in new religious movements, those of purification and healing. These two kinds of rituals are related, as we shall see, but, in general, they are *not* both present in the same kind of group. Purification rituals tend to appear in the kind of group which is called 'counter-cultural' (Glock and Bellah, 1976) (usually of Eastern origin), while healing rituals are relegated to the neo-Christian groups. Each type of ritual—the purification rituals of a yoga group and the healing rituals in a Catholic charismatic group—will be considered in only one group each, but in fact these rituals are similar to those present in a wide variety of new groups.

II. Body Rituals in New Religious Movements[1]
a)*Purification Rituals*

On a weekend retreat of a prominent yoga group in Montreal, the Integral Yoga Institute of Swami Satchendananda, the following rituals took place:

Meditation: defined in group literature as the "concentrating of the rays of the mind."

Chanting: termed "rescuing the mind from habitual oppressive thinking."

Hatha yoga: "to give the body greater physical flexibility."

Pranayama: defined as breathing exercises which both teach adherents "to breath correctly and deeply...and to remove impurities from the lungs."

Kriya yoga: "internal cleansing of toxins through the use of enemas, induced vomiting, swallowing and withdrawing cloth, cleaning the nasal passages with string and with water, swallowing and ejecting air."

Dietary regulations: "Separation of 'pure' food from food considered toxic including meat, alcohol and drugs."

Massage: "to relax the body."

While all these rituals focus on the mind or the body, and it may be argued that the mind (or head, including the sense organs) is also used symbolically, we will for the moment concentrate on the physical body and the rituals which deal with its purity. There are three of these: kriya yoga, pranayama and dietary regulations.

The most striking of these are, of course, the kriya yoga exercises. It is clear that, as in the example given earlier of the "dirty word," these particular rituals are concerned with thoroughly cleansing and purifying the orifices of the body to rid them of toxins. "Toxins" is a term much used throughout the literature of these movements. It seems at various times to indicate pollutants in the air, water and food (such as chemical wastes and additives, or poisons) which accumulate in the muscles and organs because of tensions and the chemical effect of such "stimulating" food as meat, alcohol, drugs, etc. These toxins are variously accused of causing disease, violent passions, tension and crime. In terms of Mary Douglas' four types of threats to system boundaries, kriya yoga rituals seem to focus on the external margins of the system and on the orifices which permit penetration of foreign (and harmful) matter into the system. The response on the ritual level is to purify or purge this matter.

Two other purification rituals, kranayama or breathing exercises and dietary regulations, seem to express similar concerns. The breathing exercises are designed to rid the lungs from impurities and both the breathing exercises and the dietary regulations seem aimed at keeping further impurities from entering the system. On a symbolic level we might say that once the system is purged the external defenses are stored up to prevent further contamination.

While these rituals may be seen as extreme, they are not uncharacteristic of purification rituals in a variety of groups, such as Dharma Datu, Sri Chinmoy, Hare Krishna. Most eastern inspired groups have similar dietary restrictions and may have physical exercises to cleanse the systems. There is no sense of sin or guilt connected to these rituals. Contamination is not the fault of the adherent, it exists in the very air he breathes. His concern is merely with attempting systematically and regularly, with an eye to spiritual hygiene, to cleanse himself of this dirt.

b) *Healing Rituals*

Quite the opposite is true of the healing rituals of the Charismatics (and indeed of most healing rituals): the guilt of the adherent plays a very important part.

There has been an upsurge in interest in non-medical healing in the last decade, primarily among Christian and Christian influenced groups. These include the Spiritualists (in Quebec there is a National Federation of Spiritualist healers), the Anglican and Catholic charismatics, various psychic healing groups (such as Silva Mind Control), and of course the Christian Scientists.

While there has been much discussion (among believers) about the different types of healing, psychic, faith or spiritual, most of these rituals share common characteristics. All involve a relation between a healer and a healee (while purification techniques are performed by an individual on his own body, healers rarely, if ever, heal themselves) in which they become united with each other in a larger whole. In some cases (such as the Christian Scientists) this unity is purely mental. The healer goes into an altered state of consciousness and attempts to build a kind of subject-object bridge to link him to the patient. In other cases, actual physical contact is established between healer and patient in the "laying on of hands." This is the case in the healing ritual of the Catholic Charismatics. The healer sees himself as the transmitter of the healing power of the Spirit, which is actually sometimes felt as a 'flow' through the hands. Healers in the charismatics have a 'gift of healing' which is often recognized after joining the group. In the ritual itself, the healer will put his or her hand either on the head or on the injured part of the patient and pray. In some groups other members who may not have the gift themselves will nonetheless join with the healer, placing their hands on the patients as well.

The notion of guilt enters into this ritual with the conception of disease and illness given by group members. The famous maxim of Mary Baker Eddy, that disease is 'invalid' permeates most groups practicing healing rituals. Although on some levels it is acknowledged that illness, like evil, is ever-present in the environment in the form of germs, accidents, ill or evil will, and that doctors, medicine and care should be used to keep illness at bay, it is also thought that the internal state of the individual is an important determining factor. Christian Scientists suggest that negative thinking, lack of faith or malicious animal magnetism causes an individual to 'contact' disease. The Charismatics are more likely to interpret it as a lack of faith or an alienation from the healing power within.

Whatever the interpretation, it is this internal aspect, the individual's own responsibility, which is the focus of the ritual (rather than preventive or protective measures). Many charismatic testimonials concerned with healing, begin with confessions about how the sick individual shut himself away, harbored feelings of anger, resentment, vanity, refused the Lord entrance to the heart and mind, neglected to seek the help from within and without that was available. Disease is equated with self-destruction. To be healed, the healer must re-examine and reorder his priorities. He must subdue the doubting, confused, mistrustful or prideful aspects of himself and open himself through confession and prayer to the ministration of the healer without and the Spirit within.

The ritual of healing is thus one of gaining access to neglected aspects of consciousness, of opening oneself internally to neglected healing powers. If the ill person can open himself sufficiently to these healing influences, he experiences an 'in-rushing' of the Spirit: a sense of wholeness or integration is produced, the malfunctioning corrected, the guilt relieved.

Finally, it should be noted that in all healing rituals, group interaction is seen as ultimately important. The individual who shuts himself away from the group and from the Spirit after the healing will ultimately become sick again.

While the body symbolism in terms of threats to boundaries is not as clear in healing rituals as in the purification rituals, we would argue that the dangers are perceived in terms of a confusion of internal boundaries or of a 'system at war with itself.' The object of the ritual seems to be to regulate internal relations, to subdue negative thoughts and make the powerful healing presence within felt. The idea is to make 'whole' and to correct the self-destructive thought processes of the sick individual. This is more vividly demonstrated in such groups as Christian Science, but in such groups as Charismatics it is felt that the individual must himself 'have faith' or believe in the Spirit that is with him if he is to be healed. It is the sick individual who is guilty of 'cutting himself off', of internal confusions and failures.

Despite the fact that both groups recognize an outer and an inner danger associated with contamination on the one hand and disease on the other, their emphasis is consistently different. Indeed, they form a kind of counterpoint to each other (see Table 1).

The purification rituals locate the source of harm as outside the individual and the source of cure inside. The healing rituals are precisely the reverse, locating the genesis of the problem inside the individual and the solution outside him in the hands of the Spirit.

On a social or group level this opposition is maintained. In the case of purification rituals, there is little or no interaction between members and no sense of guilt. In fact, the ritual functions symbolically to remove or defend the self from the outside world. On the other hand, the healing ritual depends upon group interaction, often physical as well as emotional. Guilt is experienced by the ill person, and the concern is with re-establishing links, opening the mind and reuniting with the healing influence of the Spirit.

Table 1

A Typology of Healing and Purification Rituals in Two Religions Movements in the Montreal Area

	Purification Rituals (IYI)	Healing Rituals (CCR)
Nature of contamination of disease	Environmental pollution: additivies in food, dirt and noise in the air, physical stress of modern life	Germs, contagion, accident, evil, ill-will, divine judgement
Cause of harm	Unseen agents which, if allowed to enter the body, create toxins which poison and destroy the system	If the internal systems (mental, spiritual and emotional) are confused, imbalanced or distorted and if the individual has 'cut himself off', disease enters
Responsibility for harm	Outside the individual — no guilt is experienced	Inside the individual — guilt is experienced
Bodily boundaries seen as threatened	External boundaries: focus on orifices	Internal boundaries: the system at war with itself
Nature of ritual for purification or cure	Preventive — breathing exercises postures diets	Curative — laying on of hands prayer mental concentration
Cause of purification or cure	Harmful agents expelled. Self defended from future intrusions of foreign environmental material	Internal balances corrected: links to community re-established, individual opened to healing influences
Responsibility for purity/cure	Inside the individual: the self	Outside the individual: the Holy Spirit
Bodily boundaries seen as effected	External: points of contact with world purified and defended	Internal contradictions and confusions regulated: system made whole
Number of participants	One	Two or more
Interaction between members	Minimal, except in initial instruction	Intense: emotional and physical contact between healer and healed, healed and other group members

III. Ritual and Social Dilemma

What is the relation between ritual and social dilemma? Douglas suggests that threats to the physical body expressed and resolved ritually mirror threats to the social body. In the case of purification rituals, the threat is penetration of the outer boundaries and with healing rituals, the threat is to internal confusion and self-destruction. How can these be translated into social norms?

The answer to this depends largely on how the term 'social body' is translated. In the case of these movements, this may be translated either as the social unit of the individual chapter of the group or as the larger North American society of which these groups are subsystems. Both definitions have implications for the kind of research needed, and the kind of answers sought. Each also presents problems and solutions.

a) *The Social Body as the Individual Group*

If the groups with purification rituals are analyzed with this definition in mind, the following relations may be hypothesized between ritual and social dilemma:

1. The ritual reflects a concern with the outer boundary of the group, that separating the group from the rest of society. It suggests that this boundary is seen as shaky and easily penetrated.

2. The fact that the group is not being physically attacked (except perhaps by a constant influx of new members which might threaten the ideology or beliefs of the group) suggests that it is felt to be symbolically weak, i.e. the social reality as defined by the group is a shaky one and easily destroyed or penetrated, and may only be preserved by isolated, blocking out the foreign and disruptive material.

3. As fears of contamination are in fact pollution fears (which Douglas notes as fears of disorder or 'matter out of place' and are particularly prevalent in situations of moral ambiguity) (Douglas, 1966), it is hypothesized that the all-inclusive, morally relativistic philosophy which Anthony and Robbins (1976) among others have suggested characterize counter-cultural groups, results in a weak structure (where right and wrong are no longer clear) which must be defended by isolation from competing or 'foreign' ideologies which slip in easily.

If the groups with healing rituals are analyzed, using the definition of social body as the individual group, the following relations may be hypothesized between ritual and social dilemma:

1. The ritual reflects a concern with internal confusions and self-destruction. The group feels that the internal relations between members is easily disturbed and disordered, resulting in social sickness.

2. The ritual emphasis on guilt suggests a need to reassert a moral order. Guilt results from having neglected, confused or broken moral imperatives. The emphasis in the ritual of connecting individuals into larger wholes suggests that the particular source of concern is in the relationship of one individual to the group.

3. Group members probably feel that the clear hierarchical and moral distinctions *to which they are accustomed* are breaking down and must be reasserted.

For example, it has often been noted that the CCR grew up in the wake of Vatican II, and the increasingly lax view of the church toward many moral issues and accepted patterns of hierarchy. This is felt by some members as a threat to moral order... the healing ritual is then a response to this internal threat.

These statements are hypothetical. They are suggested in an effort to show how dilemmas of the physical and social body may be linked. To test such hypotheses, long-term ethnographic research in such groups is needed. Such research, focusing on the relationship between social and ritual concerns, could chart the influence of the one on the other. As threats to the social body occur corresponding changes in body rituals should appear.

The difficulty in focusing on individual chapters is that these new religious movements are not isolated bodies, but subsystems of a larger (albeit pluralistic) American culture. For the most part, these movements are not exclusive, and members continue to participate in that larger culture. It is that larger culture which socialized most members. It is risking distortion, therefore, to regard these groups as complete or closed systems, whose rituals reflect only that closed group life.

b) *The Social Body as the Larger Cultural Unit of Middle Class American Society (From Which Group Membership is Recruited)*

This alternative interpretation is also fraught with problems. Not only is there the difficulty of defining the cultural limits of 'middle America,' but at this level any comparison between ritual and social dilemma is apt to become little more than a literary device. This, however, is a criticism of much of the work in the area of contemporary or popular culture. And, despite these difficulties, the approach has advantages. It allows us to view these groups (as many theorists have attempted to do) in the context of the wider culture, as expressions of/or responses to that wider culture.

As Wuthnow (1976) has indicated, much of the experimentation found in these groups has a wider, more popular base. A similar concern with purity, such as the one which has been explored, is behind the widespread health-food and environmental protection movements. As for the concern with healing, Illich (1976) pointed out that at no time in our history have health concerns and health professions held such sway in our lives.

Interestingly, on this wider cultural level our notions of disease and pollution are linked. The most dreaded diseases today, and increasingly the most virulent among the middle class urbanites, are those diseases termed 'environmental diseases,' including cancer, arthritis, heart disease (Lerner, 1975; Illich, 1976). All these diseases are characterized by two features. Their origins are not completely understood but seem to be linked to the absorption of invisible foreign particles from the environment which cause the body to malfunction and self-destruct. In the case of cancer, this self-destruction takes the form of cell growth gone berserk; in the case of heart disease, the form of failure of the blood to form the normal breakdown of cholesterol which then clogs the arteries; in the case of arthritis and other auto-immune diseases, the body quite simply appears to be revolting, forming antibodies against itself.

The term environmental is applied to these diseases for two reasons. First, the stress of urban life in a technological society seems an important, pre-conditioning factor. Second, the destructive effects of the chemical by-products or industrial wastes are prime suspects in the preciptation of these diseases.

It is these same chemicals, by-products and additives which are at the root of our ideas about pollution. The environment becomes polluted, the pollutions then penetrate our bodies through our lungs and stomachs and trigger a process of self-destruction.

While the above statements may reflect scientific fact, it is ill-advised to take our own conceptions of dirt and disease merely literally and overlook their symbolic and expressive significance. As Douglas notes:

> There is no such thing as absolute dirt; it exists in the eye of the beholder. Nor do our ideas about disease account for the range of our behavior in cleaning and avoiding dirt. Dirt offends against order. (M. Douglas, 1966: 12)

When regarded symbolically this 'popular medical model' of disease and pollution can be seen to contain the elements of *both* the purification and the healing rituals. A threat is felt in terms of penetration of external boundaries and in terms of internal self-destruction and confusion. Moreover, the two are seen as related. This suggests an interesting possibility: that if in fact purification and healing rituals are a response to a threat to the larger social body of American society, as articulated in the 'popular medical model,' then they are each only a *partial* response to that total problem.

To push this possibility and this discussion further is to enter on to very shaky ground. Translated into social and symbolic terms, as Douglas would have us do, the 'popular medical model' reads "What enters the cultural group of middle America and causes the system to self-destruct?" Such questions begin to sound like riddles (of the "what is black and dangerous and lives in trees?" variety) and one begins to suspect that the answers will be more entertaining than instructive. Not to be deterred, here are several tentative suggestions.

The most fitting, if not the most original, is that the two threats of penetration and confusion may be symbolic of a situation of competitive moral systems or cultural relativity which many theorists have used to describe the appeal of new religious movements (Eister, 1974; Glock, 1976). This theory suggests that because of the widening gap between Biblical religion and utilitarian individualism (Bellah, 1976) coupled with the increasing awareness (particularly among the college educated) of the relativity of all moral positions many Americans (and particularly middle class Americans) are experiencing a crisis in morality or meaning systems. Competing values or anti-values (which have entered our system from other cultures via the mass media, the Vietnam War and the social sciences), have caused a further breakdown of the already weakening moral and ethical structure of American society. Penetration of foreign and incompatible matter causes internal confusion and self-destruction.

In support of this hypothesis, according to Robert Wuthnow (1976) the people who are attracted to the counter-cultures new religious movements (themselves an example of a competing morality) are much more likely to be those most open to experimenting with a variety of alternative lifestyles. It is fitting, therefore, according to Douglas' theory that they would experience the weakest and most easily penetrated boundary as that which separates one social group from another. It is also fitting that the neo-Christians, who do not seem to be as attracted to any of the alternative lifestyles and who for the most part were at least nominal Christians to begin with should not be so concerned with outer boundaries as with counter-acting the confusion developing within their own system (Harrison, 1974).

Finally, one other related interpretation is suggested. It could be argued that in the economic realm the megolithic growth of business, to the point where control of the economy is outside not only the community but the nation, results not merely in a sense of weakened national unity but in times of economic stress, in a system inflexible to the needs of an individual economy. This inflexibility, linked with recession results in a system fraught with strikes and price wars which seem both incomprehensible and self-destructive. Another way of putting it is that a pluralistic society such as ours is much more likely to seem to be in a state of economic civil war when resources get short. When control of these resources is even partially outside the society itself, the situation is exacerbated.

In conclusion, both the above theories (and probably several others) have the necessary elements of penetration and confusion to qualify as possible answers to the riddle. Whether in fact they represent the social threat to which these groups and their rituals are a response can only be answered by intensive study of the members themselves and their views of and experiences in the larger economic and cultural systems or with the kind of world systems approach which can see them as a part of large-scale historical trends such as that employed by Wuthnow, (1977).

In the meantime, however, if we follow Douglas' maxim, and do not overlook the symbolic aspects of the notions of environmental disease prevalent in our culture we must also note that *whatever* social problem is there symbolized does not seem to be resolved in either ritual (purification or healing). Neither deals with the entire dilemma of penetration and disorder. These are partial and in some ways extreme responses, on the one hand recommending isolation and putting all blame on outside agents; on the other, suggesting a reassertion of an old morality and order and putting all blame on the self. Neither is particularly ritually constructive, either at pinpointing the cause of difficulty or offering a resolution. Of course, only one particular ritual has been discussed. There is considerable work to be done in looking at the overall ritual patterns of different groups. But it is through a detailed study of rituals that the symbolic message of these groups to North American society, and its interpreters in the social sciences, may be revealed.

F.R. Westley is a professor of Sociology at University of Western Ontario, in London, Ontario. Her previous work has been in the area of the structural analysis of popular culture phenomena and in the study of new religious movements.

Metaphor in the Rituals
Of Restorative and Transformative Groups

Joseph W. Bastien & David G. Bromley

PARTICIPATION IN CULTURAL rituals and ceremonial occasions has waxed and waned throughout recent American history. In the 1960s and early 1970s participation in a number of traditional ceremonies (college graduations, church weddings, Sunday church services and commemorative occasions such as Memorial Day and the Fourth of July) seem to have reached a periodic nadir. Further, a number of traditional ceremonies have come under legal attack, all the way from fraternity hazing to masses in Latin, to prayers in school. During this period, informal and individual ceremonies supplanted the more traditional conventional observances. In the last few years there has been a revived interest in ceremonies and ritualistic occasions (e.g., increased attendance at church services and graduations).

However, over the long course of American history, the amount of ritual and ceremony shared by the entire society has gradually but continually declined. In general, modern secular societies evidence less ritual and ceremony than pre-industrial societies as a result of the processes of secularization, social differentiation and scientific knowledge creation which limit the kind of mystery around which rituals can easily be constructed to a very limited sphere of social life. The most obvious example is the reduced importance of religious symbolism and imagery in structuring individual's day to day activities. Among modern secular societies, America is even less inclined to formal ritual and ceremony because of Americans' adherence to the Protestant Ethic and their historical opposition to the hierarchical traditions of our European forefathers. Numerous observers have described America as almost contemptuous of traditions (Lerner, 1957; Riesman, 1950).

Yet human experience has shown that ritual and ceremony are vital to human societies (Turner, 1969). Some evidence is found in the fact that although a number of traditional formal rituals and ceremonies have declined in social importance, new rituals are constantly being created. One example at a national level is Super Bowl Week, which has become the occasion for numerous ritualistic

48

celebrations quite apart from the athletic event itself. Others involve subsegments of the population, such as the current religious revival in which ritualistic innovations, such as speaking in tongues, have become institutionalized. Similarly, among youth, beginning with Woodstock, rock concerts have become a quasi-institutionalized form of collective celebration. Thus even in modern societies, rituals and ceremonies are being continually recreated and rejuvenated. What is it about ritual and ceremony which make it so indispensable to society?

Ritual and ceremony serve at least three important functions for the social organization in which they occur by structuring individual and collective experiences. First, they provide either continuity or movement. For example, the (until recently) unchanging nature of a Latin Mass links the participant with the centuries old traditions and hence provides a sense of continuity. On the other hand, rites of passage, such as puberty rites, marriages and funerals, delineate transitions in individual's statuses within the community (Van Gennep, 1909). Secondly, ritual and ceremony enhance communality and solidarity within a group. For example, Fourth of July celebrations, rock festivals, Super Bowl and church services are all occasions at which individuals collectively express their commitment to common value and beliefs. Even ritualistic occasions at which an individual is excluded from the community in some sense (e.g. trials) serve to enhance unity by more clearly defining the boundaries of the community. Third, ritual provides an occasion for the mystery and majesty which inevitably are part of human social life (Turner, 1969:6). A Catholic mass, for example, provides the individual with an opportunity to experience transcendence. The Super Bowl provides an opportunity for collectively sharing drama, suspense and celebration. Trials and their various forms allow individuals to vicariously experience good and evil. In sum, ritual and ceremony serve as occasions which separate the ordinary from the extraordinary, the mundane from the important, the sacred from the profane (Douglas, 1970). By so doing, ritual helps to create social order, and to link an individual's emotional life with collective experiences.

Assuming the crucial significance of ritual and ceremony in all human groups, the question remains how are meaningful rituals and ceremonies created? How do human beings construct symbolic systems around which they can orient their social activities and social relationships in a meaningful way? One crucial condition for the creation of meaningful rituals and ceremonies is the construction of metaphorically based belief systems. Following Fernandez (1974:123), by metaphor we mean a predication upon a subject of an object from a domain to which the subject belongs only by a stretch of the imagination. For example, Charles Lindbergh was commonly called the "Lone Eagle," King Richard of England was referred to as "Richard, the Lion Hearted," Rommel was dubbed the "Desert Fox," George Washington is popularly referred to as the "Father" of America, and the U.S. Government is nicknamed "Uncle Sam." Similarly, sports teams are named bears, lions, tigers, falcons and longhorns, and sports stars are called "snake," "iceman," "crusher," "monster," "doctor" and "rocket." Individual experiences and feelings also are described in metaphorical terms. For example, people will refer to themselves as "turned on," "laid back," "born again," "hot as a fire cracker," "spaced out," "in tune" and "jived up." Finally, collective experiences are conceived metaphorically. For example, the Catholic mass is seen as the "Last Supper" and the Fourth of July is treated as a "birthday." In each of these illustrations, what people are doing is attributing to themselves, others or social occasions characteristics which belong to another order and suggest an analogy. It is by linking an individual, object or occasion to one from another order that the former is imbued with a transcendental, mysterious or powerful quality.

Metaphors come alive during rituals, which are a series of performative acts creating the imagery of the metaphor. The participants can become totally involved in these experience activities; all the senses can be affected so they audibly, visually and kinesthetically perceive the metaphor (Haydu, 1974:136). For example, because people emotionally and imaginatively believe themselves to be vessels of the Spirit, they experience what otherwise would be nonsensical talk to be divinely inspired, "speaking in tongues." Similarly in communion people may literally experience a wine and a wafer as the body and blood of Christ. In each of these illustrations, metaphor provides a symbolic construct which allows individuals to transcend immediate mundane experience and reorient social relationships in some way. Socially, then, the significance of metaphor lies in its capacity to allow human beings to have kinds of relationships that would otherwise be difficult or impossible to sustain (see Bastien, 1973, 1976, 1978; Boas, 1911; Boulding, 1965; Levi-Straus, 1962; and Sapir, 1977).

Two excellent examples illustrating the importance of metaphor for rituals and ceremonies are the contemporary American groups, The Society of Creative Anachronism (hereafter SCA) and Sun Myung Moon's Unification Church (hereafter UC), more popularly known as the "Moonies" (Bromley and Shupe, 1979). These two groups differ in several ways. First the membership of SCA is primarily adult, whereas UC members are largely of college age. Second, SCA is largely a fraternal association devoted to intellectual and recreational pursuits; members thus participate on a limited part-time basis. By contrast, the UC is organized communally and individual involvement is total and full-time. The UC's goals are sweeping in nature, literally the salvation of humankind and the restoration of man to God. Finally, the SCA is essentially *restorative* in perspective (i.e., it seeks to recreate what they perceive to be valued historical parts of their cultural tradition) while the UC is *transformative* in nature (i.e., it seeks to usher in a new utopian order and, in this sense, literally tries to create the future).

A Comparison of SCA and UC

SCA was founded in Berkeley, California, in 1966 and currently has more than 10,000 members in the U.S.[1] The members of SCA emulate life as it is believed to have been lived in the Middle Ages. They adopt names, clothing and speech patterns associated with the feudal order of that era (Rigel, 1978c). They hold tournaments, where the members duel one another, sing songs and recite poetry from that period and entertain one another with revels and tournaments similar to those of medieval times (Rigel, 1977). The central metaphor of the SCA is a feudal order as that is perceived through literature and historical accounts. In the context of SCA activities, members act as if they actually were inhabitants of the medieval age and assume roles appropriate to that social order.

The UC was established on the West Coast of the U.S. in 1959, but languished in relative obscurity until the 1970s when the Church's founder and leader, Sun Myung Moon, arrived in the U.S. to personally direct the Church in the U.S. Currently the UC has approximately 3,000 or 4,000 members. According to Reverend Moon, in the Garden of Eden Eve was literally seduced by the archangel Lucifer who was jealous of God's human creation. This was the "fall of man." As a result of that sexual indiscretion all future human generations became Satanic in the sense that they emanated from Satan and not from God. The concept of fall is further extended to the slaying of Abel by Cain which created two lineages within mankind: the godless forces of Cain (equated with godless communism) and the god-fearing forces of Abel (equated with political democracies). In order for man to be restored to his original proper relationship with God, he had to pay indemnity for his sins. Periodically, sufficient indemnity had been paid that God offered man the opportunity for restoration. The present era represents one of those opportunities which if lost would not recur again for thousands of years. Thus, UC members frantically engage in trying to publicize their message and construct the necessary conditions for mankind's physical and spiritual salvation. The central metaphor for UC, then, is the Fall of Man, along with the closely related metaphoric concepts of "restoration" and "true family" (i.e., families physically and spiritually reunited with God).

For both SCA and UC there are certain implications of the metaphor construct for 1) redefining time and space, 2) creating social organization and 3) transforming individual identities. Each of these three processes has important consequences for constructing and maintaining ritual and ceremonies within each group.

Redefinitions of Time and Space

The SCA redefines the continental U.S. into medieval kingdoms. Six such units are derived from the political division of Europe in the Middle Ages: Caed (Southern California), Western Kingdom (Northern California, Oregon and Washington), Atenveldt (Arizona, New Mexico, Colorado and other Western states), Ansteorra (Texas and Oklahoma), Middle Kingdom (Middle West states), Merides (Old South), and Eastern Kingdom (Eastern states above Kentucky). As they were in the Middle Ages, kingdoms are subdivided into hierarchical orders of principalities, baronies, shires and cantons. These geographic kingdoms become the basic organizational units within which the ceremonies and rituals take place. Further, at individual tournaments, revels and feasts, the primary activities of the SCA, the space in which the ceremony or celebration takes place is decorated to resemble as closely as possible the interior of a feudal manor: thrones, low tables, tapestry, oil lamps, murals and table settings (Rigel, 1978a&b). Enormous attention is given to making every detail as authentic as a Shakespearean play at Stratford-upon-Avon.

For the UC the world is divided geographically into the Cain and Abel forces which are engaged in a titanic political and spiritual struggle. Countries are assigned specific roles in this cosmic battle; for example, Korea is the new Israel, and the U.S. is the archangel (opposed by its Satanic counterpart, the Soviet Union) which has the responsibility for ultimately defeating the forces of godless communism. There are certain locations in the world where the forces of God and Satan are poised in active confrontations, such as East and West Germany, North and South Vietnam, and North and South Korea. On a local level within the U.S., specific geographical locations which the UC has purchased and which have been blessed by Reverend Moon personally are defined as "restored." These are locuses where the communication between God and man is most readily achievable and hence are particularly propitious for various rituals and ceremonies.

Time also becomes significantly reoriented by the groups' respective metaphors. The SCA essentially attempts to replace the present with the past which tends to create a timelessness by diminishing the importance of recent history while reviving the past. Further, contemporary times are divided by occasions characteristic of the medieval era. For example, SCA has its distinctive holidays, such as the Twelfth Night (a feast and celebration held on January 6), a Midsummer Revel (corresponding to Summer Solstice on June 22), and special days designated regionally at which kings and queens are crowned and tournaments are held (Naff, 1978).

The UC has literally reinterpreted all of biblical history on the basis of their unique interpretation of the fall of man and created an elaborate numerological schema which supports their view of history as a continuous struggle for restoration. It is on the basis of this schema that the present is viewed as uniquely propitious for another restorative attempt and Moon's own biographical characteristics are linked to and found congruent with the postulated appearance of a new messiah. Moon was born at the divinely designated time (1920) in the New Israel (Korea), married at the appropriate age (40), and had the divinely ordained number of children (12). Further, like the SCA, the UC recalibrates the year in terms of holidays such as God's Day (January 1), and the birthdays of Moon and each member of his family which become the occasion for celebrative ceremonies. The UC literally tries to replace the present with the future. According to its spiritual timetable, 1981 has been designated as the year in which major events beginning the course of restoration will occur. For each group, then, the metaphor allows a symbolic redefinition of space and time which are related to the context or occasion for important rituals and ceremonies. At least for these two groups the redefinition of time is particularly salient. Both treat the present as trivial and almost meaningless and try to transcend it: the SCA by reaching into the past and the UC by reaching into the future. The future and the past become not distant eras but rather are readily accessible, as if members of each group possessed a "time machine" by which they could transport themselves through time or history. For both groups it is ritual and ceremony which provide the structure for this time travel and it is the groups' respective metaphors that lend symbolic meaning to those rituals and ceremonies.

Creating Social Organization

Two important aspects of social relationships emanate directly from the groups' respective metaphors: 1) their status hierarchies and a corresponding means of creating mobility within those hierarchies and 2) specific roles, events and activities in which members are involved. In the case of SCA, according to the feudal metaphor, a king and queen rule each kingdom as well as the principalities, baronies, shires and cantons which are their constituent units. Beneath the king and queen are the following series of royal offices: 1) The seneschal is the authorized legal representative of the society; 2) The herald informs members of forthcoming events and decisions of the SCA nation ruling body; 3) The knight-marshal referees the jousting tournaments; 4) The master and/or mistress of the arts encourages the study of medieval art; 5) The reeve keeps the financial accounts; 6) The chronicler takes minutes of the meeting; and 7) The poet laureate recites medieval verse (Rigel, 1977, 1978a,b,c). The most important status distinction involving differential prestige and power relates to knighthood, an achieved status, which is the principal source of mobility within the group. Mobility is achieved through jousting tournaments which are constructed to resemble their medieval counterparts. Combatants duel with bamboo swords covered with styrafoam, garden hose and duct tape. Tournaments begin at the shire level and winners proceed to the barony level. Victors at this level are bestowed knighthood. Tournaments are also held at the principality and kingdom levels until a victor has emerged at the latter level. This person becomes king and remains so until he too is beaten on the tournament field. It usually takes several years to fight all the duels necessary to be king. Kings remain in office from several weeks to a year, depending upon their ability to beat emerging competitors from lower levels.

The hierarchy of the UC is necessarily much truncated. The fact that Moon is regarded as having communicated directly with God gives him a certain charismatic status to which no other member can aspire. At least in theory, then, all others stand equal as "brothers" (i.e., there is a fictive kinship system which binds individuals together as family members) and "sisters" beneath his paternal guidance. While a limited bureaucracy has in fact developed, these tendencies have been vigorously opposed within the church. However, it is possible for people to gain prestige and to some extent power. Much of the activity of the church is oriented around gaining new converts and fund-raising. Proselytizing and fund-raising are conducted in a highly ritualistic fashion. In the case of fund-raising, for example, UC members at least in theory interpret the solicitations-donations exchange as follows. The UC member approaches a person on the street and asks for a donation to further the missionary work of the church. From the former's perspective the implicit request is for both to stop and acknowledge God—the donor through his contribution to God's work, the solicitor through his acceptance of the gift and the responsibility to employ it for God's purpose. If a donation is received, the solicitor responds with a gift (i.e., pin, flower, flag) to acknowledge the loving exchange and their mutual recognition of God. In each case, one's success at these activities is attributed to the member's level of spiritual understanding. If one is able to truly love others (or as members put it to act "heartistically"), then financial contributions and new converts (referred to as one's "spiritual children") will naturally follow. Success in proselytizing and fundraising are to a significant degree linked to mobility opportunities within the church such as the chance to attend its seminary or to head-up witnessing and fundraising teams.

Prestige and power are, of course, important dimensions of any social group, and so it is not surprising that the occasions which mark transitions in one's vertical status and the process by which vertical mobility is achieved are heavily laden with ritual and ceremony. For the SCA it is the ritualized combat in tournaments which provide the context for social mobility; in the case of the UC it is ritualized encounters between solicitors and donors. The power of the metaphor is again apparent. Physical strength and skill in the one case and the ability to relate "heartistically" in the other gain their social significance directly from the groups' respective metaphors.

With respect to specific roles, events and activities in the SCA each ceremonial occasion ultimately derives its meaning and organization from the feudal metaphor. In November 1978, for example, the Shire of Border March had a revel and tournament outside Beaumont, Texas, in a farm house owned by one of the members. Tessa of the Gardens, Seneschal, presided, decorated the house in medieval castle style and prepared a gourmet banquet of suckling pig, duck, lamb, potatoes, vegetables, fruit, pudding and mead beer. About twenty-five guests arrived on a Friday evening, including Lady Wench Constance Greghall the Insatiable, Lord Tilbyrne Morningstar, Master Lloyd von Eaker the Grimm Executioner, John the Plain of Shein, Adelicia de la Saul Etol Ambassador from Merides to Ansteorra, and Lady Janet Shadowhawk. The gathering included entire families and individuals of all ages. Formal greetings and pleasantries were exchanged in medieval English (e.g., "Shall we go a hawking in the earlie morn?") Men were dressed in 13th century tunics, 15th and

16th century doublets and jerkins; the women wore blouses, skirts and headsets from the same period.

Friday evening was devoted to consuming a sumptuous feast. The next day everyone gathered for the Field Tournament which consisted of competitive sword fighting. Although the bamboo swords were well padded and combatants wore metal helmets and padding, this protection did not prevent individuals from receiving painful welts. Tournaments continued through Saturday and Sunday with breaks for eating, drinking, making love and listening to poetry and music. The tournament champion who emerged became eligible to participate in jousts at the barony level.

Two unforseen events occurred. Sir Randal von Hordlichwold the Giant, a special guest, had recently attained knighthood, and so Lady Angelina initiated him into the Rite of the Knight's Virgin Belt (several maidens made love with him in a corner of the room). At another time, festivities got out of hand when two men wrestled each other and crashed down upon the banquet table, injuring a lady. A knight restored order and the revelry continued until morning.

In this illustration it is clear that the ceremonial structure of the weekend lent significance to each of the individual events and linked them together in a meaningful way (i.e., created a context of meaning) and that the feudal metaphor provided the central symbolic imagery running through the rituals and ceremonies. SCA members were able to engage in a diverse array of activities which offered fun and excitement (e.g., feasts, sexual encounters), or intellectual interest (e.g., demonstrating mastery of old English and medieval history), allowed expression of personal interests in a social context (e.g., poetry, culinary arts) and included both elements of cooperation (e.g., staging ceremonies and competition, athletic contests). While members could have undertaken some of these activities individually, certainly it was the social context (the ceremonial structure) which was the source of much of their sense of pleasure, mystery and adventure and the feudal metaphor which facilitated the transcendental quality of the rituals and ceremonies.

Each of the major daily activities within the UC similarly can be linked directly to the metaphors of fall, restoration and family. Indeed, the entire round of life of UC members can be seen as a series of rituals and ceremonies guided by these metaphors. For example, praying and singing of religious songs are the first and last activities of each day and also accompany other mundane daily events such as the eating of meals. These activities are designed to constantly enhance communality and solidarity within the "spiritual family." For many members the rest of the day is given over to witnessing and fundraising. Such exchanges are perceived as mutual acknowledgments of God. However, they also have a collective significance since new members and donations are defined as restoration of individuals or money to God. Thus, like Moon's tours and rallies which are undertaken to fulfill a divine mandate, each donation and new member achieved contributes to man's ultimate physical and spiritual communication with God for their success. If they are unsuccessful in their daily endeavors, they will immediately stop and ritualistically through prayer attempt to "recenter" themselves on God. Each of the projects the group undertakes also is legitimated through the metaphor. In one incident we observed, a UC team entered Houston, Texas, to combat pornography (recall that sexual indiscretion caused man's fall). Faced with an apathetic public and hostile shop and movie owners, UC members finally adopted a plan of unilateral action. They spent several days designing paper clothing which they then surreptitiously pasted over pictures on the marquees of pornographic establishments. While to the public this seemed like a college prank and to members themselves was a source of fun and adventure, it also was interpreted as a victory over Satan in the struggle for restoration.

Transferring Individual Identities

In both the SCA and the UC, individual identities are to some extent transformed. However, the degree of identity change is less in the former group since individuals play at their feudal roles on a more limited part-time basis. In the UC members act out their roles on a full-time basis and discard all external and competing roles. However, even in the SCA because members consider their metaphorical space and time to be their real world, at least temporarily, their participation is more than role-playing in a theatrical sense. As they participate in the group's rituals and ceremonies in their designated roles, they consciously strive to take on the qualities of those personages in a variety of ways. They assume the proper dress, decorum, language and even personality for their roles in the process of striving for authenticity. Thus, they strive to become Sir Lancelot or King Arthur or Lady Guenevere; and to the extent that these identities are supported by other members of the group, they are able to become these historical individuals. It is the rituals and ceremonies which provide the vehicle for asserting these identities. The very process of acting out the rituals such as feasts and tournaments lends form and substance to the metaphor.

In the UC the transformation of identity is more profound primarily because individuals are members of communal groups in which identity shaping is more crucial and feasible. For example, members give up virtually all personal possessions, may adopt new names and recalculate their birth dates from the day when they joined the church. A variety of rituals serves to dissociate the individuals from their former identity and relationships and cement their new identity. For instance, the constant social reaffirmation of oneness with the members of one's new spiritual family and the designation of outsiders (even one's biological family) as satanic have this effect. Another example of rituals which build new identity relate to sexuality. Of course given the UC's ideology, sexual indiscretion constitutes a major threat, a problem compounded by the constant proximity of members of the opposite sex in communal setting. Thus a series of rituals and related behaviors have developed to handle problems of containing sexual relations. In addition to avoiding provocative clothing members dispense with many of the daily grooming rituals typical in American society as well as ritualized dating behavior. In place of these rituals reaffirming brotherly and sisterly behaviors, periodic confessions or daily diaries in which members acknowledge their struggles with their fallen natures and the openly discussed, institutionalized individual and group practice of taking frequent cold showers to reduce sexual needs. In each of these illustrations individuals are orienting their behavior relative to the UC's central metaphor, striving to overcome fallen nature and to become part of the spiritually pure family which will act as the vanguard for the new messiah.

Summary and Conclusions

So ritual and ceremony are integral to human societies. They provide human groups with means of creating a sense of continuity or transition, solidarity and communality, and mystery and majesty. The fact that even in modern secular societies rituals and ceremonies persist and are continuously created offers compelling evidence of their significance. With the SCA, a restorative group which seeks to recreate the past, and the UC, a transformative group, which seeks to create the future, the central metaphor of the group structures its rituals and ceremonies. Metaphors allow individuals to sustain relationships which would otherwise be problematic or impossible. Metaphor permits individuals then to transcend the mundane, in the one case acting as if they were still in the feudal era and in the other as if they were stepping into the future.

Finally, the importance of the metaphor in our society becomes most apparent in those cases where an appropriate and an accepted metaphor is lacking. For example, increasing divorce rates and diversity of marital life-styles have made it difficult for participants in those relationships , as well as outsiders, to know how to relate to one another. Similarly, release from prison and recovery from mental illness are points of transition for which there is no ritual or ceremony or guiding metaphor.

To employ a metaphor of our own, our society is between a rock and a hard place; we value the concomitants of social change but also suffer the consequences of the dislocation which it produces. Indeed, perhaps the most eloquent evidence for us of the importance of metaphor, ritual and ceremony lies in the awkwardness and disorientation we experience when these symbolic guideposts are not present.

Notes

[1]We wish to acknowledge Arlene Naff and Mishi Shannon, who assisted us in gathering information about the SCA.

References

Bastien, Joseph W.
1973 *Qollahuaya Rituals: An Ethnographic Account of the Symbolic Relations of Man and Land in an Andean Ayllu.* Monograph 56. Ithaca: Cornell University Latin American Studies Program.
1976 "Marriage and Exchange in the Andes," *Actes du XLIIe Congres Internacional Des Americanistes*, Vol. IV: 149-64.
1978 *Mountain of the Condor: Metaphor and Ritual in an Andean Ayllu.* Monograph 64. American Ethnological Society. St. Paul: West Publishing Co.

Boaz, Franz
1911 "Introduction" in *Handbook of American Indian Languages.* Bureau of American Ethnology Bulletin 40(1).

Boulding, Kenneth
1956 *The Image.* Ann Arbor. Univ. of Michigan Press.

Bromley, David and Anson D. Shupe, Jr.
1979 *"Moonies" in America: Church, Cult and Crusade.* Beverly Hills: Sage Publications.

Douglas, Mary
1978 *Purity and Danger.* London: Pelican Books.

Evans-Pritchard. E.E.
1956 *Nuer Religion.* Oxford: Oxford Univ. Press.
1969 *The Nuer* Oxford: Oxford Univ. Press.

Fernandez, James
1974 "The Mission of Metaphor in Expressive Culture," *Current Anthropology* 15:119-45.

Griaule, Marcel
1965 *Conversations with Ogotemmeli*. London: Oxford Univ. Press.

Haydu, George G.
1974 "Reply to Fernandez." *Current Anthropology* 15 (Jun): 136.

Lerner, Max
1957 *America as a Civilization*. New York: Simon and Schuster.

Levi-Strauss, C.
1962 *Totemism*. Boston: Beacon Press.

Naff, Arlene
1979 Conversation with Ms. Naff on June 23.

Riesman, David
1950 *The Lonely Crowd*. New Haven: Yale Univ. Press.

Rigel, Aureliane and Airlie
1977 "From the Regional Pursuivant," *Palantir*, Jan. 11 (Monthly Publication from the Region of Ansteorra, in the Kingdom of Ansteorra).
1978a "Southwind," *Palantir*, March 12.
1978b "Tournament Illuminated," *Palantir*, April 11.
1978c "Black Star," *Palantir*, Dec. 12.

Sapir, David and Christopher Crocker
1977 *The Social Use of Metaphor*. Philadelphia: Univ. of Pennsylvania Press.

Turner, Victor
1969 *The Ritual Process*. Chicago: Aldine Publishing Co.

Van Gennep, Arnold
1960 *The Rites of Passage*. Trans. M. Vizedom and G.I. Caffee.
(1909) Chicago: Univ. of Chicago Press.

Ritual in Architecture:
The Celebration of Life

Dennis Alan Mann

TO UNDERSTAND ARCHITECTURE one must realize that it envelopes life. Any single position which argues that architecture is purely physical shelter or that architecture exists for the sake of the architect alone merely begs the question. The late American architect Louis I. Kahn often told his students that when they were faced with a difficult architectural question, they should search out the beginning of the question and there they might see it in its essence, unadulterated by the burdens of history and tradition. There they might discover First Principles. To better understand the relationship between ritual and architecture we ought to begin by placing ourselves outside of ourselves in order to see ourselves more clearly. Life is a celebration and architecture is the stage upon which that celebration takes place. This is most clearly highlighted when there is thrust in front of us an unfamiliar society; one whose customs, traditions, beliefs and rituals are so unlike our own that we are forced to look anew at ourselves.

Deep in the central highlands of New Guinea in the Grand Valley of the Balim River live a group of people known as the Dani. The Dani culture was presented in a classic ethnographic film, *Dead Birds*, made in 1961 by Robert Gardiner.[1] Embedded in the film as it is in Dani culture one discovers the importance of ritual and ceremony as an affirmation of Dani life and as the main structuring element of Dani belief. The two most important rituals, waging war and the pig feast, are inseparable parts of their culture and serve as important determinants in the structuring of their physical environment.

The lives of the Dani are ruled by a great variety of ghosts, but especially the ghosts of a villages' own dead friends and relatives. These ghosts cause a great deal of havoc by spoiling crops or hiding on paths waiting to accost an unsuspecting passerby. Most Dani ritual is an attempt to influence these ghosts to cease and desist and to induce them to remain in specially constructed shelters. Especially vulnerable to ghosts is a soul matter or psyche which exists within each Dani and which waxes and wanes with their well-being. Participation in war or in the pig ceremony restores the strength of the psyche and appeases the ghosts.

War is a complex issue and is waged for many reasons, some of which arise out of interpersonal disputes, theft of pigs or territorial conflicts. But it is the ritual phase of war, the war that leads to the death of an enemy tribesman and thus avenges the death of one of their own tribal members, that strengthens the soul matter and placates the ghosts. Unavenged ghosts bring sickness, unhappiness and potential future disaster. War is waged to restore the balance that was lost in a previous battle when one of their own tribe members was killed. Without this balance the ghosts would cause trouble and the spiritual well-being of each individual would retreat to the backbone and cause each person to become vulnerable to ghostly attack.

Along the whole frontier between warring tribes are high watchtowers put up by each side to command a better view of the No-Man's-Land between their territories and to guard against enemy raids. These 30' high watchtowers are manned by warriors who also guard the nearby garden plots and the villages beyond. From time to time the watchtowers need repair and, because of their functional as well as symbolic importance, any work connected with the repair is a ritualized ceremony. A small toy bow and arrow are put in the tower and roasted grass leaves are placed around it to induce the ghosts to guard against enemy attack. Each tower has a little field around it where the warriors who man the tower can celebrate the death of an enemy.

The structure of the "neighborhood" where various allied villages or compounds are located, where the valley floor gardens are tilled for their staple sweet potato crop, and where the watchtowers exist perched precariously on the edge of No-Man's-Land, is strongly determined by the ritual phase of war. Although this ritual sounds irrational from our point of view, to the Dani it is a significant social act which links their supernatural beliefs to their day-to-day activities.

Most of the Dani ritual is designed to avert ghostly danger.[2] Paths are often barred to protect a wounded man from ghosts and within each village compound a little fenced enclosure, a ghost house complete with a path leading to the doorway is put up as a resting place for wandering ghosts and as an inducement to keep ghosts away from peoples' houses. The war ritual maintains a social pattern that has existed for centuries and as such sustains a social order. More importantly this ritual transmits those patterns to the villages' youth since two groups of boys—each the enemy to the other—will often play a game of throwing grass spears. The game is the grown-up ritual in miniature.

Another means of influencing ghosts is the *wam ganekhe,* or "pig treasure," and the more important "Pig Feast." During both ceremonies many people gather together to slaughter pigs, exchange gifts and renew the group soul matter by performing magical acts upon their ceremonial sacred black and green stones. These pig festivals, as well as marriages and funerals, are held in the long central courtyard formed by the low houses which are connected by short segments of fence. Behind the houses are the banana yard, pig sties and small, unroofed, ghost houses. The entire compound is surrounded by a five foot high fence to keep the pigs in and the ghosts out. Within the compound and among the various compounds which rest in the Grand Valley along the Aike River the Dani understand, though not in the self-conscious and rational way of Westerners, that it is their ritual which is an affirmation of life and which allows them to fashion the fate that in the end awaits all people. The Dani have a clear body of ideas, they have beliefs about nature and man, and they have a concept of a structured human society.

Their ritual is a concretization of those ideas and it forms for us a clearer understanding of the meaning of ritual as a coherent and important act within any society. Furthermore, the artifacts that they make, the objects that they construct, and the spaces that they define, all serve their ritual. For the Dani, as for all people, architecture is the stage upon which this ritual, both formal and informal, is enacted.

Ritual

Ritual is the symbolic transformation of beliefs, ideas, myths, ethics and experiences. Susanne Langer has pointed out that ritual acts are a natural activity to human beings and satisfy the basic human need for expressive acts which carry and transmit value.[3] Langer concludes by stressing that "some more or less organized system of beliefs and sentiments is an absolute necessity for the carrying on of social life."[4]

There are two ways that we can discuss ritual and ceremony: formal and informal. The traditional anthropological usage is formal when it *fixes* a collection of human sentiments into a form which clearly *transmits* cultural patterns from one person or group of people to another, or from one generation to the next.[5] Ritual is a form of communication which relies on objects which carry a high symbolic content and messages in language which clearly spell out the significance of the act. Religion is a classic example of formal ritual when it fixes the connection between the action, its meaning and a supernatural power. Ritual is also composed of a series of parts (sub-rituals or ceremonies) which must occur in a fixed order and have a direct relationship to each other.

Informal ritual is more open and flexible. Although it is still a collective expression of human sentiments, its form is more loosely connected. Games, festivals, fashion and fad, shopping excursions, vacations and many different life style activities are examples of informal ritualistic behavior. While formal ritual apprises us about our roots, our ethics and mores, and our permanent beliefs, informal ritual, or social drama to use Hugh Dalziel Duncans' terms, is a window into the future. Informal ritual is the realm of change. It captures and gives form to emerging beliefs, if only for a moment. It drags us out of the rut of habit and routine. It shatters timeworn beliefs. Nevertheless, both formal and informal ritual are necessary to create and sustain social order and transmit cultural patterns.

Hugh Dalziel Duncan makes a key distinction between formal and informal ritual which shall provide an important point of departure for this paper. Duncan suggests that religious ritual, for instance, can be understood as formal ritual since it is used "as a means to fix collective sentiments through communication with some great supernatural power believed to sustain the principles of social order on which the society is based."[6] As Duncan shows, religious ritual is beyond question; its goal is to uphold authority. Art, on the other hand, can be understood more as informal ritual because it changes. Again, according to Duncan, "Art is a socially sanctioned realm of change, ambiguity and doubt."[7] Little is fixed; there are no absolute truths. Duncan concludes this distinction by saying that "Art institutionalizes change in society, just as religion institutionalizes 'eternal' and 'fixed' principles of social action."[8]

Religion And Art

When Religion is used metaphorically it can stand for all of the institutions of society which provide canons by which we can guide our lives. Procedures for advancement in the corporate world, shopping for a new car, selling our house, attending an opening at an art museum or the regular Saturday evening at the symphony hall, and the presentation of candidates for public office, all produce a type of ritualistic behavior which is nearly as rigid and fixed as the most dogmatic religious rite or ceremony. They are the ways we use today for transmitting the values and beliefs of our highly technological, consumer-oriented society. Therefore the term Religion can be expanded to stand for all of the conventionalized institutionalized rituals which we accept without question, take for granted, or engage in unconsciously. It has been shown in many anthropological studies that religion is a restatement on another plane of the social, political and economic values of a society.

When Art is used to encompass the informal rituals of a society it can act as a symbol of changing values. Today in the Western world Art captures in form, in language, in song and in image the emerging beliefs and new social values of a dynamic society. In this sense Art can make us aware, perhaps for the first time, of what might have been previously unrecognized ritual. The painter, the sculptor, the photographer, the architect, the playwright, the novelist or neo-artists like the ad writer, the fashion designer, the TV scriptwriter or the pop artist are, because of the nature of their work, closely tuned to society. Their work reflects the fickle character of the changing needs, demands, desires and tastes of their social milieu. Therefore what we might on first sight perceive as avant-garde or nonconventional art might turn out to be merely a shift in social values first recognized by the artist. Art then can fall into the realm of informal ritual. It forces us to look at ourselves from a different perspective and rather than seeing our own reflection we discover Hyde or Alice or Mickey Mouse or Archie Bunker or Ronald McDonald staring back at us.

Both formal ritual (Religion) and informal ritual (Art) often, though not always, require both space and artifact for their enactment and commemoration. Traditional architecture, both vernacular architecture and high architecture, concretize formal ritual and ceremony and cast in stone the stage upon which ritual takes place. This is precisely why the study of archeological ruins is so revealing. It tells us much about the beliefs of a long lost culture. In another way Popular architecture because it is more flexible, more adaptable, more subject to fashion and fad, and more democratic than traditional architecture acts as the testing ground for emerging rituals and changing social beliefs. Both forms of architecture—Traditional and Popular—like Religion and Art, are a necessary component of a healthy and stable culture. Stability, represented by Traditional architecture, forms the foundation upon which change, represented by Popular architecture, can occur.

Ritual And Ceremony In Traditional Architecture

Ritual and ceremony in Traditional Architecture is best

illustrated by investigating its manifestation in four aspects in the design of buildings: 1) the location of the building in the landscape, 2) the symbolic quality of the building, 3) the spatial organization of the building, and 4) the uses of public open space.

Building In The Landscape

The decision as to where and how to locate a building in the landscape is seldom made accidentally. Important buildings which serve the major institutions of a society are carefully sited to best serve the formal rituals connected with the building. Greek temples, which housed the image of their gods, for instance, were thoughtfully placed in a landscape made sacred by the immortal presence of the god. For the Greeks the landscape and the building had to be experienced together.[9] As Edith Hamilton observed:

> To the Greek architect the setting of the temple was all-important. He planned it seeing it in clear outline against the sea or sky, determining its size by its situation on plain or hilltop or the wide plateau of an acropolis.[10]

Moreover, the temple was the termination of a religious celebration. In Athens the annual Panathenaic procession led from the Dipylon gate at the city's wall to the Acropolis. There the Temple of the goddess Athena "rose above that earthbound view like a liberated being"[11] (see Figure 1). The Panathenaic procession was a

Fig. 1 Parthenon or Temple of Athena, Athens, Greece

ritual which existed for the purpose of bringing a new garment to the goddess Athena. The procession, which involved all the citizens of Athens, gave a central theme to the cultural development of the city and played a significant role in its architectural development.[12]

Ritual also determined the design and location of tipis for many of the nomadic Indian tribes of North America. Douglas Fraser has shown in his studies of village planning in primitive cultures that when the Cheyenne tribes assembled for ritual purposes, they grouped their dwellings according to a fixed plan.[13] Both the Renewal of the Sacred Arrows ceremony, which symbolized their cohesion as a tribe, and the Sun Dance, which symbolized world renewal, were religious rituals.

The layout used for these rites consisted of a plan of tipis shaped like a large "C." The opening of the "C" was oriented in a direction determined by the significance of the ceremony; east for the Sun Dance, northeast for the Medicine Arrow Renewal ceremony, and sometimes west toward the sunset if a hunt or a raid in which a life might be lost was taking place.[14] Indian land was sacred and the circle, when the "C" was a mostly completed circle, was a sacred form endowed with many symbolic meanings. Many Indian tribes believed that the power of the world worked in circles, that the seasons formed a great circle, that our life was a circle from childhood to childhood, that the sky was round, that the wind blew in circles and that the sun and moon were round and moved in great circles.[15] Black Elk of the Oglala Sioux dictated in his autobiography that

Our tipis were round like the nests of birds and these were always set in a circle, the nation's hoop, a nest of many nests where the Great Spirit meant for us to hatch our children.[16]

Black Elk's words remind us that ritual not only determined the location and formal organization of the village but also the shape and symbolic quality of the tipi itself.

Symbolic Quality Of The Building

Both vernacular architecture and high architecture are more than merely the construction of a building envelope to surround and contain simple functions. To be significant to a great portion of society, important buildings, whether they exist in primitive or advanced societies, must have a symbolic quality comprehensible to everyone. This symbolic quality enshrines ideas which transcend the immediate day-to-day concerns of people. Many times ritual operates as the metaphysical base for the formal development of a building. This, then, endows the building with a symbolic dimension.

For instance, the Dogon of northwestern Africa construct their entire physical world around such a metaphysical base. The continuity of life for the Dogon is made possible by a variety of rituals which accompany the construction of a basket, a house, a village, or guide them in the layout of their fields. Aldo Van Eyck has described the complex symbology which determines the design of the Dogon house:

> The house is built in the image of man: the actual place where cooking is done represents the respiratory organ and is always situated where a fruit of the nono plant (nono equals perpetual) is walled-in during the building process, whilst the kitchen itself is the head. The entrance represents the vulva (the cooking place lies in the axis: kitchen—central living space—entrance).[17]

The rituals which are carried on throughout the building process have been described as "the imprint of the house's image which commences."[18] Even marking the house's plan on the site where it is to be built calls for complex rituals. In addition the houses are based on symbolic proportions, the universal arch from which all space and all living beings originated, and analogously, on the human form lying on its side procreating.

Ritual can influence the form of buildings in many other ways. The complete revitalization of Rome by Pope Sixtus V was mainly generated for ecclesiastical reasons. Medieval Rome was a clogged, chaotic and tangled city, not unlike many of our older cities today. Sixtus V's master plan was prepared to connect the seven votive churches and holy shrines which were visited by the Popes' faithful followers during a single day's pilgrimage. Prior to the architectural and urban alterations of Rome the procession to the churches was, according to Edmund Bacon, a meandering and undirected movement inducing "no clearly organized sequence of purposeful architectural impressions, but rather a series of blunted visions of scattered houses, churches and rolling countryside."[19] Sixtus V's plan organized the procession into a consciously planned sequence meant to provide the highest religious experience by dramatizing the churches and thereby reinforcing the symbolic character of the ritualistic pilgrimage. Here, urban design is clearly used to serve ritual and reinforce the symbolic quality of the churches.

The Spatial Organization Of A Building

Ritual is most often reflected in the spatial organization of a building. The House of Commons in London is organized around a spatial pattern where opposing political parties face each other across a narrow aisle. This is the opposite of the pattern in the

United States where opposing parties are separated by an aisle and both parties face the speaker. When the House of Commons was damaged by German bombs during WW II there followed a great debate on the restoration of the House. The most forceful argument for reconstructing the House exactly as it had been was made by Winston Churchill with his oft-quoted words, "We shape our buildings and then they shape us." Churchill felt that if the physical appearance and spatial organization of the House was changed it might alter the character of Parliamentary debates and in the long run affect English democracy. This basic concept is what anthropologist Edward T. Hall has called "fixed-feature space."[20] The important point about fixed-feature space is that it is molded by conventional, everyday behavior. When it changes, behavior is modified. Thus the ritual of government, the transmission of clearly defined patterns from senior members to juniors is closely linked with the fixed and clearly understood spatial organization of a building.

A more dramatic example of the relationship between spatial organization and ritual can be seen by examining the plan of a Shaker community. The Shakers were a millenial religious community who founded more than twenty-five settlements in America between 1780 and 1826. They believed in a gradual redemption of the world through the transformation of earthly rural settlements into the heavenly sphere of a New Jerusalem. Shaker spatial discipline emphasized the relationship between earthly space and heavenly space. In a society which considered the concept of "architecture as aesthetic effect" to be absurd, wasteful and abnormal, the Shakers evolved a style of building based on traditional vernacular construction. The total physical environment served as a stage for their daily ritual of work and prayer. Dolores Hayden has shown how Shaker ritual, simulating the earthly sphere, has generated a spatial organization based on a consistent orthogonal order.[21] Everything from cutting bread and meat to village planning was based on the right angle. Furthermore, since the Shakers believed in the strictest separation of men and women, all public buildings had to have two doors, two sets of stairs, and an invisible boundary which separated men's space from women's space. The orthogonal order of the earthly sphere was a sharp contrast to the flowing movement characterized by the frenzied "shaking" during their religious services. In the main religious space the imaginary boundary separation was called the spiritual altar. Hayden has suggested that "the altar seems to provide the crucial transition between the earthly space of the dwelling axis on which it rests and heavenly, imaginary space, since the worshiper's acknowledgement of the invisible altar precedes the elaboration of imaginary spatial experiences during the service."[22] The interior space with its richly painted dark green-blue woodwork, red-brown benches, blue-white plaster walls and ceiling and yellow stained wood floor is aimed at forcing a transition from the earthly space to heavenly space by providing an appropriate setting for religious ritual.[23] All taken together, the entire visual sequence from fields to church was designed for religious ritual while all other spatial organization reinforced their communitarian beliefs.

The Use Of Public Open Space

Public open space can serve as the stage for innumerable performances of semi-public and public ritual and ceremony. Public festivities are symbols of civic pride and reflect a rich tradition which can sustain people over a long period of time. In many cases urban open space was intentionally designed to support those festivities. The Piazza del Campo in Siena, Italy, is an excellent case in point. The construction of the Piazza and the Town Hall, the Palazzo Pubblico, which fronts it, were undertaken in an effort to unify the internal disparities in the social and political organization of the city.[24] Since 1342 when the Piazza was completed, thousands of religious processions, public ceremonies, and other civic, military and sports events have taken place in the Campo. The design of the space supports these many different activities by defining circulation, by providing a strong sense of enclosure, and by establishing a series of visual and functional nodal points. A plan of the Piazza is roughly similar to that of a cockle shell or a fan. The south side of the space, the edge upon which rests the Palazzo Pubblico is flat. The other three sides are defined by a series of buildings which form a segmented curve (see Figure 2). Circulation occurs around the perimeter of the space while the interior of the plaza is separated from the circulation by heavy stone bollards. Visual counterpoints are created by the Torre del Mangia, the tower of the Palazzo, and the Fonte Gaia, the public fountain, at the north end of the Piazza.

The one particular event which best exemplifies the use of this space for public ritual is the Festival of the Palio or the Banner Horse-Races. Held during mid-August, the day after the Feast of the Assumption, the race re-enacts the competitive struggle among rival societies in Siena. The modern palio is a public ceremony with music, banners, floats and richly costumed participants. The race around the irregular and sloping course of the ancient Campo still promotes a sense of community and camaraderie among the Sienese

Fig. 2 Plazza Del Campo, Siena, Italy

who are vying for the banners of victory. There are many other public open spaces around the world which serve a wide variety of uses. We are all familiar with the ritual surrounding the announcement of a new Pope. Only a space the size of St. Peters Square in Rome could accommodate the tens of thousands who wait anxiously for the first sight of that puff of white smoke. Other public spaces vividly support the inauguration of public officials, the celebration of national holidays, or the growing ritual of public protest of government policy.

Ceremonial open spaces can also be found in pre-industrial societies. The pueblos of the southwestern United States are always clustered around an open court or plaza. This sacred place is integral to Pueblo life and ritual. It is within this space that the sacred rooms, or kivas, are built. These rooms are council chambers for men and are the location for their sacred ceremonies. In addition, the courtyards contain ovens for baking bread for fiestas and serve as the enclosure for the important dance rituals and ceremonial games. In Taos pueblo (see Figure 3) a stream, which comes from the sacred Blue Lake in the mountains above the village and provides the primary source of water for the inhabitants, flows through the plaza. All community life is centered within the plaza.

All these examples illustrate the importance of the building in

Fig. 3 Taos Pueblo, Taos, New Mexico

the landscape, the symbolic quality of the building, the spatial organization of the building, and the use of public open space in the support of formal ritual. If the concept of both formal and informal ritual holds, we can expect to uncover in Popular architecture new and emerging rituals and ceremonies. Perhaps in some cases these informal rituals might become the formal ritual of the future and embed itself more deeply in culture than at present. In other cases, it might fade into obscurity. Nevertheless today's Popular architecture serves as a type of modern day archeological ruin pointing out the informal rituals that have momentarily become important to contemporary American life.

Ritual And Ceremony In Popular Architecture

In the phenomenon of building in this country during the decade of the 1970s there are three areas in which there was a great surge in construction, centering around the activities of shopping, housing and recreation. If the premise of buildings as a stage for ritual holds true it also might be possible to discover evolving rituals in relatively new building types. The middle section of this paper looked at architecture as a stage for known ritual. The last third turns the process around and looks at existing architecture and infers an informal ritual which has somehow become attached to the building. The conclusions can only be considered hypothetical since there is no firm evidence of a necessary mutual interdependency of ritual to architecture. Nevertheless, each of the three building types that will be described in the following section are connected to informal ritual in contemporary American society. They are 1) Regional shopping centers and the "atrium" building with the "Ritual of Shopping," 2) high density housing developments with the "Ritual of Life Style," and 3) recreation communities and the "Ritual of Renewal."

Regional Shopping Centers And The Atrium Building
The Ritual Of Shopping

If there is any one single item that captures the changing character of American life style since World War II it is the rapid increase in disposable income. In spite of periods of rampant inflation the typical American citizen has had more money available for impulse spending than his father or grandfather. This fact, coupled with the movement to the suburbs in the 1950s and 1960s and a new investment in the deteriorating center city that has occurred during the last decade, has led to the construction of vast regional shopping centers on the fringes of metropolitan areas and huge spacious atrium centers like the Toronto Eaton Center, Philadelphia's Market East and Watertower Place in Chicago in the center of the central business district. These new centers have changed the ritual of shopping from the bartering activity that our grandparents experienced when they haunted the bazaars, open markets and shopping stalls on a daily basis in the old country. The experience of wandering between those ragged, chaotic and dusty canopies filled with the smells of garlic, fish, freshly woven wool, mingled with the garbled shouts of merchants offering special deals has been replaced by a pleasant sojourn into the air-conditioned, multileveled, heavily planted, Muzak-filled, "architecturally dynamic" shopping mall. These new malls have radically changed shopping behavior. In fact prior to their development one could describe most small suburban shopping centers as buying centers. The shopper had little choice, each store was physically independent from the other, and the shopper usually had to make a mad dash through pelting rain, blowing and drifting snow or unbearable heat and humidity to get from one oasis to another. Shopping was something you did in the shortest period of time possible and with the least pleasure. What was missing, of course, was the realization that *shopping* is a human act that should be celebrated. Moreover, pleasant experiences can be profitable. Multilevel indoor malls celebrate shopping and have, in many ways, become the new piazzas of America. Shopping in one of these centers is an experience which often encompasses a full day. Families travel across town or from outlying areas, friends from opposite sides of town meet, and teenagers hang out among the splendor of yuccas, fig trees, fountains, lights, car shows, craft exhibits, and every type of shop imaginable. All of the potential for new ritual, informal though it might be, exists in these centers. Ritual, we must remember, is a series of acts (or sub-rituals or ceremonies) closely linked with each other. Alone each action is simply a normal activity. When linked together in a fixed order, each depending on another, then simple activities become informal ritualized behaviors.

Spending a day at the shopping mall involves planning and preparation, choosing the appropriate clothes, reviewing credit card balances, and heading off across the vast wasteland of suburban America to that great, gleaming oasis. Once there, protected from pollution, urban guerillas, bill collectors, and the tedium of day-to-day life, the shopper is free to wander from store to store, comparing prices, name tags and quality of merchandise. Lunch at one of the many restaurants provides a brief break in an otherwise continual ritual. For some, especially young teenagers, an afternoon at the mall is part of a "see and be seen" ritual, a peer group ceremony that demonstrates to your friends that you're in touch with the latest fashions and hang out with the right clique. The day might end with a movie in one of the mini-theaters attached to the mall. Atrium centers (see Figure 4), with their emphasis on dynamic vertical space add to the shopping experience by creating a greater sense of excitement and anticipation. This entire shopping experience holds great promise of becoming one of the truly popular American pastimes—a way to spend disposable income while celebrating a day or even an hour away from daily routine.

High Density Housing—The Ritual Of Life Style

In addition to an increase in disposable income, another factor which has radically affected the character of American life has been the greatest mobility among industrialized societies, Americans moving their place of residence on an average of once every 4 1/2 years. Moreover, each move reflects a subtle change of life style usually taking one to an area of the city where he perceives social values to be similar to his own. In addition to the well-known suburban neighborhoods which have been flourishing since the post World War II housing boom, a more recent housing phenomenon has been developing in and around most major cities. This phenomenon is the result of the desire on the part of many

Fig. 4 Hyatt Regency, Los Angeles, California

Fig. 5 Condominiums, Balboa, California

Fig. 6 Public Housing, Cincinnati, Ohio

people to live in a community where they will find people like themselves. Because of this we discover that new apartment complexes, condominiums, planned unit developments and even government subsidized apartments house only a narrow slice of the social strata. Some developments are mainly aimed at older adults or empty nesters, others at swinging singles and young unmarried professionals, others principally at young families with preschool children, while still others cater to retired adults on fixed incomes or groups who require a rent subsidization program. Although this homogeneity is not always the rule, it appears that when one has economic mobility he prefers to live among people whose values are similar to his own. Advertisements in local newspapers clearly point out the advantages of location, the elegance of the surroundings, the types of recreational activities available, the magnificent views, or most importantly the fact that you will find people like yourself in the particular apartment complex. There is also the word-of-mouth communication or the personal visit that entices someone to change locations. Moving to a new location where we can find a life-style more suitable to our own aspirations and standards is one of the most powerful forces behind most moves that occur within the same metropolitan area. Each move brings with it a set of informal, predetermined behavior patterns which assimilate the new tenant into the new subculture.

Singles' apartment complexes are known for their multiple Saturday night parties, long and lazy Sunday afternoons around the pool playing volleyball while finishing off the twelve-pack started the night before, and dinner of thick crusty cheesy pizza delivered by the local pizzeria. Housing complexes of older adults display more sedate behavior but still on a regular basis. The point is simple: if one wishes to follow a certain life style, then moving into one particular housing or apartment complex brings along with the move a set of informal rituals. Not adhering or conforming places one outside the community.

The architectural character of these high density housing developments reinforces the informal ritual of life style that is carried out in each complex (see Figures 5 and 6). Large areas devoted to recreation, game rooms, party rooms, tennis and racquet ball courts, play areas for small children, large green, sunny areas for small flower and vegetable gardens, jogging trails or bicycle paths, generous balconies overlooking swimming pools, extra large parking lots for sailboats and small recreational vehicles, exterior walls which surround the housing clearly delineating one world from another, stylistic applications, and lush landscaping, all *signal* or *communicate* a different life style connected to a different set of rituals.

We can expect that the future might bring us more specialized living environments as American society becomes more stratified into clearly different economically and socially determined living patterns. At the same time developers and their architects, ever sensitive to minute changes in the market, leap at the opportunity to provide new stages for the different informal rituals.

Recreational Communities—The Ritual Of Renewal

Every year between the months of June and August, millions of Americans pack the family station wagon full of luggage, air rafts, fishing gear, coolers and triptiks and take to the Interstate highway in a two week search for R and R and the Fountain of Youth. In addition to disposable income and greater mobility suggested in the two previous sections as being at least partially responsible for changing the face of the American landscape, American society has profited from, or suffered from, an increasing amount of leisure time. This free time, along with the release from the day-to-day pressures that it brings, has unleashed in Americans a new spirit of travel. Travel and vacations re-energize the human psyche and re-create the human body.

For a growing number of American families the annual two week vacation has expanded to three and sometimes four weeks. This longer time period makes either extended vacations possible or it allows a family to take two or three vacations a year. Consequently, the vacation and tourist industry which serves our leisure life has become, especially in certain places, a year-round operation rather than just a summer business. Still the summer vacation, that old favorite standby, remains the most ritualized. The entire procedure of long range planning, reservations, AAA triptiks, car tuneups, taking the dog to the kennel, arranging for house care, and message and mail forwarding act as a pre-ritual warmup to what follows. The day or two of solid driving with brief stops at McDonald's, Colonel Sanders Kentucky Fried Chicken, Howard Johnsons or Holiday Inn prepare the vacationers by exhausting them. Safe arrival at their destination is received with enthusiasm and uncontrollable joy by all.

More and more American families have been spending their vacation time at one place in what is coming to be called a recreation community. These communities are usually located along the seashore, in the mountains, along lakes or adjacent to National Parks or wilderness areas. They have been designed to provide a comprehensive range of recreational activities and to satisfy all tastes. Just as the yearly vacation has become an annual ritual to renew the spirit and body, the recreational communities have grown to serve all facets of that ritual. Seasonal sports, lots of restaurants, mini excursions to nearby points of interest, babysitters supplied, and fully scheduled evening programs all guarantee that every waking hour is booked up. When the mind, spirit and body have been rejuvenated and our two weeks used up, we repack, collect up the memorabilia, gifts and snapshots and head home along the Interstate. Those more fortunate than the average American family jet away to Aspen, Hilton Head, Acapulco, Martha's Vineyard, Boca Raton, the Catskills or Palm Springs while shorter vacations are spent at Las Vegas, Atlantic City, the Bahamas or dude ranches. There is a place for every style and a style for every taste. Recreational communities are continuing to grow as Americans find more time to spend worshipping alternate ways of life. The ritual of the summer vacation is becoming as regular as the ritual of Christmas shopping, the Thanksgiving dinner, Saturday night at the Disco or the family photograph gathering.

Conclusions

If a Dani warrior could be enticed to visit America, he would observe at almost any hour of the day or night and any day of the week what would appear to him to be an important religious ritual. He would see people standing patiently in line in front of a large red wall full of graphics, symbols and images. Each person in his turn would walk up to the red wall with a small piece of paper or card which would be offered to an opening in the wall as a gift. When the gift had been accepted and the wall touched a number of times, it would utter strange sounds unlike any the Dani had ever heard. A moment later, the red wall, obviously satisfied that the proper offerings had been made, would flash some lights and give up a few small pieces of green paper to the devoted pilgrim. To the Dani warrior this behavior would be a form of unfamiliar ritual, but clearly a common act to Americans. Using our Visa or Mastercharge cards to get instant cash is a regular routine for most. To the Dani it would appear to be a religious ritual complete with icons and prayers.

Perhaps an instant cash machine will never qualify as a great work of architecture, but then neither will the watchtowers that line the frontier of the Dani in the Central Highlands of New Guinea. For the Dani the watchtowers are connected to a static way of life, a way which centers around religion and in which all ritual is formal. Until quite recently their life had not changed for hundreds of years. On the other hand, the American way of life has welcomed change as ubiquitous and greeted the artifacts that change brings with open arms. Artifacts like CB radios, food processors, pocket calculators, microwave ovens and video recorders are an affirmation of a life style which celebrates changing human sentiments and the informal ritual that accompanies change. In a dynamic society formal ritual and informal ritual are both necessary.

Notes

[1]Most of the information on the Dani has been taken from the film *Dead Birds,* by Robert Gardiner and from "The Dani of West Irian," by Karl G. Heider; Warner Modular Publications, Module 2 (1972), pp. 1-75.

[2]See *Under the Mountain Wall* (1963), Peter Matthiessen; *Gardens of War* (1969), Robert Gardiner and Karl G. Heider; *The Dungum Dani* (1970), Karl G. Heider; or the bibliography cited in note 1.

[3]Susanne K. Langer, *Philosophy in a New Key,* 1942, 1951 (Cambridge, Mass.: Harvard University Press), pp. 50-52.

[4]Ibid., pp. 50-51.

[5]See Al Kuhn, *Unified Social Science* (Homewood, Ill.: Dorsey Press, 1975), pp. 167-68; Hugh Dalziel Duncan, *Symbols in Society* (New York: Oxford Univ. Press, 1968), p. 185ff.

[6]Duncan, *Symbols in Society,* p. 185.

[7]Ibid., p. 190.   [8]Ibid., p. 190.

[9]Vincent Scully, *The Earth, the Temple and the Gods: Greek Sacred Architecture* (New Haven: Yale Univ. Press, 1962), p. 2.

[10]Edith Hamilton quoted from Scully, pp. 201-202.

[11]Ibid., p. 133.

[12]Edmund Bacon, *Design of Cities* (New York: Viking Press, 1974), pp. 65-73.

[13]Douglas Fraser, *Village Planning in the Primitive World* (New York: Braziller, 1968), p. 20.

[14]Ibid., p. 14.

[15]T.C. McLuhan, *Touch the Earth* (New York: Outerbridge and Dienstfrey, 1971), p. 42.

[16]Ibid., p. 42.

[17]Aldo Van Eyck, "Design Only Grace, Open Norm. Disturb Order Gracefully; Outmatch Need," *VIA 1 Ecology in Design* (Phila.: Univ. of Penn., 1968), p. 110.

[18]Ibid., p. 112.

[19]Bacon, p. 136.

[20]Edward T. Hall, *The Hidden Dimension* (Garden City, N.Y.: Doubleday, 1966), p. 100.

[21]Dolores Hayden, *Seven American Utopias: The Architecture of Communitarian Socialism, 1790-1975* (Cambridge, Mass.: MIT Press, 1976).

[22]Ibid., p. 71.   [23]Ibid., p. 92.

[24]Ferdinand Schevill, *Siena* (New York: Scribner's Sons, 1909).

The Tnevnoc Cult

David G. Bromley & Anson D. Shupe, Jr.

THE 1970S HAVE witnessed a profusion of new religious movements ranging from the traditional Christian-based "Jesus Freaks" to groups of oriental origin such as the International Society for Krishna Consciousness (Hare Krishna), Guru Maharaji Ji's Divine Light Mission, and Sun Myung Moon's Unification Church. As these groups have grown in size and wealth and apparently in permanence there has been a parallel spread of alarm at the tactics incorporated into the ceremonies and rituals by which they recruit and hold members. Allegations of systematic deception, seduction, drugging, hypnosis and brainwashing in their ceremonies and rituals have been leveled at these groups by distraught parents of members and former members who have "escaped" or been deprogrammed and have told their horror stories. Many of these stories have been recounted in recent books such as ex-Moonie Christopher Edward's *Crazy for God* (1979) and ex-People's Temple devotees Bonnie Thielmann's *The Broken God* (1979) and Jeannie Mills' *Six Years With God* (1979). A number of behavioral scientists and other investigators have lent their support to these accusations and have attempted to formulate explanations for these swift and seemingly bizarre "conversions." These include Flo Conway and Jim Siegelman's *Snapping* (1978), arch-deprogrammer Ted Patrick's *Let Our Children Go!* (1976) and Carroll Stoner and Jo Ann Parke's *All Gods Children* (1977).

The issues of manipulative "mind control" and apparently absolute submissiveness (interpreted as automaton, zombie-like behavior) have been the most inflammatory allegations running through this popular literature. The content of these accusations creates the impression that these new religions have innovated or rediscovered techniques of indoctrination and built them into their rituals so as to transform otherwise normal individuals into followers who resemble robots or automatons in their slavish zeal, unquestioning obedience, and lack of individuality/free will. In the course of our research, however, (Shupe and Bromley, 1979; Shupe, Speilmann and Stigall, 1977), which has included an historical examination of the social context of these groups, we have discovered past cases which are remarkably similar in many respects to these new religious groups.

In fact, what has been termed the "cult menace" is not a novel development on the American religious scene but has been a persistent feature of our history. Specifically, here we examine the ritual recruitment used in indoctrination and retention of members of the Tnevnoc cult, a once powerful and widespread religious movement of the nineteenth century that has since declined in membership and become less visible by virtue of assuming a more accommodationist stance toward the larger society. The Tnevnocs were rigidly separated by sex; therefore, since our data presented here deal only with the female Tnevnoc component of the movement, we make no claim to generalize about the entire movement.

A Brief Ethnography of the Tnevnoc Cult

Like their modern-day counterparts in the current "cult explosion," such as the Unification Church and the Divine Light Mission, the Tnevnocs made a point of attempting to recruit members in their teenage and young adult years. They apparently felt that the earlier they got the young women indoctrinated the more thoroughly the ritualistic patterns would be ingrained in the individual's personalities. Much of this recruitment was openly conducted in schools and on campuses. On the basis of their limited contacts with cult members, young girls committed themselves totally to the cult. If the cult succeeded in gaining control over these individuals they were subjected to such thorough indoctrination that they became totally dependent on the cult and in many cases lacked the will to free themselves from it.

Once a girl had been induced to join the cult she was immediately subjected to total cult control. As the Hare Krishna and the Children of God members were forced to surrender all aspects of their former lives, virtually all personal possessions were taken away, and individuals were prohibited from developing any outside involvements and commitments. Indeed, members were required to devote literally all their time and energies to cult activities. The round of cult life was relentless and consuming. Members were routinely wakened at 4:30 A.M. and faced an arduous day of menial labor interspersed with long hours of prayer, meditation, mind-numbing chanting and compulsory religious ceremonies. Like the Hare Krishna sect members who always carry prayer beads in cloth sacks attached to their wrists, the Tnevnocs likewise carried such beads which they used in their repetitive, monotonic chanting. Members gathered in candlelit, incense-filled rooms closed to outsiders for a variety of special rituals involving chanting and meditation. One particularly bizarre observance was a type of love/unity feast involving ritualistic cannibalism. Members consumed food which they were told symbolically represented parts of the dead founder's body.

The time not taken up with such rituals was devoted almost entirely to largely menial labor such as washing clothes, preparing food and scrubbing floors. Indeed, only one hour of "free time" was allowed each day, but even during this brief period members were forbidden to be alone or in unsupervised groups, being required to remain together and monitored by cult leaders. All luxuries and even basic amenities were eliminated. For example, members slept each night on wooden planks with only thin straw mats as mattresses. They subsisted on a bland, spartan diet; food deprivation was even more severe than the meager diet implies, members being permitted to eat sweets only once a year and often placed under considerable pressure to fast periodically. This combination of limited sleep, draining physical labor, long hours of compulsory group rituals and worship—all supported by a meager subsistence-level diet—left members without sufficient time or energy to preserve even their own senses of individual identity.

All of members' former sources of emotional support also were severed upon joining the cult. Since during the first year members were forbidden to leave the communal (and often remote rural) setting in which their training took place and could receive no outside visitors beyond one family visitation, it became virtually impossible for parents and friends to maintain regular and frequent contact with members. For example, members were permitted to write only a maximal four letters per year. Further, just as do Unification Church leaders, Tnevnoc cult leaders deliberately disrupted family ties by creating a fictive kinship system in which they assumed parental roles which were intended to replace members' natural parents and siblings. Any other relationships which threatened cult control were likewise strictly forbidden. For example, sexual attachments of any kind were, without exception, tabooed. Lone Tnevnocs were never allowed to be in the presence of individuals of the opposite sex and they were forbidden to maintain close personal friendships with each other or even to touch physically. All loyalty had to be channeled to the cult, and its leaders, in authoritarian fashion, enforced those strictures. Leaders went so far as to assert that they were God's direct representatives on earth and therefore due absolute obedience by all members. This subservience was formalized in each member's written promise of absolute obedience for three years, after which time individuals often were led to make similar commitments for the remainder of their lives.

Perhaps most striking was the emergence of cult-induced personality changes. This began with the alteration of each individual's exterior appearance. Like the Hare Krishna, Tnevnoc cult member immediately upon joining underwent certain physical rituals, had their hair cut off and were dispensed long flowing garments specifically designed to render members indistinguishable from one another. This concerted ritual effort to wipe out any sense of individuality was carried to such extremes that members were never permitted to own or even look into mirrors. The cult literally attempted to destroy the old individual, her identity and her former life's associations by assigning a new cult name and designating the date of her entry into the group as the individual's "real" birthdate. Of course such identity changes were more difficult to monitor than behavioral conformity. One way cult leaders maintained close surveillance over the most private aspects of members' lives was to require members to reveal publicly and record in diaries even the most minor infractions of elaborate cult rules as well as, by cult standards, improper thoughts and wishes.

This total environment, with its rigid, all-encompassing ritual of behavior that individuals could not possibly follow without some minor infractions, engendered within members constant and inescapable feelings of inadequacy, self-doubt, anxiety and guilt. Cult leaders deliberately exacerbated these nagging feelings by instituting a series of humiliating, ego-destructive punishments for even the most trivial infractions of rules. For example, daydreaming or entertaining "improper" thoughts, however fleetingly, called down upon members ceremonies of public degradation. Members were forced to ritualistically prostrate themselves in front of cult leaders and kiss their feet or, alternately, were denied food and reduced to crawling from member to member on their hands and knees at dinnertime begging for the dregs of other members' meals. Such punishments became more severe as time went on and members were even expected to punish themselves regularly for these deviations from prescribed ritual. The cult went so far as to issue each member a ring to which were attached several lengths of chain with barbed points on the ends. Members were required to return alone to their beds at night at regular intervals and flagellate themselves with such cruel devices as atonement for their infractions.

Not surprisingly the grueling demands of cult membership and the ever-present feelings of guilt and anxiety created the potential for members to "give up" or defect. In addition to the docility created by the harsh conditions of the daily round of cult life, members were constantly pressured by cult leaders for greater personal sacrifice and evidence of complete commitment. Indeed, members competed with one another to express total selflessness and dedication. These constant exhortations and punishments designed to destroy any vestiges of individuality were reinforced by ceremonies intended to bind the individual inextricably to the group. One particularly ghoulish example was a macabre nuptial ceremony in which members were required to become the living brides of the dead cult leader.

Cults—Historical and Contemporary

What we have described in the foregoing paragraphs is, of course, not a cult in the disparaging sense in which the term is currently employed to describe new religious movements but rather a traditional Roman Catholic *convent* (Tnevnoc spelled backwards). From one perspective this description constitutes only a caricature of a convent as it fails to convey the sense of majesty, purpose, personal fulfillment and belonging which nuns experience individually. It also ignores the order, harmony, stability and integration of the convent as a social organization. However, these same details also are missing from most contemporary accounts of new religious movements. It is precisely this lack of personal and organizational context and purpose which creates a sense that some of their rituals are illegitimate or destructive.

What has been conveyed fairly accurately in our description of the "Tnevnocs" are some of the recruit/socialization rituals by which both convents and modern religious movements have sought to create and maintain deep commitment on the part of their members. Certain types of groups historically have tried to harness all their members' personal energies on a voluntary basis. These include not only convents and monasteries but also elite military training units, communes and social movements seeking to effect radical social change. In order to gain control over all members' time and energy such groups must develop high levels of commitment to them. In our own research on the Unification

Church and other new religious movements we have found that intense commitment can be generated and maintained to the extent that the individuals' interests and group interests become *congruent*, that is, to the extent that individuals wish to act as it is socially requisite for them to act. This process involves totally immersing individuals in a set of rituals which render them unavailable for other lines of social action and in constructing a ritually symbolic system which provides a rationale and meaning for involvement in those activities. In a dynamic sense the process of building total commitment involves a *detachment* of individuals from former involvements and lifestyles, sources of emotional support and bases of personal identity, and *attachment* to new roles, sources of affective support and identity bases.

There is, in short, a simultaneous process of *desocialization* and *resocialization*. The extensiveness and intensity of desocialization/resocialization depends in part on the amount of selectivity any groups can exercise in their recruitment activities, such as how readily they can attract individuals who already possess characteristics they require. However, since most newly formed groups and movements, such as the "new religions," initially have rather low selectivity and yet at the same time high needs for member recruitment, intense socialization practices usually are socially imperative.

Thus, if the practices of promoting total commitment in members are similar for various historical and contemporary religious groups, the different societal reactions to them cannot be explained solely in terms of these practices. Indeed, societal response depends on the *degree of legitimacy*, defined in terms of the number and power of supporting groups, accorded to a given religious body. The lower a group's legitimacy the less resistance it can muster to counter social repression and the less control it has over its own public image. The major difference between the current treatment of Roman Catholics and Moonies, Krishnas or Children of God, then, is that the former group has now been accorded legitimacy, the persistence of at least some of the commitment maintenance practices described in this paper nothwistanding, while the latter groups have not.

Yet, as even a cursory review of American history reveals, during much of the nineteenth and the first half of the twentieth centuries Catholics also were treated as a "new religion." Indeed, the parallels with contemporary religious groups are striking. Much as the Unification Church, Hare Krishna, Children of God and People's Temple are currently labeled "cults," the Catholic Church once was perjoratively lumped together with groups such as the

Mormons and Masons despite enormous doctrinal and organizational diversity. The stereotypes and litany of charges leveled against contemporary "new religions" also are remarkably reminiscent of allegations against the earlier "new religions": political subversion, unconditional loyalty of members to authoritarian leaders, brutalizing of members, sexual indiscretions and possession of mysterious, extraordinary powers. And the atrocity stories told by apostates such as Rebecca Reed's *Six Months in a Convent* (1835), Maria Monk's *Awful Disclosures of the Hotel Dieu Nunnery at Montreal* (1836) and Ann Young's *Wife No. 19: Or, the Story of a Life in Bondage, Being a Complete Expose of Mormonism* (1875) read much like the lurid tales told by former members of contemporary "new religions."

It is not our intent to argue that none of the accusations leveled against contemporary "new religions" are false. Groups with lofty ideals frequently do assume airs of moral superiority based on the assumption that "the ends justify the means" and engage in duplicity and deception. However, it is also true that groups which seek to initiate sweeping social change become the focus of hysterical reactions well out of proportion to the real threat they present. It is easy to be drawn into simplistic calls for repressing current religious "cults," either through anti-cult legislation or more vigilante-style actions such as "deprogramming," on the basis of caricature descriptions such as we have offered on the Tnevnocs. Yet it should be kept in mind that contemporary scholars look back on the nineteenth century movement which fueled anti-Catholic sentiments as a mixture of undisguised xenophobic zeal and religious bigotry. It should also be kept in mind that most religious movements through American history have gradually been forced to accommodate to the larger society. Indeed, our history is replete with illustrations of this process, and there is no reason to think that this same process will not be repeated.

Roman Domestic Religion:
The Archaeology of Roman Popular Art

David Gerald Orr

"sed patrii servate Lares: aluistis et idem,
cursarem vestros cum tener ante pedes."

Tibullus 1. 10. 15-16.

THE ROMAN POET Tibullus summed up the essence of all
Roman domestic forces when he mentioned in his poem *Against
War* that his Lares (tutelary domestic deities) watched over him and
reared him when he was a boy. Beyond every other element
contained in the cult of the Roman domestic deities stretched the
idea that these religious forces of the hearth and home guarded their
wards and averted evil from the home. A Roman's protective gods
followed him throughout life and their favor was sought through the
continual practice of an ancient ritual and the maintenance of
traditional concepts of piety. It was this venerable household cult
that persisted late into the waning years of the Roman Empire. It
was this cult which meshed with Christianity in the home and it is
this cult which still survives in domestic Italian religious practices.
The idea that one popularly conceived domestic institution
syncretically blended some of its material culture and much of its
mental template with a later cultural change is not a new one. Yet,
the simple domestic ceremony and practices of the Roman
household does unite physical objects (the shrines of Campania)
with what little we know from other sources left to us from ancient
Rome. The result forms what George Kubler[1] denotes as the
"collective identity," a point of reference to the future. With such a
"community of objects"[2] linkages can be clearly structured which
depict the visual flow from the world we have lost to the world we
live in. In such a perspective the remarkable persistence of aspects
of the Roman household ritual may not seem so remarkable. This
essay hopes only to elucidate the cult as it existed under the Roman
Empire. Those elements suggesting its survival in various areas of
the Mediterranean will only be generally described. It is a clear
invitation to more extensive modern ethnographic research.

For the ancient Roman the cult of the domestic deities primarily
concerns itself with a quest for their special individual protection.[3]

As the cult evolved, separate and distinct groups of divine powers (or *numina*) were venerated in a clearly defined household ritual.[4] Although we are not clear on the exact nature of this ritual, it nevertheless played an important role in the household, first by the ancient male head of the family (the *paterfamilias*) and his own servants and family, and then later by non-Romans, freedmen and eventually Christians. This worship survived and its material forms create the background for much of the iconography found in modern Italian domiciles. The domestic cult signified much to the Roman: reliance of the family for its survival on the household deities, ritual piety and simplicity, and encouragement to the family for well-being to name just a few functions. The formal religions of the Roman Empire, both indigenous and oriental, offered status, gregarious social activity, but little intimacy. Within the private seclusion of the Roman household the Lares and Penates were propitiated in quiet and deep devotion. The nexus of all activities relating to the domestic cult was the household shrine (lararium).[5] Here also was demonstrated the flexibility of the cult since it enabled the worshipper to introduce into the home many strange deities and sects. Perhaps Christianity penetrated into the Roman home as such a newcomer in the simple lararium niche, altar, miniature temple, or painting. Three peculiar sets of powers were incorporated within the framework offered by the domestic shrine and its ritual. Each of these was represented by separate deities and by special ceremonies.[6] The central protective force caring for the health and continuance of the family was propitiated at the hearth and was in fact symbolized by the living fire of Vesta, goddess of the hearth. Originally agricultural deities, another group moved from the field into the home at some early point in time. Here they were honored as an additional set of tutelary *numina* within the home. The final group of deities guarded the storerooms and cupboards and never were iconographically depicted. Simply reduced, these above three sets of powers were known as Vesta, the Lares, and the Penates, respectively. Each of these elements needs to be examined.

One characteristic of Roman domestic worship which must constantly be kept in mind is that there was no priestly college to make the cult concrete and there was no written dogma to express its ancient history. No area in the Roman house better expresses this aspect of household worship than the hearth. From earliest times it was the center for religious activity in the home.[7] Here was found the "living flame" of Vesta.[8] Vesta's public cult in which her fire was tended as a symbol of Roman permanence and power is fairly well understood but her more primitive and intimate nature is only to be comprehended in relationship to the domestic hearth. Here, in simple paintings located in kitchens, near the hearth fire, Vesta was depicted anthropomorphically.[9] Since Pompeii became a Roman town rather late in its historic existence, the presence of Vesta in the lararium painting indicates the Romanization of the town. She was the patron deity of millers and bakers and in Pompeii is found on shrines located near ovens and mills. The round shape of Vesta's temple in the forum in Rome may have antecedents going back to the prehistoric period of the city.[10] Her presence in the houseshrines thus connoted both ancient tradition and political power. Yet her early amorphous religious power was reflected in her Roman temple where she was not represented by images but by fire.[11] Similarly, Vesta preserved her abstract nature in the household where her fire was tended by the daughters or wife of the *paterfamilias*. She maintained her close linkages to the purity symbolized by flame at the domestic hearth.[12]

The origins and early history of the Lares are sharply disputed.[13] Simply put it was the nature of these *numina* to resist precise areas of influence and defy clearly delineated functions.[14] The evidence suggests that the vague character of the Lares and their position in Roman domestic worship led to the practice in imperial times of using the word "Lar" as a substitute for home, household, hearth and even areas far removed from a domestic ambience.[15] The cult of the Lares had developed by the first century A.D. into a highly diversified one which could offer different services to the family. In the home, however, the tutelary character of the Lares never lost its force. The Lar (or Lares) of the family protected a Roman sent out on military service,[16] watched closely the daily lives of the home's residents,[17] and exercised constantly the role of the familial protector.[18] The survival of ancient agricultural festivals, like the *Compitalia,* demonstrates the manner in which the Lares prospered in the Roman household.[19] By the early imperial epoch, the Lares were guarding particular places, not necessarily homes. Thus there existed Lares of roads and travelers, soldiers and military camps, games, the imperial residences and even the state of Rome itself.[20]

In the household the Lares were offered sacrifices of grapes, table scraps, garlands, grain, honeycakes and wine.[21] They were worshipped on special feast days and probably were venerated in daily acts of homage. When a Roman boy and girl came of age, they dedicated to their Lares the small emblem of their childhood, the *bulla,* which was worn around their necks before adulthood.[22] A *bulla* was found in a house in Pompeii tied carefully around the figure of a domestic deity. In the house the Lares promoted the health and welfare of the family.

The image of the Lar as it is known to us from the days of the late Roman Republic and from the pictorialization of it in ancient Pompeii somehow does not convey the *gravitatas* and sobriety generally associated with the *paterfamilias* of a Roman home (fig. 1). They are shown as happy sprites, holding a wine cup overflowing with the fruits of Campanian harvests, and pose in a light, tip-toes dancing position. Their total impression is one which relates to Hellenic Dionysiac depictions; indeed their source probably was located in Magna Graecia to the south of Pompeii.[23] Non-Roman elements in the Lar's costume and makeup include the rhyton (Greek drinking vessel), the posture of the Lar itself, and the treatment of the footwear.[24] Hair length differs greatly from Lar to Lar; some are shown with closely cropped locks while others are given long flowing curls. The "Liberty Cap" (*pileus*) is also occasionally shown on Lares (fig. 2) and probably reflects the political status of their masters.[25] The high-girded skirt, however, is definitely meant to represent the Roman *tunica*.[26] Iconographically, the idea of placing paired Lares in lararium painting became popular and was the commonest canon in which the domestic deities were couched (fig. 3).

Fig. 1 Lar depicted holding rhyton (wine vessel) which is shown spouting wine into a small sacrificial pail. This is from a lararium painting found in Pompeii. The numbers refer to the Region, insula (block), and house number respectively. First Century A.D. I. xii. 3.

Fig. 2 Lararium niche with flanking Lares, each wearing the Liberty Cap *(pileus)*. A crescent moon (perhaps the moon god *Men)* crowns a finely modeledgorgon head within the niche. An incredibly thin serpent is shown beneath the lararium. Pompeii, First Century A.D. I. xii. 15.

Fig. 3 The standard lararia painting canon. Two Lares flanking a togate and sacrificing Genius figure (with female equivalent (?) Juno (?)). Two small sacrificial attendants complete the painting. First Century A.D., Pompeii, House of Polybius, IX. xiii. 3.

The position of the Penates in the Roman home is not disputed. Their function clearly related to the *penus,* a place usually located at the back of the atrium (open roofed central court) of the home.[27] Although they were also present at the hearth in company with the Lares, their main activity centered on the storeroom. Their abstract nature resulted from their earlier utilization as wards of the cereal storehouse.[28] Yet, at ancient Pompeii the Penates have significantly changed. Here, the meaning of the Penates encompasses all the domestic numina of the home.[29] Thus the Penates mean Vesta, the Lares, and any diety who is worshipped in the home. Making the muddied picture of the Penates even more difficult to see is the fact that the state cult of the Imperial Penates must have filtered down into the Roman home of the first century A.D., especially in the domiciles of those freedmen who felt strong allegiance to the imperial house. The worship of the Penates, at any rate, was an integral part of the household cult.[30] Unfortunately, our understanding of its relationship to the ancient Roman deities of the storehouse is, at the best, imperfect.

Other religious forces were present in the house shrines of ancient Roman homes. The most significant by far is the Genius. The genius was the alter-ego or spiritual "double" of an ancient Roman.[31] He was responsible for the procreative force present in the *Paterfamilias* and encouraged the continuation of the Roman family.[32] Versatile and flexible, it too could be used to protect places and things like the Lar and other fixtures of the domestic cult.[33] Both kinds of Geniuses were found in the domestic shrine. The household Genius was honored on the *dies natalis* (birthday) of the Paterfamilias.[34] Sacrifices included not only the customary honeycakes and wine but blood offerings such as pigs and lambs.[35] Oaths were sworn by the Genius and members of the Roman home regarded the concept as one of blood relationship.[36] Yet its most important power was that of continuing the roman *gens* and insuring its maintenance from one generation to another.

In ancient Pompeii, the Genius appears as both a public and a private religious being. Street shrines dedicated at the *compita* held imperial dedications and gestures (mostly by Freedmen) while in the lararia of the residential quarter the Genius was venerated as a domestic numen.[37] The Lares also seem to share in this duality; perhaps it was the simple idea that the household shrine and deities of the emperor protected the entire empire. At any rate the Genius is depicted in the shrines as a togate male figure, usually carrying a cornucopia and sacrificing with a small *patera* (fig. 4).

Closely associated with the Genius and also an ubiquitous element of the Roman household shrine is the house snake. This is

Fig. 4 Togate Genius figure sacrificing over lighted altar; Genius serpent before. First Century
A.D., Pompeii, I. xvi. 2.

not the place to examine the multitudinous ways in which serpents
penetrated Roman religion and the diverse character of that
symbolic force.[38] In the home the serpent plays two roles. First, he is
the guardian of a particular spot; the Genius of the place.[39] Here he
and the earlier cult of the Genius have obviously been combined.
One aspect of the Genius serpent's role in the home has apparently
survived in Calabria (Italy) today. Harmless snakes are still
welcomed in the home as protectors and even pets.[40] This use of the
"house snake" is still common in Balkan areas of the Mediterranean
and even as far north as Sweden.[41] In rural South Italy serpents are
seen as examples of "bon fortuna" whenever they are encountered

in the fields. All these aforementioned examples attest to the second and most important role played by the serpent in Roman domestic religion—that of familiar protector and Genius attribute.

Both the Genius (depicted anthropomorphically) and the serpent are common in the house shrines of Campania. Most of the reptiles are shown as viperine, large necked, rough-scaled animals (fig. 5). It must be stressed that the depictions of both Hellenic and Roman house serpents iconographically related to long established Mediterranean forms and are not indicative of those snakes introduced into Italy as part of the cult of Oriental or Egyptian sects.[42] They not only serve apotropaically in the home but are used frequently on mural frescoes both inside and outside the Roman house or building.[43] Here they mean simply that the place is sacred and should not be treated impiously. Curiously enough, when the Roman house cult serpent confronted Christianity (and with it the connotation of the snake as evil) it yielded its formal precedence but preserved its deep-rooted agrarian nature. Thus the house snake endured as animate arm of the procreative Genius force, together with its tutelary function of guarding special spots and places. Able to accommodate a great many religious ideas, the Genius (and its serpent) became a significant element in Roman domestic worship.

Fig. 5 Crested and bearded Genius serpent approaching altar upon which is an egg and pine cone. Pompeii, I. xii. 3. First Century A.D. Lararium painting.

All the aforementioned elements are bound together by the ceremonies and rituals which once centered on the house shrines themselves. Pompeii has by far the most dazzling assemblage of objects and shrines to be found anywhere in the Roman world. By the fortuitous and timely application of basic volcanism some 1900 years ago, Pompeii has preserved for us a collection of about five hundred lararia. The entire remaining portion of known Roman house shrines from sites other than ancient Campania actually amounts to about twenty examples. Nevertheless, certain caveats should be underscored at the onset of our final discussion. First, the surviving shrines are typical of the immediate region surrounding Vesuvius, "happy Campania," and may in fact be atypical of those found in Rome and other more densely populated areas and provinces. Specific details of the iconography encountered in Pompeian lararia, for example, probably were not indicative of those common, let us say, to Iberia or Africa. Yet the literary evidence does confirm the presence of the main elements of the Roman house shrine; elements we have summarized above. Thus their general character is not singularly distinctive and may respond closely to a general canon found elsewhere; perhaps couched in different styles and symbols.[44] They must, moreover, be considered typological reference points for what we know of Roman culture elsewhere.[45]

All the shrines excavated in Pompeii have two basic key attributes. They must provide for the veneration of deities symbolized by the paintings and sculpture found on the shrine, and they must accommodate the simple needs presented by the worshipper. Since portions of the sacrifice ritual involves burnt offerings, the lararia area must have access to the open sky. Altars can be provided as tile shelves attached to the shrine or can be temporary in nature and used wherever the need arises. Scale does not seem to be a factor; lararia range from tiny foot square niches to the freestanding platformed "temples" occasionally present in the central halls of Roman houses. Of course, it must be admitted that sacrifice can be accomplished along with acts of domestic piety without lararia or altars. Yet, in the formal domestic ritual, the lararium becomes indispensable. Three major areas of the Roman house appear to be the most frequently encountered sites for house shrines. The grandest and most monumental shrines are usually found in the atria (central open roofed hall) of Roman domiciles. Kitchens, the room containing the hearth fire, and gardens account for most of the lararia present in Pompeii. Many houses (and shops) have multiple shrines and some rooms within Roman homes may have more than one shrine.

Four types of shrine are present in Pompeii. The most common form is simply an arcuated niche or recess in the masonry wall; either painted or unpainted. These niches are usually furnished with a roof tile or masonry ledge for sacrifice and object display[46] (fig. 6). More elaborate variations on this type is repeated by adding

Fig. 6 Niche-type lararium. The painting shows a togate Genius figure sacrificing before a small altar; an attendant can be seen behind him. Pompeii, First Century A.D., I. xvii. 4.

two-dimensional temple facade surrounds.[47] Some shrines are created by wall paintings fronted with small portable altars[48] (fig. 3). Most impressive of all forms is the miniature freestanding temple type, or aedicula (fig. 7). This lararium is generally built of rubble masonry stuccoed and painted, and roofed by rubble masonry columns; one unique example even sheathed with marble slabs covered with bas-relief depictions of the earthquake which demolished Pompeii in 62 A.D.[49] Rare indeed is the sacellum; a separate building devoted exclusively to the propitiation of the household deities.[50] Only a small group of these structures are

Fig. 7 Aedicula-type lararium. The roof has been destroyed but the stuccoed brick columns are still present. Two painted and stuccoed serpents can be seen on the shrine's inner panels. Painted winged griffons are also visible on either side of the aedicula. Pompeii, Probably first century A.D., I. xvi. 2.

known.

The paintings and sculptures found in the Pompeian house shrines document an incredible spectrum of religious concepts and practices. Fortuna, Vesta and Bacchus are among the most popular

Roman deities and they respectively referred to basic aspects of Pompeii's economic and social makeup. Fortuna, more precisely the good luck of Pompeian commerce and trade, reflected the mercantile character of Pompeii. Vesta mirrored the newly acquired "Romanity" and with it its central Italic religious traditions. She was also the patroness of bakers: an important industry in Pompeii.[51] Like Vesta, the wine god Bacchus embodied the economic activity of Campania. The rich viticultural farming land surrounding Pompeii is encapsulated in the iconography of Bacchus shown sometimes as a figure completely enveloped in grapes! He is additionally the most popular patron deity for the numerous hostels and taverns located in the town. Pompeii's Roman protectoress was Venus, the family goddesses of Sulla who captured the town in the first century A.D. and who later became an important deity in the imperial pantheon. Finally let us not ignore the presence of Mercury in the household shrines; the god of tavern owners, commerce, finance and thieves.

But it was the dramatic infusion of oriental religions into the Pompeian home which gives the shrines their most exciting character. Egyptian gods and goddesses, most notably those of the Isis and Serapis cults, are found in many of the lararia. The active commercial links with Alexandria probably accounted for their great popularity. Stranger still were the Hellenistic Greek-Egyptian syncretisms such as Isis-Artemis and Isis-Fortuna. Even the river Sarnus which flowed by Pompeii was honored by an elaborately painted household shrine which depicts scenes of trade and pleasure on the river.[52] Lastly, Christianity may be present in Herculaneum during the same period as Pompeii, i.e. the late first century A.D. A possible imprint in the wall near a wooden lararium found in a Herculaneum house appears to be cruciform in shape.[53]

The paintings found in Pompeian lararia differ markedly from the regular mural decoration encountered as one visits the houses and public structures of the city. Even more remarkable is the fact that each individual depiction, although many follow the canon previously described, displays its own personal hallmark. No two house shrines have been found to display similar qualities of line, color and design. More often than not the work is spontaneously rendered and intimately postured. Thus the Pompeian house shrines confront us with a "primitive" quality not found in the more elitist "high-style" standard mural compositions scattered throughout the city. These paintings have long been ignored since they do not take part in the "loftier" and more Olympian world of the great four Pompeian styles. But the study of art is an historical and sociological phenomenon which must not bog itself down in the swamps of truth and teleology. More to the point, the Pompeian shrines reflect a different intellectual and phenomenological sense of time and place. As such they partake in traditional passages of time and share attributes which usually are more permanently immeshed in the cults of house and hearth. At the same time the paintings show interesting innovations. For example, the full face frontality more generally associated with early Christian and later Byzantine art can be found in many kitchen paintings found in Pompeii. The sense of humor deeply ingrained in many of the shrines, e.g. a painted smiling snake emerging from a real hole in the plaster, underscore an additional quality present in such paintings. The eighteenth-century aestheticians chose to ignore high style Roman painting as well as popular depictions since they were not consistent with a Polyclitan ideal they so much admired in Hellenic sculpture. Here at Pompeii, on the lararia surfaces, these paintings serve as strong testators for the continuing debate as to the nature of art and the nature of the designed material world. Another essay may offer some clarity on these troubling waters.

It may be that the individually executed house shrine paintings, with their attendant variety, expressed ideas which were later to mature into a new European artistic force. In the House of Polybius, a fine lararium painting was recently discovered; one which was apparently left unfinished at the time of the eruption in 79 A.D. (fig. 3). A detail of one of the Lares shows the thin drawing which preceded the shading and coloring that completed the painting (fig. 8). Here we can appreciate the personal nature of these paintings with the greatest attention given to facial physiognomy and expression. Exceptional as this painting is (few are as monumental in scale and detail), the Polybius shrine manages to convey to us the force and power of the Roman house shrine. One imagines the Roman youths, male and female, who first donned their adult clothes before it in their "coming of age" rituals. It truly gives us a participatory experience in the traditional power of religious images.

Roman household worship, as exemplified by these shrines, became the vehicle used by Christianity to penetrate into the Mediterranean home. Christians quickly took advantage of the simple provisions for domestic piety already framed by the household shrine. As Christianity spread throughout Europe, the house cult, now duly converted, went with it. It easily combined with sacred house corner traditions already present in Germanic lore and prospered in every European region. In the Mediterranean it survived practically unscathed. The graceful polychromed terracotta garden shrines now seen in the Naples area recall the Roman

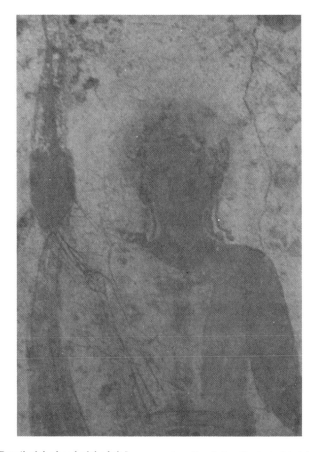

Fig. 8 Detail of the head of the left Lar present on the shrine illustrated *in toto* as Figure Three. The unfinished character of the work demonstrates the painting techniques utilized. Pompeii, 79 A.D. ca., IX. xiii. 3.

house cult vividly. Madonnas, proudly ensconced in Neapolitan homes, evoke still the tutelary nature of the Lares. The mountain shrine in Greece still serves the weary traveller in much the same manner as the Roman roadside lararium. Above all, the continual flow of domestic numen still protects and keeps the home. The importance of Roman domestic religion as a significant catalyst in this process is undisputed. The needs so wondrously identified by Roman household rituals never have been displaced by the violent patterns of western history.

Notes

[1]George Kubler, *The Shape of Time*, New Haven: 1962, especially p. 9.

[2]Bernard Herman and David Orr, "Pear Valley, *et al:* An Excursion into the Analysis of Southern Vernacular Architecture," *Southern Folklore Quarterly* V. 39, no. 4, Dec., 1975, pp. 307-325.

[3]See Warde Fowler, *Roman Ideas of Deity in the Last Century B.C.*, London: 1914, pp. 15, 25. See also R.M. Ogilvie, *The Romans and Their Gods in the Age of Augustus*, London: 1969, pp. 102-105.

[4]For the early development of the cult see Jesse Benedict Carter, *The Religion of Numa*, London: 1906.

[5]For *lararia* see George K. Boyce, *Corpus of the Lararia of Pompeii, Memoirs of the American Academy in Rome*, 14, Rome: 1937, and David Gerald Orr, *Roman Domestic Religion: A Study of the Roman Household Deities and their Shrines* (Ph.D. dissertation, University of Maryland, College Park, Md, 1972).

[6]David Gerald Orr, "Roman Domestic Religion: The Evidence of the Household Shrines," in *ANRW*, Band II. 16. 1. Berlin: 1978, p. 1559.

[7]Ovid *Fasti* 6. 301-308; *Trist.*5.5.10. Cato *R.R.* 143.2. For the hearth see H.J. Rose, *Religion in Greece and Rome*, New York: 1959, p. 178.

[8]For Living Flame, "vivam flammam," see Ovid *Fasti* 6. 291. For Vesta see also Gerhard Radke, *Die Goetter Altitaliens, Fontes et Commentationes 3*, Muenster: 1965, pp. 320-324 and H. Hommel, *Vesta und die fruehroemische Religion, ANRW* I, 2, Berlin: 1972, pp. 397-420. For the State cult see Thomas Worsfold, *The History of the Vestal Virgins*, London: 1952.

[9]See Boyce, op. cit., no. 77 and no. 420.

[10]Michael Grant, *The Roman Forum*, New York: 1970, pp. 55-60.

[11]Ovid *Fasti* 295-398.

[12]The sanctity of the hearth fire seemed to be an ancient element of Greek household worship as well. Hestia, the Greek analog to Vesta, was also never completely anthropomorphized. In both Greek and Roman religion the hearth was versatile—it served both secular and non-secular functions.

[13]Two opposing theories have been formulated concerning the early history and evolution of the Lares in Roman religion. The first group holds that the Lares were originally agricultural deities and moved into the house from their early hegemony of the fields and crops. See Kurt Latte, *Roemische Religionsgeschicte,Handbuch der Altertumswiss.* V. 4. Munich: 1960, pp. 166-174; R.E.A. Palmer, *Roman Religion and Roman Empire, Five Essays,* The Haney Foundation Series 15, Philadelphia: 1974, pp. 114-115 and p. 117. The other concept argues that the Lares embodied the spirits of the dead ancestors of the family. See E. Samter, *Familienfeste der Griechen und Roemer,* Berlin: 1901, pp. 105-108. Perhaps this view was a Greek one which melded with the earlier Italic idea that the Lares came from the arable fields. See Margaret Waites, "The Nature of the Lares and Their Representation in Roman Art," *AJA,* 24 (1920), pp. 241-261.

[14]An inscription found recently at Tor Tignosa, outside Rome, further attests to this idea. See M. Guarducci, "Cippo latino arcaico con dedica ad Enea," *Bull. Com.* 76, *Bull. del Mus. della civilta Romana 19,* 1956-58, pp. 3-13. *Numen* was always recognized as being a kind of religious force which could be attached to objects and thereby increase their supernatural power.

[15]Virgil *Georg.* 3. 344. Martial 10. 61. 5.

[16]*Corpus Inscriptionum Latinarum* (afterwards CIL) III 3460. Ovid *Trist.* 4. 8. 22.

[17]Cato *R.R.* 143. 3.

[18]Plautus' *Aulularia* contains a prologue spoken by a Lar! In this passage is contained one of the best summations of their tutelary nature. *Aulularia* 1-5.

[19]A good description of the festival is given in W. Warde Fowler, *The Roman Festivals of the Period of the Republic,*London: 1899, pp. 279-80. See also Louise Holland, "The Shrine of the Lares Compitales," *TAPA,* 68 (1939), pp. 428-41. *Compita* were sacred spots located where four properties intersected or where four streets converged at right angles. Since Roman mensuration used squares and rectangles for city planning, many such spots existed in Roman towns. Pompeii's main east-west axis is provided with a street shrine at almost every *compitum.*

[20]Roads and travelers: CIL II 4320, CIL XIV 4547.
Soldiers and Military Camps: CIL III 3460
Games: CIL VI 36810
Imperial Residences: CIL VI 443, 445-449.
State: Ovid *Fasti* 5. 129.

[21]Tibullus 1. 10. 21-24. Horace *Carmina* 3. 23. 3-4.

Horace *Sat.* 2. 5. 12-14.
[22]For the *bulla* see Petronius, *Sat.* 60. 8.
[23]Boyce, op. cit., Plate 18, no. 1; Plate 24, nos. 1 & 2. Orr, dissertation, Corpus A, no. 3.
[24]Waites, op. cit., pp. 257ff. Georg Wissowa, *Religion und Kultus der Roemer*, Handbuch der altertumswiss., IV, 5, Munich: 1902, p. 172. For the Rhyton see Orr, *ANRW*, p. 1568, no. 67.
[25]Orr, *ANRW*, p. 1569, n. 74.
[26]Lillian M.Wilson, *The Clothing of the Ancient Romans*, Baltimore: 1938, pp. 55-56.
[27]W. Warde Fowler, *The Religious Experience of the Roman People*, London: 1933, pp. 73-74. Orr, *ANRW*, p. 1563, n. 28.
[28]Martial 8. 75. 1.
[29]Horace *Carmina* 2.4.15; 3. 23.19. The *Di Penates* were all the divinities worshipped at the hearth.
[30]Cicero *Rep.* 5.7. See also Orr, dissertation, pp. 42-43.
[31]Fowler, *Religious Experience*, p. 74. See also H.J. Rose, "On the Original Significance of the Genius." *CQ* 17, pp. 57-60.
[32]H.J. Rose, *Religion in Greece and Rome* New York: 1959, p. 193. Women were represented by their Juno. This concept also suggested the youth concept in the representation of procreative force.
[33]Orr, *ANRW*, p. 1570.
[34]Tibullus 1.7.49; 2.2.1.
[35]Ovid *Trist.* 3.13.17.
[36]Orr, *ANRW*, p. 1571.
[37]Street Shrines: Orr, dissertation, Plate XI, pp. 125-27. Also V. Spinnazola, *Pompei alla luce degli scavi di Via dell'abbondanza* 3 volumes. Rome: 1953, pp. 177ff. Domestic Numen: CILX 860.
[38]For example, the serpent in Greece was also the guardian of the house and an animal associated with good luck. They were also used as instruments through which the future could be read. See Martin P. Nilsson, *Greek Folk Religion*, New York: 1940, p. 71. Pliny mentions that snakes were kept as pets. See *N.H.* 29.72. He also distinguished between those which were poisonous (Aspides) and those which were non-poisonous (Dracones).
[39]Persius *in Georg.* 3. 417.
[40]Nilsson, p. 71. See also M. Nilsson, *The Minoan-Mycenaean Religion and its Survival in Greek Religion*, Lund: 1927, p. 281.
[41]Nilsson, *Greek Folk*, p. 71.
[42]Orr, *ANRW*, p. 1573.
[43]Ibid., pp. 1574-75.
[44]For example, certain representations, the Lares for instance, resemble those found elsewhere; see the images of the Lares and Genius shown on a street shrine altar found in Rome and now in the Palace of the Conservators, Rome, Italy.
[45]Orr, *ANRW*, p. 1585.
[46]Ibid., Plate One, Fig. one.
[47]Ibid., Plate One. Fig. two.
[48]Ibid., p. 1578.
[49]*Boyce*, Plate 30, Fig. four.
[50]Ibid., p. 18.
[51]Ibid., Number 77.
[52]Orr, *ANRW*, Plate Seven, Fig. fourteen, p. 1582.
[53]See Margherita Guarducci, "Dal gioco letterale all Crittographia Mistica," in *ANRW*, 16.2., Plate seven, Fig. eleven.

Bibliographic Note

Articles on Roman domestic religion can be found in the following standard handbooks: Latte, K., *Roemische Religionsgeschicte,* Handbuch der Altertumswiss. V 4 (Munchen: 1960); *Oxford Classical Dictionary,* 2nd ed., 1970; Wissowa, G., *Religion und Kultus der Roemer,* Handbuch der Altertumswiss. IV 5

(Munchen: 1912); De Marchi, A., *Il Culto privato di Roema antica* (Milan: 1896). Although out of date this monograph constitutes the only real separate study of the house cult; Ogilvie, R.M., *The Romans and their Gods in the Age of Augustus* (London: 1969); a concise little essay on domestic worship is included in this splendid study; Orr, D., "Roman Domestic Religion: The Evidence of the Household Shrines," in *Aufstieg und Niedergang der Roemischen Welt,* Band II.16.1. (Berlin: 1978), pp. 1557-91.

There exists at this time no serious study linking the Roman household cult with modern practices in Italy.

Acknowledgments

This essay is based on research done in Italy in 1966, 1970, and during the course of a Rome Prize Fellowship in Classics at the American Academy in Rome. Many fellows and scholars at that institution stimulated the author in his work there. Parts of this essay formed portions of the author's dissertation at the University of Maryland. The help provided by Professor Wilhelmina Jashemski is immeasurable; her constant encouragement made the author's labors an easy task.

This essay appeared in Fred E.H. Schroeders' *5000 Years of Popular Culture* (Popular Press, 1980) 155-172.

Miami's Little Havana:
Yard Shrines, Cult Religion and Landscape

James R. Curtis

IN THE SUMMER of 1978 a brief article entitled "Neighbors Irate Over Family's Shrine" appeared in *The Miami Herald*.[1] The story told of a group of residents in the predominantly non-Latin city of South Miami who feared that a newly-erected, seven-foot shrine in the front yard of a Cuban neighbor would lower property values. City officials called in to investigate found that the shrine was located too close to the front property line, and thus was in violation of municipal building and zoning laws. Confused and saddened by the turmoil created the Cuban family stated that the shrine had been built (at a cost of $1,500) in gratitude to Santa Barbara "for answering all of our prayers."

More than an isolated human interest story, the above incident is perhaps symbolic of the bicultural social adjustments, and urban landscape transformations, which have taken place and are continuing to occur in the greater Miami area as a result of Cuban in-migration. In the short span of only twenty years, beginning in 1959, the Cuban population of Dade County has ballooned from about 20,000 to a current estimate of 430,000.[2] Counting the 94,000 non-Cuban Latins residing in the county—mostly Puerto Ricans, Mexicans and Central and South Americans—Latins constitute approximately 35 per cent of the county's population, as compared to only five per cent in 1960.[3] Moreover, Latins have settled in distinct residential concentrations, thereby greatly accentuating the "Latinization" of selected locales.[4] The city of Miami, for example, is almost 56 per cent Latin (207,000 out of 370,000); Hialeah, with a population of 133,000, is over 65 per cent Latin, most of whom are Cuban. The impact of such sudden and fundamental change in the pattern of ethnicity has profoundly altered both material and nonmaterial elements of culture in the region. Nowhere are these transformations better manifested than in Little Havana, a four-square-mile enclave of Cuban culture located a scant mile southwest of downtown Miami (Fig. 1).

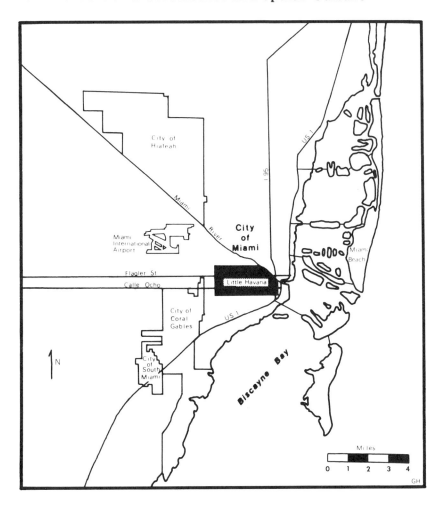

Little Havana

Often referred to as "a city (or "nation") within a city," Little Havana is the nucleus, the core, of Cuban life in Miami. Once a healthy middle-class Anglo neighborhood, dating from the immediate post-World War I era, by the mid-1950s it had deteriorated and was declining in population as urban growth and increased mobility opened up newer housing areas for the middle-class in the outlying suburbs.[5] For the newly-arriving Cuban refugees this area was preferred in respect to having available and affordable housing units and vacant shops for potential business endeavors.[6] It was also served by public transportation and near the central business district where social services and employment opportunities were most abundant. The neighborhood was reborn as "Little Havana" almost literally overnight. Although its function as the principal receptor area has declined in recent years as the Cuban population has grown in numbers and affluence,[7] and has since spread out to other settlement areas, Little Havana remains in spirit, if not landscape, the traditional Cuban quarter.

In most important respect, Little Havana is a self-contained community which has evolved, by design, to suit the needs and tastes of its residents, and in so doing has embellished the landscape with a pronounced Cuban flavor. Along West Flagler and Southwest Eighth Streets (the latter known locally as "*Calle Ocho*"), the two principal commercial strips which cut through the district, a full complement of goods and services is offered which cater to the Cuban population. If so desired, a Cuban who lives in Little Havana and speaks only Spanish, could shop, dine out, be medically cared for, attend churches, schools, shows and theaters, die and be buried without a word of English being uttered.

The commercial landscape of Little Havana reflects in both vivid and subtle ways this impress of Cuban culture. From the older stucco buildings of Spanish and art deco styles, and from the small shopping plazas which have been built of late, neon store signs flash "*Joyeria*," "*Ferreteria*," "*Muebleria*," "*Farmacia*," "*Mercado*," "*Zapateria*," and so on. One frequently encounters small groups of three and four gathered at the countless vest-pocket, open-air coffee counters to sip the syrupy-dark, bittersweet *cafe cubano* and consume fresh *pasteles* (pastry.).

The newsstands and bookstores in the district display a plethora of Spanish-language books, magazines and newspapers, including *El Miami Herald* with a circulation in excess of 50,000. The acrid smell of cured tobacco wafts from the thirty or so small cigar factories located in the area where old men (*tabaqueros*) patiently roll cigars *a mano* (by hand).[8] At Antonio Maceo Mini Park, on *Calle Ocho*, men play continuous games of dominoes on permanently-fixed tables and benches designed specifically for that purpose. Fresh fruits and vegetables are sold in open-air markets and stands which dot the district. The sweet smell of simmering garlic hangs heavy over the hundred-plus restaurants featuring Cuban and Spanish cuisine, ranging from elegant super clubs with valet parking to four-stool cafes.

The life and vitality of these places, however, stand in stark contrast to the somberness surrounding the Cuban Memorial Plaza, where flowers and wreaths are faithfully placed at the base of the Bay of Pigs monument in memory of loved ones who fell during that ill-fated invasion. To be sure, the landscape of Little Havana conveys a strong feeling of pre-revolutionary Cuba, but the sense of a people in exile remains pervasive. The existence of nearly one hundred officially recognized "municipalities in exile," which function as social and quasi-political organizations composed of former residents of particular municipalities in Cuba, attests to their vitality.[9] Many of these groups, in fact, have converted houses and other buildings in Little Havana into meeting halls where lectures, concerts and dances are periodically held, and where informational and historical newsletters are published.

Thus, as befitting a people caught inextricably between two cultures, Little Havana is not an isolated community devoid of contact and consequence with the surrounding society and environment. Rather, in culture and landscape, it is a mixture of both Cuban and American influences. Cuban and American flags, for example, proudly bedeck the streets of Little Havana during national holidays of both countries. Cuban (grocery) shoppers may patronize the neighborhood Winn Dixie or Pantry Pride supermarkets, and then walk to the back parking lot of these stores and barter with itinerant Cuban peddlers selling fresh fish, poultry, fruit and vegetables. Teenagers sip on *batidos* (exotic fruit milkshakes) from Cuban ice cream shops and eat *grandes macs* from the local McDonald's. In language as well, especially among the younger Cubans, one now hears a curious mixture of Spanish and English ("Spanglish," as it is known).[10] Signs on some store windows, for example, announce "*Gran* Sale." Young people may be heard shouting to one another, "*Tenga un* nice day."

Although the housing area of Little Havana has been significantly up-graded and changed as a consequence of the Cuban tenure, the residential landscape is not nearly as "Latinized" as the commercial strips in the district. In fact, a quick drive through the area would probably leave the impression that it is largely indistinguishable from neighboring Anglo residential areas. Yet, upon closer inspection, differences unfold. Fences, for example, now enclose many front yards, and wrought iron and tile have been added to some houses for decorative purposes. Even these characteristically Hispanic features, however, remain relatively minor in comparison to what one might expect to find in most Latin communities. If anything, one is impressed more by how little these embellishments reflect the fundamental replacement of culture groups which has occurred in the area. This observation, however, is somewhat misleading, for it fails to include the single most conspicuous landscape element which clearly distinguishes Little Havana from non-Cuban residential areas.

Yard Shrines

If the Cuban family in the story recounted at the beginning of this article had lived in Little Havana, it would not have aroused the resentment, or even stirred the curiosity, of neighbors over the construction of its yard shrine. City officials would not have been brought in to search for some minor infraction of local building or zoning laws to force its removal. More commonplace than exceptional, there are literally hundreds of yard shrines gracing the cultural landscape of Little Havana.[11]

The shrines may be found anywhere in the yard area—front, back or along the sides—although the front yard, especially near the sidewalk, appears to be a favored location. Regardless of placement, however, the front of the shrine always faces the street. Since these are personal shrines, built to suit the religious needs and preferences of individuals, no two are exactly alike; diversity is the standard. In size, the shrines range from about two to ten feet in height, and two to six feet in width. Most are rectangular in shape, although octagonal and circular structures are not uncommon. The most frequently used building materials include brick, cement, stone and glass; wood is rarely, if ever, used except for trimming. Exterior walls, though, are often stuccoed or tiled. A single cross may adorn the top of a shrine, and use of latticework and other forms of ornamentation are occasionally found, but in general the degree of exterior embellishment is more austere than ornate.

Regardless of size, materials used, or shape, the interiors of the shrines remain visible through either sealed glass side panels or a single glass door enclosing the front of the sanctuary. Pedestalled inside, usually on an elevated platform or altar, stands a single statue. At the base of the statue, and occasionally on a small stairwell leading to the base, one often finds an utterly baffling array of items, including, for example, fresh-cut or artificial flowers, candles, crucifixes, jars or leaves, bowls of water, beads, stones, miniature figures of men or animals, and other assorted paraphernalia.

The statues themselves are of Catholic saints, the Madonna and Jesus, each identifiable (at least to the knowing eye) by sex, colors, adornment, and particular symbols, such as a cup, a cane or a cross. By far, the three saints which are enshrined most commonly in Little Havana are, in order, Santa Barbara, Our Lady of Charity (patron saint of Cuba), and Saint Lazarus. Other saints, particularly Saint Francis of Assisi, Saint Christopher and Saint Peter are also found, but with much less frequency. Likewise, shrines built in honor of the Madonna and Jesus are not nearly as numerous as those erected to the main three saints.

Santa Barbara is most often portrayed as a young woman dressed in a white tunic with a red mantle bordered with gold trimming. She wears a golden crown and holds a golden goblet in her right hand and a golden sword in her left (Fig. 2). Our Lady of Charity is similarly represented as a young woman dressed in a white tunic. Her cloak, however, is either blue or white. She holds a child in her left arm. At her feet, seated or kneeling in a boat, are two or three small male figures looking reverently upward (Figs. 3, 4). Saint Lazarus is usually depicted as a bent and crippled man of middle-age, with open wounds and sores, supported with the aid of crutches. Two or three small dog figures often stand at his feet (Fig. 5). This particular portrayal of Lazarus is not the image officially recognized or sanctioned by the Church; it has evolved from Cuban tradition.

Sacred elements in the landscape often convey much less religious context from which they spring than observation alone would suggest. The religious beliefs which inspire the construction of yard shrines in Little Havana are illustrative of this contention. Considering, for example, that a vast majority of Cubans are Roman Catholics, and that most of the shrines are built in apparent homage to saints, one might logically suspect that these shrines are erected by followers of the Catholic faith. This assumption, however, is neither entirely correct nor incorrect. In truth, many of the shrines are built by Catholics, but perhaps an equal number, if not more, are erected by followers of a fascinating, syncretic Afro-Cuban cult religion called *Santeria*.

Santeria: An Afro-Cuban Religion

The history of the West Indies is rich in examples of the spontaneous melding of European and African culture traits and complexes. This process of transculturation—in which different cultural elements are jumbled, mixed and fused—played an important role in the shaping of present cultural patterns in the region, particularly in the nonmaterial aspects of culture such as language, music and religion. More notable examples of religious syncretism in the New World in which elements of Catholicism were combined with ancient African tribal beliefs and practices include *Vodun* (i.e., "voodoo") in Haiti, *Xango* in Trinidad and *Santeria* in Cuba.[12]

Santeria, like other syncretic Afro-Christian folk religions, combines an elaborate ensemble of ritual, magical, medical and theological beliefs to form a total magico-religious world view. The *Santeria* religion evolved among descendants of the Yoruba slaves who had been brought to Cuba from Nigeria beginning in the sixteenth century, but particularly in the first half of the nineteenth century.[13] These descendants—known in Cuba as the *Lucumi*—learned from oral history the tribal religion of their ancestral home.

It was a complex polytheistic religion involving a pantheon of gods and goddesses called *orishas*.[14] It was also colorful in its mythology. In many respects it was extraordinarily reminiscent of ancient Greek mythology.[15] The African religion was rather quickly altered, however, as the Cuban *Lucumis* fell increasingly under the sway of the Spanish culture.[16] Exposure to the Catholic religion, particularly its veneration of numerous saints, greatly influenced the nature of the emergent folk religion.[17] In time, the Yoruba deities came to be identified with the images of Catholic saints.[18] The *orishas* then became *santos* ("saints"), and their worship became known as *Santeria*—literally the worship of saints. Thus, to the *santero* (i.e., the practitioner of *Santeria*), a shrine may be built to house a statue in the image of a Catholic saint, but the saint is actually representative of a Yoruba god. It is exceedingly difficult to determine accurately, based solely on appearance, whether a yard shrine in Little Havana actually belongs to a Catholic or a follower of *Santeria*. In general, however, yard shrines built by practitioners of *Santeria* are more likely to contain non-traditional religious items such as bowls of water, stones and jars of leaves.

The followers of *Santeria* believe in a supreme god called *Olodumare, Olofi* or *Olorun*. He is thought to be a distant, lofty figure. Contact with this supreme deity is attainable only through the *orishals* who serve as intermediaries.[19] Thus, worship of god-saints serves as the focus for formal and informal devotional practices; there are no subcults or special rites exclusively in honor of *Olodumare*.

The saints—who are known both by their Catholic names and their Yoruba appellations—are associated with specific colors, particular symbols or "weapons," such as thunder, fire or swords, and are considered to have the same supernatural powers ascribed to the African deities.[20] Each is believed to possess specific attributes, which in total govern all aspects of human life and natural phenomena. A *santero* might seek to invoke the power, for example, of *Babalu-Aye* (associated with Saint Lazarus), god of illness and disease, to cure a particular ailment, or *Orunmila* (associated with Saint Francis of Assisi), god of wisdom and divination, to bestow knowledge. Others, purportedly, can assure success in a job, ward off an evil spirit, bring back a former lover, and so on.

The numerous deities, however, are not all venerated equally; some are more favored than others, often leading to the formation of a special subcult devoted to a particular god-saint. In Cuba, as in Miami now *Chango* (associated with Saint Barbara), god of fire, thunder and lightning, is the most popular of all the *orishas*.[21] *Chango* represents a curious form of syncretism involving a change of sex from the male Yoruba god to the female Catholic saint. *Oshun* (associated with Our Lady of Charity, patron saint of Cuba), god of love, marriage and gold, and *Babalu-Aye* are also extremely popular in Miami. Seven of the most revered and powerful *orishas* are often worshipped collectively. This group is known among *santeros* as the "Seven African Powers." The *orishas* which make up this septet, their associated Catholic images, colors, human aspects controlled, and weapons are shown in Table 1.

The ritual and devotional activities of *santeros* are confined, in most cases, to private residences. The more important functions, such as an initiation into the cult, a funeral, or a consultation in which some form of divination is sought is presided over by a high "priest" of the religion, called a *babaloa*.[22] Lesser orders of priesthood attend to the more mundane rites and rituals. The rituals themselves are primitive, bizarre affairs, often involving the consumption of beverages concocted from exotic herbs and roots, the use of incense, oils and foreign perfumes, drumming, dancing, trance inducement and animal sacrifices.[23] Many of the liturgical practices including phraseology used in prayers and incantations, as well as various paraphernalia needed for ritualistic purposes, are also borrowed from Catholicism. A *Santeria* priest might even suggest to a follower that he or she attend a Catholic mass; in many cases simply to obtain holy water or even a piece of the consecrated host for use in a subsequent ritual.[24]

The Expansion of Santeria

As surprising as it may seem *Santeria* today is neither a predominantly rural nor a lower socioeconomic class phonomenon. Indeed, authorities on the religion confirm that *Santeria* has permeated all racial groups and socioeconomic classes in Cuba, and now in the Cuban community in exile.[25] With the Cuban immigration to the United States, *Santeria* is known to be thriving in the larger cities where Cuban refugees have settled, including New York, Los Angeles, Detroit, Chicago and particularly Miami. A precise determination of the numbers of adherents to *Santeria* in Miami is virtually impossible to ascertain, since they do not build public churches or publish membership records. It is believed, however, that their numbers run into the thousands. One rough indication is provided by anthropologist William Bascom who estimated in 1969 that there were at least 83 *babaloas*, or high priests, practicing in Miami.[26] This may be compared to Havana, which is the stronghold of *Santaria* with tens of thousands of followers, where Bascom estimated the number of *babaloas* at about 200 just prior to the Cuban Revolution.[27] Perhaps a better indicator

Table 1

The Seven African Powers

Orisha	Catholic Image	Colors	Human Aspect Controlled	Weapons or Symbols
Chango	Santa Barbara	red/white	passion, enemies	thunder, sword, cup
Eleggua	Holy Guardian Angel	red/black	messages	iron nails, small iron rooster
Obatala	Our Lady of Mercy	white	peace, purity	all white substances
Oggun	Saint Peter	green/black	war, employment	iron, knives, steel
Orunmila	Saint Francis of Assisi	green/yellow	divination	Table of Ifa (a divination board)
Oshun	Our Lady of Charity	yellow/red/ green	love, marriage, gold	mirror, seashells, pumpkins
Yemaya	Our Lady of Regla	blue/white	maternity, womenhood	canoe, seashells, fans

Source: Migene Gonzalez-Wippler, Santeria: African Magic In Latin America. New York: The Julian Press, Inc., 1973.

is the existence in Miami of over 12 *botanicas*, which are retail supply outlets catering to the *Santeria* trade.

By all scholarly accounts, *Santeria* is becoming increasingly popular among certain segments of the Cuban exile community. The reason most commonly cited for this kindling of interest is the fear of some Cuban refugees of losing their cultural identity through acculturation to the American way of life.[28] Such a conversion would perhaps represent an attempt to maintain linkage to a more stable past in the face of rapidly changing values and lifestyles. Disenchantment with the Catholic faith is another factor also frequently mentioned as contributing to the apparent expansion of *Santeria* in the United States. In this respect, the Catholic church's questioning of the historical validity of certain saints who were popular in Cuba (such as Saint Lazarus and Saint Christopher), the elimination of many rituals practiced in Cuba, and just the size and institutionalized nature of the Catholic religion have reportedly prompted some Cuban-Americans to seek out alternative religious affiliation, including *Santeria.1*[29] Furthermore, the adaptive nature of the *Santeria* religion itself has apparently contributed to its expansion. Mercedes Sandoval, for example, concludes that: "Its intrinsic flexibility, eclecticism and heterogeneity have been advantages in helping ensure functional, dogmatic and ritual changes which enable it to meet the different needs of its many followers."[30] Evidently one of the more important and attractive aspects of *Santeria* for the Cuban community in Miami is its function as a mental health care system.[31]

In the process of change and modification as practiced in the United States, however, many African chants and dances, the use of certain herbs and roots and other medicinal and ritualistic elements have been abandoned. One of the more interesting adaptations, for example, involves a change in the Oil of the Seven African Powers, used in the worship of those deities. The "oil" is now available in *botanicas* in Miami as an aerosol spray. Directions on the side of the container read as follows: "Repeat as necessary. Make your petition. Make the sign of the cross. Air freshener, deodorizer."

Perhaps the apparent expansion of interest in *Santeria* among certain members of the Cuban exile community is only a transitional phenomenon which will subside, or die out completely, as the process of acculturation speeds ahead; which occurred, for example, in Italian-American cult religions.[32] At the present time, however, as one follower of *Santeria* said, "... when we hear thunder in Miami, we know that *Chango* is in exile."[33] Regardless of the future of this particular religious cult, the yard shrines and other contributions to the cultural landscape associated with the Cuban sector reflect the growing social diversity of this rapidly changing cosmopolitan city.

Notes

[1]Sam Jacobs, "Neighbors Irate Over Family's Shrine," *The Miami Herald* (July 2, 1978), section A, p. 23.

[2]Strategy Research Corporation, "Latin Market Survey," Miami, Florida, 1977, p. 78; Metropolitan Dade County Office of the County Manager, "Profile of the Latin Population in the Metropolitan Dade County Area," Miami, Florida, 1976.

[3]Strategy Research Corporation, p. 78.

[4]Metropolitan Dade County Planning Department, "Ethnic Breakdown By Census Tract," Miami, Florida, 1975.

[5]Metropolitan Dade County Office of the City Manager, "Impact of the Community Development Program on Private Involvement in the Commercial Rehabilitation of the 'Little Havana' Neighborhood," Miami, Florida, 1978, p. 2.

[6]Kimball D. Woodbury, "The Spatial Diffusion of the Cuban Community in Dade County, Florida" (unpublished M.A. thesis, University of Florida, Department of Geography, 1978), p. 33.

[7]F. Pierce Eichelberger, "The Cubans in Miami: Residential Movements and Ethnic Group Differentiation" (unpublished M.A. thesis, University of Cincinnati, Department of Geography, 1974), p. 83.

[8]William D. Montalbano, "Vanishing Hands," *The Miami Herald* (Feb., 4, 1979), Tropic section, pp. 19-21.

[9]Ileana Oroza, "The Traditionalist," *The Miami Herald* (July 4, 1978), section A, p. 16.

[10]John Dorschner, "Growing Up Spanglish in Miami," *The Miami Herald* (Sept., 11, 1977), Tropic section, pp. 6-13.

[11]Matthew Creelman, "Count Your Built-In Blessings," *The Miami Herald* (July 21, 1979), section D, p. 3.

[12]George E. Simpson, *Religious Cults of the Caribbean: Trinidad, Jamaica, and Haiti* (Rio Piedras, Puerto Rico: Institute of Caribbean Studies, 1970), p. 11.

[13]Migene Gonzalez-Wippler, *Santeria: African Magic In Latin America* (New York: The Julian Press, 1973), p. 1.

[14]D.E. Baldwin, *The Yoruba of Southwest Nigeria* (Boston: G.K. Hall, 1976).

[15]J.O. Lucas, *The Religions of the Yorubas* (Lagos: C.M.S. Bookshop, 1942).

[16]William Bascom, "The Yoruba in Cuba," *Nigeria*, 37 (1951).

[17]William Bascom, "The Focus of Cuban Santeria," *Southwestern Journal of Anthropology*, 6 (Spring, 1950), pp. 64-68.

[18]Gonzalez-Wippler, p. 3; Melville J. Herskovits, "African Gods and Catholic Saints in New World Negro Belief," *American Anthropologist*, 39 (Oct.-Dec., 1937), pp. 635-643.

[19]Isabel Mercedes Castellanos, "The Use of Language in Afro-Cuban Religion" (unpublished Ph.D. dissertation, Georgetown University, Dept. of Languages and Linguistics, 1976), pp. 31-33.

[20]Gonzalez-Wippler, p. 16.

[21]Mercedes C. Sandoval, "Santeria As A Mental Health Care System: An Historical Overview," *Social Science and Medicine*, 13 B (April, 1979), p. 139; William R. Bascom, *Shango In The New World* (Austin, Texas: Univ. of Texas Press, 1972), pp. 13-15.

[22]Castallanos, p. 35.

[23]Mercedes C. Sandoval, *La Religion Afro-Cubana* (Madrid, Spain: Playor, S.A., 1975); Lydia Cabrera, *El Monte* (Miami: Ediciones, C.R., 1971); Ellen Hampton, "Drums Beating and Animals Shrieking Frighting Southwest Dade Residents," *The Miami Herald* (Nov., 25, 1979), section B, p. 19.

[24]Gonzalez-Wippler, p. 4.

[25]Sandoval, *La Religion Afro-Cubana*, pp. 270-272; Castellanos, pp. 163-164.

[26]Bascom, *Shango In The New World*, p. 20.

[27]*Ibid.*

[28]Castellanos, p. 164.

[29]Sandoval, *La Religion Afro-Cubana*, p. 272.

[30]Sandoval, *Social Science and Medicine*, p. 137.

[31]*Ibid.*, pp. 137-151; Clarissa S. Scott, "Health and Healing Practices Among Five Ethnic Groups in Miami, Florida," *Public Health Reports*, 89 (Nov.-Dec., 1974), pp. 526-527.

[32]Rudolph J. Vecoli, "Cult and Occult in Italian-American Culture: The Persistence of a Religious Heritage," in *Immigrants and Religion in Urban Culture*, ed. by Randall M. Miller and Thomas D. Marzik (Philadelphia: Temple Univ. Press, 1977), pp. 25-47.

[33]Sandoval, *La Religion Afro-Cubana*, p. 274.

This essay appeared in *Journal of Cultural Geography* I:1 (Fall, 1980), 1-16.

Television Viewing as Ritual

Michael T. Marsden

ONE OF THE classic scholastic attributes of God was omnipresence, a quality which in turn became an operative definition. Given the penetration level of television receivers in the Western world, it would seem to be quite logical to extend the argument and suggest that television has taken on some god-like qualities, not the least of which is omnipresence. In addition, the television receiver has quietly and smoothly assumed the role of household god, becoming the focal point for interior designer and homeowner alike. Television viewing is not an activity; it is a way of life, a contemporary, electronic creed. True, we are not always "watching" our television receivers when they have "power on," but they most assuredly are a part of our environment at that moment. In fact, television occupies a larger part of our waking consciousness as a society than does eating, and it is rivaling sleeping in the amount of our time it consumes.

Television viewing is too often examined in terms of content, which while an extremely important focus for the cultural analyst, is not the only valid or viable perspective. Equally important is the perspective of "flow" so effectively presented and exemplified by Raymond Williams in his book *Television: Technology and Cultural Form*. People do not watch programs, they watch television. And they read about television, not about programs in *TV Guide* or in their local newspapers. (Reading about television provides an interesting sub-ritual which exists to balance the non-linear bias of television viewing.) It is not by accident that prime-time television runs three hours per evening; Americans have regularly and systematically enjoyed a three-hour block of entertainment for an evening from 19th century popular theater (a five act play plus a one

120

act farce), to vaudeville (10 to 15 distinct acts averaging a total of three hours of programming), to a double-bill movie (two features plus a newsreel plus a cartoon), etc. The pattern was well established for a complete evening's entertainment long before the first experimental images of Felix the Cat disturbed the airways in and around New York City in the late 1920s.

But behind the patterned and timed entertainment forms were the cultural needs that these various entertainment forms so effectively fulfilled. Popular culture in general, and the popular arts in particular, do not provide the audience with an opportunity for escape *from* anything. To the contrary what they provide is the option of escaping *into* a restructured, reformulated world in which the senseless makes sense, where the logic of feeling rules, and where resolution is not only possible but demanded. It is a world which some call fantasy but which the wiser call dreaming. It is a conscious state of unconsciousness in which the human mind can deal with issues which in the "normal," destructured world would prove intolerable or unacceptable. The function of the popular arts is basically the same function served by all of art through the ages; only the aesthetic codes are different. Television as, in the words of Horace Newcomb, "the most popular art" has a most special function in our contemporary culture, serving to focus our cultural needs and wishes through programming into an extended block of time in which we can reorder our world until it is psychologically acceptable. It is time that we took television producers at their word; they are truly trying to give us what we want, and we are not always as clear as they would like us to be on what it is we want. That is why we devise rating systems and various feedback mechanisms. That is why the relationship between television producer/television audience/television programming is a highly dynamic, organic one which can and does flex to meet the deep-felt needs and desires of all parties. When the American audience did not get the trial of a President on PBS through the Watergate Hearings they turned to commercial television and *Washington Behind Closed Doors* for their sense of justice and satisfaction. But it is television viewing as a whole, not the viewing of particular programs or even programming forms, which is the major ritual in our society.

Rituals, whether religious or secular, exist as paradigms of order for the purpose of placing the immediate environment into perspective. Television programming, whether it be a highly creative 60 second commercial, a half-hour newscast, or a 90 minute made-for-television movie, exists to provide the viewer with a mediated experience which is highly emotional in nature. It has been suggested that television, unlike the print medium, emphasizes the right side of the brain. While the left side of the brain controls sequential, linear throught processes, the right side of the brain involves itself in simultaneous, non-sequential processes. We thus become emotional scanners, tuning in and out of melodramatic and dramatic scenes of restructured reality for the purposes of preparing ourselves to more effectively and efficiently deal with the non-televised world once the"power is off." The parallels to a religious liturgical service are many and obvious.

While the left side of the brain promotes the intellect, the right side is busy processing feelings. The ritual of television viewing is most heavily involved with activating the feelings of the viewers, with involving them in restructured experiences. It may well be argued that the ritual of television viewing is the most powerful secular ritual in contemporary society because of its pervasiveness. A number of separate experiments in the United States and Europe involving deprivation of television viewing (several of which actually paid the volunteers not to watch television) have resulted in notable failures.

One of the most misinformed generalizations to spring from World War II media research was that of a monolithic mass audience, the creation of the researcher's imagination but hardly a reflection of reality. Perhaps in times of world paranoia such evasions of reason are understandable; perhaps we even did have "an enemy" and needed to believe that all Germans were Nazis and all Japanese kamikazes. But in post-World War II America there should have been a return to reason within research circles, a claim on rationality, clear thinking when it came to research studies on the mass media.

Television was born full-commercial into a cultural climate of monolithic media thought in which there was an enemy who could change media forms easily and quickly: before World War II the movies were at fault, but in the early 1950s comic books received the researchers' glare. There was more than enough laser-like thinking left over for television when it began to be clearly seen as *the* major threat to American culture in the 1950s and 1960s. Intellectuals who would under almost any other circumstances question the exception to the exception to the rule found themselves quite comfortably, at times even cozily, living with and embellishing generalizations about the "mass media" and their clear-cut effects upon a poor, misguided, image-hungry audience who were simply waiting for media-generated signals to react to, whether they be signals for role behavior or purchasing habits.

Out of this intellectual clay was created the "mass viewer," who was described as passive, mindless, soulless, consumption-oriented and certainly without any normal discriminatory powers. This viewer became the "they" of countless, condescending conversations, which became so rote that they themselves were ritualized. We even created an archetypal chair for this "mass viewer," personified it as "Archie's chair," and then enshrined it in the Smithsonian. It was widely assumed that "mass viewers" could be sold anything if only they could be manipulated properly, for they were without the intellectual equipage to protect themselves. In short, advertising empires were built upon the non-logic of the monolithic audience. These ways of life, and reactions to them, were, like the conversations about them, made subconscious and the action toward and reaction to them ritualized.

In the 1970s media research began quite properly to question some of the sacred assumptions about the "mass viewers" and their habits. It became clear that the audience was not an audience at all, but an assemblage of many distinct audiences who were united only under special circumstances and for very special needs and purposes, such as the coverage of the moon landing or the broadcast of Super Bowl games. Demographics became crucial to the television industry, and to support industries to a greater extent in the 1970s than had been the case in the earlier decades, psychographics became a further refined tool for marketing research and the development of advertising strategies.

Despite the obvious and significant rise in multiple-set ownership, researchers kept working out of the pre-transistor radio listening paradigm of a "typical" family sitting in front of their radio receiver tuned into the popular culture of the airwaves *sans* interruptions. Yet the evidence was there in force in the 1960s that people were viewing television in increasing numbers in private, personal ways; they were not communally consuming the culture via this new medium as they had done with previous media. Television sets found their ways into bedrooms, bathrooms, garages, workshops, offices. etc. And programming types followed: Johnny Carson certainly knew his audience was in the bedroom in significant numbers. Television sets further merged into and began in turn to shape lifestyles.

The shift in audience utilization of hardware was further demarked in the 1970s by the advent of home videotaping equipment which moved television into new time frames and into the more private, personal realms of human behavior. Video games were but one illustration of our need to develop additional ways of manipulating and thus further utilizing the television medium.

During the 1970s researchers finally began to examine how people used the medium. We became wise enough to realize that while the average American household may have had the television set *on* for better than six hours a day, that did not mean that the set(s) was being *watched* for that length of time by any combination of viewers. What it did mean is that television programming has become a regularized part of our everyday environment for large portions of our waking days. And it also meant that people have learned to use the medium in creative ways, as background sound, as a "buffer" against other "realities" of the household, as a babysitter, a companion, another member of the family. Television "viewing" then may well not be viewing at all—it may be more properly referred to as "receiving."

Researchers are just now beginning to carefully examine the conditions under which the ritual of television viewing is occurring. Certainly the audience is not exclusively comprised of compulsively passive viewers who exercise little or no choice in programming taste. To the contrary, evidence would seem to suggest that viewers are diverse in their uses of the medium and often are quite active in their interactions with the television viewing ritual.

Virtually every member of Western civilization is involved directly or indirectly in the ritual of television viewing. The television receiver is not unlike the medieval cathedral which served as a focal point for the culture and a window to rituals which were culturally significant. Television provides a series of common, shared experiences and images which have become part of the collective, shared traditions of our society. Viewers ritualistically enter into televisionland which is not as much a world of fantasized fact as it is of fact fantasized. Television is clearly a dream world, a state of mind in which resolution and closure occur with a satisfying regularity. It is also a dream world in which the deepest needs and desires of the society are depicted in living color eighteen broadcast hours a day, seven days a week. And through reruns we share in a kind of living history of the medium and the concerns it shared with the society. Television viewing is quite simply *the* American ritual.

And it will remain the American ritual—universal, omnipresent, and apparently satisfying—until it is replaced by an equally satisfactory cultural experience. Most rituals are accompanied by considerable manifest liturgy, but the television viewing ritual has been largely internalized, thus reducing the visibility of its liturgy for the non-serious cultural analyst. The ritual of television viewing involves the mind, not the body, and in the words of Marshall McLuhan, the viewer is "transported" into a different world of mediated events whose purpose is to reassure, to reaffirm and to reestablish harmony in an essentially disharmonious world. This household god may be largely taken for granted, but that does not diminish its awesome cultural power.

American Sporting Rituals

David Q. Voigt

IT HAS BEEN the joy and despair of mankind to live in a symbolic world where words have power to exalt or degrade, caress or reject or to heal or maim. And some by their ambiguity have the power to drive writers stark raving mad. One such word is "ritual," whose essential meaning has been gutted from over-tinkering by eager wordsmiths. In fact, all the philosophical prating over the meaning of ritual threatened to drown this writer in a semantical morass until rescue came in the form of a saving lifeline from a pundit who wrote consolingly that "there is the widest possible disagreement as to how the word ritual should be used and how the performance of ritual should be understood."[1]

Thank god for relativity and its gift of choice! To cut this semantical Gordian knot and get on with the task of discussing ritual in sport, I propose an operational definition of the word. Henceforth, rituals shall be taken to mean those culturally prescribed behavior forms used by individuals or groups to cope with the pressures of reality. Certainly all societies define certain structured behavior patterns as "real"; in America it is our work world of jobs and economic survival that most see as the real world.

In embracing the work world, Americans also subscribe to a world view of scientific reality—of rational procedures, natural explanations for cause and effect relationships and rigidly structured time frames. Of course there are other worlds; included are supernatural worlds, play worlds, fun worlds, magical worlds and others. Because every man must at times enter and explore these alternative worlds, rituals exist as psychodramas serving the purpose of taking us out of one so that we might find strength and power from others.[2]

But ritual procedures differ from those ordinary procedures we

125

daily follow. Those we follow because they have proved to be useful, practical and rewarding; in short, we follow them because we think they "work." But ritual procedures are employed to unleash other powers—magical, supernatural, ecstatic, or psychological; in short, we follow these because we "must." As the late Eric Berne put it, rituals are parentally patterned. In following ritual procedures we conform like obedient children, ever fearful that if we don't follow the prescriptions precisely we run a risk of angering the very powers we seek to invoke.[3]

As scripted behaviors, rituals resemble little dramas whose lines must be learned if we hope to benefit from the release of powers. Thus, we learn the rites and routinely invoke the powers and make the rituals a familiar part of our behavior. As repetitive actions, rituals show up in all avenues of social life and their recurrences testify to the endless human struggle to manage and to cope with inevitable failure and loss of control. A ritual then "is a public act and an expression of faith in the world's orderly processes."[4]

Obviously one can learn much about the character of persons or groups by observing their rituals and attempting to lay bare their meanings. Also the pace of societal change can be gauged by studying changing ritual forms. But even a fast-changing society like America still clings to dead ritual forms, many of which survive as empty "ritualisms."[5]

The Rites of Christmas Present
An example of an all-inclusive American ritual is seen in our annual Christmas festivities. Like all rituals, Christmastide is recurrent and its other-worldly aspect carries the promise of energy renewal. As the childish jingle proclaims, "Christmas comes but once a year, but when it comes it brings good cheer."

As currently staged the Christmas ritual is a major celebration that willy-nilly yanks most Americans out of daily work routines. By dint of its promise of renewed energy, joy, sociability and love, the Christmas rites have Americans acquiescing in a month-long regimen of shopping and planning. In playing out the ritual drama, one must conform to such prescriptions by indulging in carol singing, church attendance, partying, feasting and most of all—gift giving.

So heavy is the pressure to conform to this secularized ritual drama that most Americans abide, even those beset by feelings of hypocrisy or resentment. After all, the element of child-like conformity to ritual demands is part of any ritual. Hence, it is hardly surprising to learn that there are goodly numbers of Christmas ritual resenters. Their ranks include non-Christians, workaholics who resent its disrupting obligations, skeptics who oppose its advertising appeals and phony good will, and frustrated TV addicts who cannot abide its intrusions into familiar programming.

Closet Christmas objectors might be relieved to learn that studies show nine of ten Americans suffer from "adverse emotional reactions to Christmas pressures." While some of those afflicted boldly battle the tyranny of Christmas rites by staging "anti-holiday" workshops aimed at developing substitute rituals to replace the Christmas rites, perhaps the best solution for coping with so compelling a ritual demand is simply to go along with it tongue-in-cheek.[6]

Ritual Demands of American Sport

Even more compelling than the Christmas ritual which after all lasts but a month is the all-encompassing ritual of American sport. Considered as a single institution with all its individual and group forms, sports exerts its ritualistic authority over the whole society all year long. Indeed, for an American to be utterly without interest in sport, to be uninvolved as a participant or spectator, is to be alienated from American culture.

In American culture participation in sports rituals serves a function of re-creating one's energies for fuller participation in the "real" world of work. While re-creation of energy is perhaps the most socially approved function, many participants use sports as a means of escaping the realities of the work world. Indeed, many find in sporting rituals athlete gods to worship, sporting pages as scriptures, stadiums as houses of worship, and like-minded fans as congregationalists. Together these make sporting rites serve as a kind of religious experience.[7]

Be that as it may, sports participation, at least for re-creative purposes, has been accepted ritual in America since colonial times. One of the first recorded ball games took place on Christmas day in 1621 and formally organized horse-races and other spectacles were staged throughout that period. Such rites with attendant betting and partisanship rites served the purpose of transporting spectators into another world of reality.[8]

Since those far off days American sports have multiplied and the ritual hold on the populace has been expanded. One need but compare all the varied offerings of present-day scholastic sports programs with more limited offerings of half a century ago. Back then varsity participation was limited to a handful of male athletes who participated in a small number of sports, but even then the sports functioned as initiatory rites and as rites of passage.

In initiatory rites male athletes learned the ritual codes that transported them into other worlds of competitive reality. As rites of passage they transported athletes to ever higher levels of competition, each symbolically marking the transition to athletic maturity. And as rites of passage, each succeeding sport season functioned as a calendar marking the year's passage. In bygone days like the 'Thirties the ritual transition was thoroughly satisfying in its simplicity. Springtime was baseball or track and field time, the summer game was baseball, after the World Series football ruled the fall, and winter time was basketball or hockey time. Since there was little overlap, it was possible for a gifted athlete to participate in several ritualized forms. I personally remember Jim Brown, the future pro-football Hall of Famer, dominating five high school sports. A high school student in the early 'Fifties, Brown easily slipped into starring football and basketball roles, but the spring overlap posed a bit of a problem. Still Brown managed to pitch and slug away in baseball games and then sidle over to the track meet to pick up 15 points in field events. And if he found it harder to fit into lacrosse schedules, at least he starred on off days because lacrosse happened to be his favorite game!

Today's situation is more complex and the multiplication of sports offerings is a reminder that rituals must change to meet ongoing social changes. In the thirty year period since Brown enjoyed the heady ecstasy of being a five-letter man, sports programs have greatly expanded to accommodate women and men. And along with all the variety of offerings has come increasing professionalization and specialization to profoundly alter sports rituals.

Such changes were responses to changing American values like the increasing commitment to leisure and sports or the equalitarian demands from women. The professional and specialization additives were responses to similar trends in the "real" world of work. But equally important were professional standards which seeped in from the expanding world of professional sports.

Back in the 'Fifties baseball was still the leading professional team sport, easily surpassing professional hockey, football and basketball. But the rapid growth of television undermined this pattern. Not only did television enhance the popularity and profitability of these rivals, but the new medium proved to be a powerful teaching device. From TV young athletes picked up cues and standards that turned many toward these and other participant type sports. Thus, in quick time professional standards shaped scholastic programs with one result that coaches now demanded that athletes thoroughly dedicate themselves to a single sport to the exclusion of others.

The new, varied sporting programs that emerged drastically altered the sporting rites of passage. Instead of the orderly time frame that marked the 'Fifties, a bewildering "squeezing of the seasons" came to pass. Inspired by the lengthening of seasons in pro sports, scholastic programs followed suit. Thus, by 1978 professional basketball and hockey campaigns extended from late October to May, encroaching on the baseball season and the football season. Indeed, those seasons are now longer than the expanded professional baseball season. Moreover, year-round televising of golf, soccer and tennis have added to the disturbing effect.

This new calendar effect reshaped scholastic sports programs by lengthening the basketball season which encroaches on spring programs on the one hand and limited football players from playing basketball on the other. This re-cycled sporting calendar has athletes concentrating on the rites of a single sport.

In its current manifestation American sport is a potent force for conformity. In its many forms, sport communicates an endless number of ritualistic symbols and demands. Indeed, one writer sees sport as the modern opiate of the world's masses. In America the passion for sport rivals religion, sex and politics in its persuasive ability to make "people...put their own vital interests second, maybe third to the misadventures of athletic strangers."[9]

As a shaper of behavior, pressure to conform to sport, to get with its rituals begins at the earliest stages in child development; indeed, social psychologists insist that the ritual metaphors of sport function to develop personality and speed conformity to social and cultural demands. If so, by the time one is ready for little league baseball or "mitey-mite" football, he is already versed in the rituals of these sports. And like as not, familiarity with sports and imitation of these rites have early been acquired through televised sports programs. Thus, when springtime comes, many kids fasten baseball gloves to bike handlebars and push off to imitate some major league hero; and in like manner in their seasons other sports are served.

Still most Americans seldom view sport as a monolithic structure, even if "being a sport" or "getting right" with sports are cultural imperatives. Most, it seems, identify with certain sports. After all, American sport is a congeries of diversified outlets, each with its own ritual order. Hence, it is well to focus on certain ones with an eye for exposing ritual contents and for glimpsing significant symbolisms.

Ritual Life Among Bowlers
Bowling is a sport that annually attracts upwards of 60 million

devotees, many of whom are regular league bowlers. A year-round indoor sport, most leagues run through the fall and winter. As weather conditions force indoor activity, bowling appears as a world renewal rite which allows participants to defy nature's restrictions on daylight or outdoor activity. Indeed, as a ritual drama, bowling represents a triumph of science and technology over nature. In most alleys league play can be completed in two hours thanks to efficient machinery that automatically sets pins and returns balls.

Not surprisingly many of the ritual acts practiced by bowlers are scientifically inspired. For neophytes, courses sponsored by bowling equipment companies teach them how to use a precise step by step delivery and to gauge each arc of one's swing by each step. Gripping the ball, releasing it, and following through are precise ritual acts which, when integrated, hold out hope of attaining favorable and precisely measured results. Hence, bowlers are strongly addicted to numerical scores and averages as indicators of their prowess.

As ritualists bowlers are emotionally affected by game scores and averages which are studied and pondered. To improve these, bowlers indulge in rites such as aiming at alley markers, shifting positions by counting boards, and varying speeds of delivery.

Other science-minded rites include wearing wrist supporters designed to prevent "breaking" one's wrist in the act of delivery, compulsively drying one's hands on personalized towels, and powdering fingers to reduce friction. And when waiting one's turn to bowl, a bowler often receives ritual advice from teammates in the form of phrases like "reach out," "follow through," or "slow down."

These are but few among many rites bowlers engage in as they quest after big scores and seek to control their game. But bowlers also know from bitter experience that scientific rituals sometimes fail to deliver the promised payoff. Hence, at any time religious or magical rites are likely to be injected. As a church league bowler, I regularly hear appeals to deities, indeed more then that I hear in church. True, such ritual appeals are usually expletives, curses or damnations. Likewise, magical rites are ever present. Some carry magical charms, or refuse to wash shirt or towel until a current hot streak ends; or, in search of extra *mana*, some regularly touch a high-average colleague just before throwing.

One also learns much from the tribal rites of bowling. As a team sport bowling exhibits many sociability rites, including one of playing nickels or dimes to a teammate who scores consecutive strikes or makes a difficult "split." And one prescribed rite calls for ceremonial touching, really a comradely grasping of each other's shoulders, when one bowler follows his mate to the line. With so many comradely rituals in the sport it is understandable why "Doc," in William F. Whyte's *Street Corner Society,* owed his position as leader of his gang in part to his bowling prowess; and one can also see why "Biff," in Arthur Miller's *Death of a Salesman,* replied to his younger brother's question of what is sex like with these words, "It's like bowling!"

Football—Tribalizing the Fall Season

In the years since World War II bowling grew to rival sex and pinochle as popular American indoor sports. And at the same time football threatened to outstrip baseball as the nation's most popular outdoor sport.

As staged at the scholastic, college and professional levels of performance, each football game is a ritualized public drama that mirrors the faith of its participants in man's ability to control the forces that make the world go round. In a determined effort to control the outcome of each weekly game, staffs of coaches stage daily ritualized drills and scrimmages in hopes of meshing the offensive and defensive skills of their charges into a triumphant striking force. The success or failure of a coach's game plan is tested weekly in a single engagement which is played out during a rigid time frame. Thus, it might be said that all the rites of practice and all the tactics and strategies used in the game mirror an abiding American faith in the ability of science and technology to impose order on the world.

As a fall spectacular the opening of the football wars coincides with the transition from summer to fall seasons. This suggests that football functions as a sporting rite of passage. Well adapted to cooler weather and diminishing daylight, the weekly games suggest our people's defiance of nature's attempt to force inactivity; and since the games are played against all sorts of weather conditions, the symbolic defiance of nature looms larger.

As important as each game is to coaches, each game carries a larger significance as a fall tribalizing ritual. At schools and colleges this effect is best seen at annual homecoming games when graduates return to mingle with a current crop of scholars and briefly recapture what once was a meaningful community experience. On such occasions the game itself serves as a ritualized backdrop to the world renewal rites of renewing and reaffirming once familiar traditions.

Among the prescribed rites grads are wont to sport their old school colors while attending the game; and the colors are in evidence at pre and post game parties that are themselves important rituals. But the game itself is the focal point for tribal renewal. Bands play, nubile cheerleaders lead in demonstrations of loyalty, floats pass by at halftime ceremonials, and "alma maters" are sung. Blended with the local rites are significant national tribal rites which run heavily to patriotic displays like flag raising and anthems played by marching bands. It is noteworthy that in the southland such national rites are often overshadowed by ritual reminders of a century old lost cause. At southern games then rebel flags, renditions of "Dixie," and symbols of the primacy of states are familiar rites. Suffice it to say that whether national or sectional, such rites are taken seriously and are not to be mocked. Student protestors from Ivy League schools learned this back in the early 'Seventies when halftime protest ceremonies stirred opposition, or when their bands scurried out in "standard disorganized formations," similar objections were heard. Although the times harbored protests, extending these to football games incurred anger and was censored out by television producers.

Today some tribal rituals as staged by some colleges bid fair to turn each game into a homecoming ritual. At Little Rock, Arkansas, home of the University of Arkansas "Razorbacks" or "Hogs," as they are lovingly known to loyal followers, totemic identification reaches frenetic proportions. The totem rites demand that "Hog" followers emulate their piggish ancestor, so "Hog" clansmen respond by wearing jackets, pins, sweaters, caps and even underwear—all emblazoned with hog totems. Indeed, some zealots follow the team to road games and ride in recreational vehicles adorned with names like "Hog Heaven" or "Razorback Retreat."

In the judgment of one observer these swinish rites serve the necessary function of compensating for the dismal fact that "Hog" fans live in Arkansas. Ordinarily, only Mississippi's presence in the Union saves Arkansas from the undisputed recognition of being "the Poland of the United States." And since the Razorback team is the state's major claim to fame, the rites of identification with the team take on symbolic significance as escape from reality and as forlorn expression of hopes for a better future.[10]

Perhaps, but the ritual significance of American football has been the subject of much study and heuristic assessment. One writer, spoofing Freud, viewed the spectacle as one gigantic fertility rite with the players exerting garden magic on the oval shaped ball which symbolizes the female egg!

More seriously, football's symbolic significance has been as a ritualized assertion of male dominance. In the opinion of anthropologist William Arens, this is evidenced in the uniforms worn by the all-male cast. The macho-appearing uniforms accentuate maleness, especially the cod-piece motif that fronts the knickers. Moreover, the myth of feminine evil is seen in the purifying rites imposed on players before the games. No sex the night before is the law and coaches apparently believe in the debilitating powers of sex despite scientific evidence to the contrary.[11] Mayhap this stubborn belief explains why sportswriters ritualistically treat football players as oafs; a judgment that one writer expressed in unmatchable words as he wrote of one player "who was not precisely as dumb as an ox, but in truth he wasn't much smarter."

My personal field observation of football rites has been limited to ten years as a season ticket holder which enabled me to behold the forlorn Philadelphia Eagles of the National (Pro) Football League. From 1964-1973 I watched seventy games, an experience I would wish on no man and which I accepted only because my father-in-law gave me them each year as a "gift."

Still that experience offered firsthand insights into the dynamic character of rituals and left me mightily impressed by the ingenuity of the notorious Philadelphia fans for inventing new rituals. As a season ticket holder, I experienced tribal identity with those regulars whose company I shared because they were my seatmates for each three-hour drama. Each new season and each scheduled home game was indulged in neighborly "maintenance rites," as we renewed our acquaintance, our common faith in the Eagles, and our conviction that "this might be their year."

A most important rite for Eagle fans was the consumption of ritual food and drink. Some fans came early and held tailgate cookouts in the parking lots. Many boldly passed through entrance gates loaded down with sandwiches and booze which they bore past cowed gate keepers, who knew better than to try to impose the body searches on such fans as baseball fans customarily endured. Perhaps their forebearance was charitable in that the keepers knew that boozy rites were needed, since what Eagle fans beheld in the name of football was truly a travesty.

Like all normal fans Eagle followers employed traditional team support rites like cheering their boys, booing officials, making loud roars to distract enemy signal callers. But the plain fact was none worked because in simple sooth the team was lousy. Hence, when orthodox rituals fail, you invent new ones. So Eagle fans invoked the notorious "defiance rituals" that generations of Philadelphia baseball fans had been using for so long.

These "rites of rebellion" surfaced at any time. Even during the sacred ritual of singing the National Anthem, clutches of leather-lunged fans punctuated rest stops during the singing with irreverent outbursts of "Joe [Kuharich] must go!" On one memorable visit when the management scheduled a visit from Santa Claus as part of a pre-Christmas halftime ceremonial, fans staged a ritual protest against all the miseries of a woebegone season by pelting Santa with snowballs as he circled the field on his float!

By their frequent indulgence in defiance rituals Eagle fans gained a reputation as being the nation's more irreverent fans. At their best they defied orthodox tribal rites by booing their own team unmercifully. Moreover, many adopted the protest ritual of leaving games early in hopes of beating traffic jams. But on one memorable occasion as a horde of early departees filed out a gate, one fan perched atop a battlement disdainfully pissed down upon them. For me it was the last affront: having been drenched by the "mad pisser," I chose to limit my sporting energies to baseball!

Rites of the Summer Game

For more than a century major league baseball has laid claim to being America's prima field sport. While subject to debate, there is no gainsaying baseball's significance as a tribalizing rite. Nay, it goes farther for its annual repetition makes the game a powerful world renewal rite. As a rite of passage the opening of the spring training camps heralds the loosening of winter's grip and signals the start of warm weather activity. Therefore the opening of championship play in April, the July All-Star game break, and the opening of World Series play in October are nationally accepted calendar points that testify to the game's powerful hold on the minds of Americans.

In its century long existence the game's tribalizing potential has laid its mark on Americans. Today being an American demands that one speak as one and this calls for an ability to speak the language of baseball and fit it to varied social scenes. Not the least of these is the sexual scene where swinging, striking out, getting to first base, hitting a homerun and scoring are meaningful to one's formation of a "pleasure bond."[12] In making this pitch for baseball language being a major source of verbal rituals, as a ballpark figure it is safe to say that most Americans are at home with its usage.

Yet unlike its great rival, football, which is far more nativistic, baseball has been transplanted to many world areas. But as this American game took root in different lands its rituals changed and took on different meanings. Thus, Japanese or Latin American versions of the game differ from our own. Among peripheral peoples who have adopted baseball the rituals differ strikingly. Among Eskimo villagers who play, for example, competition and victory seem to be irrelevant, and among the Cochiti village pueblo Indians, local baseball rivalries displaced hostile forms of witchcraft that threatened tribal unity.[13]

Such diverse baseball forms remind one that the world of man is made up of many tribes. Of these, Americans are but one and American baseball but one version among the world's baseball forms. Still, American baseball has had a powerful tribalizing impact on generations of Americans.

For openers, there is baseball's mythic and arrogant claim to being America's national sport, a claim that major league moguls have pushed since the close of the Civil War. It was a time when sentiments of American nationalism were feverish, when the nation cried out for unity. Certainly baseball was an athletic expression of this feeling. Owners profited from making ball games a part of the patriotic rites of Memorial Day, the Fourth of July and other national holidays. By the time of President Taft the ritual custom began of having presidents throw out the first ball on opening day in Washington. Soon after the ritual of playing the National Anthem became part of the baseball spectacle. However, America lacked an official anthem until well into this century. But during World War I President Wilson ruled that the "Star-Spangled Banner" should serve; hence, major league clubs fell in line and hired bands to play that unsingable tune. Thereafter it was played at games only on patriotic holidays, and when the anthem was officially adopted in 1931, ball fans sang it at opening days and World Series matches. Not until World War II did the anthem become the ritual curtain raiser for every scheduled game, but since then this has been a sacrosanct requirement. Hence, any promoter who dared experiment with jazzy versions or sought to exclude the rite faced stinging criticism. Thus, baseball's claim to being the National game became a two-edged sword. Aside from its blessings, the claim forced promoters to lend ritual support to war efforts, including unpopular ones like the Vietnam conflict, and to link baseball with super patriotic groups like the American Legion and other conservative forces.[14]

Meanwhile, promoters adapted other tribal rituals to support baseball. In the early years major league games were attended mostly by males whose working schedules coincided with the late afternoon starting times of games. While these starting times barred working class fans, it was early felt that profits could increase from more female fans. Indeed, manager Harry Wright of the Phillies thought that more ladies at games would be more effective than more cops in curbing boorish behavior. Perhaps so, but by the 1880s ladies days were instituted as a new ritual; and at that time a canny Cincinnati promoter hit upon the idea of pitching handsome Tony Mullane every Monday and designated that day ladies day. Henceforth, ladies days were popular tribalizing rites until the ritual fell before the rising tide of female equalitarian movements which branded it chauvinistic.

By the end of World War II ladies day fell by the wayside along with daytime major league games. Thereafter most games were staged at night and new tribalizing rituals aimed at enticing females and suburbanites. Nowadays many groups are bussed to games and a new ritual greeting lists these local groups in bright lights on electronic scoreboards. But more seductive are the ritual giveaway nights when paying fans receive such items as bats, balls, jackets, free beer, pantyhose and other designated attractions.

In addition to these promo days, clubs annually stage old timers' games and often set aside certain games for honoring popular players. More than mere tribal rites, such events resemble rites of passage for players and fans. When transporting players from ordinary status to that of demigods, such rites have religious overtones.

But the process of deifying ballplayers has a measured certainty about it which appeals to science-minded Americans. The certainty derives from the work of generations of statisticians whose annual compilations made poring over them an absorbing ritual for fans. It is safe to say that baseball yields to no sport in measuring and comparing player performances. Nevertheless, the "figure filberts," as these statistical packrats have been called, seem hellbent on drowning fans in trivia. Recent lists include triple crowns for pitchers, top pitchers for the first five full seasons, most combined homers and stolen bases, and such gems as all-time clutch teams and all-time mean teams! Adrift in such nonsense who can blame fans for paraphrasing Mussolini and saying, when I hear the word statistics, I reach for my revolver.

Statistics aside, any major league game embodies a godsplenty of rituals large and small. Included are those obvious ones whereby home fans try to bring magical powers to aid their favorites by such rites as synchronic cheering, foot stamping, booing and seventh-inning stretching. Sadly, promoters seem to have grasped this and now attempt to control such rituals by using organ music, taped bugle calls, and scoreboard cartoons to summon fans to the rites. One can only hope that gods and forces are not mocked, for such desecrations must surely piss off any baseball gods that be!

It was promoters too who long ago pushed the ritual of booing umpires. It seems as if money was their motive in encouraging fans in umpire baiting as a means of "gingering up" games. If so, it worked well and villified umpires long ago adopted little purifying rituals of their own like brushing off home plate with their buttocks aimed at players on the field so as not to moon the fans. But lately organized umps have turned tartars and refuse to countenance a proposed new ritual which would permit instant replay of their calls to be shown on electronic scoreboards.

Still the most fascinating rituals are those played out by players on the field in hopes of controlling their pressure-packed lives. Looking over the modern crop of players one sees bulging cheeks, swollen by cuds of chewing tobacco. A revival of a once descredited ritual, tobacco chewing players find it relaxing and, since it reduces the need for drinking water, conducive to speed. Of course, some overdo the rite a mite, like bachelor Richie Hebner who "even chews on dates." Chewing rites once forced pitcher Ron Guidry to leave a game after swallowing a cud while leaping for a ball. He had to leave the televised game, he said, lest "I become the first player to throw up on national TV!" Ironically, national TV viewers were treated to that television first last fall when Preston Pearson of the Dallas (football) Cowboys disgorged. In a hasty coverup, sportscaster Howard Cosell assured fans that such behavior would not become a televised ritual.

Unlike football players, modern baseball players are less hampered by purification rites like the taboo on sex relations before games. This is understandable since baseball schedules run to 162 games a year. To be sure, in the past the sex taboo was strong; in 1889 the Brooklyn Bridegrooms swore off marital sex during their stretch drive and were rewarded with victory. But modern players no longer fear the taboo. On the contrary, "beaver shooting," "scoping" female fans and consorting with "bimbos" are well established *macho* rites, so much so that Jim Brosnan reported seeing "groupies" lined up for inspection by players at one spring training site; it made Brosnan wonder if groupies went in for spring training rites. Maybe so, but one veteran player confided that whenever a player utters the ritual statement that "the game's been good to me," he means that he often "scored."

Among the serious rituals in any game is the duel between pitcher and batter. To intimidate batters, pitchers indulge in delaying rites, such as fidgeting with their uniform, rubbing the ball, or posing rigidly with ball in hand. The latter rite was already ancient in the early 1870s when a writer wondered if pitcher Al Spalding was trying to decide if he held a ball or an orange.

In defense, batters use delaying rituals such as stepping out, scratching themselves and beating dirt off their spikes. But the duel waxes ominous when a pitcher throws a brush-back pitch or deliberately tries to hit the batter. In fact batters expect to be treated in this manner, especially when a pitcher has just been hit hard. However, should the pitcher hit a batter, a vengeance ritual demands that the offending pitcher himself be hit. Although such rituals duels are an established baseball tradition, officials act as if it did not exist. Hence, imagine their embarrassment when pitcher Lynn McGlothen boldly admitted throwing at a batter, saying, "I just can't have a hitter like him [Del Unser] beating on me!"

In employing rituals for the purpose of unleashing magical or supernatural forces, it is not surprising that batters should do more. After all, even the best batters make outs seven of every ten times. This makes batting an uncertain science and where uncertainty exists, ritual thrives. Some batters prefer scientific rites, like Rod Carew who employs half a dozen different stances. Others ritually coddle bats in hopes of stirring the *mana* inside; for example, old Honus Wagner laid aside a bat after 100 hits believing that there were no more hits to be had. Others ritually fondle crucifixes or cross themselves. Once when a batter did this, catcher Birdie Tebbets called time, crossed himself, and piped: "Now that we're even with God, let's see who's the best man."

There are literally hundreds of rites to choose from, including elaborate flashing of signals by third base coaches, which, when missed, lead to imposed fines. There are the ritual duels between pitchers and would-be base stealers, and the pre-game rituals of running, batting and fielding drills that serve the function of readying players for the upcoming game.

A ball player's life is tension-ridden and tension-relieving rituals are legion. One sees these when a player ritually touches a base bag for luck, or swings nervously in the on-deck circle, or pats his glove when poised to catch a fly ball. In bullpens where relief pitchers bide their time awaiting a call to appear in a do-or-die situation, more elaborate tension-relieving rites appear. In some 'pens telescopes are used to "scope" comely females in the stands and inhabitants often indulge in ritual games of bubble gum soccer or long range tobacco spitting contests. But when a reliefer is summoned to duty, a ritual drama has him arriving at the mound in a motorized cart, shaped like a baseball cap with the totem colors of the home team emblazoned on it. To fans the ritual signals help is on the way although sometimes the "fireman" adds gasoline to an already inflammatory situation.

These and other tension-relieving rites testify to the uncertain lives ballplayers lead. After all, when a player flags or fails, his career is in jeopardy. No wonder then that veteran players long practiced elaborate avoidance rituals aimed at saving their jobs by discrediting rookies who might replace them. In the past, rookies suffered much from these; sometimes their bats were sawed in half and at the very least they were excluded from batting practice.

Happily for veterans and rookies the recent scarcity of talent has lent greater feelings of job security. Still the happiest day of a rookie's life is the day when he is afforded some rite of acceptance. With the Yankees a star like Joe DiMaggio had the power to bestow such acceptance. What he would do was invite a rookie to dinner. One rookie recalled as the proudest day of his life trying to pay for his meal, but being haughtily told by DiMaggio that "When you eat with the Dago, the Dago pays!"

Today's better paid and better defended players have gained a measure of security beyond the dreams of old timers. To a considerable extent this security is reflected in a new set of rituals. Among the newer ones none is more revolutionary than the bargaining rites which pit players against owners in salary negotiations. In the past, owners controlled the ritual and forced solitary players to listen to a litany of owner poverty and invidious comparisons with other players which had the effect of making a player settle for less money. Thus, general manager George Weiss of the Yankees used to con players into accepting the argument that a player's World Series share counted as a raise; and Buzzy Bavasi of the Dodgers boasted that he saved Dodger owner Walter O'Malley over a million dollars by jawboning players in negotiations.

But the rise of the Players Association ended this degrading ritual. Now negotiating rites are carried on with players represented by lawyers or agents who bargain for them. If dissatisfied, players no longer need stage a lonely holdout because they now can opt for arbitration procedures or, if sufficiently tenured, they can opt to enter a free agent draft. As a result this ritual revolution has sent average baseball salaries soaring to $120,000 a year.[16] If new rituals like this one can accomplish so much, I daresay that any reader would make common cause with any ritual broker who promises similar results.

Notes

[1]Edmund R. Leach, "Ritual," *International Encyclopedia of the Social Sciences*, 520-526.

[2]Ruth Benedict, "Ritual," *Encyclopedia of the Social Sciences*, 396-397.

[3]Eric Berne, *Games People Play* (New York: Grove Press, 1964), 18-19, 37.

[4]Yi Fu Tuan, *Landscapes of Fear* (New York: Pantheon, 1979), 69-70.

[5]Frederick Bird, "The Contemporary Ritual Milieu," published in this volume.

[6]Frank Trippett, "Get This Season Off the Couch," *Time*, Dec. 11, 1978.

[7]Hal Lawson, "Physical Education and Sport: Alternatives for the Future," in Andrew Yiannakis, et al., *Sport Sociology: Contemporary Themes* (Dubuque, Iowa: Kendall-Hunt, 1976), 234.

[8]Robert Cantwell, "America is Formed for Happiness," *Sports Illustrated*, Dec. 22, 2975.

[9]*New York Times,* April 13, 1969, July 2, 1978 on squeezing of the seasons. Sport as an opiate of the masses is presented by Richard Shepard in *Ibid.,* Nov. 17, 1974.

[10]Gene Lyons, "Monday Night Fever," *New York Times Magazine,* Jan. 1, 1978.

[11]William Arens, "Professional Football: An American Symbol and Ritual," in Arens and Susan Montague, *American Dimension: Cultural Myths and Social Realities* (1976).

[12]David Q. Voigt, "Sex in Baseball: Reflections of a Changing Taboo," *Journal of Popular Culture*, Spring, 1979. For more of baseball's impact on language rituals, see Tristram Coffin, *The Old Ball Game: Baseball in Folklore and Fiction* (New York: Herder and Herder, 1971), 51-75.

[13]David Q. Voigt, "Anthropology and the Leisure Frame of Reference," in Voigt, *America's Leisure Revolution: Essays in the Sociology of Leisure and Sport* (Reading, Pa: Albright College, 1974).

[14]David Q. Voigt, "Reflections on Diamonds," in *Ibid.,* 87-108.

[15]David Q. Voigt, *America Through Baseball* (Chicago: Nelson-Hall, 1976).

[16]David Q. Voigt, "A New Breed of Baseball Players," unpublished chapter of mss entitled "American Baseball: The Age of Continental Expansion."

Ritual Illustration
Functioning as Substitute Imagery:
Pornography

Alan Gowans

NO CULTURES PAST or present, and few individuals within any one culture, have ever agreed entirely on a definition of pornography.[1] But the core of it, in all times and places, is the art of exciting sexual desire. As such, it is an art almost as primaeval as that symbol-making and using which sets humans off from animals. For just as no animal both makes and uses substitute images as symbols, so no animals artificially excite sexual desire; in their kingdom, sexual relations are so physiologically fixed and predetermined that no such art is requisite.

The basis for all pornography is substitute imagery;[2] insofar as painted or photographed or carved bodies serve the purposes of the real thing *in absentia*. But pornography is effectual only insofar as those substitute images are involved in some kind of action—i.e., the illustration of a sequence or process. In theory, a nude body or bodies alone might have the desired effect, as Praxiteles's Cnidian Aphrodite (to give the kind of chaste classic example professors are supposed to) was reported to have so inflamed youths visiting the shrine that they attempted to violate the statue.[3] In practise such an account merely arouses derision—and laughter of any kind, even derisive laughter, is the death of pornography. Some kind of sequence is required. Modern popular/commercial arts provide two sorts: one, a single figure in some kind of provocative action and the other representations of sex acts going on. Both sorts have abundant ancestry in historic arts and reveal a good deal about the past.

That our popular/commercial single-figure pornography is more illustration than substitute imagery becomes self-evident

141

when you realize that even a single picture is always thought of as in some kind of action, a frame on a film-roll, if you like; and that it is in the form of movies that pornographic arts have flourished most abundantly and abandonedly in modern times. Whence, possibly, insight into the social function of the many historical arts with comparable social functions.

"Ancient erotic arts" used to mean Pompeii. Now Khajuraho and Konarak and Elephanta come oftener to mind—blessings of jet travel department! In all "enlightened" discussions since the 18th century, however, much is always made of an alleged contrast between repressed cultures like ours which keep pornography underground (however ineffectually), and those healthier and opener psychic times to which Indian and Roman brothels seem such enviable testaments.[4] An official (and very sober, very factual, very good) guide to Khajuraho is typical. There we read,[5]

> As the sculptures mirror their times, it is evident that the age which produced them had none of the taboos or inhibitions against sex as we have now. The people of that age took a healthy integrated view of life and gave sex its due place in the scheme of things. . . . The representation of erotic scenes, therefore, was not taken as banal or abnormal or unnatural.

Admittedly, the description goes on, "Behind the familiar human facade of the *sura-sundaris* is hidden a deeper meaning and symbolism." This is no place to venture a toe into that turgid sea of controversy over what metaphysical, mythological, spiritual or other symbolism Indian erotic imagery may involve. But it is worthwhile to explore the neglected possibility that modern popular/commercial arts might be fundamentally similar to traditional historic arts of pornographic illustration. For it does seem that, however different their outward forms and media, there is an identity of social function between what the Germans so precisely call our *Einhandigliteratur* and those decorative sculptures for which Indian temples have become so well-known.

"*Apsarases* or *sura-sundaris*," the guide goes on, "who account for the finest and most numerous sculptures at Khajuraho,

> are usually represented as handsome and youthful nymphs, attired in the choicest gems and garments and full of winsome grace and charm. As heavenly dancers (*apsareses*) they are shown as dancing in various postures. . . . But more frequently the *sura-sundaris* are portrayed to express common human moods, emotions, and activities and are often difficult to distinguish from conventional *nayikas*, such as those *apsareses* shown as disrobing, yawning, scratching the back, touching the breasts, rinsing water from the wet plaits of hair. . . . writing a letter, playing on a flute. . . painting designs on the wall or bedecking themselves in various ways by painting the feet, applying collrium, etc.

So could be described, with hardly a word changed, typical layouts in any monthly issue of *Playboy, Penthouse, Gallery, Hustler, Cheri,* etc., etc. But in these modern cases the social function is plainly establishable: not simply illustration of events, but a special kind of *tableau* (as the term "lay-out" implies) where the substitute image has a special function and greater importance than in most illustrations. Establishable with like ease, thanks to photography's ability to produce exactly repeatable images, is that these layouts represent the same figure in different poses. Could these temple sculptures not be seen the same way? Not as all different figures, but as successive images of one, then another, each thus illustrating in proto-movie style a provocative routine? Some are indeed already so identified as successive poses in erotic dance.

So seen, figures like the Khajuraho *sura-sundaris* and all comparable Indian temple sculptures function as strip-tease preliminaries to the main exterior scenes of sexual ecstasy, which in turn are carnal counterparts to and hence preparation for the inner cult images (the difference being manifested by contrast of severe vs. luxuriant style, rigidly canonical vs. lissom poses). The whole architectural, sculptural and painted complex of a Khajuraho temple would then appear unified in a grand integrated scheme. High medieval Indian architecture and arts generally then would be understandable no longer as additive compositions, mimetic shapes plus garish miscellaneous illustration (as Indian arts were in fact interpreted by Fergusson, by Toynbee, even by Baldwin Smith), but in the way Gothic cathedrals are understood, all the exterior sculpture interrelated, and in turn complimented by interior arts whose style only seems different (solid, material stone sculptures on the outside, ethereal glass and canonically-dictated crucifixes and reliquaries within). So understood in terms of social function, high medieval Indian temples thus afford parallels to the West's abbeys and cathedrals of this same time stratum—and to the age's great Buddhist temples in China and India, Islam's most impressive mosques.... All have to do with creating a visual metaphor of the promises of their several religions, to bring heaven to earth.[6] What constitutes "heaven" obviously diverges from one belief-system to another. Detailed discussion of the differences would be irrelevant here, however rewarding; to the present point is simply: the concept of a heaven which consists of endless sex play is by no means unusual. Acknowledged or not, it is a utopian element in our society quite as much as in earlier ones.

Observing how such arts as the Khajuraho sculptures functioned comparably to our popular/commercial arts of strip-tease dance, magazine and movie pornography thus leads to contemplation of one of the mysterious parallels in universal history. But that's only a beginning.

The kind of dance nowadays called strip-tease originates far back in time. Already in the first century A.D. a Latin verse describes

The Syrian cabaret-hostess, whose hair is bound back by a Grecian headband/ whose quivering thighs sway to the rhythm of castanets/ dances intoxicated, voluptuous, in the smoky tavern....[7]

And already in those times this dance was being called a secularized, lascivious variant of primitive fertility rites. Discussing such rites and fertility cults, underdocumented and overdisputed as they are, is well beyond our present purposes—even if displacement of primaeval female deities by Aryan male-dominated cults and social outlook, or the relative importance of male vs. female fetiches, were not so tediously and tendentiously bound up with prejudices pro and con contemporary feminism, church canons, Lenin's views on public morality, and whether children corrupt our comics. Only a speculation, again: could the strip tease, practised by every known people in one form or another today,[8] derive from some equally universal origin in some primaeval ritual of fertility? Considering its social function—exciting of sexual desire—it's by no means impossible.

Religion in its broadest sense is both a system of belief and a means of clarifying relationships which defy rational explanation. For the latter purpose it has always made great use of tableaux and rituals which illustrate the ineffable: Man and God, Earth and Heaven, Birth and Death. Among the most mysterious of these has always been sex and the sexual instinct. It's so inexplicable as to be often classed among forms of madness. Violence and frenzy, love and voluptuousness were joint attributes of Ishtar of Erech, of Cybele, of Dionysius. Nor do we explain sex any better; we have a choice, as a wise contemporary once put it, of the language of the nursery, or of the gutter, or of science—and all are equally unsatisfactory. Our current real religion, Science, explains what things are made of and how they work, but not what they are or what starts them working. To this day the interaction of male and female remains a profound mystery. That is why nobody to this day can define pornography, why you must start with a non-definition. That is fundamentally (obviously there could be many reasons) why in all cultures sex has been something hidden. Cybele was to be found deep in a cave. Dionysius and the Maenads held their rites in wild fastnesses. *Naturvolker* in the South Seas and Africa make puberty initiations dark tabus. According to *Genesis* secrecy and sex came into Eden together. 3rd- and 2nd-millenium cult images of the Great Mother, Earth Goddess, ritual attendants, etc., were secreted in graves.

What form of ritual illustration was used for these mysteries? About what has always been secret, posterity can expect to learn little. But there are indications. The power and madness of erotic love is made demonstrable by some ritual which excites it. What sort of ritual was involved is suggested by Ishtar's attempt to rescue Tammuz from the underworld. The "courtesan of the gods" undertook

'to journey towards that land without return, towards that house from which he who enters does not come out again,' she had the gates opened and penetrated the seven precincts, at each gate stripping off one by one a piece of ornament or dress: the great crown from her head, pendants from her ears, the necklace from her throat, the jewels from her breast, her girdle adorned with birthstones, the bracelets from her hands and from her feet; and finally the garment which covered her nakedness....[9]

Likening such a myth to strip-tease would be facetious in terms of quality or profundity. But both represent ritual illustration, with similar physiological social function: to induce a desired mood amongst spectators.

Ishtar, so associated alike with the underworld, the dead and erotic passion, has often been suggested as the Mesopotamian counterpart to the central cult figure of that megalithic culture discovered by archaeology over the last half-century[10] to have extended all round the Mediterranean littoral from the Cyclades to the Orkneys. That such megalithic building functioned as ceremonial centers, with rites of some kind at burials and regularly thereafter, has long been suggested also. That such rites could have been something like Ishtar's performance is by no means impossible. The figures being in sequential groups supports such a speculation; their not "looking sexy" to us, as art-history surveys sometimes take unnecessary pains to point out, does not imply that they had no such significance for their makers either. That grave images functioned like dolls for role-playing is long established fact.

Logically, linking sex and death accords with human instincts and practises at all times and places. In our culture that connection has been pushed underground, not by Christianity which in fact recognizes the connection in many ways throughout the centuries, so much as by our present religion, which considers death along with sin and poverty and war as something to be abolished in due course by Science, and in the interval between now and the coming utopia to be thought of seldom by people of sophistication, and mentioned never except in jest. Nevertheless the connection is real and remains in our underground in the truest sense. It bubbles up whenever and wherever pressures force up our protective scientific/utopian lid to reveal the actual continuing state of our affairs. One instance was the Dionysiac celebrations marking the end of World War I, when rioting crowds, berzerk with relief that the Great Slaughter had ended, copulated in public places while officially mourning the dead.[11] Another, public ritual sites like Forest Lawn, where symbols of sex and death mingle in defiance of science and utopia alike, in age-old interaction.

Like all popular/commercial arts, then, strip-tease and associated pornography respond to deep-seated individual and social needs. Energies expended fulminating against them might more constructively be channelled into ways of realizing their potential for promoting more humanely and metaphysically meaningful environment.

Contemporary theory makes much of a fine distinction between hard-core pornography, which seems to be actual depiction of sexual intercourse, and soft-core, depiction of preliminaries thereto. Pretentious and pedantic apparently, since in life one presupposes the other and likewise in historic arts: on the Khajuraho temples, *sura-sundaris* and *mithuna* couplings are interrelated logically, visually and conceptually.

Nevertheless, studying these arts' social function reveals a subtle difference. At Khajuraho, the group sex scenes make plain what the *sura-sundaris* only implies: how the temple functions as a metaphor of heaven-on-earth. It doesn't matter precisely how this kind of heaven was understood, whether only symbolically, as is so often claimed[12] or literally, as promised faithful Moslems in the Koran, "with ever-youthful companions, the black-eyed houris, and the *ghilman,* lovely boys."[13] The point is that it illustrates a ritual which is the justification and symbol of a new state of society still to be attained rather than actually existing in the world of time and history, a foretaste of joys forever in some future time. Utopian scenes, in fact, to be understood in some context like:

In a royal temple the idol was of gold, set with diamonds, rubies and emeralds, hung with crowns, necklaces, bracelets, anklets, studded with costly stones, and beneath it untold treasures filled a cellar in the substructure. When His Majesty the Paramarabhattaraka Maharajatadhiraja attended the service accompanied by his queens, ministers, and other relatives and friends all in fashionable, costly attire, when a choir sang accompanied by a great number of instruments when beautiful dancing girls displayed their art before the idol, furtively throwing amorous glances at the visitors, it must have indeed have been a magnificent spectacle, a masterpiece of refined showmanship built up around the divine presence in the idol. What it was worth in genuine religiousness is another matter. But official religion in an aristocratic society always tends to develop in this direction and did the same in Medieval Europe, China, and Japan."[14]

—symbol and justification of a new state of society far different from any heretofore known in time and history.

Just so, can our own "hard core pornography" be explained— not so much popular/commercial as the reverse or underside of our avant-garde Establishment High Culture.

Balanced minds find hard-core acrobatics more ludicrous than exciting; but then, this is no art for balanced minds (as ancient mythology recognized by invariably coupling erotic love with madness and folly). Hard-core pornography has nothing to do, really, with any sober, factual, existing world, as may easily be discovered from a few captions in sex magazines, a few lines of dialogue from sex films, a few pages of pontificating by any modern sex guru. It's ritual illustration of our 20th-century religion's ecstatic visions of future social bliss, times when all humanity will be liberated as only those gurus are now, when pleasure will be unalloyed by responsibility, all life as uninhibited as—I was about to say, Eden before the Fall, but remember where you are!—in that prehistoric Age of Natural Man. Mythologic, to be sure; for of that idyllic time when mankind lived free of all restraint and peacefully browsed on fruits and berries, the most diligent researchings have as yet produced no proof. But fervently believed as an article of faith nonetheless. Faith is what hard-core pornography demands if it is to carry any conviction. Faith that dirt, smells, impotence, disease, all are abolished and need no longer be taken into any account. Faith even more that Natural Man (Redux) can continue indefinite co-existence with all the benefits of high and highly-disciplined technology (central heating, no goosebumps; chemical hairsets and shampoos, no dishevellment; deodorants; nylons that don't run— and, of course, contraceptives and prophylactics that work infallibly), as our avant-garde creed has held lo these long years.

For the orgy is in fact one image of what our 20th-century religion promises its faithful (or at least, its docile), just as Khajuraho's art is one image of Candella dynasty promisings. Or perhaps only an updated version of one continuing fantasy, for counterparts inbetween abound. Lucas Cranach, recorder of Luther's Reformation, painted a *Golden Age* to come when godly princes would be firmly in control of State churches and a contented peasantry, so that lords and ladies could disport themselves in palace gardens, naked and unashamed; in that same century Rabelais gave literary form to something similar in his Abbey of Themele. Our hedonistic utopia already found literary form in H.G. Wells's 1896 *Time Machine* with its Eloi dancing through sunlit gardens free of science, free of learning, free of thought, free of responsibility—Wynwood Read realized. Zamiatin's *We* described that vision too. So did Huxley's *Brave New World*. All ignoring the Morlocks also found by that *Time Machine;* the regimentation of

We; the nihilism of *BNW.* Most of all ignoring those overtones of *Nineteen Eighty Four* where pornography was calculatedly used to divert potential protest into safe (from the Party's viewpoint) channels—add the fact that pornography may well have been used for such a purpose often before; John Rosenfield asserts that Japanese 18th-century pornography had this kind of State use.

A case, in short, of historic arts telling us something about popular/commercial, rather than the other way round.

Notes

[1]Cf. Edouard Fuchs, *Sittengeschichte* (Berlin, 1904).

[2]It was Baudelaire who first cited pornography as a major function for the new art of photography, in his commentary on the Salon of 1859, "The Modern Public & Photography," J. Mayne, ed., *The Mirror of Art, Critical Studies of Charles Baudelaire* (London, 1955). There are useful observations in Lena Johannesson, *Den Massproducerade Bilden* (Stockholm, 1978), pp. 159-165. "Scientific pornography."

[3]Pliny, *Natural History*, XXXVI, 20: "...Superior to all the works, not only of Praxiteles, but indeed in the whole world, is the Aphrodite which many people have sailed to Knidos in order to see.... They say a certain man was once overcome with love for the statue and, after he had hidden himself !in the shrine! during the nighttime, embraced the statue and that there is a stain on it as an indication of his lust.... There is another Eros by him, this one nude, in Parium, the colony on the Propontis, which is equal to sthe Aphrodite at Knidos both for its fame and for the injury which it suffered; for Alketas the Rhodian fell in love with it and also left upon it the same sort of trace of his love.... From J.J. Pollitt, *The Art of Greece, Sources & Documents* (Englewood Cliffs, 1965), pp. 128-129.

[4]A typical example: the celebrated *Worship of Priapus* by Richard Payne Knight, first published in 1783. It already has all the attributes of mdoern popular/commercial pornography: the underground publication that anybody interested can locate, the specious high-mindedness, the scientific inquiry, the unargued assumption that the ethics of derelict civilizations must be superior to his own.... Curiously, this volume was reprinted by "Collectors Publications", Covina, California, in 1967, with a copyright: "All rights including Motion Picture Rights reserved under International, Pan-American, and Universal Copyright Conventions" (!) Let freedom ring..!

[5]Krishna Deva, *Khajuraho* (New Delhi, 1977), p. 14.

[6]This age was the theme of the first, 1976, ISUH Institute in Cross-Cultural Studies at the University of Victoria. E.g., *Proceedings* (Watkins Glen, N.Y., 1977), p. 49.:
"When Abelard talks about Celestial Jerusalem in relation to Solomon's Temple, he no longer assumes that Solomon was trying to reproduce the glories of Heaven here on earth. He assumes rather—as though it were too self-evident to expound upon—that Solomon's Temple was the model for God's "regal place"; it is by studying Solomon's Temple that we can understand what Heaven is like (and, by copying it in our own churches, bring Heaven down to earth—that is the logical conclusion to any such line of thought). Suger's concept of the function of his great new Abbey follows naturally from such premises—when he wishes to have his "soul exalted to an immaterial realm" he imagines that realm in terms of St. Denis. Kings and Brahmans in India did the same—throughout all the 11th, 12th and 13th century Hindu realms, spiritual heavens were claimed to resemble the great temples which Chola and Candella rulers erected. In the case of Angkor and Java this is even more obvious. Great temples of this age there were proclaimed to be Heaven-on-earth in the most literal possible sense. Likewise the devout in Burma could envisage Heaven best from their great Sikhara temples, whether these were conceived as temple-mountains blazing with light, or as vases containing a lotus. Again, if neo-Confucian philosophers wanted to envisage ideal world harmonies, it was from Sung paintings that they could get their concepts—not the other way around. In Japan, Genshin and Nichiren taught that in this third and last world-age (beginning in the mid-11th century) the reality of Heaven would be realizable only through material things like sutra mounds and sentai-do (Halls of 1000 Images);

hence the rationale of constructing a Byodo-in which would literally create here and now on earth the Western Paradise of Amida Buddha; hence the rationale of the sanjusangendo in Kyoto with what John Rosenfield called its '...awesome array of nearly life-sized statues of the 1000-armed Kannon...the sheer quantity and bristing complexity of that ensemble of images in Kyoto is one of the most sobering experiences of the irrational power of Asian imagery.' "

[7]Quoted by Peter C. Dronke, *The Medieval Lyric* (London, 1968), p. 13. This verse, it seems, was long attributed to Virgin!

[8]One of those subjects where everybody seems to have an opinion and few have many facts. One might have supposed the matter exhaustively researched; not so. Max von Boehn is as usual careful, but *Der Tanz* (Berlin, 1925) is too early to be *a propos*. Troy and Margaret West Kinney, *The Dance* (New York, 1935) has useful material on Arabic dancing, but an unscholarly approach.

[9]*New Larousse Encyclopaedia of Mythology* (Paris, 1968), p. 58.

[10]Glyn Daniel, *Megalith Builders of Western Europe* (London, 1961); on Cycladic sculpture, Christian Zervos, *L'art des Cyclades* (Paris, 1957), and Sect. 11, Fgr. 26 and fns. 38, 39.

[11]A.J.P. Taylor, *The First World War* (London, 1963), p. 251; "On 11 November 1918 the Allied peoples burst into rejoicing. All work stopped for the day. Crowds blocked the streets, dancing and cheering... As evening fell, the crowds grew more riotous. Total strangers copulated in public—a symbol that life had triumphed over death."

[12]"According to the Hindu view the final aim of life is salvation which lies in the merging of the *atman* with *paramatman* or the individual soul with the universal. The union of man and women, wherein all sense of duality is lost, thus came to constitute a symbol of liberation. 'As a man in the embrace of his beloved wife knows naught, either without or within, so one in the embrace of the Knowing Self knows naught, either without or within.' " (Deva, *Khajuraho*, p. 19). A.K. Coomeraswamy's chapter "Sahaja" in *The Dance of Shiva* (New York, 1957, pp. 124-134) is well-known.

[13]Sura 78/34, quoted by Annemarie Schimmel, "The Celestial Garden in Islam," in *The Islamic Garden* (Washington, Dumbarton Oaks, 1976), p. 15.

[14]Herman Goetz, *Art of India* (Baden-Baden, 1969), pp. 164-165.

[15]A useful source of illustrations for this and other utopian themes is Ian Tod & Michael Wheeler, *Utopia* (London, 1978); it also has a useful bibliography for this vast theme. Typical of more scholarly studies is Dolores Hayden, *Seven American Utopias*—(Cambridge, 1976), which has a massive bibliography. Curiously, I could not find a study of group sex (orgies) as a utopian activity (there are of course painfully many "studies" of the subject on the "how to do it" level). It is of course a favorite theme of Malcolm Muggeridge's; his works abound with passing allusions to sex as the sacrament of materialistic religion, & c.

[16]Orwell clearly saw the "doublethink" inherent in legalized pornography. On the one hand, Party members in *1984* were to be rigidly puritanical, so that all their efforts should be devoted to perfection of Party and society. On the other, Winston's girlfriend Julia worked in Pornosec, churning out cheap books like "Three Nights in a Girls' School" to keep the proles content. A historical precedent is evidenced by John Rosenfield, *Traditions of Japanese Art* (Cambridge, Mass., 1970), p. 361, on three leaves from an album of shunga (-school of Katsukawa Shunsho): "During the lengthening decades of peace and internal stability, the nightlife of Edo, as of Osaka and Kyoto, became ever more boisterous.... In its indulgence, color, and romance the 'floating world' served as an emotional outlet for an intensely organized, rigid social order created by the military government to bring order to a nation that had known rebellion and disorder for many decades."

This essay is a chapter in Gowans' book *Learning to See* (Popular Press, 1981).

The Minstrel Show as Ritual: Surrogate Black Culture

David N. Lyon

AROUND 1840 THE National Theater of white America was the minstrel show, impersonations of black men by whites in black face. Recent scholarship has given us a vivid picture of this phenomenon and advanced several notions concerning its significance.[1] In addition to all their other functions, minstrel shows were structurally embedded in American culture as functional rituals answering deep psychological and sociological needs. Although something like this has been suggested before, the suggestion has yet to be given form and its fascination for so many white Americans for so long a period explained.

The white view of blacks at the opening of the nineteenth century has been shown to be a mixture of sexual myth and intellectual construct.[2] By mid-century, a symbiotic economic and social relationship of great volatility had developed between the institution of slavery in the south and the rest of predominantly white America. Whether the slave was seen as an independent child, or a subhuman member of the animal kingdom on the chain of being, the need to allay anxiety generated by the peculiar institution was always present.[3] Such anxiety seems to have assumed at least two major forms, fear of black violence and guilt over what appeared to be widespread miscegenation.[4] In this context, whites seemed to swing from seeing blacks as childlike, innocuous, loyal pleasure-seeking plantation darkies, to another perspective from which they were viewed as sexually aggressive, viscious and prone to rape and violent revolt. Two personalities, the child and the beast, seemed to predominate in the white mind.[5]

It was against such a background that a popular music which purported to be authentically Afro-American, although it was conceived and performed by whites disgused as blacks, became pervasive in American culture. In seeking to comprehend this fact, it must first be noted that African music, which had survived the havoc of dislocation and migrated to America, was organically related to African society, language and a whole pattern of social usages. It was intimately associated with cults and cult rituals, tied ineluctably to certain activities and procedures, and joined to sacred spaces and times which had a unique origin in the mythology of the tribes involved.[6] Major collections of Afro-American music assembled by whites, however, supported the thesis of missionaries that blacks were an "oppressed race sustained by religious sentiment."[7] Scholars at the beginning of this century tended to agree with Newman Ivy White, who averred that "Negro music" had its origin in the "improvising and imitative tendencies," and that black songs were "variational imitations of the white man."[8] In general, and this will be seen to be related to my thesis about minstrel music, turn of the century scholars had an understanding of Afro-American music that was not informed by any knowledge of its African origins.[9]

More recent study has argued persuasively for the existence of much black music in America containing sharply formulated race consciousness.[10] I would suggest that because of its deep connections with black identity, which extend back to African society, such music was doubtless productive of the sort of anxiety discussed at the beginning of this paper, and that there is a logic in the fact that cultural mechanisms for dealing with this anxiety developed musical forms. Generally, there must have been a systematic screening out, in a way suggested by Ralph Ellison's brilliant novel, *Invisible Man,* of all black music other than benign religious examples heavily influenced by white music. Blind spots in early scholarship undoubtedly reflect this screening out.

Ignoring the threat, however, seems to have been insufficient, so that whites went on to invent a secular black music rooted in white folk traditions, ascribed this music to blacks, and thus created a kind of security blanket which defined black culture in a manner which rendered it comic and innocuous. It was necessary to ritualize this ersatz music so that it would have the power to affect both conscious and unconscious levels of meaning, and the mode in which this was achieved was the dramaturgy of the minstrel stage, a world peopled by artificial black men who were really masked whites, whose movements, motivations and even thoughts were carefully orchestrated by their white creators.[11] Superficially, the content of minstrel shows was harmless, silly and without point other than its humor. Beneath the surface, however, seen in the necessary context of American race relations and attitudes toward race, it becomes clear that it constituted an elaborate ritual of great importance in American life.[12]

The word ritual has a fairly specialized meaning for anthropologists and students of religion. There is bound to be some question about employing a term whose meaning is bound up with traditional cultures to describe a social activity found in the midst of a budding modern, complex society. Reservations about such a procedure might be allayed by several considerations. First, there are definitely ways to generalize what we mean by ritual so that it fits nineteenth century America. Second, nineteenth century America, particularly in its early decades, was just beginning to emerge out of a traditional framework, a fact which can only suggest the presence of rituals as a coping mechanism for dealing with newly evolved conflict and strain.[12]

Fundamentally rituals utilize archetypes, and by this is meant an immemorial pattern of some sort, not an ideal type found in a putative collective unconsciousness. These archetypes convey certain structural properties of human culture. A rite, according to Eliade, expresses a complex system of coherent affirmations about the ultimate reality of things.[13] Displaying a ritual attitude toward certain objects, which is the basis of a rite, is an indication that these objects stand in some significant relation to the social order which is then affirmed by the ritual attitude.[14] I would submit that whites in nineteenth century America, and to some extent in our own time, developed clear collective expressions of social sentiment toward blacks which became ritualized in the form of minstrel shows. The impersonator in blackface was really a member of the white group, yet paradoxically not a member of the white group since for ritual purposes he was possessed by a black spirit. He was also an emblem of white fantasy, and at the same time an object of importance toward which a ritual attitude was displayed. This ambiguous existential status fitted white societal needs perfectly, since through ritual, human acts were legitimized by employing an extra-human model.[15] Attitudes expressed in the minstrel ritual about blacks and toward blacks were the reduction to some sort of order of the complex and inconsistent inventory of white thoughts on the subject. It was, to paraphrase Levi-Strauss, as if a thinking process was taking place in the mythological portrayal of blacks within the ritual.[16] The paradigm of attitudes toward blacks expressed in the minstrel show was an obvious source of social solidarity among whites. Blacks became objects of ritual because they were of such great material and spiritual importance to whites, who were deeply involved with them economically and socially in an anxiety producing context. Just as the vicissitudes of climate gave rise to many rituals in primitive society, an economic connection fraught with uncertainty and ambivalence produced a similar basis for ritual here.[17]

Generally ritual attitudes and rituals themselves serve clear functions.[18] Ceremonies of riddance and exorcism are common. Ceremonies which induce certain kinds of spirit possession, that is the occupation of bodies by certain spirits, are also well known. The beating of a scapegoat who has been possessed by the community spirit of evil is known in many cultures from the ancient Greeks to the mystery plays of medieval England.[19] Further, rituals take place in sacred spaces, and the theater, with its proscenium arch, is a clear profanation of sacred space, an observation which might also be made of a movie screen or a television set. The minstrel stage was such a space, upon which a particular ritual was played out thousands and thousands of times.[20]

Given the existence of black secular music in America, and the obvious fact that it embodied powerful and mysterious cultural survivals, it is evident that rituals designed to avert the stress and anxiety of slavery would incorporate this music in a manner which would defuse its threatening character. The power of the minstrel ritual as a structural element in the adjustment whites made to the cultural fact of slavery lay precisely in this capability. Grounding the minstrel ritual in a cultural form, music, which was primary to black society, and then linking this music to a white folk tradition, represented a direct assault upon black identity which acted to neutralize its most threatening aspects. The white performer in blackface served whites as both alter ego and scapegoat. As alter ego, he was a sort of hero, a kind of phallic hero, or eternal figure of the fantasy world, and in the words of Roheim, the fantasy or dream, is "the guardian of sleep against the demons of reality."[21] The demon of white reality in this case was the sexually aggressive, rebellious black. At the same time, whites wanted to possess the power they attributed to blacks, which was primitive sexuality, and also be free to carry on the sort of social relationship with blacks which led to miscegenation and economic exploitation. A more subliminal need was doubtless a need for some mode through which whites might expiate any guilt they felt over all these associations. The extent to which blackface constituted a mask permitted the white who hid behind it to maneuver within the hierarchy of these functions. The mask offered concealment, a subliminal "authenticating" link with real black culture in which masks played an important role, and an unmistakable sign that through the mask one had entered the ritual world. Fundamentally, the minstrel show offered whites a multifunctional mode from which they could derive affirmations of their own attitudes and inner feelings, as well as, through the depiction of the black as a harmless clown, a reassurance against whatever physical threat the Afro-American seemed to pose.

Minstrel material demonstrates the notions advanced thus far. The skit "Hard Times: A Negro Extravaganza" is a good vehicle with which to begin such a demonstration. "Hard Times" is a doggerel version of the Faust theme in which the black protagonist, old Dan Tucker, enters into an agreement with Belzebub [sic]. Typical Tucker utterances go as follows:

> For don't the big book 'spressly tell us,
> And tells us, too, without much fussin'
> Whedder we're white or color'd pusson
> "Bressed am dem dat's berry poor,
> Dey'll nothing get, dats berry sure?"[22]

Tucker rapidly succumbs to the devil's blandishments, and sells his body and soul for a peck of coal, which he might not use, however, on penalty of being carried at once to hell. It is of no matter. Through other means he is given plenty of coal, food and other essentials, although just how is never made clear.[23]

In the next scene, Tucker's son Gabe and his pal Chummie appear. They are constantly quarreling, fighting and insulting each other. Gabe boasts that "I struck a nigger last night an' he jump up and axed if lightening hit any ob de udder niggers." This element, which appears gratuitous, is very probably descended from an English mumming play in which Beelzebub is also involved, in the older version in connection with Saint George and a Turk, the two of whom are constantly fighting. Here, this element is linked tenuously to a main plot, the pact between Tucker and the devil, which is resolved through the intervention of Tucker's wife. Claiming that she already owns Tucker, exclaiming that he is "bone of my bone, and sinner ob my sinner," she contends with the devil for her husband and defeats her antagonist. Gabe and Chummie continue beating each other throughout this final scene, and matters conclude with a song commemorating the events which have just taken place.[24]

What is this all about? To begin with it is based on a very old idea, the contention between the wife and the devil who has tried to make off with a long-suffering husband who would willingly go to hell to escape the clutches of his shrewish mate. Or such at least is the attitude of the man in relatively recent versions of this story in

English and German folklore since the Middle Ages, or in a related American folk song recorded in the 1920s. Going back further, however, one recalls the Assyrian goddess Ishtar or Astarte, a fertility symbol. Ishtar is married to Thammuz, who is spring. Thammuz is stolen away by the goddess of the underworld, who is then bested by Ishtar, restoring fertility to the earth. Such "explanations" of winter, and the period of infertility, abound in primitive mythologies.[25] In addition to whatever subliminal meaning might carry over from this ancient connection with fertility rites, Dan Tucker in "Hard Times" is a demonstration of several important ritual attitudes. He is treated as a sexual object, in the nearly explicit "bone of my bone," which also shows the woman in the dual relation of mother/wife, and there are other sexual allusions in this vignette. It is also important that the devil is bested, not by ingenuity or strength, as might have been the case in antecedent versions involving white heroes, but by bungling incompetence, a putative black attribute, and through the dumb luck of the child-man, who is ultimately rescued by a woman. Fighting between Gabe and Chummie, which is a kind of ostenato figure in all this, seems to be a ritual of exorcism, descended from the ritual of the stock character—Vice—beating the devil, common on the English stage. Here Chummie and his pal represent potentially violent, sexually aggressive blacks who spend their energies upon foolish, meaningless attacks upon another.[26]

There are many other songs in which both devils and men are beaten, sometimes by female lovers, in one instance only to have the man turn around and give his female assailant a "hickory mesmerizing," probably a phallic allusion.[27] Sex, however, is very sublimated in most of these songs. It is sometimes obvious, as in the image of "breaking the sucker while pumping too hard," but is often buried beneath a series of superficial incidents and activities, such as chasing flies or having one's goose stolen.[28]

More direct are the numerous references to the incompetence of blacks and the assistance of whites in helping them get out of their comic dilemmas. Nothing blacks do on the minstrel stage is serious or important. But at the same time, blacks never come to any harm. They are neither saved nor damned. They are always happy, they are spontaneous, silly, without responsibility or concern, and violent only in jesting ways and toward one another. An occasional reference, however, can be found to a lyric which probably directly incorporates the white fear of black violence, such as this verse from the song "Juba":

> Gib me a knif sharp as a sickle
> To cut that nigger's wizen pipe
> Date ate up all de sassengers.[29]

In "My Old Dad" the element of black sexual aggressiveness and miscegenation is far less sublimated than usual. Here, a white boy is singing about his father, who has drowned. The boy goes fishing, hooks his dad, but the fishing pole breaks and the father goes to the devil. At this point one sees a device, the broken pole, similar to that found in a phallic ritual described by Roheim in his studies of aborigines.[30] Although such symbolic baggage could hardly be intended by a modern author, the link with an older, very much older, ritual becomes even more apparent as the tale proceeds. The devil, who is in blackface, informs the man that there is no room in hell for him, and sends him away until room can be found. Yet marks are placed upon this man so he will not be lost in the dark, tobacco leaf ears and a tail like a shad. In the last verse there is a clear reference to miscegenation:

> One night while mudder laid asleep
> A nigger into the house did creep
> What dat? sed she but soon felt glad
> When she found out 'twas my old Dad.[31]

The boy singing, who is white, is thus the apparent issue of a union of white and black, his father being not only a black man but a man endowed with symbolic marks, the tail and vegetable ears. What are the primary elements of this story? A man is drowned, his son breaks a pole in fishing for him, the man is revivified in some strange manner, encounters the Devil, and then is marked with vegetative and fish-like characteristics. In this ritual there seem to be clear survivals from still another fertility myth, that of the Fisher King, in which the fish, as a symbol of divine life, suddenly appears in a profane guise, but somehow saved from damnation, an indeterminate status so consistent with the sort of attributes with which black men have been endowed by the minds of English-speaking peoples from the time of initial contact.[32] Yet the "hero" is following some path, not from one physical point to another, but from one psychological point to another, a fantasy track, and yet one which lies upon a cognitive map which contains instructions as to the meaning of black identity in white society. The boy is an initiate, one who fishes with his pole, a reference perhaps to some long-forgotten *rite de passage*. The black man is an "eternal one of the dream," a totemic hero who will traverse a safe path, a guardian of sleep against the reality of sin and guilt.[33] Immediately the pervasive anxiety-ridden fantasy, that of the black man sneaking into the house and cohabiting with a white woman, is neutralized through a ritual-dramatic means. At the same time, fear of damnation is dispelled.

Discovering vestiges of older nature rituals incorporated into the minstrel framework becomes quite plausible when one considers the ready availability of such material within the Western European folk tradition. Furthermore, materials which have passed over from an active ritualistic context into the realm of literature can easily be put back at the disposal of ritual needs when these emerge. Such use in this instance becomes less mysterious when one considers the importance of slavery in American agriculture, and the critical matter of increasing the number of slaves through breeding in order to maintain an economically viable system, a need which was part of the perception of many whites whether or not it existed in fact.[34]

Since the high point of minstrel entertainment, the cult of the Negro in America has taken many forms, such as the notion of the "white Negro hipster" put forth a number of years ago by Norman Mailer, the incarnation of musical figures like Charlie Parker and John Coltrane into a pantheon of existentialist heroes, and the vast attention paid to the ritual domination of whites by black athletes like the Harlem Globetrotters, who themselves incorporate vestiges of minstrel material into their routines. In each case, such a cult represents the use of ritual attitudes by whites to defuse and render harmless a mysterious and threatening presence in their midst.

In conclusion, in the 19th century whites viewed blacks alternately as child and beast, and were driven to develop highly ritualized collective expressions of group solidarity in the face of the threat blacks posed. The minstrel show was the chief vehicle of these attitudes, and the examples used here could have been duplicated many times over. As a musical extravaganza, the minstrel show drew much of its ritual power from the fact that survival of secular African music among blacks appeared arcane and threatening to whites, particularly in view of the obvious primary place of music in African and Afro-American culture. Hence, the development of a surrogate black music was an imperative element in any ritual of the sort described here. Vital to the success of the minstrel device was a rigorous screening out of many aspects of black culture which might have contradicted the artificial constructs of the minstrel stage, and the depiction of blacks it presented. Under no circumstances did whites want to confront the reality of Afro-American music, or for that matter Afro-American culture in general, and in one sense the minstrel show might best be understood as a reaction formation to the presence of race-consciousness in the music of slaves and their descendants, a race-consciousness not even all blacks were willing to acknowledge.[35]

Notes

[1]The admirable study *Blacking Up, The Minstrel Show in Nineteenth Century America*, by Robert C. Toll (New York, 1974) might on initial consideration seem to say all that can be said on this subject. It was not Toll's intention in this ground-breaking work, however, to explain the deeper structural connections between the minstrel form of entertainment and other aspects of American culture. Toll has indicated some of the central mechanisms in this connection and presented a wealth of descriptive materials. In what follows I propose to show how and why these mechanisms work. Albert McLean,Jr., in his *American Vaudeville as Ritual* (Lexington, Ky., 1965) has also offered some useful suggestions. His notion that the minstrel show served as a barrier to the extension of slavery into the territories is a corollary of my broader hypothesis, See McLean, pp. 26-27. For a good account of the beginning of minstrel music, see Hans Nathan, *Dan Emmett and the Rise of Early Negro Minstrelsy*, Norman, Ok., 1962.

[2]Winthrop Jordan, in *White Over Black, American Attitudes Toward the Negro, 1550-1812*, (Baltimore, 1969) has advanced this thesis in magisterial fashion.

[3]The debate has focused on the thesis of Stanly Elkins, that slavery in the United States generated a depersonalized and dependent victim, and has spawned an extensive literature which is now well known. I have in mind the recent works by Fogel and Engerman, Gutman, Genovese and others. For a balanced account of the slave personality, see John W. Blassingame, *The Slave Community*, (New York, 1972), pp. 184ff.

[4]George M. Fredrickson, *The Black Image in the White Mind* (New York, 1971), pp. 52-43. Also, David Brion Davis, *The Slave Power Conspiracy and the Paranoid Style* (Baton Rouge, 1969), p. 17.

[5]Fredrickson, p. 53.

[6]Fela Sowande, *The Role of Music in African Society* (Washington, 1969). Also Bruno Nettl, *Folk and Traditional Music of the Western Continents* (Englewood Cliffs, 1973), p. 127ff. For specific information on tribes involved in the slave trades see David Wason Ames, "Music of Nigeria, Hausa Music," Commentary for *Anthology of African Music*, recording edited for the International Music Council for the International Institute of Comparative Music Studies and Documentation, Baren Reiter (UNESCO) BM 30L2306-7. And Hugo Zemp, "The Music of the Dan," Commentary, in the same series, BM30L2301. Cf. Paul Oliver, *Savannah Syncopations, African Retentions in the Blues* (New York, 1970), pp. 28-67. On sacred space, see Mircea Eliade, *The Sacred and the Profane* (New York, 1957), pp. 20-65.

[7]Thomas Wentworth Higginson, quoted in Newman Ivy White, *American Negro Folksongs* (Hatboro, 1965 [1928]), p. 13.

[8]White, p. 6. Cf. Lawrence W. Levine, "Slave Songs and Slave Consciousness, an Exploration in Neglected Sources," in *Anonymous Americans, Explorations in Nineteenth Century Social History*, ed. Tamara K. Hareven (Englewood Cliffs, 1971), pp. 101-102.

[9]Miles Mark Fischer, *Negro Slave Labor Songs in the United States* (New York, 1968[1953]), p. 13. There is an excellent discussion of these matters in Levine, pp. 99ff.

[10]Levine, *passim*. Also Fischer, pp. 183ff., and Oliver, pp. 84-101. On survivals in the later period, see also Gunther Schuller, *Early Jazz* (New York, 1968), pp. 3-66., and Bruno Nettl, *Music in Primitive Culture* (Cambridge, 1956), pp. 131ff.

[11]Toll, pp. 41ff. In a somewhat confused early account, Constance Rourke suggested that blacks picked up Anglo-Irish folklore which was then learned in the adopted form by white exponents of minstrel music. Such did the double myth of cultureless black and the "authenticity" of minstrel music persist. See *Roots of American Culture* (New York, 1942), p. 269. For a general account of this whole process, cf., Joel Kovel, *White Racism* (New York, 1971), p. 5.

[12]On ritual in modern societies, see Roland Barthes, "Myth Today," in *Mythologies* (New York, 1972), p. 109-159.

[13]Eliade, *Myth of the Eternal Return, (Princeton, 1954)* pp. xiv-xv, and 3-6. Cf. Paul Radin,

The World of Primitive Man (New York, 1953), p. 172.

[14]A.R. Radcliffe-Brown, *Structure and Function in Primitive Society,* (New York 1952) pp. 123-4.

[15]Eliade, *Myth of the Eternal Return,* p. 27.

[16]Claude Levi-Strauss, *The Raw and the Cooked* (New York, 1965), p. 12.

[17]On the power of ritual to conjoin separate groups, see Levi-Strauss, *The Savage Mind* (Chicago, 1966), p. 32. Note also the statement by Radcliffe-Brown, "Any object or event which has important effects upon the well-being (material or spiritual) of a society, or any thing which stands for or represents any such object or event tends to become an object of the ritual attitude." *Structure and Function,* p. 129.

[18]Emile Durkheim, *Elementary Forms of Religious Life* (New York, 1915), Book 3, "The Principal Ritual Attitudes."

[19]Jane Harrison, *Prolegemana to the Study of Greek Religion* (New York, 1955 [1903]), pp. 1-100, *passim.* Also Radin, pp. 105-182, and Jessie L. Weston, *From Ritual to Romance, passim.*

[20]Eliade, *Sacred and Profane,* p. 42. Rourke observed this ritual character in the 1930s, *Roots of American Culture,* p. 271.

[21]Geza Roheim, *The Eternal Ones of the Dream* (New York, 1945), p. 8.

[22]Nathan, p. 416.   [23]*Ibid.,* pp. 418-19.

[24]*Ibid.,* pp. 419-20. For a possible English antecedent see Weston, pp. 95-100.

[25]Weston, pp. 38-9. Also "Astarte," *Encyclopedia Britannica,* 11th Edition (New York: 1910), V. 2, p. 791. The song is "Old Lady and the Devil," *American Folk Music,* V. 1, Folkways LP FP251.

[26]The character Vice in English morality plays was a confidant of the devil, who later evolved into a kind of fool on the Elizabethan stage. See Robert Potter, *The English Morality Plays, Origins, History and Influence of a Dramatic Tradition* (London, 1975), pp. 196-7. There appear to be many common elements between minstrel shows in the 19th century and the earlier morality plays, pointing to a common base in a folk tradition. Mimicry, combat, dance and didactic themes all figure in both. See, for example, Richard Axton, *European Drama of the Early Middle Ages* (Pittsburgh, 1974), *passim.*

[27]Nathan, pp. 432-3.

[28]*Ibid.,* pp. 454-5 and 461-3. McLean has observed the lack of overt comment on sex in minstrel shows. *Vaudeville,* p. 29.

[29]Nathan, p. 443.   [30]Roheim, pp. 178ff.

[31]Nathan, pp. 447-9.   [32]Weston, pp. 113ff.

[33]Roheim, pp. 6 and 222.

[34]See Robert Fogel and Stanly Engerman, *Time on the Cross, The Economics of American Negro Slavery* (Boston, 1974), pp. 78-86, and Herbert Gutman, *Slavery and the Numbers Game, A Critique on Time on the Cross,* (Urbana, 1975), pp. 94-102.

[35]For example, John Work, *Folk Song of the American Negro* (New York, 1969 [1915], p. 28. Work quotes uncritically observations on the imitative character of Negro music.

The Roast:
American Ritual Satire and Humor

George A. Test

EDWIN D. CANHAM and Arthur Krock, associated for many years with the *Christian Science Monitor* and the *New York Times,* respectively, and Jack Benny, who needs no identification, called the roast a uniquely American event.[1] The Associated Press, the *New York Times,* the *Boston Herald,* the *Albany* (N.Y.) *Times-Union,* and other news media annually report the occurrences of certain roasts. Every President of the United States since 1885 has been the object of at least one roast. As an American ritual it is approaching its centennial and over the years has involved tens of thousands as participants and audiences. Yet the roast has completely escaped the attention of scholars of folkways and popular culture in the United States.

During the last several years the roast has become a fairly regular form of television entertainment bringing to viewers the kind of roast associated with the Friars Club. Three years ago the Young Americans for Freedom roasted William Simon, then Secretary of the Treasury, in the first of what has become an annual roast for political figures, economists, journalists and other public personages of conservative leanings. Meanwhile, the Gridiron Club of Washington, D.C., the Inner Circle of New York City journalists, the New York Financial Writers Association, the Legislative Correspondents of Albany, N.Y., the Clover Clubs of Philadelphia and Boston, Saints and Sinners groups around the country, and the Friars Clubs of New York City and Beverly Hills continue to hold their annual shenanigans. From all this it can hardly be maintained that the roast is undergoing a renaissance, but it is safe to say that it is alive and well.

160

Oddly enough "roast" as a noun referring to the event held by the aforementioned organizations has still to gain admittance to any dictionary. The verb form meaning to *jest at, to banter, to ridicule* goes back, according to the OED, to the early 18th century, and to refer to the act itself as a roast may go back to the Scottish *flytings* of the early 16th century. American usage includes that by Washington Irving in a mock quotation by the literary imposter George Psalmanazar as the epigraph to the *Salmagundi* papers:

> In hoc est hoax, cum quiz et jokesez,
> Et smokem, toastem, roastem folksez,
> Fee, faw, fum.

The translation which accompanies this macaronic verse reads:

> With baked, and broiled, and stewed, and toasted;
> And fried, and boiled, and smoked, and roasted.
> We treat the town.

The 1828 *Webster's Dictionary* included the word but until recently it was placed in the slang or colloquial category, as in Weseen's *Dictionary of American Slang* (1934). Bergen Evans in his *Dictionary of Contemporary American Usage* (1957) claimed that "only in America is roasting much used in the figurative and slang sense." The colloquial designation still clings to the word.

And yet the idea of a roast was always explicit in the events which came to be thus described, as in the name of the Gridiron Club, the gridiron referring to a metal or wire framework used for cooking meat or fish. The membership lapel pin of the Washington Club is in fact a tiny gridiron. Arthur Wallace Dunn in his history of the Gridiron Club published in 1915 admitted that its dinners were roasts, although he denied any "maliciousness" in the roasters, implying thereby that to roast someone was not an altogether acceptable practice. The name Friars Club is of course a pun on a word associated with cookery. Early newspaper accounts of meetings of the Gridiron Club, the Friars and such groups often called them "stunt dinners." When reporters used the word "roast" in the 1930s and '40s they placed it gingerly in quotation marks. In the late 1960s and early 1970s George Jessel and later Dean Martin conducted watered-down television versions of the Friar Club roasts and the word has attained a popular usage that dictionary makers have yet to acknowledge.

Thus roast as a figurative concept for a humorous and satiric attack on a person has a long history. As an event in which such an attack becomes a ritual, the roast has existed long enough to take its place as a curiously modern and American expression and practice similar to ritual satiric attacks found in a variety of cultures and eras.

*   *   *   *

The first dinner of the Clover Club of Philadelphia—January 19, 1882—may be looked upon as the beginning of the era of the American roast. But the word *roast* was nowhere in evidence. Instead the Clover Club constitution spoke of a "Club for Social Enjoyments, the Cultivation of Literary Tastes, and the Encouragement of Hospitable Intercourse.[2] One member even tried to entice visitors to its meetings by hinting of Bohemianism, but this ploy apparently fooled no one.[3] For the institutionalizing of "good-fellowship, broad hospitality, love of humor, wit and culture" by the professional men, men of wealth and prominence who made up the Philadelphia Club was always in the taste of a genteel age. But the spirit of the roast, as the history of the word suggests, did not spring full blown from the heads of the members of the Clover Club.

Spontaneous and intermittent roasting flourished in the clubs of 18th century London. The Beef-steak Society, whose membership pin and ring incorporated a gridiron into its design much as the Gridiron and Clovers Clubs were to do later with theirs, was "composed of the chief wits and great men of the nation," according to one early account.[4] One member of the Steaks, as they preferred to call themselves, was Richard Estcourt, an actor with advanced power of mimickry. Chetwood, an 18th-century historian of the British stage, says of Estcourt that "he entertained the audience with a variety of little catches and flights of humor that pleased all but his critics."[5] Estcourt, who was memorialized in certain *Spectator* papers (nos. 358 and 468) was also capable of poking fun at himself and was the butt of others' humor. The Literary Club boasted the talent for mimickry of David Garrick and the sarcastic wit of Topham Beauclerk, a friend of Dr. Johnson referred to in Boswell's life. The Shilling-Whist Club was famous for its practical jokes directed in some cases against a member known as Oliver Goldsmith. Another small club met at the Globe Tavern in Fleet Street and entertained itself with "songs, jokes, dramatic imitations, burlesque parodies, and broad sallies of humor."

Similar clubs in America include the pre-Revolutionary Tuesday Club[6] of Annapolis founded by Dr. Alexander Hamilton, an immigrant from Edinburgh who landed in Maryland in 1738.

Within a few years he had established a successful medical practice and apothecary shop, married well and begun to dabble in land speculation. In the spring of 1744 he organized the Tuesday Club patterned on the Whin-bush Club of Edinburgh of which he had been a member. The Club met weekly at members' homes until 1756 when Hamilton died and the group disbanded. In Hamilton's history of the Club he defended its practice of satirizing events and topics of the time as an effective way of inducing learning and of avoiding the divisiveness and acrimony that grew out of personal attacks. By the use of irony and satire the group handled controversial issues in an indirect manner. In unrehearsed skits they mocked local events and common beliefs and caricatured persons in the community.

The Knickerbocker spirit of satire and burlesque prevailed in the Ugly Club of New York (ca. 1813-15) whose purpose was to advocate and honor ugliness in all forms.[7] In letters published in the *Columbian* magazine a certain "X" described the officers in unflattering terms. Membership in the Club was extended to New York City's handsomest and manliest. Poet-laureate of the Ugly Club was Fitz-Greene Halleck (1790-1867), a friend of Washington Irving and a minor poet whose early works are characterized by a satiric bent. Although little is known of its meetings the Bread and Cheese Club founded in 1822 by James Fenimore Cooper drew into its circle leading literary intellectual and political figures during the decade of its existence. Letters and reminiscences referring to the Club indicate that it didn't take itself seriously, concentrating on "ingenious fun-making," according to one historian.[8] Halleck was also a member of the Bread and Cheese Club, as were Anthony Bleecker, a punster of great repute, and Charles A. Davis, who later wrote the *Letters of Jack Downing.* A couple of decades later an even more distinguished membership was drawn to the New York Century Club whose Twelfth Night Festivals combined Christmas spirit and humor by making trivial gifts a source of humor and genial mockery.

Isolated and unrelated examples such as these cannot be used to support the claim that a tradition of social or institutional roasting existed. But given the triple-faced nature of laughter, where the bonding and appeasing functions of convivial laughter are, there also is the possibility of aggressive laughter, but normally laughing aggression against persons outside the group. When laughter is directed at persons within the group, it must not be so aggressive as to threaten the unity of the group, or else the group must agree, formally as was the apparent case with the Tuesday Club of Annapolis, or else unconsciously as is the usual case, to make the acceptance of the aggression a socially desirable value in itself. That such behavior tends to be ritualized is illustrated by the infamous example of Mark Twain at the Whittier birthday dinner in 1877. Present were Emerson, Longfellow, Lowell and Howells, the literary establishment and its heir, honoring another member of the establishment. Mark Twain's story about the overnight visit of three drunken, card-playing, thieving persons calling themselves Emerson, Lowell and Longfellow to a cabin in the West is one of the funniest sketches ever composed by Mark Twain, but told in the midst of a friendly but serious occasion it was a disaster as was the general reception by the press for some weeks after. Not only was Mark Twain still an outsider to some extent but more importantly he attempted a "roast" where there was no ritual for it. Whatever intellectual and psychological interpretations may be used to account for Mark Twain's behavior, it must also be understood as a breach of ritual: a birthday dinner is one kind of ritual, a roast is another. Aggressive laughter at members of the establishment by outsiders is as ritualized as most other human behavior and failing to adhere to that ritual may have disastrous consequences.

Although Mark Twain apologized in writing to the principals, he vacillated for the rest of his life about the propriety of what he had done at the dinner. One wonders whether he recalled the Whittier affair when he attended a genuine roast at the Philadelphia Clover Club dinner in 1885. Some years later when he was invited to the Gridiron Club dinner he considered reading the Whittier dinner sketch but ended by reminiscing about his newspaper days.

At the time of Mark Twain's visit, the Clover Club was only three years old, but in the next dozen years it was to attain pre-eminence as a roasting club. The guest list for the first fifteen years of the Club published in Mary Deacon's history is remarkable for its number (nearly 2000) and its variety. Visitors from abroad who happened to be in Philadelphia at the time of the Clover Club's annual meeting (in January in the early days, later April) were especially welcome. Political figures from presidents and governors on down were also prominent on the guest list. Grover Cleveland was guest of honor at the Constitutional Centennial Celebration in 1887 with former president Rutherford B. Hayes and numerous senators and governors. But during that period actors, writers of all kinds, explorers, military leaders, publishers, men of commerce, industry and the professions were guests at the sumptuous dinners in the Bellevue-Stratford Hotel. The membership included thirteen editors and newspapermen, eleven lawyers, three men in the medical profession, the owner of a ship line, a banker, and a book dealer, among others. But the guest list showed the Club to be virtually an international organization, drawing as it did men of letters and arts and politics from all over the world.

Since the 1920s at least (records for the early decades of the 20th century are scarce), no president has been a guest of the Clover Club and men of letters and the arts have disappeared from the guest lists. It is still more than a Philadelphia organization since its guests come from all over Pennsylvania and the areas adjacent to the City of Brotherly Love, including Washington, D.C. with its large supply of political figures. But no longer do people of the stature of Mark Twain, Eugene Field, Edgar W. "Bill" Nye, Charles Dudley Warner, Edwin Booth, Joseph Jefferson, Edward Harrigan, Frank R. Stockton, Richard Harding Davis, General William T. Sherman and S. Weir Mitchell come. Nor do the likes of Henry Irving, Herbert Beerbohm Tree or Thomas A'Becket from England, or explorer Paul DuChaillu and actors Constant Cocquelin and his son Jean from France.

In the mid-1920s the Clover Club dinners ceased for two years because of illness over the same period among the officers, two of whom subsequently died. In 1929 the Club held its 47th annual dinner numbering it from the first meeting in 1882 even though there had been two years without meetings. Prohibition had its inhibiting influence although stock from private cellars is said to have supplied the dinners. Newspaper accounts following the repeal of Prohibition in 1932 noted the livelier atmosphere of the dinners, although an account in 1938 suggested that the day of such clubs might be past.[9] Such has not been the case and although two dinners during World War II (one within a month after the attack on Pearl Harbor and another two years later) were devoid of the usual horseplay, the Club has flourished and is now within striking distance of its centennial.

Despite these changes the rituals, symbols and roasting practice of the Club have changed very little. The motto from which the Club takes its name remains the same:

> While we live we live in clover;
> When we die we die all over.

The couplet is said to come from an old minstrel song and the phrase "in clover" connotes a kind of Big Rock Candy Mountain life. The four-leaf variety figures prominently in the decorations for the dinner. The printed menu is always clover-shaped, the clover appears on the gridiron that forms the centerpiece of the main table and is engraved on a three-handled loving cup which rests on the gridiron. Part way through the dinner the newest member of the Club who has been seated for part of the dinner in a large chair "too high from the table to eat and too low to hold onto the ceiling," serves the members and the guests of honor at the head table from the three-handled cup beginning with the Club president. The "baby member" is all the while attired in bib and baby hat. Another ritual involves the singing of the song Darby Ram while a live ram is led among the tables. The ram of the song is a prodigious beast with a tail that reaches the sky, horns that reach the moon, and wool so fine and thin that

> It took 90,000 girls, sir,
> Just 100 years to spin.
> O, what a ram,
> O, what a ram!

But the basic business of the Clover Club is heckling. From the opening gavel on, irreverence toward all speakers is the order of the evening. The president wears out his gavel trying to get a hearing for the speakers who in turn either keep their remarks short and light or suffer the consequences. As a reporter for the Philadelphia *Inquirer* noted in 1939, "the club's unwritten by-law [is] that every man has the right to speak, and every man has the right to heckle."[10] The humor is very spontaneous, topical and ephemeral. Few of the quips reported by Mary Deacon from the first fifteen years of dinners bear repeating and her disclaimer that "it was impossible to put on paper the aroma of bouquet of a Clover Club dinner" is probably well taken. But the spirit of the dinner is unmistakable and is suggested in the remark from the account of the dinner in 1939:

The legendary quips and heckling of the club's long history were dimmed by the sparkle of the spontaneous wit and humor, and the feeling of good fellowship that abounded, transcending all political, all professional, and all social lines.[11]

In the derision and mockery all are momentarily made equal, men of power and prominence are brought low and the quipper elevated by his wit and humor. A Clover Club roast is in one sense the most primitive of all roasts because it relies mainly on spontaneous irreverence. Even the intermittent reading of letters and telegrams of regret for being unable (or unwilling) to attend has no pattern. Some are perfunctory, others, as that from Robert J. Burdette in 1896, are elaborate. Burdette's consisted of an illustrated nine-stanza poem. Eugene Field declined since he said he was "not ripe for crucifixion." Those who come are not obliged to make a speech; some have recited verse ("The Midnight Ride of Paul Revere" was once delivered in a Pennsylvania Dutch dialect), others have rendered songs. Occasionally mock gifts are presented. In 1884 when William M. Bunn was appointed Governor of Idaho, then a territory in the wild west to Easterners, he was given a return railroad ticket, a toy gun, a bow and arrow and other items for survival in an uncivilized country. Many years later a governor of Pennsylvania who had recently fallen off a stool while trying to milk a cow at a farm show was surprised to receive a three-legged milking stool at an annual dinner. At a recent dinner the guests were presented with a slide show of baby pictures of prominent Pennsylvanians present and absent. Parody songs have begun to be presented more frequently than was once the case. But spontaneous heckling remains the distinguishing characteristic of the Clover Club roast dinner. Freedom to be humorously irreverent to others, especially those who occupy positions of power, wealth and influence, is its function, a permission that is unspoken and unformulated but nevertheless stylized, formal, accepted, regularized—in short, ritualized.

Unlike the Clover Club whose roasts have become relatively localized, the ritual roasts of the Friars Club are the best known of all roasts since they involve people in the entertainment world and have been broadcast on radio and seen on television, most recently on the "specials" known as the Dean Martin Roasts. Whereas most other roasting groups tend to be small and informal organizations which exist mainly for their dinners, the Friars Club (and this is true of the New York City Club as well as the Beverly Hills, California, Club) has grown to well over a thousand members. Each group has a club house (known as a monastery) and each carries on extensive and varied philanthropical activities. The New York group holds that a majority of its members have to be directly connected with the entertainment world in some capacity, but it fills out its membership with people from the non-entertainment world who have an interest in or admiration for those in show business. The West Coast group became independent some years ago when it allowed its membership to expand to allow ninety-five percent to be non-show business types, thereby drawing down upon it the disapproval of the parent group.[12] Even though the two groups are no longer legally connected, their activities do not differ.

The New York Friars Club began in 1904 as a group of press agents who joined together to put an end to the practice of those who were giving press agentry a bad name by fraudulently soliciting free passes to shows. The group succeeded and in the process found a common ground for additional meetings and for changing its name from the Press Agents' Association to the Friars Club and beginning the long tradition of holding roast dinners. The first guest of honor was playwright Clyde Fitch in 1906 and before the year was out, Marc Klaw, a successful theatrical entrepreneur,

Henry Miller, a well-known actor and producer, and the composer Victor Herbert were afforded the same honor. At his dinner Victor Herbert contributed the Friars Song (words by Charles Emerson Cook) which is still sung at all testimonial dinners. The idea behind the testimonial dinners has remained the same, although changes in the format have occurred over the years. For each dinner (or luncheon) a guest of honor is invited, generally someone in the entertainment business although political figures are sometimes chosen. Then a panel of guests is chosen, each of whom is afforded a turn in roasting the main guest. When each has had a turn the main guest is allowed to retaliate in kind. Guests of honor are usually persons in the full bloom of their fame so that the roast is ideally a gesture of recognition and a reminder that fame and power are not sufficient unto themselves. In the early years of the tradition guests made speeches about the main guest and sometimes showed a degree of cleverness in their remarks. A.L. Erlanger at the roast of George M. Cohan in 1910 referred to Cohan throughout his speech as "Jesse Cohan's son," Jesse Cohan being present and a well-known stage performer in his own right.[13] Erlanger, probably the most influential producer of his time, gave a humorous account of his acquaintance with Cohan and a history of Cohan's career. He invited the audience to become a jury to try Cohan, although his instructions were to find Cohan guilty of being the "possessor of super skill in everything he undertakes." Milton Berle once said that the roast is a "crazy way to tell a person you love them."[14]

Although he probably had in mind the widespread use of insults that has come to characterize the televised roast, a closer look reveals a curious mixture of hostility growing out of a certain amount of truth telling and a large dose of sentimentality that is characteristic of show folks in their public dealings with one another and their business. ("There's no business like show business," and all that sort of thing.) The Friars Club roasts have in fact always been performances. Large numbers of guests are invited who pay large sums of money as contributions to the charities supported by the Friars. The roast is then a staged affair and the guest of honor is "on trial" in that everyone has come to see whether he or she can take it. Whatever home truths are revealed are clothed in joke form and veiled in laughter so as to make them at least momentarily palatable. This format prevailed down to the time of World War II.

What has evolved since then even at the so-called X-rated stag luncheons is more a performance and less a roast than was once the case. As comedians have come to dominate the guest lists, what were once speeches have come to be routines, with the guests of honor made to fit into jokes that often have little or no relation to the guest's life and personality. Roasters generally confine themselves to the stereotyped characteristics known to the public. Howard Cosell's egotism, Milton Berle's penchant for stealing jokes, Dean Martin's drinking and so on. The television roasts and those reported in Joey Adams' book *Here's to the Friars* (1976) are not so much watered-down versions as they are perversions of the original function, concerned not so much with roasting the guest as with using the occasion for a series of one-liners with the guest of honor as subject for a gag rather than the object of satire, fellow performer rather than ritual victim. The original function has virtually disappeared, but the ritual lingers on.

Not so with the Gridiron Club of Washington, D.C. where the roast continues to flourish. Since 1885 a group of journalists stationed in the nation's capitol have roasted every President except Grover Cleveland and a great many other political figures as well. In their early years the Gridiron Club and the Clover Club went on outings and excursions together and conducted their roasts in a similar manner. The Gridiron Club was in fact a copy of the Philadelphia Clover Club.

The circumstances that caused the Washington journalists to come together was their embattled status in the early 1880s regarding the right to certain seats in the Congressional galleries. Meetings growing out of this brouhaha became dinners which in turn metamorphosed into the Gridiron Club in 1885. Like the Clover Club it has only a set of officers to manage its affairs and dinners and no known place of residence. The dinners are held annually, although at one time they were semi-annual. The dinner scheduled for December 9, 1941 was cancelled in the wake of the attack on Pearl Harbor and no dinners were held again until 1945. The early dinners were attended by only several dozen people, but they now draw close to a thousand.

Gridiron Club roasts are by far the most elaborate of all roasts. While the dinner is being served, members of the Club perform skits or stunts designed to satirize political figures and current events. Drawing on a wide variety of songs, members provide new lyrics which comment on the political vagaries of the guests, including the President. Current popular tunes, Gilbert and Sullivan numbers, hymns, melodies from operas and musical comedies are all dragged in with new words. "Stand up, stand up for Jesus," became "Stand up, stand up for Lyndon." Cole Porter's dermatology complaint became "I've got it under my skin,/ The White House, deep in the heart of me." And Gilbert and Sullivan's "I am the very model of the modern major general," has probably been adapted to more situations than any other single song. Costumes, make-up and props all contribute to the humor. Because the humor is topical in the extreme it dates almost overnight and articles retailing some of the more telling points of the skits tend to be flat or obvious. Like the atmosphere of the Clover Club the stimulation of the event apparently does wonders for the humor of the Gridiron Club dinners. Yet readers of the newspaper accounts following the dinners can still get a certain satisfaction from having those bigwigs lampooned.

As though to counteract the ephemeral nature of the dinner, the Club provides its guests with menus and other souvenirs that also carry satirical messages. Playing cards, military orders with a map of the "bottle-field," a primer, a calendar, a who's who, almanacs, a book of dream interpretations, a tour guide to Washington and a theatrical program have been used as devices for roasting the politicos. C.K. Berryman, for many years a political cartoonist for the Washington *Post,* illustrated some of these souvenir items.[15] The tables at the banquet are set up to resemble a huge gridiron. The membership pin of the Club is a tiny gridiron. From the beginning, the events of the dinner were guided by two rules: reporters are never present, women are always present. The first was meant to deter those present from rushing out and reporting the details of the satire. The second was a figurative way of keeping the proceeding from becoming raunchy since until 1927 women were not invited to attend the dinners. The first has been honored mainly by keeping the President's remarks off the record as well as those of his political "opposition." Another tradition makes each new president of the Club the target for humor at the dinner at which he is inducted. The United States Marine Band has for many years provided the musical accompaniment. No other outsiders help in the performances which are worked up during the four to six weeks before the dinner. Prior to World War I the Club issued its famous "Advice to Orators." Although every period and circumstance has its own cliches, the "Advice" still has a certain timelessness that makes it worth repeating:

The members of the Gridiron Club know that it is the most unique club in the world and the most famous.
They know that it gives the best dinners in the world.
They also have a fair knowledge of the newspaper business.
They know that they MOULD PUBLIC OPINION; that they MAKE and UNMAKE PUBLIC MEN.
They understand all about the POWER OF THE PRESS, and what ought to be their MISSION IN LIFE.
They also know that you ARE GLAD TO BE HERE; that you DID NOT EXPECT TO BE CALLED UPON, etc., etc.

Remember that your time is short and soon you may be called down, so omit all references to hackneyed themes and phrases.

Time magazine once referred to the Gridiron Club as the "Hardened Arteries Club," observing that it was run by the Washington journalistic establishment.[16] Others have agreed, as for example in 1970 when the annual dinner was picketed by women protesting the stag audience. For no woman had ever attended a Gridiron Club dinner with the exception of Jeannette Rankin, the first woman elected to Congress who was invited in 1917. Although a few women were invited in 1972, it failed to satisfy the critics who held a counter-gridiron event the following year. In 1975 Betty Ford and Happy Rockefeller attended and since then no further protests have been reported. The Gridiron Club accepted Carl T. Rowan, its first black member, in 1973. Attacks on the Gridiron Club were nothing new, since Raymond S. Tompkins writing in the *American Mercury* in October 1927 indicted the Club for insincerity claiming that its mockery of public figures was really meaningless. President William Howard Taft would have disagreed, for in 1914 writing on "Personal Aspects of the Presidency" after having left the position, he said,

The Gridiron dinners, at which of late years I was a regular attendant, are worthy of mention. They furnished a great deal of fun, some of it bright and excruciating, all of it of a popular flavor, because it was at the expense of those guests who were in the public eye. After some training, both as Secretary of War and as President, I was able to smile broadly at a caustic joke at my expense and seem to enjoy it, with the consolatory thought that every other guest of any prominence had to suffer the same penalty for an evening's pleasure.[17]

Although President Taft was speaking of the Gridiron Club, his sentiments could apply to the guests of the Clover Club of Philadelphia and of the Friars Club. For among them they represent three different styles of roasts. The Clover Club of Philadelphia uses direct, spontaneous and generally unstructured heckling. The Friars Club also uses the direct heckling approach although in a somewhat structured format. The Gridiron Club uses an indirect approach that features preparation and organization. All other roasting groups use either the Friars or the Gridiron format. The Circus Saints and Sinners, a national organization with "tents" in various cities, and the newly instituted roasts by the Young Americans for Freedom use the Friars Club approach. The Gridiron Club format is used by the Clover Club of Boston, the Inner Circle of New York City journalists, the Financial Writers Association of New York, the Legislative Correspondents Association of Albany, N.Y. and the defunct Caveat Club of Philadelphia barristers.

Despite the varied formats the intention is the same, to satirize the folly of men and events, or if not to satirize at least to generate some humor at the expense of men of influence and power. Given the touchy nature of such an endeavor, how is the appropriate atmosphere established? Could the opening remarks at the first meeting of all the roasting groups be discovered, they would make a useful study. How are men of power or wealth or fame to be convinced that they should sit still while they are the subject of jibes, quips, barbs and other forms of verbal aggression that make the typical roast? When the Financial Writers Association began in 1938 the remarks of the President of the Association set the ground rules for the dinner. He pointed out that the evening's entertainment was going to be in the "spirit of frolic," as the *Times* reporter phrased it. The president then added: "If any person were to feel that he had received rough treatment in song and story, it was because the association had thought that the individual could 'take it'."[18] This statement effectively "traps" the roastee, for to object publically to being roasted calls into question the Association's judgment and shows moreover that he can't in fact "take it." So the target is not so much displaying tolerance and good humor as he is gritting his teeth and taking it, knowing, as President Taft pointed out, that others will eventually receive the same treatment and he can then laugh at their expense.

Having created the appropriate atmosphere for their roast, what do the roasters believe they are accomplishing? Arthur Krock, writing in late 1947 in the aftermath of World War II, said "the break in tension, so far as Washington is concerned, and the brief rush of lighter air that are the contributions of a Gridiron evening are especially useful and welcome at such a time."[19] James Reston, a little more than ten years later, agreed. Likening the Gridiron Club to a court jester he saw its function as the easing of the "terrible oppression of official responsibility." But the court jester he said also provoked "laughter by dramatising the sharp contrast between pretense and reality,.... [to] remind the big shots that they are really very small objects in a large and complicated drama."[20] At the fortieth anniversary dinner of the Gridiron Club in 1925 the history of the group was reviewed in a letter from Chauncey Depew, at 91 the only member still living who had been present at the first dinner of the Club in 1885. In the letter he said:

> The Gridiron Club is a mirror; it reveals the statesman to himself as he is; it is the greatest most benevolent and beneficial creation to reduce the abnormal swelling of the head and the enlargement of the chest. It is doing a great work in giving its guests the best evenings to be found anywhere in the United States. It rescues a large

number of statesmen who are so obsessed with the idea that they may become President that they live in a rarefied atmosphere and can do no more work.

The Gridiron Club dissipates the brainstorms and makes them useful Senators. For many years Punch has restored sanity to English public life; the Gridiron Club has done and is doing the same patriotic work for the United States.[21]

Depew's sentiments were echoed some years later in a *Times* editorial, "Spoofing the Great," which said, "To laugh at ourselves is a philosophical stature that most of us are unable to attain. In the [Gridiron dinners] we reach that objectivity by proxy, it may be said: we are tickled by the spectacle of our favorite or most detested politicians reduced to absurdity."[22] In short, by deflating those of power and influence the roast provides a moment of psychic cleansing and social unity for the participants.

As Chancey Depew noted, the Gridiron Club was performing a patriotic function, and others have taken pride in the roast as a unique American phenomenon. James Reston and Arthur Krock have been bemused by what might have been going on in the minds of foreign, especially Russian, observers at Gridiron dinners. How do such observers view these free-swinging attacks on men in high places? Surely people in other countries enjoy no such freedom. And in one sense this is undoubtedly true. In some countries public criticism of political figures is dangerous, not to say fatal. But there are many ways to poke fun at leaders as the presence of satiric and humor magazines, political cartoons and cabarets and nightclubs with stand-up comics testify. Since such phenomena are often transient, even ephemeral, the longevity of the American roast gives it special significance. On the other hand, in the context of the seemingly universal impulse to mock those in positions of wealth and power the roast can be seen as an interesting contemporary example of such an impulse and not at all unique. How then is it special and American and how is it universal?

The oldest of the roasting clubs began at a time in the history of the United States when voluntary associations were springing up so fast and in such numbers that observers were to characterize Americans, as deTocqueville had already done, as a nation of joiners. The bewildering number and kinds of associations were an expression of a decentralizing tendency in American society that countered the centralizing growth of business and government. But the roasting groups carried the decentralizing tendency one step further by becoming unofficial critics of those who by their power and wealth were often the instigators and proprietors of the centralizing movement. For this reason roasts can be seen as an instrument of that indigenous American radicalism that seeks a fuller realization of the potential of the system of which it is a part.

But that critical function did not extend to its concept of membership because the roasting groups remained for many years totally male organizations. The Friars Club allowed a woman on the dais for the first time in 1953 when Sophia Tucker celebrated fifty years in show business. The Gridiron Club and the Inner Circle began admitting women to its dinners for the first time in 1972. Membership in the clubs has been dominated by newspapermen, lawyers and others either of wealth or influence, with the guests drawn from similar circles. Morally and democratically this homogeneity may be reprehensible, but ritually it is probably indispensible. Shared values and assumptions about manners and behavior are necessary if deviations from them are to be satirized. The injunction which opened the Gridiron Club dinners that ladies are figuratively always present served to set their dinners (and all other roasting groups except the Friars Club followed the spirit) apart from other all-male gatherings which are often stereotyped as being preoccupied with raunchy humor. To this extent the earliest groups were a product of the Genteel Tradition in American life even while reserving a place for all-male gathering for the purpose of laughing. But the exclusion of women was based on more than the desire for a night out with the boys. There were those who held that women did not have a sense of humor, and the issue was seriously debated in respectable journals in the last part of the 19th century and the early part of the present one. With few exceptions humor in American culture of that time was largely a male preoccupation.

The humor and satire, as has been noted, was sometimes direct, sometimes indirect. The informal heckling of the Philadelphia Clover Club and the formal heckling of the Friars Club are in the tradition of direct attack satire which Robert Elliott in his book the *Power of Satire* has traced back to the magic of the curse. Its most highly developed literary expression is the formal verse satire of Roman literature and includes the diatribe. It is a minor but virulent strain in the history of satire. Heckling can be seen as an undernourished and distant cousin of the diatribe, a form not much cultivated in American literature (Philip Wylie's *Generation of Vipers* is the best known recent example of the ancient art), but alive and well in political oratory and on the editorial page since the beginning of the Republic. The most apt term to describe the kind of satire in the skits and songs of the Gridiron Club and its relations is the "higher vaudeville." The adjective higher is appropriate since their routines contained few examples of the anti-ethnic humor of many vaudeville shows of the late 19th and early 20th centuries. The minstrel show format, however, was used occasionally, even as recently as the 1930s. But the content of the higher vaudeville was supplied by men whose tool in trade was language and whose cultural background included an acquaintance with literature and the arts. While far from high-toned, they could assume a common body of knowledge about English and American writers, the Bible, popular and operatic music, and of course current events—in short, the culture of the genteel tradition in the late 19th century, the culture of an upper-middle class establishment today.

But if the roast has its American flavor, it is by no means a uniquely American phenomenon. It has something in common with what can only be described as ritual sacrifice by verbal abuse practiced by pre-literate African tribes. In the *Apo* ceremony practiced by the Ashanti and described in 1705 by a Dutch explorer and again in 1923 by an English anthropologist, the people of the tribe were allowed to discharge all their accumulated ill feelings against chiefs and nobles.[23] Paul B. DuChaillu, a French explorer and later a guest of the Philadelphia Clover Club, described a similar ceremony conducted in the early 19th century by the people of Gaboon, a West African tribe, when they elevated a new ruler.[24] He said that the prospective king "kept his temper, and took all the abuse with a smiling face," just as William Howard Taft admitted doing.

The roast also has something in common with the rich variety of festivals and ceremonies in which roles are reversed and practices burlesqued. The Roman Saturnalia was such a festival, well known from Horace's Satire (II, 7) in which he has his servant Davus tell him off in permissible Saturnalian freedom. The most elaborate of such role reversal festivals was the medieval Feast of Fools in which the lower clergy of the large cathedrals held mock-elections of "officers," ridiculed holy ceremonies, profaned the sacraments, delivered mock sermons, and otherwise behaved in a fashion not ordinarily allowed. Slowly banished from the cathedrals the festivals were taken over by craft and professional guilds which became known in France as abbeys of misrule or fool societies. Out of the fool societies came the *sottie,* a simple satirical revue performed by semi-professional actors in fools' costumes who engaged in acrobatic clowning, uttered dialogues with patter-like delivery, presented simply plotted farces full of puns, songs and obscenity. One such society was the Basoche made up of the bailiffs, scribes and law clerks of Paris. They wrote and presented a variety of plays including mock trials which dealt with on occasion the lives of persons in or known to the audience. Groups which perform in a similar spirit have been reported in India, Mexico and Newfoundland.

The roast then can be seen as an American expression of an

impulse that has manifested itself in a variety of ways in other times and places. It is the most successful and longest-lived American expression of such ritual satire and humor. Law school "libel shows" such as those held recently at Syracuse University Law School, April Fool's Day issues of high school and college Class Days have never achieved the status of the roast. Such organizations as the National Nothing Foundation dedicated to National Nothing Day on which nothing is celebrated, honored or observed; the Procrastinators Club of America dedicated to putting things off until tomorrow or later; and even the annual Dubious Achievement Awards of *Esquire* magazine tend to get swallowed and lost in the media. On the other hand, newspapermen have played an important even dominant role in most of the roasting clubs which has made them much more visible than if they had been the concern say of biology teachers or bus drivers. Moreover the fourth estate performs a special and indispensible function in American society, making it at once hated and feared and courted. This ambivalence is very like that which Robert Elliott has noted as the position occupied by the satirist in society who is seen as both attacker and defender, as social prop and social threat. In the roast, however, the two roles are combined. Calling into question the excesses, the hypocrisy, the pretensions of those in positions of influence the roast carries out a mock sacrifice for the health of the community, a purgation of those misguided and socially inefficient values and behavior that are antithetical to the psychological and social health of individuals and the successful functioning of society and social groups. The roast thus takes its place among the many and varied forms and expression of ritual satire and humor.

Notes

[1]Canham made his statement in an article, "In the Glow of the Gridiron," in the *Christian Science Monitor Weekly Magazine Section,* 6 April 1940, pp. 4, 15. Krock's statement appeared in his column, "In the Nation," in the *New York Times,* 12 Dec., 1947, p. 26. Benny is quoted in "TV Roasts: A Crazy Way of Telling People You Love Them," in *TV Guide,* 11 May 1974, p. 15.

[2]Cited in Mary R. Deacon, *The Clover Club of Philadelphia* (Phila.: Avil, 1897), p. 3.

[3]Albert Parry, *Garrets and Pretenders: A History of Bohemia in America* (New York: Dover, 1960), pp. 153-55.

[4]Quoted in John Timbs, *Clubs and Club Life in London* (London, n.d. 1873?), p. 105.

[5]Timbs.

[6]Elaine G. Breslaw, "Wit, Whimsy and Politics: The Uses of Satire by the Tuesday Club of Annapolis, 1744 to 1756," *W&MQ,* 32 (1975), 295-306.

[7]Nelson F. Adkins, *Fritz-Green Halleck: An Early Knickerbocker Wit and Poet* (New Haven: Yale University Press, 1930), p. 33.

[8]Adkins, "James Fenimore Cooper and The Bread and Cheese Club," *MLN,* 47 (1932), 72.

[9]"Men and Things: Gay Old Clover Club's Fifty-six Candles," *Philadelphia Inquirer,* 20

January 1938, p. 15.

[10]Alexander Kendrick, "Clover Club Marks 57th Anniversary, Honors Gov. James," 20 January 1939, p. 5.

[11]Kendrick.

[12]Sam Zolotow, " 'Bless Our Bank' Shifts Directors," *New York Times,* 23 August 1962, p. 24.

[13]"Cohan Dined by Friars," *New York Times,* 4 April 1910, p. 9.

[14]*TV Guide,* 11 May 1974, p. 14.

[15]Arthur Wallace Dunn, *Gridiron Nights* (New York: Stokes, 1915), p. 178.

[16]24 December 1945, p. 70.

[17]*Saturday Evening Post,* 28 February 1914, p. 32.

[18]" 'Financial Follies' Given by Writers," 17 December 1938, pp. 23, 25.

[19]Krock, "In the Nation," 12 December 1938, pp. 23, 25.

[20]*New York Times,* 16 March 1958, Section 4, p. 10.

[21]"Gridiron History Reviewed by Depew," *New York Times,* 24 April 1925, p. 10.

[22]14 October 1937, p. 24.

[23]William Bosman, *A New and Accurate Description of the Coast of Guinea....*Letter X (London, 1705), p. 158; cited in R.S. Rattray, *Ashanti* (Oxford University Press, 1923), p. 151.

[24]Paul B. DuChaillu, *Explorations and Adventures in Equatorial Africa* (1861; rpt. London: Laurie, 1945), p. 19

The Cult and Ritual of Toughness in Cold War America

Donald J. Mrozek

DURING WORLD WAR II millions of Americans in and out of military service experienced physical training and participated in sports that the federal government had organized to raise the national quotient of physical fitness and to impart "combative" values to individual citizens. Many affected by this program, including prominent coaches and athletic managers, slipped beyond the practical purposes of the federal programs in countering the Axis threat and carried a general enthusiasm for physical and moral toughness into the post-war period. To the large extent that political and spiritual struggles assumed a concrete, physical symbology, the conflict between the Soviet Union and the United States to win converts around the world and to stand as the champion of world society's future encouraged the development of a cult of toughness, built on ritual, in America, the seeds of which had already been scattered in the war years. As distinct from fitness, toughness explicitly characterized an aggressive, action-oriented attitude—one that turned abruptly away from the rather dilatory spirit that many Americans read back into the 1930s. Heartened by the experience of World War II, which seemed to prove that Americans were capable of decisive action on an unparalleled scale, various figures in government, organized athletics and physical education used sport and physical training in increasingly ritualized forms to generate a tough and winning attitude in the Cold War.

A comparable error developed with respect to the use of a military draft which gradually became confused with American

178

tradition, despite the fact that it had not previously been a standard measure even in time of war. This kind of misinterpretation fostered alarmist visions of decay and decadence within American culture. Kinkead himself concluded that, in the case of the American POWs in Korea, "it was not just our young soldiers who faced the antagonists, but more importantly the entire cultural pattern which produced these young soldiers.[6]

Tellingly, Albert D. Biderman has pointed out that "we can learn less about pathologies of our society from the behavior of the Americans captured in Korea than we can by attempting to understand the reasons for the complaints that have been made against them."[7] Much of the lesson to which Biderman directs us rests in the growing belief that political ideas and moral values depended on physical toughness. Thus Kinkead could write with unconcealed satisfaction that the Army had embarked on survival training programs that simulated the environments and practices that soldiers might encounter if separated from their units or taken as POWs. Kinkead clearly agreed with the Army which, he noted, "now realizes that a man's prior knowledge of a situation" might be critical to his survival if he should fall into that situation. Then, however, he showed that "knowledge" had a special meaning: "If captured, they are subjected to treatment, which, although not as severe as the real thing, approximates Communist handling."[8] Knowledge and learning now assumed so specifically physical a meaning that torture, in the general manner of a Korean POW camp, became accepted procedure. The American would learn not with his imagination but with his body.

Although the cult of toughness had roots in the 1940s, its ritualistic practice grew strong and spread most impressively in the following two decades, stimulated by a debate over the physical and spiritual implications of American performance in the Korean War. The early reports of "brain-washing" left many Americans unwilling to believe that extreme physical conditions—the imposition of pain and torture—were effective means of altering value and behavior.[1] The discrimination that Americans in the safety of their home territory made between collaborators and victims helped to define the contours of this belief. Those prisoners of war who had not been subjected to overt physical torture might be the source of some embarrassment; yet, in these cases, some degree of cooperation could be understood, if not accepted. It was specifically the physical nature of the conditioning that Americans identified as central in altering behavior.[2]

This emphasis on the effectiveness of physical stress in ritualistically shaping values and behavior had precedent in the

American past, and it enjoyed new attention during the Cold War in the two decades following World War II. Particularly after the reports of collaboration by Americans in Korean began to arouse concern about the physical and ethnical toughness of the average citizen, there was renewed interest in taking "corrective measures." Among them was the use of painful physical stress to train or to condition Americans either to achieve or to resist. The desire for physical toughness for its assumed uses as a conservator of values hastened the movement of using pain in a practical, creative ritual. Painful and stressful experience was integrated into sporting events, enhancing their ritual and ceremonial importance.

Not that Americans of the late 1930s and early 1940s were unconcerned with the durability and resolve of the young. In the early stages of World War II, newspaper editors and illustrators promoted a new and tougher image of American youth. A Joseph Parrish cartoon for the Chicago *Tribune* of May 3, 1942, for example, expressed the hope that Axis sneers at American youth as a "hothouse plant" made fragile by the American standard of living are misguided.[3] Parrish answered the charge with a sketch of "fighting American youth" ensconced in "The Greenhouse," the gunner's station in a U.S. bomber. So, too, both the young American fighter and Uncle Sam himself were presented as strapping, muscular, powerful men.[4] Uncle Sam lost a good many of his years and most of his paternal reserve and distance; the young American shed frivolity and self-indulgence. All reacted strongly against the sensation of weakness so deeply rooted in the experiences of the Depression, and the sense of challenge and of fulfillment that the war afforded was commanding. Yet, if there was a touch of toughness in the self-image of the American in those years, it was without the complicating touch of pain which can temper inclination into total dedication. Even in cartoons that would imply objective suffering, such as one in which a "fiendish enemy" Japanese is bayoneting a prisoner tied to a post,[5] the principal emphasis rested on outrage, not on suffering. The agony was of the spirit, not of the body—an agony of purpose, and not of experience.

But for critics of the performance of Americans taken as POWs, the realms of spirit and body commingled. In this respect, the attitude of Cold War America toward physical toughening deviated from that of Americans in the interwar years. In addition, the growing vogue of behavioralism itself jeopardized confidence in the priority or primacy of ethical values or in the belief that they were spiritually generated and sustained. In this regard, perhaps behavioralism just proved to be an extreme variant of American pragmatism.

Yet it is important to observe that many problems with this new emphasis on stress and pain were simple and practical. The erroneous assertions of critics such as Eugene Kinkead that the Code of Conduct (1955) for the military represented traditional American policies reflects the tendency, after World War II, to mistake the exceptional and abnormal for the customary and the ordinary. Americans had, for example, accepted parole and favors from captors from the War of American Independence on; and prisoners of war had talked with interrogators well beyond the limits of "name, rank, and serial number only." Kinkead's misunderstanding of history, however, is itself revealing, in that it reflects a wider willingness in the 1950s to accept extreme interpretations of American tradition and behavior.

A far more elaborate program, and one that soon received broad publicity, was the Air Force's survival program at Stead Air Force Base in Nevada. During the last days of the training cycle, after schooling in evasive maneuver and living off the land was complete, the "captive" Air Force personnel were taken to a simulation of a Prisoner of War camp. Here, according to the most prominent and perhaps most sensational report, at the discretion of the training personnel, they could be forced into boxes about 18 inches wide, with a slanted bottom, and set too short to allow the confined person to stand straight. In some cases, interrogators used electric shock from low-powered generators. In yet others, those persons being shocked knelt on broomsticks so that their reflexes, when stimulated by electricity, drew them painfully off the sticks to the floor. Still others were confined in pits filled with water, left there for long hours. During the public discussion of the program in 1955 and afterwards Air Force representatives did not dispute the facts as reported. However, they emphasized that participation should be considered voluntary. Indeed, their cooperation had been essential in making possible *Life* magazine's extensive photo-essay of the program. Moreover, the preponderance of those reporting about the program at Stead concluded that it was tough but necessary.

Dispute developed as to the nature and scope of the program. But the coverage in *Life* magazine left strange implications about the directions of the flying service. The Air Force's torture program reflected an extreme conversion to behavioralism and an embracing of the primacy of material phenomena. Knowledge would rise through experience, and future behavior would be shaped by controlling current physical experience. Thus, to enable flight crews to resist or survive torture in POW camps, the service would torture them now to prepare for the later unpleasant possibility. The logic was both grim and faulty. After all, to "learn" to accept death, one need not be killed.[9] Nor need everyone be raped in order to learn of ways to respond in such extreme conditions. The logic behind the Air Force program failed to distinguish realms in which creative imagination might be a more effective as well as humane mode of learning from those in which actual physical experience proved best.[10]

Since one can hardly presume that all Air Force personnel had rejected in theory all forms of learning other than physical experience, this Air Force program suggests at least that some missions were considered too sensitive to be left merely to searching minds and loyal sentiment. Such a notion, suggesting the dominance of the material world, pointed toward philosophical nihilism. The genealogy of both belief and action was becoming a genealogy of force.

It is striking that by late 1955, 29,000 men would have gone through this program with so little indication (none reported, in fact) of objection. Despite the repetition of Stead's scheduled activities, the staff members appear never to have conceived of them as mere routine. The values to be imparted loomed so large that repeated actions likely assumed the quality of rite rather than rote. For the participants in the Stead program, unfamiliarity and the unknown further strengthened this tendency to see special value in the experience of stress and pain. One senses an authentic acceptance of the program, and in a sense an enjoyment of it. Not only was it something to pull through, something to tough out; it suggested that values were developed in this peculiar crucible. It was, in short, a rite of passage in which pain and suffering were the avenue to distinctive and higher identity. This traditional use of suffering, however, raises relatively few problems of interpretation or understanding. It is the far more arbitrary direction of suffering to a political and military function that requires more sensitive evaluation. For the former hastens acculturation, while the latter aims at specific achievement. Rituals also may be mild or savage, pacific or bellicose. Hence their specific content reveals much in the character of the culture that practices them.

In large part, the Air Force's survival program—even the phase that dealt with the experience of torture—was designed to encourage imagination and ingenuity in evading the worst impact of interrogation, if capture itself could not be avoided. The survival program did encourage wit, although it also made most graphic the physical stress in which that wit would have to be exercised. In covering the story, on the other hand, magazines and newspapers— even when they acknowledged this concern for wit and ingenuity— concentrated on the extreme physical treatment, in this way illustrating the values that they believed were represented by the program. In short, as an indicator of values, the nature of the public attention to the Stead program was even more broadly revealing than the program itself.

Such public sentiment began to gain institutional support. The interest that the Kennedy Administration showed in promoting physical fitness has been widely acknowledged. But the rationale behind that interest has received less attention. It is difficult to ignore the advantages to health and vitality that many have gained from this emphasis, but it is correspondingly easy to note the somewhat self-indulgent quality of the fitness and sporting culture since John Kennedy.

For the leaders of the fitness culture of the Kennedy era, however—including the president himself and his adviser on fitness, "Bud" Wilkinson—physical training and sport were aspects of the Cold War, as well as avenues toward personal fulfillment. Indeed, the promotion of physical education and athletics was couched in a highly Social Darwinist language of competition with possible international rivals, especially the Soviet Union. Increasingly, combative games and sports became the special rites of a Cold War political culture that rested on the premise of struggle and competition. Consistent with this impulse, publicists—such as magazine writers and editors—railed against the alleged "softness" of American youth and became adherents to a cult of toughness. The very word toughness itself, so richly freighted with social implications, soon virtually replaced the more neutral term fitness.

President Kennedy himself addressed the issue in articles for national magazines including "Our Unfit Youth" and "Vigor We Need." In the latter article, published in *Sports Illustrated* in July 1962, Kennedy wrote of colonial and early national history and the stamina of the Americans who carved out the national domain. Then he emphasized that "physical hardihood" enabled Americans to overcome "tenacious foes" in World Wars I and II. Physical fitness was a valuable asset in military action in particular and in international confrontation more broadly. Moreover, he thus sought to place new ritual practices within the sanction of history. Then he associated the improvement of the physical condition of American youth in his presidency with meeting military demands in Europe and in the "jungles of Asia." Physical fitness was the price to pay for guaranteeing peace and the continuation of American civilization and celebrations of physical culture were even more convincingly the components of nationalistic ritual.[11]

The dire implications of Kennedy's articles ran as an *idee fixe* through the pronouncements of appropriate personnel, from

Secretary of Health, Education and Welfare Abraham Ribicoff through special consultant on physical fitness Wilkinson. Wilkinson, in an interview-article in *U.S. News and World Report* in August 1961, had agreed with the magazine staff that the Soviet youth were probably "far, far ahead of us" in physical condition. The reason for concern, at least for the magazine's responsible editors, became clear in the headline warning: "At a time when the world is full of dangers, a number of authorities say American youngsters lack muscle." The title question, quite consistently, asked whether American youth was "too soft" in the perilous world around them.[12]

It is important to attend to the logical leaps in these statements. First, they presume a rather precise correlation between physical condition and what one may fairly call "moral stamina" in a convoluted world conflict. If there is a real causal link, it has hardly been conclusively demonstrated; and so the periodic enthusiasm for such views itself assumes historical consequence. The proposition that muscle equals fitness is equally tenuous; and the reigning bias that fitness is, in fact, toughness is all but impossible to sustain objectively. The reason for this last assertion is simple: fitness describes a medical phenomenon; toughness defines an attitude toward personal and social conduct.

As a group the Kennedy Administration gained a reputation for being fitness-oriented—an impression boosted by coverage of specific measures undertaken to enhance the physical condition of American personnel. Typical was the coverage of Marine Corps Commandant David M. Shoup's effort to reinstate the standards of fitness demanded by President Theodore Roosevelt. Described in *Time* magazine as a "physical fitness bug," Shoup was given photographic space in the article reporting his demand that company grade officers be capable of marching 50 miles within 20 hours, with the last 700 yards at double-time. President Kennedy gave his encouragement to Shoup, who was pegged in a caption as "tough to the Corps."[13]

The choice of such a word as tough, with remarkable frequency in the Kennedy years, was assuredly not conspiratorial. But it reflected a combative attitude toward life that many not connected with the Administration itself also shared.

For example, in June 1962, about the time that John Kennedy was featured in *Sports Illustrated, Saturday Evening Post* heralded an article told to W. Gill by R.M. Marshall entitled "Toughening Our Soft Generation." In touting a Pennsylvania Boy Scout program and railing against "coddling" of the young, Marshall couched his sternest warnings in international terms. Marshall observed that

40% of men called under the military draft between 1948 and 1962 had been declared ineligible, most for physical defects. Inadequate fitness meant military weakness. So, too, he cited reports suggesting that nearly 60% of American children showed failure in tests of physical performance that only 8.7% of European children failed. Americans might well, then, be losing physical supremacy to other peoples. Perhaps most tellingly, Marshall then pointed to the Soviet Union's "trouncing" of Americans in the Summer Olympics of 1956 and 1960. Be it understood that the article made measured recommendations on the whole, and its author evidenced a strong concern to avoid "regimentation." Yet there appears here—in explicitly international terms—a sense of the need to compete for survival and to prepare for the competition by becoming personally tough. Marshall underscores this by referring to rough treatment he received in his own conditioning program before World War I which he regards as an indisputable enhancement of his personal security.[14] It is also suggestive that strength for international conflict was to come from a program in the Boy Scouts, traditionally an agency of passage for young males.

The cult of toughness ranged widely through American culture; and, in the early 1960s, it became something of a fad—associated with the glamor of action and youthful vitality. For all the intrinsic merits of such programs, as Outward Bound then, it is relatively easy to see them as reflections of the "strange enthusiasms" of the Kennedy days. After describing some of Outward Bound's strenuous and exciting mountain-region activities for *Reader's Digest,* author Lydia Lawrence then hastened to associate them with other of the nation's heroic images, saying that the events did not occur at "a Marine training site." Outward Bound's director, Joshua Miner, spoke of the thrill and excitement available to young people who, until then, had lived "in a cult of comfort and safety...." Miner may indeed have had in mind only a cult of confidence and thrill to replace the cult of comfort and safety, yet there remains a probably unintended kinship with many of the drives that motivated Kennedy's statements and policy.

The fusion of toughness and pain (or at least the impression that pain is a part of societal progress) was a significant ancillary aspect of the Kennedy era's cult of toughness; and this sentiment spread widely beyond official Washington. In April 1964, *Life* magazine portrayed a new style of swim training as "All-Out Agony at Indiana U." and prominently featured an Indiana swimmer in his exercises so as to emphasize his "achievement" of agony in isometric contraction. Such effort was justifiable as part of a team effort and also because its method of attainment smacked of current technologies and a bit of pseudo-science. Isometric exercise was rather *chic* and voguish, after all. For a new generation of Americans purportedly willing to "pay any price, bear any burden" for the policies of their nation, swimmer Lary Schulhof served as a photographic example that the road to victory could wind through stages of hurt, pain and agony. A caption for a photograph showing this achievement described it as "Training by Torture."[15] To appreciate the distinctiveness of the characterization of training provided in that article, one may contrast it with a 1939 article concerning a swimming team from Mercersberg, Pennsylvania.[16]

The Mercersberg swimmers showed effort, exertion and determination. But the photographer did not present them in pain, literally agonizing in their training to sweat out the last beads of decadence and softness. Indeed, the coach himself emerged as a warm and decent man, parental and kindly in his attention to his charges. In one photograph, the coach bicycled among the members of the team as they ran, poking them good-humoredly with a pole to encourage the occasional slacker. No one shows much self-consciousness at the coach's actions, and smiles are all but universal. In another scene, the coach gives advice to a swimmer at poolside in a manner that might easily be styled "fatherly." In yet another, the coach personally administers doses of honey to the team. In short, human kindness and consideration closely accompany physical effort. If there is an overriding philosophy in such a training program, it conforms best to *Kraft durch freude,* the achievement of strength and effective performance through the joy—not the pain—of training and competition.

That the Mercersberg swimmers of 1939 had times when, in the casual sense, they were in pain would be difficult to doubt. A photographer with a mind to do so could certainly have found opportunities to catch them in grimaces no less agonizing than those of the Indiana swimmer. What is significant, then, is that the editors, writers and photographers of 1962 did choose those relatively few moments of intense reaction to physical stress and accorded them centrality in their treatment of the training program. Pain was portrayed not as an accident of training but as its very core. Surely swimmer Schulhof experienced stress—whether hurt, pain or agony—in his training exercises. But the article itself has a life of its own. In the portrayal of the less extreme degrees of hurt and pain, for example, Schulhof's facial expression could just as easily have been the grimace of someone having a hard time opening a jar of pickles—it is not a photographic trick, but an act of editorial selection. Not only had Coach Jim Counsilman changed a training program; the magazine staff had redefined the essence of training and identified in it a spirit different from that shown by the Mercersberg team of 1939.

The reassessment of the utility and desirability of pain that appears in the magazine coverage of swim-training was by no means unique. In 1937 *Life* showed its displeasure with professional wrestling in an article headed "Cruel Crowds Demand Mat Torture." The author took the wrestlers' ring antics at face value and deplored the brutality of the performers and the spectators alike. Yet in 1958 *Look* could speak of the "Wrestlers—the New Heroes."[17] Although this article described the rise of wrestling in the schools, its author did not ignore professional wrestling, noting that even its lack of respectability could no longer deter young boys from committing themselves to this tough, combative sport that promised popularity and status as sports heroes. In a day when greater emphasis was being placed on the physical condition and "toughness" of all boys regardless of size and body-type, wrestling's weight-divisions allowed even-handed and more intense competition to all comers. The tone of decrial of 1937 had long since yielded to adulation by 1958. For maturity had as one of its key components the stoic acceptance of the painful effects of violent behavior.

The emphasis had not always been nor need always be on the suffering associated with achievement. For example, *Look*'s 1958 coverage of high school wrestling strongly underscored the supposed ease with which schoolboy wrestlers won admiring fans (and dates) among the females in the student body.[18] Yet popular coverage of the President himself attended periodically to his physical ailments (associated with war injuries) and so all the more emphasized his stoic, Spartan toughness in overcoming the weakness that might putatively have constricted his presidency or even precluded it in the first place.

Yet another article extolled the values of strenuous athletic competitions for boys, even if they included the risks of suffering and injury. The August 18, 1962 issue of *Look* reminded its readers that, even for high school boys, "Football Is Violence"; and so it included the risk of pain and injury, even "an occasional fatality. There were ten last year." But these dangers paled before the advantage that the young athletes were believed to gain in their competition. Risk of pain and suffering, the authors asserted, was often inseparable from life. Hence it was all the more important that football "demonstrates the value of work, sacrifice, courage and perseverance." For the authors, football provided the moral equivalent of on-the-job training, allowing boys to experience the risk and suffering of life while still within the moderating confines of the school system. Photographs accompanying the article included portrayals of young players in pain from injuries sustained in games. The captions emphasize both pain and its value. One injured player, from a team designated the "Knights," is shown as he "grimaces in pain." A photograph that does not show a player suffering an injury nonetheless illustrates that "tackling confronts tackler and runner with the challenge of bodily risks and teaches them to meet it."[19]   The cooperative relationship that players appear to enjoy with their coaches and doctors implies that these painful experiences build ritualized links to the adult world of order, dedication and purpose. Nor is this taken to be a minor benefit. When the authors aver that football develops the characteristics of sacrifice and courage, they cannot resist noting that "these lessons are especially salutary in our modern society with its delinquency problem, lack of discipline and physical softness." At once the writers assert the ability of physical activity to control spiritual vision and reveal their horror of "softness" and decadence.

The values extolled in "Football Is Violence" lingered from an older, more traditionalist America, whose heirs now praised work in a culture that generated proportionately fewer meaningful jobs each year. They praised sacrifice when their own cultural experience became increasingly decadent. They lauded courage in an age at least rhetorically made timid by the "shadow of the Bomb." They called for perseverance from a culture increasingly eager for immediate gratification. In a political sense, such views were conservative; and those who harbored them confounded them with physical and sexual biases as well. Decadence, then, became moral, political and physical so that liberals could best be labelled "panty-waists" and communists could be associated with homosexuals in what their detractors regarded as the liaisons of distastefully appropriate bedfellows, literally and figuratively. The politically perverse must be morally and physically so, and *vice versa*.[20]

When *Look* magazine chose to provide a corrective for the physical deficiences it perceived in American youth, it spotlighted Carmichael, California's La Sierra High School for showing "How America Can Get Physically Tough." The La Sierra program, designed by the school's football coach and physical education director, Stan Le Protti, centered on a system of compulsory exercise for boys which encouraged them to move from group to higher group defined by the level of physical skills demonstrated. Each group had its own emblematic colors, sharpening the adjustment of identity. The article's authors seemed pleased that "A normal or even underdeveloped boy can become a superior physical type." They recorded the opinion of Bud Wilkinson, football coach at the

University of Oklahoma and special adviser to President Kennedy on physical fitness, that the La Sierra program would "help make America's youth as agile and physically tough as any in the world." (*Look*'s words, Wilkinson's opinion.) Reflecting its relatively conservative and utilitarian bias, *Look*'s authors asserted that graduates of Le Protti's programs would more than meet the physical demands of military service. Moreover, since the program included requirements of "neatness, good grooming and citizenship," the authors concluded that it produced not only "physical fitness, but. . . good Americans." By close implication, the authors had associated good grooming with patriotism and toughness with the citizenship appropriate for good Americans. The direction of behavior in matters such as grooming would preclude the emergence of alien political and social views. Physical effort in the "rites of autumn" on the gridiron would produce proper, traditionally American views; and perhaps even carefully orchestrated mass physical training could work to the same end.

In a small way at least, the article's authors hinted that the program worked effectively even over the short term. All nine photographs in the article showed boys in their exercises. The authors recorded that girls accepted the program enthusiastically; they "admired the boys for their achievements and sometimes tried to emulate them in the easier tests." La Sierra's system was envisioned in a man's world, in which strain and striving showed in the faces of the male photographic subjects pictured in the article. The quality of these youth was portrayed specifically in the effort that marked their faces and tensed their muscles. Muscular extension and contraction served both as the sign and the source of the boys' dedication and as the badge of their achievement.[21] Toughness had become the virtue Americans at large required, and La Sierra's youth served as ritual models for its achievement.

When John Kennedy died in 1963 there were many who were available to insure that the political value of the cult of toughness would not come to an abrupt end. Not the least promiment was the President's brother Robert. Writing for *Sports Illustrated*'s July 27, 1964 issue, Robert Kennedy began with as clear a statement of the place of sport and physical education in world affairs that the opinion-makers of the Kennedy era could offer. "Part of a nation's prestige in the cold war," he avowed, "is won in the Olympic Games." So, then, the United States owed it to itself in its international responsibilities to make major improvements in its system of physical culture. Excellence in the international celebration of sport would ratify the renewed aggressiveness of Americans. The advantage Kennedy foresaw for Americans at home was the intensifying of their "inner glow of pride." Abroad there would once again be projected "the picture ... of a young America bursting with enthusiasm."[22] The self-conscious imitation of the days of Teddy Roosevelt carried the Kennedy era "cold warriors" into yet another realm of competition. Physical culture would give Americans the chance to achieve a Social Darwinist *succes de prestige*.

Americans have by no means been unique in being interested in the physical performance of the citizenry. Yet though not unique, Americans have had a deep and special relationship to the material world and to physical experience. Indeed it is difficult to conceive in American culture of an idea existing apart from and independent of physical experience. Formalist and idealist systems have fared none too well among this people. So, then, the nation tends to express its ideas through ritualized actions. In its preparation to meet the challenges of the cold war, then, it is perhaps the more understandable that some in the Kennedy Administration should have equated individual physical "toughness" with the ability of a nation to win its way in international affairs. The fitness, or "toughness," measures that the Administration proposed and that others supported may have offered the individual the benefits of health and conditioning. But they also assumed an important role as cultural rites. For the advocate of "toughness" the appeal of these measures ranged beyond the individual realm to a ritualized social and international confrontation with all that the term means. Personal experience in ritualistic activities accumulated in a ritualized stance of the nation in world affairs.

Notes

[1]There is a large and growing literature on the nature of pain, and no real agreement on what pain is. Mark Zborowski, *People in Pain* (San Francisco: Jossey-Bass, 1969) suggests that the definition of and reaction to pain are culturally conditioned. Also useful is Matisyohu Weisenberg (St. Louis: The C.V. Mosby Co., 1957) which also contains a very helpful bibliography.

The emphasis within Christianity on the concept of sacrifice lent itself to the laification of religious sacrifice into pain for the benefit of team, government or military unit. Pain illustrated that people were committing themselves to a cause, and it signified that they were making progress along the route toward greater fulfillment of their objectives of team effort, military mission or government service. As practiced in America, Christianity could be a religion of resistance as easily as a religion of tolerance and acceptance; and it is the former variant that showed itself as often as the latter.

[2]The best known imputation that American prisoners of war behaved discreditably in Korea and that this was due to inadequate discipline in the U.S. Army and in the American culture is Eugene Kinkead, *In Every War But One* (New York, 1959), released in England in 1960 as *Why They Collaborated*. An impressive rejoinder to Kinkead, arguing that American POWs in Korea performed with considerable merit under extreme and unusual circumstances and under extraordinary and new demands from their superior authority, is Albert D. Biderman, *March to Calumny, The Story of the American POWs in the Korean War* (New York: Macmillan, 1963).

[3]Cartoons referred to in this paragraph typify the attitudes of the period. These used here are reprinted in John T. McCutcheon, Carey Orr, Joseph Parrish and Carl Somdahl, *War Cartoons* (Chicago: Tribune Publishing Co., 1942). The "hothouse plant" of May 3, 1942, is on p. 88.

[4]The muscular Uncle Sam appears, for example, in cartoons for Dec. 11, 1941; Dec. 24, 1941; Jan. 26, 1942. On Dec. 15, 1941, he even wears an "athletic" cut undershirt. Typical of the muscular Americans in the Navy and Army are cartoons of Dec. 10, 1941 and Dec. 11, 1941, respectively.

[5]See McCutcheon et al, *War Cartoons*, 60 (March 12, 1942).

[6]Kinkead, p. 9-10.

[7]Biderman, 12.

[8]Kinkead, 203-204.

[9]The single most striking article concerning the program at Stead AFB is "Is This Brutal and Degrading? Air Force Survival School," *Life,* 39:40-5 (Sept. 19, 1945). Opposing the Air Force's program is "Schools for Sadists? Brainwashing at Fort Stead, Nevada," *Saturday Review* 38:22 (Sept. 24, 1955). Another interesting article supportive of the program is "We Took the Torture Course," an interview with C.E. Buckingham, W.F. Keating and L. Clary, Jr., *U.S. News and World Report,* 39:42-4 (Sept. 23, 1955).

In this paragraph I have used the word "torture" to describe the forms of treatment that were often called simply "stress" by Army and Air Force officials. This departure from the terminology of the military is, I think, in the interests of simple accuracy. Were these same forms of treatment applied to Americans by other nationals, I have little doubt that the military would regard it as torture.

[10]One recalls the officer in Franz Kafka's "In the Penal Colony" who explains that there is no need to tell the condemned man what his sentence is. The machine of execution will print out the sentence, and the process of informing the condemned is simultaneously the process of executing him. "There would be no point in telling him. He'll learn it on his body." Kafka, *The Penal Colony, Stories and Short Pieces,* trans. Willa and Edwin Muir (New York: Shocken Brooks, 1948), p. 197. As the mode of execution in Kafka's story symbolizes a whole approach toward living, so does this Air Force program reflect deeper philosophical suppositions of its practitioners and its subjects.

[11]See John F. Kennedy, "Vigor We Need," *Sports Illustrated,* July 16, 1962, 12-15. Also see Kennedy, "Our Unfit Youth," *Good Housekeeping,* Jan., 1962, 123-5.

[12]See "In a Dangerous World, Is American Youth Too Soft?" interview with C.B. Wilkinson, *U.S. News and World Report,* August 21, 1961.

[13]See "Nip-ups, Anyone? Fitness of White House Staff," *Time*, Feb., 15, 1963, 27. For coverage which maintained a completely humorless, stiff approach toward these measures, see "Physical Fitness on the New Frontier," *U.S. News and World Report,* Feb., 18, 1963, 10.

[14]See "Toughening Our Soft Generation," R.W. Marshall as told to W. Gill, *Saturday Evening Post,* June 23, 1962, 13-17. Note once again the emphatic use of the term "tough."

[15]"All Out Agony at Indiana U." *Life* 56:94-6 (April 10, 1964). Also see articles in *Time* 82:42 (Aug., 23, 1963) and *Sports Illustrated* 20:48 (March 23, 1964).

[16]See *Look*, 1939, for coverage of training at Mercersberg.

[17]See "Cruel Crowds Demand Mat Torture," *Life,* Jan. 25, 1937. Also see "Wrestlers—the New Heroes, *Look,* Feb. 4, 1958, 82-84.

[18]See "Wrestlers—the New Heroes," *Look,* Feb. 4, 1958, 82-84.

[19]"Football is Violence," *Look,* 26:18 (Aug., 28, 1962), 72-8. In certain situations pain is accepted—perhaps even welcomed—as a means through which to achieve heights of stoicism, self-control, and character development. For example, one commentator studied the attitudes of high school coaches (all male) toward pain suffered by their players. One by no means unique response demanded that the player "react as a real man, try to endure what pain there may be and not to be showy about the whole ordeal." Another implied similarities between military character and athletic propriety: "Being an X-service man, I expect my players to behave as my boys in the service——Brave——and not go into any fanfare for the people. It is not the end of the world and time will heal all injured persons."

See Frances P, Noe, "Coaches, Players, and Pain," *International Review of Sport Sociology,* 2(9), 1973, 47-61.

Apocalypse Now:
Viet-Nam as Generative Ritual
William P. Kelly

CRITICAL RESPONSE TO Francis Ford Coppola's *Apocalypse Now* has been remarkably consistent. Virtually all of its reviewers have judged it an incoherent work only partially redeemed by its brilliant passages. Its concluding sequence, which climaxes with the ritualistic slaughter of the renegade Colonel Kurtz (Marlon Brando), has been the object of particular disdain. Intellectually and artistically muddled, the film's denouement, its critics have maintained, defuses Coppola's narrative energies and strands his audience in a morass of bathos and pretension. Coppola's misstep has been most frequently attributed to overbearing ambition. Where *Heart of Darkness*, Coppola's major source for the film, acknowledges the futility of naming the unnamable, *Apocalypse Now* succumbs to the temptation to show, to designate, to fix the horror that Conrad preserves as an ineffable presence. Language as the creation of culture, this argument suggests, is incapable of particularizing the pre-cultural darkness Conrad's and Coppola's narrators confront.

Surely Coppola's conclusion invites these charges of hubris. By eschewing irreducable enigma as the inevitable telos of a journey into darkness, Coppola resists not only the example of Conrad but that of other American artists who have attempted to engage their culture's confrontation with the primitive. The Twain of *Huckleberry Finn*, the Cooper of *The Last of the Mohicans* and the Melville of *Benito Cereno* and *Moby Dick* come immediately to mind, but other precedents ranging from Puritan captivity narratives to Robert Montgomery Bird and to William Faulkner and Robert Frost might as easily be cited. Indeed *Apocalypse Now* is less an attempt to render Coppola's literary sources—most notably *Heart of Darkness, The Waste Land,* and Michael Herr's *Dispatches*—in cinematic terms than it is an effort to efface them.

Certainly too, the film's conclusion is seriously flawed. While Coppola's treatment of Captain Willard's (Martin Sheen) river journey is by no means a model of restraint, every aspect of the film's concluding segment is visually and intellectually extravagant. Coppola's ability to control and to exploit the film's surreal and acid-laced tone prior to Willard's arrival at Kurtz's temple is compromised by a disintegration of narrative progression. When the structuring power inherent in Willard's journey ceases to function, the film's productive counterpoise evaporates. Coppola finds himself in the untenable position of attempting to derive system from a film abandoned to madness. The gore that envelopes Kurtz's temple fails to convey either the horror of the film's earlier carnage or an image of violence released from all restraint. There are simply too many bodies, too many severed heads, too many scattered limbs. Like the temple itself, which is more suggestive of the film's earlier references to Disneyland than of the genesis of civilization, Coppola's corpse-littered field is too obviously a prop. If the external set of the film's conclusion betrays the hand of a designer intoxicated by Hieronymus Bosch, the darkly lit interiors of the sequence suggest the chiaroscuro of Rembrandt and Caravaggio. Coppola intrudes on our suspension of disbelief. We are no longer viewing a film; we are witnessing self-conscious artistry. Nor are Coppola's sets the only examples of this disruptive presence. By pointedly calling our attention to the copies of *The Golden Bough* and *From Ritual to Romance* on Kurtz's desk and by having Brando read from "The Hollow Men," Coppola again asserts his aspirations toward high art and serious intent. Not only do these signals render Coppola vulnerable to charges of pretension, but they violate as well the distance and dislocation which the rest of the film has carefully imposed on its audience. Whether we are offended because Coppola has underestimated our intelligence or are impelled to consciously "read" the film, our capacity for shock and numbed horror has been seriously eroded.

This roster of aesthetic misprision could be considerably extended. The eccentric performances of Brando and of Dennis Hopper as an American photo-journalist fail to distill character from caricature. It seems unlikely, if not ludicrous, that Kurtz's Montagnard guerrilas would interrupt their campaign to enact the ritual sacrifice of a carabao. The dialogue throughout the film's concluding segment is fatuous. Symbols, allusions, and portentious posturings crowd each other off the screen. We are constantly assaulted by what Andrew Sarris has termed "strained seriousness." Coppola's struggle to forge meaning from the chaos of Viet-Nam is well intentioned to be sure, but that effort vitiates the film's initial power.

While Coppola has certainly mismanaged his conclusion, the critical tendency to dismiss the sequence as inorganic is unwarranted. Willard's ritual slaughter of Colonel Kurtz stands at the heart of Coppola's ambition, organizing and extending the argument he advances throughout Willard's journey. Indeed ritual itself is the central concern of *Apocalypse Now*. To dismiss Coppola's climactic treatment of that theme as "muddled," to fail to engage its relation to the artistically more successful river sequences, is to abandon any meaningful explication of the film. That abdication of critical responsibility is particularly unfortunate, because *Apocalypse Now* is an enterprise of some significance. While the film fails to fully realize Coppola's intentions, the nature of his objective and the trajectory of his vision ultimately provide an illuminating perspective on Viet-Nam and its impact on contemporary American culture.

II

Apocalypse Now's interest in ritual is a doubled one. During the course of Willard's river journey, Coppola's efforts are directed toward defining ritual—which he conceives of as the sustaining prop of culture and of identity—as mediated violence. Having unmasked the horror, the darkness at the heart of civilization, Coppola concludes the film by attempting to resuscitate the very mechanisms of catharsis and control which he has dissected and discredited. While he is more successful in realizing the former intention, it is his flawed attempt to reinvoke ritual that defines the intention of the film as a whole and establishes the measure of its ambition.

A recognition of this polarity—and hence of the film's coherence—depends upon an alignment of the ritualized violence of Kurtz's temple with that of the American presence in Viet-Nam. That relationship, as Coppola conceptualizes it, is not one of chronology, of causation, or of analogy, but one of identity. The Montagnard ritual, which initiates the climactic sequence of the film, begins as revel. In a setting dominated by corpses and death, a catalogue of unchecked violence and reciprocal vengeance, Kurtz's tribesmen dance around a fire to the mounting rhythms of their drums. The unanimous and overwhelming malice of the tribe is called forth and then discharged against the sacrificial carabao. By focusing communal violence on a powerless target, catharsis is achieved without the innauguration of an endless cycle of vengeance. Violence intrinsic to the human condition is safely channeled; the tribe is unified against a designated other. The carabao, a domestic animal, at once a part of and separate from the community, is both an appropriate and a non-threatening surrogate for violence that might otherwise be directed against other members of the tribe or against enemies capable of reprisal. It is ultimately inconsequential whether the ceremony is regarded as symbolic, as Sir James Frazer would argue, or as the re-presentation of an actual event which Rene Girard describes as "an original, spontaneous 'lynching' that restored order in a community by reestablishing [social accord] around the figure of a surrogate victim."[1] What *is* crucial is that the ritual sacrifice establishes differentiation, meaning and order through the creation of a symbolic register. By distinguishing between same and different, us and them, corrosive and sanctioned violence, their sacrifice permits the Montagnards to master and channel their aggression. Like language itself, ritual creates signification by establishing unanimously recognized and shared distinctions.

By cross-cutting from the Montagnard ritual to Willard's assassination of Kurtz, Coppola visually establishes the unity of the two events. Kurtz is, for Willard, the other. Like the carabao, he is, as an American officer, an adequate surrogate for Willard's violence; and as a madman, whom Willard has been authorized to "terminate," a non-threatening victim whose death will not provoke progressively escalating vengeance. Willard's capacity for unmediated violence, which has been unleashed by the events of his journey, is, like the malice of the Montagnard revel, focused and safely discharged. The symbolic register, the system of differentiation, which Willard lost in the course of his voyage is reclaimed. By killing Kurtz, he reestablishes his identity and his separation from Kurtz himself and from the unmediated violence he represents. In becoming Kurtz's double, a transformation he undergoes during the course of his journey, Willard abandons the system of signification upon which his identity and his cultural location are predicated. The world he enters is not merely amoral; it is without demarcation of any kind. By sacrificing Kurtz, Willard reorders his universe, redefines the boundary between sanity and madness, and purges the violence he has come to recognize as the irreducible core of his being. For both Willard and the Montagnard tribesmen, the twin rituals at the film's climax initiate history and culture. From an undifferentiated chaos shaped only by a violent will, a symbolic register capable of generating order, culture, and signification is born. Man's determining aggression is acknowledged, evoked, and defused through a cathartic ritual. Identity is defined through the designation and sacrifice of an other.

Far more important, however, than the unity Coppola establishes between his concluding rituals is the identity he structures between these climactic events and the American enterprise in Viet-Nam. By locating the American war against the North Vietnamese within the contexts of racial and economic exploitation, Coppola defines the war not as a violation of American experience but as its most characteristic expression. The preponderance of black soldiers, the constant racial epithets directed against the Vietnamese, and the arrows and spears of Kurtz's army invoke, as a crucial subtext for the film, the long history of American violence directed against racial others. The recurrent targeting of Indians, blacks, and other ideological and cultural minorities is, Coppola suggests, a fundamental mechanism of American life. The Vietnamese War, as Coppola engages it in *Apocalypse Now,* becomes yet another episode in that history. Like the Indian Wars, racial lynchings, and xenophobic eruptions, the Vietnamese conflict discharged the tensions of a heterogeneous culture, beset by domestic and foreign adversaries, against a racially recognizable and fundamentally non-threatening other.

Of equal importance, Coppola's characterization of the American Army as a corporation and his emphasis on the technology it employed establishes the Vietnamese War as the product of industrial capital. The ruthless competition encouraged by that economic system, its dependence on warfare for nourishment, its implicit imperialism, and its substitution of nationalism for private identity require the designation and elimination of a surrogate target to deflect internal discord. In a secular culture bereft of religious and civil rituals, war plays a crucial role in the unification of community and the preservation of order. Like the carabao, and like Kurtz, then, the Vietnamese themselves become surrogate victims sacrificed by a culture to preserve the security of its social organization.

Coppola's intent in *Apocalypse Now,* however, transcends the identification of ritualized violence as the mainspring of American culture. The film's major concern involves a phenomenon which Girard has termed "sacrifical crisis." The function of ritual, Girard maintains, is the re-presentation of a mechanism which has redirected the reciprocal violence of a community toward a recognizable surrogate. When that event, be it the slaughter of an animal, a racial lynching, or a war, loses its power to signify, to purge, and to unify, social order is threatened. The potential for reprisal, for chaos, and for the blurring of shared values, which that crisis engenders, undermines the very existence of culture. A language deprived of syntax, a society which loses faith in its rituals must, Girard argues, recapitulate the experience of Babel.

The Vietnamese War provoked, for Coppola, that sacrifical crisis. Ritual depends for its efficacy on the blurring of its mediations. Once the primal violence which it masks and directs is recognized, it loses its generative power. The dark sources implicit in the extended and victoryless Vietnamese conflict became, Coppola argues, too overt. Rather than unifying American culture, the war bifurcated its citizens. Nightly broadcasts of its napalmed victims blurred the designation of the Vietnamese as the other. The domino theory's failure to arouse cultural insecurity, the ideological ambiguities implicit in America's intervention against the cause of revolution, the injustice suggested by the alignment of American technology against primitive guerrillas, and perhaps most importantly, the failure of the conflict to generate recognizable heroes and villains undermined the war's power to focus and discharge communal violence. Rather than externalizing that energy, the Vietnamese War spawned a cultural implosion. Lyndon Johnson and Jane Fonda, Richard Nixon and the hippies, and not Ho Chi Minh, became the targets of American outrage. Generational, racial and economic conflict, drug-induced fantasies, widespread disaffection, alternative lifestyles, and a loss of faith in civic and economic institutions were its disruptive legacies. Apocalyptic rather than patriotic rhetoric dominated public discourse. Slouching beasts were set loose in the land. Communal violence discharged against a racial other, which had long been a regenerative device in American life, seemed to turn on its source, threatening cultural signification and identity.

It is this disorientation, this failure of cultural syntax, that besets Willard and Kurtz in *Apocalypse Now*. The film begins with Coppola's vivid depiction of the disintegration of Willard's personal coherence. Past and present, dream and reality are obscured as Willard's nightmare of an exploding jungle intrudes on his consciousness. The fan blades in his hotel room become helicopter propellers. He is startled to find himself in Saigon rather than in the jungle. Coppola inverts his image and juxtaposes it to a stone idol's head. The demarcations between civilization and the primitive are blurred; the order which the projector's lense imposes on the cinematic field is violated. Coppola's recording of the Doors' "The End" serves as an aural counterpoint to his disorienting images. The Doors' acid-rock, the nihilism of their lyrics, and the self-destructive posturing they affect associates Willard's trauma with the domestic turmoil of the Vietnam era. In a voice-over narration, Willard describes his divorce and his alienation from "home." "When I was there," the disembodied voice entones, "all I could think of was getting back into the jungle." Assuming the identity of a guerrilla, Willard crouches on the floor. He then drives his fist against a mirror, shattering the coherence of his image. Civilization and jungle, Viet-Nam and home, self and other become one.

The disintegration of signification which this opening sequence details becomes the dominant motif of the first two-thirds of *Apocalypse Now*. Coppola characterizes the Vietnamese War as failed ritual. Its power to unify culture and to channel aggression is undermined by the transparency of its mechanism. The blurring of intention and the discrimination between self and other which secure the generative potency of communal violence become, Coppola argues, progressively more untenable in Viet-Nam. The ideological sanctions which mask episodes of communal assaults on surrogate targets here unravel. Coppola conceptualizes the relation between intrinsic violence and its cultural mediations not as one of base and superstructure but as one of competing texts. With the decline of its repressive capacity, the war's power to define private aggression as cultural imperative—and hence its ability to unify and to create signification—evaporates.

III

After Willard's assault on the mirror, messengers arrive to take him to Intelligence Headquarters where he is to receive an assignment. There he learns that he is to assassinate a renegade colonel, who, with his Montagnard army, is conducting an unsanctioned campaign. The Headquarters compound is a model of order and civility. Mounted trophies adorn the walls; luncheon is elegantly served; the commanding general's (G.D. Spradlin) tone is cultivated and reserved. Colonel Kurtz's "methods," he tells Willard, have become "unsound." He had been "a brilliant officer," a "humanitarian," but now he operates "without any decent restraint." When the general orders Willard to "terminate Kurtz's command," his manner is paternal. His posture is that of a deeply concerned therapist and not that of a superior officer authorizing an execution. This discrepancy between form and content, between the civility of "terminate" and the reality of "murder" is further advanced by Willard's refusal to acknowledge his CIA activities when he is interrogated by the general's aide (Harrison Ford). In full possession of the facts of Willard's career, the aide asks him to confirm the unquestionable accuracy of his dossier. Willard, however, conforms to CIA convention and disavows all knowledge of his activity. There is no question of preserving security. The aide is aware of the details of Willard's secret operations; Willard knows that he possesses the facts of the case. The two men play a game, the rules of which require Willard not only to become a murderer but also to profess ignorance of his actions even to the men who have ordered them. The object of Coppola's attention here is not hypocrisy but disintegration. The burden of the Headquarters compound is to preserve an illusion of system and control. The general's manner, the accoutrements of his command, and his concern for "Walt" Kurtz signify an enlightened vision that sincerely regrets the necessity of war and bloodshed. He must distinguish between Kurtz and himself, between the madness of Kurtz's Cambodian campaign and the clarity of the larger American enterprise in Viet-Nam. The absurdity of that effort is apparent to Coppola's post-war, post-watergate audience. Coppola is not, as some of his critics have argued, belaboring the obvious by discrediting American policy in Viet-Nam. Rather, he is demonstrating the deterioration of the mechanisms which disguise the sources of communal violence. The paternal rationalism of Intelligence Headquarters no longer masks the aggression it seeks to mediate; base and superstructure are co-extensive. The semiotics of the Headquarters compound fail to convey the desired messages of order and control. The arbitrary character of that sign system gives way and bespeaks what it is intended to hide.

This unravelling of signification and cultural mediation is not lost on Willard. The figure in the general's carpet is all to clear. As he leaves the compound to begin a mission he is told "will never exist," he recalls other terminations he has effected. "But this time it was an American and an officer," Willard's voice-over remarks, "that wasn't supposed to make a difference to me, but it did...charging a man with murder here was like giving out speeding tickets at the Indianapolis 500." The distinctions between self and other, murder and duty, which have already been blurred for Willard, are further undermined. His target is no longer a racial other but a fellow American. It is, of course, crucial for the army and for Willard himself to classify Kurtz as an other, because like Willard's mirror, Kurtz presents a too threatening image of self. The destructive impulses which have been projected against racial others throughout the nation's history are here, of necessity, focused on Kurtz.

This sense of sacrificial crisis, of the unravelling of cultural signification, mounts as Willard embarks on his mission. The crew of the naval patrol boat that is to transport Willard to Kurtz's camp attempt unsuccessfully to preserve cultural demarcations in the jungle. Lance (Sam Bottoms), a surfer from California, water skis behind the patrol boat, while Clean (Larry Fishburne), a refugee from the South Bronx, dances on deck to the Rolling Stones. Chief (Albert Hall), the boat's middle-aged black captain, tries to impose discipline in the midst of chaos. Chef (Frederic Forrest), a New Orleans *saucier,* ventures into the jungle in search of mangoes for his recipes. They vigorously attempt to blind themselves to their location and to the nature of their task by invoking the symbolic register of home. The futility of that effort becomes manifest when their speeding boat swamps the primitive skiff of some local fishermen. Although that incident is in itself a minor one, it is indicative of an intrusive disjunction between signifier and signified. While they themselves are not initially aware of the bankruptcy of their defensive strategies, Willard immediately recognizes the crew as "rock and rollers with one foot in the grave." Throughout the journey section of the film, Willard provides this clarifying perspective on the madness of Viet-Nam, a role Coppola underscores by continually cutting from the central activity of his scenes to a shot of an isolated Willard. The vision of America that perspective offers is one of a culture whose sustaining rituals are eroding; whose ceremonies of purgation are in eclipse.

That state of crisis is particularly apparent in the initial sequence of Willard's journey. The patrol boat has linked up with an air cavalry troop under the command of Lieutenant Colonel Kilgore (Robert Duvall). Kilgore makes a conscientious effort to identify his unit with its military forebearers, the horse cavalry of the American west. He wears a peaked cavalry hat and a yellow foulard and adopts the pose of a Custer or a Sheridan. Within this formulation, of course, the Vietnamese become the Indian tribes that stood in the way of westward expansion. Kilgore has a cavalry officer's contempt for these primitives and terms them "gooks," "dinks," and "slopes." Nor is his wild west affectation the only system of signification he employs to locate himself in the jungles of Viet-Nam. He is addicted to surfing, and at every opportunity, unstraps his board from his gunship and takes to the waves with his "boys." When one of his soldiers dismisses a beach with particularly promising surf because it is a Viet Cong stronghold, Kilgore bellows "Charlie don't surf," and orders an attack. This reduction of the world into cavalry and Indians, surfers and non-surfers maintains the discrimination between self and other, same and different that is the source of signification. But like the futile efforts of Willard's crew, Kilgore's struggle to naturalize his aggression through the invocation of a comforting symbolic register is self-deluding. When he gathers his troops for a post-battle beach party complete with steaks, beer, and bonfire, Willard sadly observes that "the more they tried to make it like home, the more they missed it."

Again Coppola's intentions are quite clear. Kilgore's system of signification and the world view it generates are at odds with the reality that surrounds him. Signifier and signified have become disjunctive. The conception of his troops as heroes who ride to the rescue, as preservers of culture against the onslaught of the savage, which Kilgore's cavalry trappings suggest, is undermined by Coppola's depiction of the overkill they unleash against the Vietnamese. While Kilgore's targets are indeed "the enemy," they are largely women and children whose means of defense are limited. Coppola recurrently cross-cuts from the high technology weaponry of the air cav to shots of junks, carts and primitive bridges. The initial scene of the sequence in which Kilgore's troops are mopping up after a victory is particularly harrowing. Kilgore walks among the dead and dying, leaving playing cards on the corpses to identify them as his victims. That gesture suggests that the war is a contest between Kilgore and an equal but absent force who will read the message Kilgore's "death cards" leave behind. The effect of that strategy is to distance the immediate devastation of Kilgore's attack (many of the dead are children) and to posit a real enemy whose power requires the exercise of the air cav's overwhelming force. Indiscriminate slaughter, then, is both defined as necessary and proper and is naturalized within the heroic context of the old west. The sacrifice of the mass is offered in the corpse-strewn field, while a bullhorn announces that "we have come to extend a welcome hand." The respective ideologies of religious rite and poltical statement, are, of course, disjunctive with the carnage that Coppola depicts, and like Kilgore's death cards, suggest a futile attempt to subsume violence under a system of comforting signification.

It is an error to assume that the argument Coppola constructs in this sequence is limited in its scope to an indictment of American policy in South East Asia. By aligning Kilgore's mad aggression with the cavalry and the Indian Wars, Coppola invokes a more far-reaching concern. Certainly the cavalry's assault on the western tribes was no less unjustified and indiscriminate than Kilgore's attacks on Vietnamese hamlets. As a cathartic ritual, however, that war was far more effective. The plains wars of post-Civil War America unified a divided nation and redirected the corrosive internal violence of that catastrophic conflict against the Indians. The communal sacrifice of a racial other helped to restore equilibrium, direction, and signification to a cultural fabric that had been badly frayed. The Indian wars succeeded as ritual where Viet-Nam failed, because their mechanism remained blurred. Cavalry massacres were mediated through correspondents' reports which preserved the dislocation necessary for the successful enactment of ritual. Through distance and time, heroes could be created, signification safely assigned. In Viet-Nam, however, the presence of film crews and television journalists foreclosed that possibility. Coppola makes this point, not only by cross-cutting to Willard, an outsider whose faith in ideological mediations has been lost, but more importantly by filming himself as a journalist filming Kilgore's attack. Coppola argues that, like Willard, we were privy to the disorienting evidence of Viet-Nam. As a result, not only did the war fail to serve the purgative functions of a generative ritual, but it also exposed the mechanisms of cultural signification to the light of consciousness. The war became, then, divisive in and of itself, and at the same time, threatened, by analogy, the integrity of America's historiographic vision. The signification traditionally assigned to racial violence, to the male bonding invoked by Kilgore's beach party, and to the power of technology was disrupted in a manner profoundly threatening to cultural assumptions and social order. When Kilgore rather mournfully tells Willard that "some day this war will end," the film's implications are clear. The discharging of aggression which warfare authorizes is essential not only for the preservation of Kilgore's identity, but for that of the culture he represents as well. The technology he employs so lovingly, the male bonding he promotes, and his need for both victory and surrogate targets are determining hallmarks of American culture. Coppola refuses to permit us to dismiss Viet-Nam as an aberration but forces us to confront it as a symptom of social disease.

As Willard and the crew of the patrol boat proceed toward Cambodia and Kurtz, each of their encounters invokes a similar vision of unravelling syntax. Signifier and signified collide to suggest the arbitrary character of meaning. When Chef and Willard leave the boat to search for mangoes in the jungle, they meet a tiger and barely escape with their lives. Chef's conception of the wilderness as a tranquil larder, a notion supported by the lush cinematography of this scene, is rudely assaulted. "Never, goddamn never, leave the boat," is the lesson Chef derives from this experience, but Coppola's point is more broadly based. Never, goddamn never, he argues, confront the beasts that lurk in the jungles masked by our language, our assumptions, and our categories of perception. Therein lies chaos.

The USO show that the crew stops to see at Hau Phat strengthens that paradigm. Playboy bunnies, the icons of sexual fantasy, appear on a stage ringed by illuminated phallic shells. As the bunnies mime intercourse with M-16's, the symbolic register decays and soldiers intent on actualizing their fantasies rush the stage. The system of signification which this theatrical event embodies deteriorates; unlicensed sexuality is unleashed. Just as Kilgore's cavalry affectations erode when they are juxtaposed with the reality they purport to represent, the power of the centerfold to displace desire disintegrates when it confronts the violent passion it seeks to organize. Comforting symbols collide with disruptive realities to call an entire system of signification into question.

Willard, who stands apart at the USO show, demonstrates the fully emerged clarity of his vision in the following scene. Chief orders a sampan to stop and submit to a routine search for contraband. During that inspection, Clean panics and fires into the sampan killing everyone on board except a young girl who is badly wounded. When Chief tells Willard that they must evacuate her to an aide station Willard coldly shoots the girl. "It's a way we had of living over here," he offers by way of justification, "we cut them in half and then give them a Band-Aid. It was a lie." Any uncertainty that may have troubled Willard has evaporated. He will participate in the army's violence but not in its lies. The real dilemma Coppola confronts is now apparent. Willard recognizes the army's humanitarian and ideological mediations as the shams that they are. But in embracing the violence that they unsuccessfully mask, he becomes, like Kurtz, a monster driven only by the dictates of an aggressive will. His options are untenable. He may blind himself to the repressed realities of mediating rituals or alternatively abandon civilization itself. Both paths lead inexorably to madness.

In the bridge at Do Lung sequence, perhaps the most visually striking episode of the film, Coppola extends his consideration of this destructive paradox. Do Lung, the final outpost of the American army is under constant assault by the Viet Cong. The bridge there is rebuilt during the day and destroyed by enemy mortars at night. The chain of command that sustains military order has been disrupted. Soldiers hurl themselves from the river banks and attempt to claw their way aboard the patrol boat. Willard's efforts to locate the commanding officer are fruitless. When he asks a black soldier, who wears a necklace of bones around his neck, whether he knows who is in command, the soldier freezes him with his glance and answers only "Yeah." Clearly no one is in command at Do Lung. Civilization has collapsed, leaving only the law of survival in tact. The precarious bridge the men daily erect as a symbol of military control is reduced to rubble by the unseen forces of the jungle. The nightmare landscape of Coppola's set serves as an organizing metaphor for his consideration of sacrificial crisis. Rather than enacting a generative ritual, the Vietnamese War, as Coppola engages it in *Apocalypse Now,* exposes the very mechanisms which give that ritual its power. The discriminations between sustaining order and corrosive violence, between sign and signifier, are violated. Base effaces superstructure. Chief begs Willard to turn back, to shield his eyes from the horror of Do Lung, to abandon his pursuit of Kurtz. But for Willard there is no choice. "Part of me was afraid of what I'd find there," he says, "but much stronger was the desire to confront him."

In the final scene prior to Willard's arrival at Kurtz's camp, the patrol boat comes under attack from the bows and arrows of the Montagnards. Initially the men believe that the tribesmen are only trying to frighten them, but then Chief is felled by a spear. Before he dies, he looks at his wound, says "a spear," and attempts to strangle Willard. At this moment, Chief confronts the darkness that has blighted Willard's vision. The demarcation between self and other that has sustained Chief finally disintegrates. He recognizes the unity between himself, the descendent of slaves, and the spear-wielding Montagnards. The dynamics of American violence become clear. The bankrupt ritual in which he participates is unmasked, and he strikes against Willard as an emblem of his true racial other. When Lance, who by this point in the film has become addled on acid and violence, lovingly buries Chief in the river, the entire ambivalent history of race relations in America—the territory Leslie Fiedler has so carefully charted— is evoked. Natty and

Chingachgook, Huck and Jim, Ishmael and Queequeg come to mind as Lance kisses Chief's forehead before letting him slip below the water. The unity shared by these outcast characters is here even more clearly the subject of fantasy and futile longing. Chief is dead; Lance is irretrievably damaged.

IV

Willard finally arrives at his destination and confronts the unmediated violence of Kurtz and his army. The bloated figure of Marlon Brando is an appropriate representation of the horror he must engage. Kurtz is a grotesque extension of the character Willard has become. Like Willard, Kurtz has recognized the disjunction between rhetoric and reality in Viet-Nam. The mechanism of ritual violence are clear to him; he has dismissed these mediations as "lying morality" and embraced the hidden text of the war. He pursues his purposes without Band-Aids, pacification programs, or cavalry uniforms. He regards justice and law as fictive structures which organize and mask primal violence. "You have the right to kill me," he tells Willard, "but no right to judge me." Free from the "lying morality" of culture, Kurtz wallows in indiscriminate violence. His temple is a tableaux of a world released from the mediations of culture.

Willard's confrontation with Kurtz does not generate new insight or dispell illusion. His experiences on the river have prepared him to embrace the inescapable horror of Kurtz's doctrine. Unable to refute the logic of Kurtz's vision, Willard is faced with the temptation of joining Kurtz as the first assassin dispatched to kill him has done. There is no longer any official imperative to complete his mission. "They would make me a major for this [the assassination of Kurtz]," Willard says, "but I wasn't even in their fucking army any more." If he is to resist the logic of joining Kurtz, he must do so on individual and ultimately irrational grounds.

Willard kills Kurtz not because it is his duty or because he disputes the accuracy of Kurtz's world view, but because he realizes that it is expedient that this man die. Kurtz's logic is flawless, but it is ultimately destructive. Kurtz himself recognizes this truth and cooperates in his execution. Willard's sanity, his faith in ritual and culture, is not entirely restored, he leaves Kurtz's camp a blasted man who can only repeat Kurtz's invocation, "the horror, the horror," but he does leave. Having seen Medusa, he returns like Ishmael or the messengers of Job to tell his tale.

Having unmasked the mechanisms of culture to reveal the violence that supports them, Coppola concludes his film by reenacting a redemptive ritual. Willard saves himself by forging signification in a context that denies its possibility. Kurtz, whom he recognizes as a version of self, is defined as other. As surrogate victim, he becomes a conduit that bears away the force of Willard's violence. Coppola is not suggesting that Willard has rediscovered a transcendent moral order that mandates the execution of Kurtz. Rather he argues that Willard recognizes the necessity of distributing speeding tickets at the Indianapolis 500. It is not justice that he seeks in killing Kurtz but order. The discriminations he makes between Kurtz and himself, between his assassinations and Kurtz's murders and between system and chaos are clearly fictions, but they are necessary lies. He is not blind to his duplicity, but he embraces it nonetheless.

The ambition of this denouement is striking, for *Apocalypse Now* replicates on a larger scale Willard's ritual murder of Kurtz. Coppola's objective, as he describes it in his program notes, is the purgation of the cultural malaise engendered by Viet-Nam. By laying open a festering wound, he attempts to promote healing. He acknowledges the source of that affliction by recapitulating the sacrificial crisis the Vietnamese conflict provoked, and then through the generative violence of his concluding sequence, he argues for the necessary resuscitation of culture and its rituals. That enterprise is, of course, not an original one. His intention is anticipated in the works of the major figures of modernism, and like those writers, Coppola ultimately fails to fully achieve his ends. Culture can not create ritual. Its mediations, once revealed, are beyond repair. The restoration of faith is finally inaccessible to the power of reason and conscious artistry.

More significant, however, than Coppola's failure to realize his intentions in *Apocalypse Now* is that unlike Pound, Yeats, or Eliot, Coppola works in a popular medium. If, as Richard Slotkin has argued, "the myth of regeneration through violence is the structuring metaphor of the American experience," the debunking of that paradigm in a film intended for a mass market is a troubling harbinger indeed.[2] Coppola does not, however, merely exploit the currency of this crisis of faith. In *Apocalypse Now* he attempts to respond to and to redress that cultural scepticism. Coppola's faith in the social power of art is in itself encouraging in this era of private vision and escapist discourse.

Notes

[1] Sir James Frazer, *The Golden Bough* (New York: Macmillan, 1963); Rene Girard, *Violence and the Sacred* (Baltimore: Johns Hopkins, 1977), p.95.

[2] Richard Slotkin, *Regeneration through Violence* (Middletown: Wesleyan, 1973), p.5.

Myth, Ritual and the Comic Strip G-Man

Richard Gid Powers

ATTEMPTS TO UNLOCK the secret of political success cannot neglect the mythic and ritualistic aspects of politics: politics as psychodrama, the expression of cultural needs and their symbolic satisfaction on a grand scale; the political leader as actor in the ritualized role of mythological hero. No episode better illustrates this phenomenon of mythology and its sustaining ritual coming to the aid of a political career than the story of J. Edgar Hoover and the F.B.I. A prime example of this was his foray into the mythopoeic world of the comics, an officially-sponsored strip in 1936 called *War on Crime.*

If the comics are any indication, American popular culture's mood during the thirties was made for mythology, its thirst was for ritual. By the end of the twenties comic strips were no longer merely "the funnies." As early as 1924 *Little Orphan Annie* had carried melodrama into the comic strips. In 1929 Hank Foster's *Tarzan* and Philip Nowlan and Dick Calkin's *Buck Rogers* borrowed two characters from the adventure pulps and turned the comics into a vehicle by which the public could identify with heroic characters in epic adventures. Once they had broken with realism, adventure comic strips began to add other elements of mythology and ritual to their stories while they discarded the fetters of probability and possibility. As heroes sailed through outer space and swung from jungle vines, they became projections of their readers' fantasy selves, selves freed from the bonds of cowardice, stupidity, weakness and, worst of all, childhood.

Since the paramount function of myth is, adopting Richard Slotkin's formulation, "to reconcile and unite... individualities to a collective identity,"[1] and ritual is the mechanism for perpetuating

206

this reconciliation it hardly needs to be pointed out that depression America, its economy in collapse and its leadership in paralysis, needed the reassurance offered by mythology and ritual. What is worth noting is how pulp and comic strip writers of the thirties seized on one variation of the heroic archetype as *the* adventure formula of the decade. This was the action detective story.

In *Regeneration Through Violence* Slotkin describes how Americans turned the archetype of the struggle between Themis (rational authority) and Moira (the primitive urges of the unconscious) into the national myth of the Indian hunter.[2] This collective American dream perceives society as a struggle between the lawless and the lawful. This makes the climax in almost all American mythic adventures a showdown between a hero of the law (sheriff, detective or cop) and a symbol of rebellion against society, be it the public enemy or the outlaw.[3]

Unlike the detective hero of the mystery story, the action hero is essentially a man of action, not intellect. In the mystery formula the climax comes when the villain is unmasked. In the action story the villain's identity is usually known from the start. Its resolution requires full poetic justice: the villain has to be punished as befits the evil he symbolizes, preferably by death though for reasons of decorum a conventionalized right to the jaw often has to suffice.[4] With Chester Gould's *Dick Tracy* (1931), the action detective emerged as a major factor in the comic strips. Soon the comics were full of private eyes, plainclothesmen and cops, all pitted against monstrous emblems of criminal anarchy.

J. Edgar Hoover loved these comic strips. He said they were "highly important influences in creating a public distaste for crime," and it was said he derived "a keen inward satisfaction from seeing their flinty-jawed heroes prevail over evil."[5] One of his favorite strips was *Dick Tracy*. Another was *Secret Agent X-9*. Early in 1936, however, he began to notice something in *X-9* that he didn't like and decided to stop. Slowly but surely X-9 was turning into a G-Man, a special agent of the F.B.I.

To see why this bothered Hoover it is necessary to know two things: the first is the impact that American popular culture had had on Hoover's career up to that point. The second is the fundamental differences between popular culture's image of the G-Man and Hoover's own.

In 1936 J. Edgar Hoover was probably more famous, more highly acclaimed, than any other man in Washington save Roosevelt himself. He was a star, and popular culture had made him that star.

Chronology tells the story. When Roosevelt came into office in

1933 Hoover's outfit, then called the "Bureau of Investigation," was unknown to the general public and to most government officials. It had been out of the news ever since Hoover took command of the tiny scandal-ridden unit in 1924.[6]

In 1933, when Homer Cummings became Attorney General, the American public was convinced the nation was in the grip of a major crime emergency. Crime statistics, then in rudimentary form, would later reveal that there *was* no crime wave, that crime levels had been declining since about 1919 and would continue to decline until 1940.[7] Nevertheless, failure to solve the Lindbergh kidnapping of 1932 and the brazen activities of a few highly-publicized Prohibition era gangsters convinced the public that law enforcement had broken down.

Herbert Hoover's response to demands for federal action against crime was to remind the public that the constitution made crime a local responsibility, so solutions ought to be sought on the local level. Roosevelt's New Deal was, as much as anything else, the result of the realization that the new national communications media had "nationalized" public opinion, so that once the public had decided that a problem was national in scope the federal government would have to "do something" about it or risk losing its leadership image and its moral authority.[8]

In this case "something" was a federal war on crime. Homer Cummings selected certain cases, notably the so-called Kansas City Massacre of June 17, 1933, and dramatized them as the underworld's "declaration of war" against organized society. He named Assistant Attorney General Joseph Keenan as his field lieutenant, re-named Hoover's agency the "Division of Investigation" (calling it his "super-police force") and acquired the military prison at Alcatraz as the "super-prison" for the super-crooks he was planning to round up.

The public's response to all this hoopla was ecstatic and the Department of Justice became the nation's hottest beat during 1933 and 1934. When Cummings proclaimed the manhunt for John Dillinger during the summer of 1934 to be the ultimate test of strength between crime and the law, the nation participated in it (by way of the press) as a national blood ritual, and when Dillinger was shot editorialists across the nation hailed Cummings and his men as the country's saviors. By the end of 1934 Homer Cummings was a national hero, a man who had managed to satisfy a vital cultural need in depression America. As Hugh Dalziel Duncan observed in *Symbols in Society,*

when there is no community drama of social order, with a struggle between a hero and a villain who personify good and bad principles of order, then chaos . . . results. The emotional counterpart in the individual of chaos in society is the kind of deep anxiety which passes into "formless dread."[9]

In mythological terms Cummings had given the culture villains, he had given it a struggle between good and evil and he had given it a hero of order—himself. The adulation Cummings was receiving at the end of 1934 was the public's way of saying "thank you" for rescuing it from Duncan's "formless dread."

Because of what was going to happen in 1935 it is important to emphasize that it was Cummings, not J. Edgar Hoover, that the public regarded as the leader of the government's triumphant anticrime crusade. During the course of the cases that would be the basis of Hoover's reputation and the myth of the F.B.I., the newspapers invariably referred to the special agents of the Division of Investigation as "Department of Justice" agents (Cummings' men), and reporters went to Cummings, not Hoover, for press releases about the cases. For example, when special agents shot Baby Face Nelson, it was Cummings who called reporters into his office and sputtered "We got him!"[10] When Dillinger was killed it was Cummings who got the reflected glory of being the boss of Melvin Purvis, "the man who got Dillinger." So closely was Purvis associated with Cummings in the public mind that newspapers sometimes mis-identified Purvis as the "head" of the Division of Investigation. (How that must have riled Hoover!) The most conclusive proof of Cummings' pre-eminent position in the law enforcement community was the "Attorney General's Conference on Crime" that he hosted in Washington in December, 1934, a gala convocation of the country's cops that all but canonized Cummings as the leader and guiding spirit of a national law enforcement movement.

At the very moment Cummings was savoring his new role as the nation's symbol of the law, however, Warner Brothers was putting together a movie that would shove him out of the law enforcement picture, installing in the Attorney General's place the director of the by-now-once-again-renamed Federal Bureau of Investigation. The movie was *G-Men,* starring James Cagney, which Warner Brothers billed as the "documentary history" of the just-concluded federal war on crime.[11]

G-Men took the most notable cases of 1933-34, with special reference to the Kansas City Massacre and the Dillinger manhunt and wove them into a plot that had Cagney join the Bureau to avenge the death of a friend murdered by gangsters. The picture capitalized on the public's interest in everything having to do with federal agents by putting Cagney through the course of training for special agents before turning him loose on his enemies, a job complicated by the mob's taking his girlfriend as a hostage.

All this was, as we shall see, straight action detective formula stuff, highly ritualized for impact. The political impact of the film lay in the way it handled the relationship between the F.B.I. and the rest of the government.

It had been Attorney General Cummings who, with Roosevelt's backing, had planned, led and symbolized the federal war on crime. That was not how *G-Men* told the story. In the movie version it is F.B.I. Director Gregory who appeals to Congress to

make it a federal crime to kill a Governmental Agent.... Arm Governmental agents... and not just with revolvers! If these gangsters want to use machine guns—give the Special Agents machine guns... shotguns... tear gas and everything else! This is war!

From the committee room the scene shifts to a joint session of Congress, and then to a series of newspaper dissolves: "GOVERNMENT DECLARES WAR ON CRIME...CONGRESS RUSHES THROUGH NEW CRIME LAWS...DEPARTMENT OF JUSTICE STARTS DRIVE."[12]

As he watched this scene Homer Cummings must have felt control of the F.B.I. slipping from his grasp. The movie had taken the very words *he* had spoken to Congress and put them in the mouth of another man. Cummings knew too much about public opinion and its manipulation—he had done almost nothing else for two years—not to realize the significance of this deft substitution of F.B.I. Director for Attorney General. Whether the movie was cause or effect—and in popular culture the two are impossible to separate—a momentous shift had taken place in the public's image of the F.B.I. In *G-Men* the F.B.I. was no longer what it had been just a few short months earlier, a conventional government agency in the normal chain of command, a bureau that carried out the orders of constitutional superiors. The movie G-Men and their director got their mandate, not from the President, not from the Attorney General, but from the nation itself represented by a joint session of congress. In short, popular culture had begun to create an image of Hoover as an autonomous symbol of the law, in command of a band of heroes responsible not to governmental authority but to the people, the popular culture audience. And that was the popular culture-created image that Hoover was enjoying in 1936 when he decided that someone was going to have to teach Secret Agent X-9 a lesson.

X-9 began in 1934 as the Hearst chain's answer to the Daily News Syndicate's *Dick Tracy*, but in the early going the strip suffered because the hero lacked a strong identity and a distinctive crime fighting style. Alex Raymond and Dashiell Hammett created the strip, but never made it clear who X-9 was secret-agenting for. He started as a millionaire playboy who moonlighted as a sort of free-lance avenger *a la* Lamont Cranston or (later) Bruce Wayne. He even had the traditional oriental valet.

Raymond and Hammett abandoned the strip in 1935. The artwork was then taken over by Charles Flanders, the writing first by Leslie Charteris (famous for *the Saint)* and then by Robert Storm. Under Storm's direction X-9 began to display unexpected expertise with the microscope and the fingerprint powder. Even more unexpectedly, it turned out that he had a boss back in Washington he reported to. Early in 1936 he got rid of the valet, pinned on his badge, stuffed some ID in his wallet. The comic strips had their first G-Man, and the F.B.I. had an angry Director.[13]

Secret Agent X-9 was a well-plotted, dramatically-drawn strip with plenty of Hoover's beloved scientific detection and hardly any rough stuff. The F.B.I. got nothing but respectful, even worshipful, treatment, and there were regular flashbacks to Washington where Hoover himself made stately appearances in the crime labs. So where was the problem?

The problem was that in the image of the F.B.I. Hoover was promoting, the individual G-Man was supposed to be a loyal, obedient, faceless cog in the F.B.I. machine. *Secret Agent X-9's* G-Man was cut from the same mold as the popular culture heroes in all action detective formula adventures. He had a personality distinctive enough to distinguish him from the other heroes competing for the audience's attention, and he had all the other characteristic traits of popular hero: he was strong, smart, dominating and, as befitted an *American* popular hero, he was self-reliant and self-directed.

More than just a little ego was involved in Hoover's hostility toward G-Men who made names for themselves. (He drove Purvis out of the Bureau after he became famous, and he criticized Cagney's G-Man for being an "Individual.") Hoover's strategy for leading a transformation of American law enforcement depended on the public's seeing the F.B.I. *idea* as the hero of every G-Man adventure. If the country began to give credit for the Bureau's success to the heroics of individual G-Men, then Hoover's carefully crafted Bureau, his finely-honed law enforcement program, Hoover himself—all became irrelevant.[14] To convert popular culture to F.B.I. orthodoxy Hoover was going to have to launch his own comic strip G-Man, with his own ritual.

What ensued would merely be a footnote in the history of

popular culture and a comic interlude in the F.B.I. story if it did not have a bearing on one of the most important questions in the study of the political significance of popular culture. Is the popular image of politics merely a reflection of the political process, or does popular involvement with politics grow out of the political process' resemblance to the patterns and rituals of popular mythology? Does the politician become a popular hero because of what he does, or because the popular audience interprets his actions as the "fulfillment" of popular myths? Did Hoover and the F.B.I. become heroes because "They did the job; they got the Machine Gun Kellys and the John Dillingers," as an assistant director told me,[15] or did the public idolize them because their exploits conformed to the pattern of the popular action detective formula?

If Hoover's success was independent of popular mythology he should have been able to tailor the popular culture G-Man to reflect accurately the real F.B.I. If, on the other hand, he actually owed his success to popular mythology, then he could retain his popularity only if his image continued to fit the expectations of the popular culture. Now let us see what happened.

On May 16, 1936, Hoover's comic strip, *War on Crime,* opened in forty-five papers across the country.[16] Hoover had put together the whole package. He had gotten an artist, Kemp Starrett, an editor, Doug Borgstedt, and a writer, his closest friend in the Washington press corps, Rex Collier of the *Washington Star,* and he had arranged for the *Ledger Syndicate* of Philadelphia to carry the strip.

Hoover involved himself and the Bureau massively in promoting the strip, and the theme of the ballyhoo was that this was a TRUE history of the gangster wars, one that rejected any trace of melodrama or sensationalism and clung tightly to the facts. Every day's episode carried an affidavit of authenticity: "True Stories of G-Men Activities Based on Records of the Federal Bureau of Investigation—Modified in the Public Interest," and advertisements for the comic played up the contrast between *War on Crime's* historical accuracy and the improbabilities of the formula-ridden competition:

Daily millions of readers are following fictitious thrillers and dime novel desperadoes in their wild comic-strip adventures! Imagine, then, how this great public audience will welcome and support a strip whose characters are actual people, whose heroes are real G-Men, and whose villains are John Dillinger, Machine Gun Kelly, and Baby Face Nelson.

REAL G—MEN VERSUS REAL GANGSTERS, not lurid tales of fictitious underworld, but actual case histories showing the actual people involved...FACTS—NOT FICTION!

So here was Hoover's chance to make the F.B.I. story mean what he thought it meant, to tell it in his own words, to shape it according to his own ideas. And what was the result? What format did Rex Collier (with Hoover's express approval) adopt in *War on Crime?*

From the first episode to the last (which was not too long a span of time—the strip died before the end of 1936), *War on Crime* adapted itself to the demands of popular mythology. Every episode conformed to one of the demands of the action detective formula, but with one fatal deviation. And that one omission was, as we shall see, enough to do the comic in.

The most graphic example of how *War on Crime* obeyed the conventions of the comic strip action detective formula was the opening episode that introduced the strip during the first two weeks. As a rule every new comic book hero is identified in an episode known as the "origin story." This seeks to explain how the hero acquired his extraordinary powers, and why he dedicated himself to the welfare of others instead of simply enjoying being the strongest, bravest, smartest and best-looking man in the world.

Batman's origin story, for example, describes the murder of Bruce Wayne's father and mother during a hold-up. A few days later Bruce kneels by his bed and swears "by the spirits of my parents to avenge their deaths by spending the rest of my life warring on all criminals." Then he begins a strenuous course of training designed to prepare him for his crusade. "He becomes a master scientist, trains his body to physical perfection until he is able to perform amazing athletic feats." Sketches show Bruce peering through a microscope and hefting a barbell. The last sequence in the episode brings the origin story to a climax. "I am ready," he tells himself,

but first I must have a disguise. Criminals are a superstitious, cowardly lot, so my disguise must be able to strike terror into their hearts. I must be a creature of the night, black, terrible . . . a . . .

Just then a huge bat flies into the room.

"A bat! That's it! It's an omen. I shall become a bat!" And thus is born this weird figure of the dark—this avenger of evil—the Batman.

In the final frame Batman appears in full costume and in a dramatic pose against the night skyline, a new action hero ready for every adventure his writers and artists can dream up.[17]

Batman's first episode has all the marks of the biography of Joseph Campbell's "hero with a thousand faces." He makes his first appearance as a fledgling, in this case a boy, though other heroes first appear as infants or raw adult recruits. Then something happens—in the case of the action detective, someone dear to him, a parent, a sweetheart or a friend, is murdered—and he vows to seek revenge, not just against the individual villain who injured him, but against all criminals. He declares war on crime. Then he strenuously prepares himself for his new role, strengthening himself in mind and body. At least he is ready. He adopts a heroic name, usually revealed to him in a fabulous manner, often by his foe during his first adventure, and then sallies forth in a series of preliminary adventures before entering into mortal combat against the foe he was born to face, the arch-villain who stands for evil itself. That evil genius defeated, the action detective hero embarks on a perpetual routine of battling each new villain the fates—his writers—designate as the next symbol of crime. Minor criminals may continue to exist, but CRIME itself is now under control; that seems to be the subliminal message of the comic book crime story.

War on Crime's first frame showed a pair of idealized special agents in snap-brimmed hats gunning down a gang of brutish-looking thugs. "On a thousand fronts," read the caption,

the crackle of government guns and the upraised hands of cringing desperadoes have marked Uncle Sam's "WAR ON CRIME." One by one America's public enemies have been sent to prison or, if they resisted with arms, to the morgue, by the courageous men of the F.B.I.—the G-MEN.

This tableau of F.B.I. men shooting down gangsters, the G-Man hero's characteristic pose, as much an identifying detail as Batman's crouch or Superman's pose in full flight, was what had to be accounted for in *War on Crime*'s origin story.

The next frame all but announced that the F.B.I. story to follow was going to be cloaked in mythology. There was a heroic portrait of J. Edgar Hoover over a caption that read

Directing this round-up of kidnappers, extortionists, bandits and other predatory criminals is a keen-eyed, broad-shouldered lawyer, John Edgar Hoover, Federal Bureau of Investigation.

Behind Hoover's skull, as though emanating from his brain, floated the two classic personae of the G-Men: a white-garbed scientist peering through a microscope, and a stereotypical square-jawed special agent in the snap-brimmed fedora.

The next two weeks showed the G-Man developing from an idea in Hoover's brain into the machine gun-wielding hero of the law shown in the comic's first panel. This was to be, in short, the mythological enactment of the special agent's metamorphosis from brainchild to G-Man.

First Hoover was shown gaining control of the Bureau in 1924. Before that epochal event, a caption stated, the F.B.I. was "an obscure agency steeped in politics and burdened with inefficient agents, some with police records."

For the next few days the strip showed the fledgling G-Men going through the same kind of training that had turned Superman and Batman into heroes. Instead of leaping tall buildings and outrunning locomotives, however, the young G-Men learned how to prepare evidence; they studied jiu-jitsu, ballistics, X-rays, invisible ink, marksmanship, lie-detector tests and handwriting identification. They practiced high-speed auto chases and nighttime raids. Hoover's special pride and joy, the fingerprint collection, took three full days to describe.

As had been the case with Batman, the death of someone dear to the G-Men brought their training to a close and called them to their destiny, incidentally supplying them with the motivation of revenge that would carry them through the rest of their careers. The Kansas City Massacre[18] served as the insult the new heroes were going to have to avenge. The comic appropriated Homer Cummings' interpretation of the incident: it was, a caption read, "Gangland's bloody challenge to the law."

That challenge accepted, *War on Crime* could bring its origin story to an end by displaying the G-Man hero armed and ready for combat in the pose that would be his trademark: an immense and spectral agent looming over a quivering bandit. The G-Man floated in the air surrounded by an other-worldly nimbus, machine gun trained on a cowering crook. "We are ready," the origin story concluded, "to begin an amazing account of the actual exploits of the G-Men, based on the official files." The stories may have come out of the files, but the formula came out of popular mythology and age-old ritual.

War on Crime's origin story was not the only way the action detective formula crept into this avowedly realistic strip. The cases that illustrated the Bureau's history also followed a mythological pattern. The principle of selection that guided the choice of these cases seems to have been the classic series of stages in the life story of the mythic hero: birth, training, winning a heroic name, the call to destiny and, finally, the epic struggle against the enemy who symbolizes the ultimate danger to the race.

The G-Man hero's first case in *War on Crime* was that old standby, Machine Gun Kelly's kidnapping of Oklahoma oilman Charles Urschel in 1933. This was, to be sure, a notable case purely from the standpoint of scientific crime solving and deductive reasoning, but Collier and Hoover seem to have chosen it as *War on*

Crime's first adventure because of its importance in the development of the G-Man myth. For J. Edgar Hoover and his publicists, the Urschel case was first and foremost "the case in which we got our name." It was the adventure that lifted the F.B.I. from the level of ordinary mortality and made it the stuff of legend by giving it its imagination-gripping nickname of "the G-Men." Forty years later[19] Hoover would still be retelling this (possibly fictitious) incident in which Machine Gun Kelly shouted "Don't shoot, G-Men, don't shoot" at his F.B.I. captors, this supposedly being the first time the agents had ever heard the term. The episode would hardly have merited the overwhelming significance Hoover attached to it (the incident is a prominent feature of every authorized F.B.I. book or movie) if Hoover, like the public, had not viewed the adventures of the Bureau in the light of mythology and ritual.

Every mythic hero has to have a name that sets him apart from the common herd as one destined for great deeds, and he acquires this name in the conventional ritualistic way. In the great religions God Himself pins the new name on the hero—Saul-Paul on the road to Tarsus, Simon-Peter being placed in command of the other apostles. In popular mythology a comic book god is sometimes conjured up for a pop christening. Billy Batson, for example, an orphan newsboy, wanders into an underground throne room where Shazam, "an ancient Egyptian Wizard" gives him the name of Captain Marvel and explains the allegorical significance of Shazam's magical name: "S" for the wisdom of Solomon, and so on. More often in popular culture the story's premise does not permit God to officiate, so another popular convention comes into play. The new hero's first enemy comes up with the new name at the moment of his defeat. Cooper's Natty Bumppo, for example, gets his warrior's name of "Hawkeye" from a dying Mohawk.

In the myth of the G-Man Machine Gun Kelly played the dying Mohawk. The F.B.I. agents who raided Kelly's room were ordinary detectives when they went in. Kelly's shout of panic turned them into the figures of romance. The new hero now had his epic name.

The next case in *War on Crime* was another milestone in the development of the G-Man myth. The hero had his heroic name, properly bestowed. Now he needed a mission worthy of that name. Thus the Kansas City Massacre, which Collier had already described in the origin story as "gangland's bloody challenge to the law," the beginning of the "war on crime." There was further symbolism in this case. It gave the G-Man hero a personal stake in the war on crime—revenge of the death of a fallen comrade. A popular culture hero cannot be a bureaucrat, going into combat for legalistic reasons; his ritualistic role repels mundane motives. He has to live by a personal code of chivalry. The Kansas City Massacre showed him subscribing to such a code. The death of the F.B.I. agents at Kansas City's Union Station also demonstrated the full significance of the symbolism the F.B.I. agent had taken on by becoming a G-Man. He was no longer simply another cop: now he was the symbol of the law. An attack on a G-Man was an attack on law itself, and would be personally avenged by the whole G-Man clan.

The comic's Kansas City Massacre episode began like a chapter in *Prince Valiant:*

Accepting gangland's challenge at Kansas City, Director Hoover of the Federal Bureau of Investigation ordered a relentless hunt for the slayers of Agent Caffrey.

Before long Pretty Boy Floyd, the F.B.I.'s prime suspect, begins to go to pieces under the relentless "G-Heat," and he makes a "proposition to Uncle Sam": he will surrender if Hoover will guarantee his immunity from the "hot seat." Hoover's reply conforms to the rule that only full poetic justice can slake the action hero's thirst for revenge. "Tell Pretty Boy Floyd for me," he says, "that we don't bargain with gangsters.... He is going to pay the full penalty for those murders at Kansas City."

This tale of insult and revenge could end only with Floyd's death. The finale was titled "The Massacre Avenged," and showed Floyd going down before an impromptu firing squad of G-Men. Thus "the F.B.I. avenged completely the gory massacre at Kansas City."

The G-Man hero—born, trained, named and blooded through the appropriate age-old rituals—was now ready to enter into mortal combat with the greatest criminal the publicity machinery of the thirties could produce: John Dillinger, "The Mad Dog of the Midwest," billed by *War on Crime* as the ultimate American criminal, the archetypal American bad man. In the myth of the G-Man the Dillinger case is the main event—Goliath to his David, Hector to his Achilles, Grendel to his Beowulf; High Noon. The preliminary events over, the hero has to face the enemy champion in a battle to the death.

Once Dillinger was stretched out on a slab in the morgue, the G-Man hero had achieved full legendary stature as a mythic hero. He was ready for a perpetual series of crusades against the ungodly.

But this was not to be. Soon after the Dillinger episode the strip began to run out of gas. It vanished from the newspapers by the end of the year.

What blighted the promising future of the official G-Man hero? He had everything demanded of a popular culture hero except one thing—a personality. That his personality was a blank was no accident. Hoover let *War on Crime*'s writer cast the F.B.I. story in the pattern of popular culture mythology up to a point, but he insisted that the G-Man hero not be the kind of free-wheeling operative he objected to in *Secret Agent X-9*. Hoover had started *War on Crime* to show that organization, not individual heroics, was the F.B.I. secret. Therefore, instead of having one sharply defined star agent pass through the heroic life cycle, gaining audience recognition and identification along the way, *War on Crime* had a group hero, a crowd of anonymous F.B.I. agents, all with the same square jaws and poker faces, all acting in unison, all taking orders at every turn from their director. *War on Crime* was cast in the form of the action detective formula, but it was a myth without, properly speaking, a hero. It was all launching pad with no rocket.

Collier and the Ledger Syndicate had not somehow gotten the urge to create a comic strip version of the collective novel. An examination of the rough drafts and page proofs for the comic shows that it was when characterizing the G-Man hero that Collier and his collaborators were most closely controlled by Hoover and his officials. Hoover simply would not permit Collier to give the field agent the self-reliance and independence that an action detective hero needed. Agents could not be turned into stars. They had to remain spear-bearers for Hoover, and Hoover was a thousand miles away from the action, a sort of brooding off-panel presence, felt but for the most part not seen.

Collier tried manfully to give readers some one person in the strip to identify with, somebody with a name and a face. As far as was humanly possible, Collier gave them Hoover. The desk-bound director was repeatedly involved in the plot by cutting from the heroics in the field back to strategy sessions in Washington where Hoover was shown barking orders into a telephone. But all the intercutting made hash of the plot and, even worse, comic strip readers were not used to identifying with a hero whose only weapon was a telephone that seemed to be growing out of of his ear.

There was also a practical problem. Even though Hoover was insisting on anonymity for the strip's field agents, at least one of them needed to have a name so that Hoover's orders would not have to be addressed "To Whom It May Concern." In response to Collier's pleas headquarters said that if there had to be a field agent with an identity it ought to be Sam Cowley, Hoover's roving personal representative who had been killed during the Baby Face Nelson case.

Collier tried to go along with Hoover, who was at this time using Cowley as a rival to Melvin Purvis in the ace agent sweepstakes.[20]

The trouble was that Cowley did not really figure in all the cases Collier was writing about, and he was not in on the kill in some of the cases he *had* worked on. This made the use of Cowley as a source of continuity for a strip a contradiction in terms. He was a hero who kept disappearing from the action when things got hot, only to show up when the fight was over to deliver the blood-thirsty moral of the episode and then disappear again.

With the strip's continuity in tatters, Collier tried to make some sense of the confusion by inventing a "generic" agent named Inspector Thomas Woodrow, "veteran nemesis of crime," carefully described as Hoover's personal representative in the field.

In the Kansas City Massacre episode, disagreement between Hoover and Collier over how the star agent should be characterized turned the strip into a farce. In this instance Sam Cowley had not been involved in the initial stages of the case, nor was he present when Melvin Purvis shot Pretty Boy Floyd, the Bureau's designated villain in the story. The first draft of the episode had "Inspector Woodrow" in charge. Then Hoover demanded that Collier make Cowley the star, so Cowley's name was substituted for Woodrow's in the strips that had not yet appeared. Then Hoover told Collier to get Cowley out of Floyd's death scene, evidently being reluctant to tamper with the facts in a case that was still fresh in the public's mind. Once again the proofs were revised, and Woodrow's name was put back in. Finally, Collier, in desperation, wrote his editor:

> Since sending you the final week of the Massacre case I have gone over the whole case and find that the elimination of Cowley's name and substitution of Woodrow's in the last week may cause confusion. The facts are that Cowley was in general charge of the hunt, but was not at the scene of Floyd's slaying. Earlier in the story I have had Inspector Woodrow in charge of the round-up of Massacre murderers. At that time Cowley was not in charge—yet the F.B.I. wants to give Cowley credit for the final capture.

By this time Woodrow and Cowley were being shuffled in and out of the strip bewilderingly. At the Bureau's insistence, for example, there was a picture of a plane overhead, with an agent on the ground gazing at it and saying, to no one in particular, "That must be Inspector Cowley and his squad. Washington ordered him to drop the Stoll case temporarily and take charge of the hunt for Floyd."

In a last ditch effort to rescue the continuity of his strip, Collier went through the proofs of the Massacre finale and crossed out *all* proper names. Thus a line that at first had read, "Disregarding repeated demands of Inspector Cowley of the F.B.I. that he surrender" was changed to "Disregarding repeated demands of Inspector Woodrow of the F.B.I." and finally emerged as "Disregarding repeated demands of the F.B.I."

The end result was that there was no one at all for the reader of *War on Crime* to identify with. The final absurdity was Floyd's death scene. In any action detective formula story—in any mythic adventure, for that matter—when the villain dies the hero *has* to be the one who does the killing, and he has to stick around to pronounce the epitaph. But in *War on Crime* the climactic line, "All right, men, fire," emerges out of a mob of anonymous agents. Every adventure story has to close with the hero posing over the body of the fallen villain. The best that *War on Crime* could manage was to assign "an Inspector" to strike this pose over Floyd's corpse.

In his history of the daily comic strips Ron Goulart guessed that *War on Crime* failed because its artwork, writing and plotting were just too good for its audience. They weren't getting enough "Kapowie's" and "Pow's." From the standpoint of popular culture studies, though, there was more to it than that. J. Edgar Hoover was trying to collaborate with American popular culture in the production of an official G-Man myth, but he was trying to do it on his terms. He was trying to withhold one ingredient essential to any myth—a hero.

American popular culture's response to Hoover's mythopoeic parsimony was what might have been expected. If the official F.B.I. denied it an official G-Man hero, then it would manufacture bogus G-Men. The result was that while the F.B.I.'s officially sanctioned entertainment during the thirties was, without exception, short-lived and of limited popularity, American popular culture was swarming with unsanctioned, bootleg G-Men—Secret Agent X-9, "G-Man," Dan Fowler, Captain America, The Shield, and dozens of their lesser-known colleagues. By a process of association the real F.B.I. profited from the public's appreciation of the heroics of these bogus G-Men. This popularity, however, like the popularity the F.B.I. gained from popular culture's action formula re-enactments of the great gangster cases of 1933-1934, was essentially irrelevant to the role Hoover had planned for the F.B.I. in American law enforcement. In fact the action detective image, while it undoubtedly made Hoover a formidable figure in the American political calculus that equates being well-known with being important, may have worked against his master plan.

Hoover's goal throughout his career was to integrate *all* American law enforcement into a coordinated structure under F.B.I. leadership, with the F.B.I.'s technical expertise and its training facilities as the organizational glue holding the country's constitutionally independent local law enforcement agencies together. Not only was the action detective image of the F.B.I. incompatible with this organizational concept, but it was bound to cause friction and jealousies among the very agencies Hoover hoped to cooperate with.

And friction and jealousy were, in fact, the most pronounced results of a bizarre series of action by Hoover between 1936 and 1939 when he seemed to be presenting *himself* to the public as the action detective G-Man hero that popular culture craved.

Beginning with the arrest of the last of the gangster era big-name crooks, Alvin "Old Creepy" Karpis in 1936, and culminating with the capture of Louis "Lepke" Buchalter in 1939, Hoover himself went into the field to make the captures, lead the raids and direct the shoot-outs in some of the Bureau's most publicized cases. For example, after one such operation on December 15, 1936 the New York City Police and the New Jersey State Police charged Hoover with "violating an agreement with them in order to steal the glory that was rightfully theirs."[21] That even J. Edgar Hoover, who more than anyone else should have known that this was not in the interest of sound law enforcement, should have had his head turned by the action detective image shows the enormous pressure the popular culture exerts on American law enforcement to conform to the expectations created by popular mythology. Needless to say, this impulse toward psychodrama has not helped the country deal with its crime problem.

Judging by the evidence of the comics, American popular culture had a hard time taking Hoover seriously as an action hero. He *did* become a fixture in mythology during the late thirties and the wartime years, but as a sort of grey eminence managing a stable of action heroes—not as an action hero himself. He seemed to function as an intermediary figure between out-and-out fantasy and newspaper reality, between heroes like Captain America and official America. He was something like a humorless Wizard of Oz: he could pull the strings and make the noises of the ritual but he could not act in the ritual itself. He was a comic book fantasy's connection in Washington—and Washington's link with fantasy. For example, he had a role in the origin story of the most famous of all the F.B.I.-inspired super-heroes, Captain America.

Captain America was born in March 1941.[22] On the origin story's first page, "as the ruthless war-mongers of Europe focus[ed] their eyes on a peace loving country," a crew of saboteurs prepare to dynamite "American Munitions, Inc."

Back in Washington there are discouraging reports from the Chief of Staff:

I tell you, Mr. President, there's no stopping these vermin.... They're so firmly entrenched in our ranks that I hesitate to give a confidential report to even my most trusted aide.

Roosevelt wisecracks:

What would you suggest, gentlemen, a character out of the comic books? Perhaps the HUMAN TORCH in the army would solve our problem! But seriously, gentlemen, something is being done.... Please send in Mr. Grover!
Enter J. Arthur Grover, head of the Federal Bureau of Investigation.

Grover takes them to a secret laboratory where they watch Grover's scientists exhibit their solution to the nation's security problem.

The doctors take a frail young volunteer, rejected as unfit for military service, and inject him with "a seething liquid" that will turn him into "one of America's saviors." The military leaders "gape in awe" as

the serum coursing through his blood... [builds] his body and brain tissues, until his stature and intelligence increase to an amazing degree.

Go back to *War on Crime* for a minute. In that comic recruits were injected with the Director's inspirational leadership by way of classroom lectures, firing-range instruction and gymnasium workouts. Obviously imparting the G-spirit via hypodermic needles had a certain style the official comic lacked.

The volunteer's feeble muscles surge and grow. At last he towers like a mountain of flesh over his scientist-creators. "Behold," one of Grover's scientists announces,

the first of a corps of super-agents whose mental and physical ability will make them a terror to spies and saboteurs.... We shall call you CAPTAIN AMERICA, son! Because, like you... Americans shall gain the strength and will to safeguard our shores.

Then the spies attack. They kill the serum's inventor, wound Grover and smash the only bottle of Captain America serum. The Captain annihilates the spies, but the damage is done. Instead of a legion of Captain Americas there will be just one. So he will not have to face Hitler singlehandedly, however, he organizes a fan club called "Captain America's Sentinels of Liberty," each of whose members solemnly pledge "to uphold the principles of the sentinels of liberty and assist Captain America in his wars against spies in the U.S.A."

Captain America was the most famous of the fantasy G-Men spawned by the adventure comics. With his red, white and blue leotard and his shield marked with the scarlet letter "A" he was also the most gorgeous. Almost as pretty was "The Shield," billed as "The G-Man Extraordinary," who pre-dated Captain America by a year. Hoover made regular guest appearances in The Shield's adventures: in the first panel giving the hero his assignment, in the last to give him a medal. Like Captain America, The Shield was "no importation from another planet nor accidental freak of nature." He was "the product of years of painstaking toil, the climax to brilliant scientific research." The Plastic Man was another superhero G-Man; at least he had Hoover (a.k.a. F.B.I. Chief Banner) for boss.

Hoover's ultimate place in American comic book mythology received its definitive characterization in the origin story of "The Justice Society of America." This was a showcase for new and rising comic book heroes, and first appeared in the Winter, 1940, issue of *All Star Comics.* Its charter members were The Atom, The Sandman, The Spectre, The Flash, Hawkman, Dr. Fate, The Green Lantern and Hour Man. Superman and Batman made occasional guest appearances.

During their first meeting, while the guys swapped yarns about their favorite cases, The Flash stepped out and returned an instant later. He had just been to Washington for a meeting with J. Edgar Hoover, and he had news: "He wants all of us members of the Justice Society to come down and see him—all together! I thought next Thursday night would be okay." "Incidentally," The Flash added, "he's one swell guy."[23]

This encounter between Hoover and the Justice Society of America may be taken as popular mythology's final pigeon-holing of the Director and his Bureau. Neither would henceforth be permitted to assume center stage in heroic adventures. Hoover would remain in the comics to send costumed crime fighters into the fray and to welcome them home. The G-Men themselves would continue to appear, but only as a team of faceless and nameless avengers who made an appearance in the last panel of a gangster comic to mete out poetic justice with their Tommy guns.

What is the significance of the comic strip G-Man? It suggests that success or failure in what Walter Bagehot called the "dignified" side of politics, Murray Edelman's "politics as symbolic action," depends upon the political leader's making his personality and actions conform to the formulas that govern the area of popular culture corresponding to his field of action. Since the formula that governs crime entertainment is that of an action hero performing rituals of crime and punishment (the action detective formula), a symbolic leader like Hoover will prosper to the extent that his image conforms to the formula, and his popularity will decline when his image deviates from it. Real-life crime fighting, therefore, will interest the public only when it provides the same satisfactions offered by crime entertainment: an identification "in action and passion with heroes who struggle to uphold principles of social order." Hugh Dalziel Duncan, whose phrase this is, adds that "in this identification with leaders and causes, anxiety, fear, and loneliness vanish."[24]

The function of crime and punishment in society, Emile Durkheim argues, "is to maintain social cohesion intact.... [It] violently pushes all...toward one another and unites them in the same place."[25] When real life dramas of crime and punishment (the Dillinger case, for example) appear closely resembling rituals of crime and punishment, the public will insist on seeing the actors as action heroes and formula villains, and their encounters will be read as popular mythology. When the image of the real-life crime fighter deviates from the formula—as did the image of the G-Man that Hoover promoted in his publicity and in *War on Crime*—the public will lose interest and go back to entertainment more faithful to the desired ritual. In other words, it will skip the news and go straight to the comics. But ... that's democracy for you.

Notes

[1]Richard Slotkin, *Regeneration Through Violence: The Mythology of the American Frontier, 1600-1860* (Middletown, Conn.: Wesleyan University Press, 1973), p. 8. Slotkin quotes with approval Joseph Campbell's definition of myth as "traditional metaphor addressed to ultimate questions"; a more political definition, such as Roland Barthes' notion that the essential "principle" in myth is the transformation of "history into nature," (Roland Barthes, *Mythologies* [New York: Hill and Wang, n.d.] p. 129) might have made more explicit the cultural process that Slotkin describes in his magnificent book. Following Barthes, myth gives a culture an explanation of things that are happening in terms of *the way things have to be.*

[2]Slotkin, p. 11; Slotkin is adopting a thesis of J.L. Henderson's in *Threshold of Initiation.*

[3]Slotkin should not be held responsible for this extrapolation from the frontier story to the crime story. It is almost a cliche to call the detective story an "urban Western." I think the conventional wisdom here is essentially correct.

[4]For a fuller discussion of this, see my "J. Edgar Hoover and the Detective Hero", *Journal of Popular Culture* (Fall, 1975), pp. 270-273.

[5]Jack Alexander, "The Director, I," *The New Yorker* (Sept. 25, 1937), p. 20.

[6]Hoover went to work for the Justice Department in 1917 at the age of twenty-two. He had been Assistant Director of the Bureau of Investigation since 1921 when Coolidge's Attorney General, Harlan F. Stone, picked Hoover to reform the Bureau which had been discredited during the Teapot Dome Scandal.

[7]*The Challenge of Crime in a Free Society* (New York: Avon, 1968), p. 102.

[8]For a discussion of the political necessity of doing *something* when a problem arises, see Murray Edelman, *The Symbolic Uses of Politics* (Urbana: Univ. of Illinois, 1964), pp. 7, 78, 79.

[9]Hugh Dalziel Duncan, *Symbols in Society* (New York: Oxford, 1968), p. 139. Duncan's book is a collection of stimulating suggestions served up in a "take it or leave it" manner.

[10]*New York American,* November 29, 1934, p. 1.

[11]For a full discussion of *G-Men* and its political effect, see my "The Attorney General and the G-Man: Hollywood's Role in Hoover's Rise to Power," *Southwest Review* 62 (Autumn, 1977).

[12]These quotes are from the copy of the script in the possession of the author.

[13]Background on Secret Agent X-9 can be found in Ron Goulart, *The Adventurous Decade: Comic Strips in the Thirties* (New Rochelle: Arlington House, 1975) and *Nostalgia Comics* 1 (n.d.).

[14]For an analysis of the logic behind Hoover's publicity see my "Reading His Own Publicity: The Influence of Public Relations on the F.B.I. Program," *Mass Comm Review* 4 (Fall, 1977), 2-22.

[15]Louis B. Nichols, 26 June, 1975.

[16]This discussion of *War on Crime* is based on interviews with the writer Rex Collier, and on materials lent by Mr. Collier to the author.

[17]See the reprint of the Batman origin story in Jules Feiffer, *The Great Comic Book Heroes* (New York: Bonanza, 1965), p. 69-70.

[18]On June 17, 1933 five F.B.I. agents and three local police officers escorting escaped convict Frank "Jelly" Nash from Hot Springs, Arkansas, to Leavenworth prison were attacked by three gunmen at Kansas City's Union Station. Three of the local police and F.B.I. agent Raymond Caffrey were killed, and two of the other agents were wounded. The F.B.I.'s handling of the case was based on the theory that the gunmen were Vern Miller, Adam Richetti and Charles "Pretty Boy" Floyd. Whether or not Floyd was actually involved has always been a matter of controversy.

[19]For example, in his introduction to Andrew Tully's *The F.B.I.'s Most Famous Cases* (New York: Morrow, 1965), Hoover wrote: "Machine Gun Kelly occupies an...important place in the F.B.I.'s history, for he tagged our agents with the indelible nickname of 'G-Men' on September 26, 1933, while surrendering at Memphis, Tennessee." (p. x). Actually "G-Men" was never used in public print, as far as I know, until after the Cagney movie appeared in Spring, 1935. It certainly did not appear in any contemporary accounts of Kelly's capture.

[20]Hoover hated Purvis, and when Purvis wrote a book (*American Agent*) after leaving the Bureau in 1935 Hoover changed Purvis' resignation to "resignation with prejudice." In an effort to denigrate Purvis, Hoover and his publicists claimed that Sam Cowley, not Purvis, had been in charge of the final stages of the Dillinger case. My conclusion, based on the deportment of the F.B.I. agents at the Biograph shoot-out, is that Purvis *was* in charge. Purvis definitely was in charge of the Pretty Boy Floyd case. When Purvis turned the Baby Face Nelson manhunt into a highly publicized personal vendetta, Hoover pulled him off the case.

[21]Fred J. Cook, *The F.B.I. Nobody Knows* (New York: Macmillan, 1964), p. 197.

[22]The Captain America origin story is also reprinted in Feiffer, *The Great Comic Book Heroes*.

[23]Jim Harmon, "A Swell Bunch of Guys," in *All In Color For A Dime*, Dick Lupoff and Don Thompson, eds. (New York: Ace, 1970), p. 179.

[24]Duncan, *Symbols in Society*, p. 237.

[25]Emile Durkheim, *The Division of Labor in Society* (New York: Free Press, 1964), pp. 103, 108.

American Beauty Rituals

Christine A. Hope

JUST AS WE learn about "primitive" cultures by observing the people's rituals we can learn much about ourselves by examining our seemingly trivial and taken-for-granted ritual behaviors, especially when we examine beauty rituals engaged in mostly by women.[1]

An overview of American beauty rituals indicates that they might be categorized in any number of ways. A few of these rituals are taught to us early in life, are tied to health as well as to beauty considerations, and are considered obligatory on a daily basis until we die. For example, little girls as young as two or three are encouraged to take pride in having shiny hair; at age ninety, "getting their hair done" in the nursing home beauty shop may well be the highlight of the elderly ladies' week. Other rituals of this sort are face-washing and tooth-brushing. Then there are beauty rituals which usually occur once in a lifetime, require the intervention of professionals, involve actual reshaping of the body, and are too expensive for most Americans to consider. Straightening the teeth by the use of metal braces, plastic surgery to reshape or renew the face, and silicone injections to enlarge the breasts are examples. In between these two extremes are a large number of rituals which women usually begin practicing in early adolescence or slightly before. Most often, these rituals are learned about and experimented with in secret and often with the initial disapproval of the elders. These are the rituals written about in fashion magazines and heralded in television commercials and magazine ads. They most often do not involve permanent changes in the body. The practice of such rituals is concentrated in the courtship years but may well continue (or even intensify) throughout middle age and into old age.

Such rituals may take place on a daily, weekly or seasonal basis. They may or may not require the intervention of professionals. Examples include applying color to the eyes, lips, nails and face; removing body hair; styling head hair; padding some areas of the body while constricting others; and altering overall skin color by lying in the sun. The rituals of this intermediate type, with some investigation of the more permanent rituals, provide interesting food for thought.

One theme which ties together numerous beauty rituals in the United States is the theme of "femininity." That is, women and girls are encouraged to engage in rituals to make themselves "more feminine," to do things to their bodies which will emphasize the ways in which women are different from men. One beauty practice which has been promoted on this basis is the painful ritual of removing female body hair. According to conventional wisdom on the subject, hairiness equals masculinity; hairlessness (except on the head) is feminine. As a book published by the cosmetics industry expressed it, "One of the things that distinguishes woman from man is the lack of hair on her face, forearm, and legs. . . . Whatever the reason, it is an assured fact that both men and women are proud of the difference. The body hair of the male denotes strength and manliness. The smooth, fair skin of the female denotes gentility and womanly charm."[2] So ingrained is this assumption that men without body hair feel just as uncomfortable as women with it do. A letter which appeared in "Dear Abby" provides a good illustration:[3]

Dear Abby: I've never seen a problem like mine in your column. I'm a 33-year-old normal man, except that I have absolutely no hair on my chest, arms or legs. And that is where I want hair the most. I have plenty of hair on my head and a thick growth in my pubic area, so I know I can grow hair. But, I'm so ashamed of my hairless body I avoid going to the beach.
Is there some kind of treatment I can take to promote the growth of hair where I want it? I am miserable in my hairless state. I want to be like the other guys.

Abby advises the man to see an endocrinologist and, in the meantime, to buy "paste-on hair for chests" in a "better men's shop."

While men without body hair may have to *add* some in order to feel at ease on the beach, most women have to *remove* naturally-growing hair in order to avoid comment and to conform to the feminine ideal. The practice usually begins in early adolescence when the female first acquires underarm and pubic hair and notices the darkening of her arm and leg hair. Aware of the cultural maxim that hairiness is masculine and after a childhood of seeing pictures of beautiful adult women with tanned, perfectly smooth legs, thighs, chests and arms, the almost-adolescent girl confronts the darkened body hair now cropping up on her own body with a mixture of curiosity, horror and determination. She is determined to get rid of the foreign hair and may have vague ideas about how to do so.

If the girl asks her mother for help in this matter, she will probably be told that she is too young to be concerned with shaving yet. Robin Morgan, for example, recalls ". . . wanting to shave your legs at twelve and being agonized because your mother won't let you" as one of the "barbarous rituals" of being female in America.[4] But the daughter will often persist. An acquaintance of mine met resistance from her mother in this matter until she threatened to sit out in the front yard and cut her newly darkened leg hair with a pair of scissors. Other mothers meet their daughters' requests with incredulity, expressing disbelief that the girl could possibly be worried about so trivial a matter at so tender an age.

Meeting this initial resistance on the part of her elders (or being too embarrassed to bring it up in the first place), the girl engages in her first experiments with hair removal in secret and without instruction. The usual implement is Dad's (or Mom's) safety razor; the usual result is a blood-stained bathmat, blood-streaked towels, a wastebasket full of small pieces of blood-soaked toilet paper used to dab the smaller nicks, and a pair of moderately hairless, bandaid-patched legs. As Morgan puts it ". . . being agonized at fourteen you finally have shaved your legs, and your flesh is on fire" is another barbarous ritual.[5] Much to her dismay, our young battle-scarred veteran discovers that, within a very few days, the hair on her legs reappears and that this new growth seems tougher and more stubbly than the baby-fine hair of last week. She may very well be sorry she ever began the never-ending ritual, but, in the name of femininity, she persists.

Although most women get somewhat better at wielding the razor over time, the ever-present danger of bloody nicks from a new blade or a moment of carelessness remains. Emily Prager, an adult in her mid-twenties, writes about the hazards like this: "I used to shave my legs just before the date. I wanted to be sure they were ultra-smooth for the evening ahead. It took years of frantic last-minute efforts to 1) wash out the blood-spots on my panty hose while 2) trying not to reopen the shaving nicks while 3) somehow detaching the sticky nylon from the severed skin, before I realized that one hour before a date is no time for me to have a razor in my hand."[6]

The advertisements in beauty magazines which push hair removal products and processes most often stress methods other than shaving with a safety razor. Bleaches, electrolysis, tweezers, chemical depilatories, electric shavers, and waxes (hot, cold and "thermostatically controlled") are among the methods mentioned. Most American women, however, choose shaving, and most use safety razors rather than electric shavers.[7] Their choice is not surprising given the painfulness, messiness, ineffectiveness and even danger of the other methods. Prager notes some of the traumas which accompany the use of a depilatory to remove hair from her thighs, "If I don't stand upright with my legs apart, odd patches of my pubic hair will be removed; if I'm not completely motionless, drops of depilatory will fall on the rug, leaving discolored brown spots among the pink fuzz; and that ten endless minutes, despite possible skin irritation, is required for sure removal of unsightly body hair. It's a hellish experience all around."[8] While Prager describes some of the minor annoyances of depilatory use, the women who used an expensive depilatory by the name of Koremlu during the 1920s to remove hair from their faces and arms developed symptoms similar to those of lead poisoning and ended up as case histories in medical journals.[9] Beauty, it seems, has its price.

At various times since hair removal rituals became established in the years after World War I, a few people have suggested that they be abandoned. A 1942 health book, after noting the hazards of depilatory use and electroylsis, suggested "Perhaps the best solution for the problem of superfluous hairs on arms and legs is to accept them, not as a disfigurement but as a natural condition which one should leave alone."[10] More recently, supporters of the Women's Liberation Movement have suggested that such painful, enslaving rituals be abandoned. After all, the lack of dark hair in places other than on the scalp is naturally characteristic of *children*, not adult women. By persisting in the practice, feminists would argue, women are rejecting their own bodies and confirming their age-old identification with children. Most American women have not heeded these arguments. Consumer surveys report that between 70% and 98% (depending on the age group) of American women remove body hair[11] and that women are more willing to appear in public without a bra than without having shaved.[12] It would appear that old definitions of femininity and masculinity and the practices which embody them are very persistent.

The practices undertaken to enlarge, shape and control the female bustline are also beauty rituals which reflect the femininity theme. Once again males and females are seen as polar opposites: females have breasts, males don't; therefore breasts are feminine, flat chests are not. It is not strictly true, however, that American cultural beliefs specify that the larger the bustline, the more feminine the woman. The ideal breast size for women varies with fashions and has changed several times during the twentieth century alone. It probably does make sense to say, however, that large-breasted women are perceived as being more desirous of sex and more sexually available than women with small breasts. Eve Babitz, writing about her life as a 36DD, notes that she frequently hears comments such as "Shit, she must really be horny," directed toward her.[13] The assumption made about big-breasted women is that they are continuously desirous of sex and, therefore, open to public propositions, Babitz concludes. Interestingly, Nora Ephron found that the opposite assumptions are made about small-breasted women like herself; a woman who anticipated that Ephron was going to be her daughter-in-law presented her with a book on frigidity—"You have small breasts, she was saying... therefore you will doubtless have sexual problems."[14] These observations reveal that women's anxieties about breast size are not simply personal hangups. Women take steps to shape and control the bustlines they show to the world because the breast size others perceive has real consequences for women. A flat-chested woman will not be initially perceived as sexually available (or even perhaps as a mature woman) unless she does something to increase her breast size; the woman with larger-than-usual breasts will be initially perceived *only* as a sex object if she doesn't take steps to disguise her endowment. Both women have the problem, at least in some situations, of presenting themselves to be something other than what they really are in order to be taken seriously.

The problems associated with being flat-chested are perhaps most acute during the courtship years when most females *want* to be recognized as potential sexual partners. Ephron notes that having breasts is a confirmation both to the individual girl and to those around her that she really is female. About her own experience, she writes: "I wanted desperately not to be... a mixture of both things [male and female], but instead just one, a girl, a definite indisputable girl. As soft and as pink as a nursery. And nothing would do that for me, I felt, but breasts........ .... you could see breasts; they were there; they were visible."[15]

Once the adolescent girl with small breasts recognizes that they are probably not going to get much larger, she might undertake any number of ritual actions to either 1) actually increase her breast size or 2) make it appear to the world that she has. Most of the possibilities under the first category are either shams (Ephron tried a Mark Eden Bust Developer, sleeping on her back, and splashing cold water on her breasts every night)[16] or impractical for a girl of this age (e.g. silicone injections, getting pregnant). Among the most common rituals under the second category is stuffing the training bra with Kleenex. Unfortunately the effect is a somewhat lumpy appearance and there is not much to hold the Kleenex in place. The padded bra is likely to be the solution finally settled on. Even this artifice is not without its hazards. Ephron notes that each of her three padded bras was a different size and shape, undoubtedly creating much confusion (or amusement) amongst onlookers, and that her swimsuit with the built-in bust stabbed her in the rib cage and left red welts on her body.[17]

The greatest danger of the padded bra, of course, is being discovered in your deception. While the discovery of fraudulence may not break up many romances, it does make courtship rituals rather awkward. The heroine of *Kinflicks* recalls one such moment: "Joe Bob with his left hand poked tentatively at my right breast, or rather poked the mound of my maroon uniform jacket, poked the padding of my Never-Tell bra."[18] If all else fails, the flat-chested young woman can always accept her condition and resort to ritualized joking with her fellow flatties. She might refer to her breasts as her "pirate treasure" (a sunken chest) or suggest to an equally flat friend that her back really has more use for a bra than her front (to support the protruding shoulder blades).

The small-breasted or flat-chested woman may eventually discard her bras entirely or come to appreciate the freedom from street comments which comes with being flat. Some women discover that an impressive bustline seems much less important to men in their twenties than to boys in their teens. One delighted young woman recently wrote to "Dear Abby" about her man: "With his love and reassurance, I have thrown away all my padded bras (after 12 years) and I am no longer the least bit ashamed of being flat-chested." The letter was signed "Flat But Fulfilled."[19]

On the other hand, some women never lose their desire for large breasts and, as adults, take steps to permanently change their bustlines through breast implants or silicone injections. One woman who has undergone four breast implant operations (the last three to correct the first) explained her initial decision like this: "I was so flat I wanted to hide every time I undressed. And I'd only make love with the lights out."[20] The complication rate of such operations runs at about 60% with hardening, scar tissue formation and misshapen, assymetrical breasts the most frequent side effects.[21] Despite the high complication rate of such operations (so high that many physicians oppose doing them at all), demand remains high. Many flat-chested women have apparently been convinced that their worthiness as women depends on the size of their chests.

The problems faced by girls and women with large breasts and the ritualistic actions they take to deal with them are less often discussed. During the 1920s when the flat-chested look was fashionable, there were undergarments designed to hold back the breasts. Such garments are no longer widely available and large-breasted women who wish to present themselves to the world as something other than sex objects seem to depend mostly on outergarments to do the job. Eve Babitz explains her techniques as follows: "Whenever I go into the street, I have to cover myself with clothes that flow and drape. I cannot wear a tight anything on the street if I hope to have a moment's peace.... Putting on disguises is one of my daily tasks. 'Now what shall I wear today that'll billow around?' I say to myself, squinting into my closet. If I'm going to see friends and I have to go on the street first, I usually have to wear a coat... and then take it off (sweating) upon arrival."[22] In each case, the woman with less-than-usual sized breasts feels compelled to correct her condition in the pursuit of beauty and social acceptance.

The rituals associated with female weight control share certain characteristics with the hair removal and bustline control rituals already discussed. Like both of these other sets of rituals, the rituals associated with weight control (almost always meaning weight reduction) are undertaken in hopes of becoming more beautiful. Weight reduction, like hair removal, involves the taking away of part of the body. Like bustline control, weight control is practiced at least partly because it is believed that a woman's overall size says something about her character. In contrast to the other rituals discussed, however, it cannot be argued that the rituals associated with female weight loss are derived from some naturally occurring difference between men and women. In fact, one of the major natural differences between men and women is that the fat-to-body weight ratio is higher in women than in men.[23] If the logic used for justifying other beauty rituals were followed here, women would be striving to add to their fat in order to appear more feminine just as men try to become more muscular to appear more masculine. Women in some traditional West African societies have done just this, spending time in "fatting-houses" eating fatty foods and going without exercise.[24] Such is not, of course, the case in contemporary American society. Instead, both men and women are expected to control their body weight and avoid obesity. Men are expected to do so mostly for health considerations, women for reasons of beauty.

It is the women who are more concerned about their weight and they are much more likely than men to be dieting. Like the other beauty rituals discussed, dieting is more common among adolescent girls than among adult women. It is not at all unusual to find *both* adolescent and adult females who are not overweight according to medical definitions putting themselves on diets or belonging to weight-watching organizations.[25] Although weight reduction is often urged for health reasons, the beauty reasons seem to be more compelling.

There are both group and individual rituals associated with female weight loss. One important aspect of female weight control in the United States is the discussion of it. Conversations about the fear of becoming fat, about how much one "gained" over the holiday weekend, and about the merits of various diets are extremely common among American women of all ages and weights and in a variety of social situations. Secretaries on coffee breaks, club women at bridge parties, and adolescents at slumber parties all discuss the topic. I will never forget the scene: at one of the most experimental colleges in the country during one of the most radical of times (the late '60s) the women students at my lunch table were discussing—not the war, not oppression, not politics or philosophy—but how *fat* all the starchy cafeteria food was making them! Learning to talk about one's weight or dieting attempts is essential for good adjustment in many all-female groups. For example one learns that the socially acceptable thing to say when offered some sweet, calorie-rich dessert is not, "Yes, please," but rather,"I really shouldn't ...but ..." or, "Oh, oh, there goes my diet!" By following such unwritten rules, one presents oneself to others as a responsible woman who is concerned about her appearance.

Ritual conversation about weight loss and dieting has, in fact, become institutionalized in the form of self-help organizations dedicated to helping women lose weight. At the meetings of organizations with names like Buxom Belles, International; Weight Watchers; and the TOPS (Take Off Pounds Sensibly) Clubs, women who feel that they have a weight problem gather to weigh in (with prizes given for those losing the most weight), compare diets, give testimonials and offer support to one another in their endeavors.

Actual reducing rituals (as distinguished from talking-about-reducing rituals) are also often performed in group settings, many of them commercialized establishments. Those who can afford it go to exclusive spas or clinics where dieting is combined with exercise, sunbathing and other health and beauty rituals. An ad for one such clinic ("for the committed woman who cares about herself and her family") mentioned a whole range of exotic-sounding techniques including "blood chemistry, nutrition guidance... jacuzzi, ionization, theraffin wrap, and massage on the cellular level."[26] For younger females with weight problems and sufficient money, there are summer camps for overweight girls. Those with more moderate incomes might perform their reducing rituals in commercial establishments with names such as "Slender World," "Nutri/System" and "European Health-Spa." These establishments claim to offer a range of services including diet counseling, exercise and "Contour Treatments" using "a specially formulated cream."[27] They promise happiness, fulfillment, and improved personal relationships as well as the loss of pounds and inches.

Most women who practice reducing rituals, however, probably do so alone; even those who belong to organizations or visit weight-loss clinics must put their lessons into practice in their own kitchens. There are any number of diet articles in beauty magazines and diet books on the market to help them. In the past several years alone, potential dieters have been deluged with high-fiber, high-protein, high-carbohydrate, superenergy, liquid protein, "save-your-life," and "last chance" diets. The creation of new diets is a major industry and one which is extremely prone to faddism. The fact that so many diet books are best-sellers and that each year brings a new crop of diets indicates both the American dedication to self improvement in terms of weight control and the ultimate ineffectiveness of most of the diets. Exercise books have recently come to be equally popular, at least partially for reasons related to weight loss. For those who don't want to bother with menu-planning, calorie-counting, or jogging, doctor-prescribed amphetamines which suppress the appetite might be seen as the solution to a weight problem. Those who prefer self-medication can find appetite-suppressant candies and over the counter drugs on the shelves of their neighborhood drug store and low calorie versions of regular foods in the "diet" section of their supermarket.

What explains the American obsession with weight loss, particularly among women? A large part of the explanation certainly has to do with social factors. Women are more often judged on the basis of their appearance than men are and an important element of appearance is overall size. While some aspects of appearance (such as height) are not under the individual's control, it is believed that one's weight is. Thus, the woman who is overweight is believed to be one who doesn't care about appearance, one who cannot control herself, one who is lazy and perhaps even immoral. Such were the conclusions of one sociological study of public reactions to obesity: "... fatness is assessed negatively as unaesthetic and as an indication of self-indulgence. In a society which has historically been suffused with a Protestant Ethic, one characteristic of which is a strong emphasis on impulse control, fatness suggests a kind of immorality...."[28] Obese people (being part of the public) often incorporate this cultural judgment and apply it to themselves. Said one overweight woman, "The fear of fat, the fear of being a monster, is the fear of having no control—of being taken over by something that rises up inside of you."[29] The assumptions made about overweight people extend to their mental capacities as well. One woman who has experienced life both fat and thin noted: "Besides actual discrimination, like landlords not renting to fat people, most everyone thinks if you're fat you're not very bright. You're oafish and dull."[29]

Given these assumptions about the obese, it is not surprising that women struggle to control their weight in much the same way as they struggle to control their hair, bustlines and wrinkles. For some, particularly adolescents, the struggle results in literally starving themselves to death or near death. Anorexia nervosa is a disease whose symptoms include the rejection of food, cessation of menstrual periods, extreme forms of dieting, and an obsessive fear of being overweight.[30] In the recent past, as many as 15%-20% of those with the disease died, with others resigned to lifetime treatment.[31] While the disease clearly has physical and psychological components, its causes are also partially cultural. Anorexia nervosa is most prevalent in societies and subcultures where thinness is idealized and fatness ostracized.[32] The comments of adolescent females who are receiving treatment for the disease reveal the extent to which social and cultural factors led them to engage and persist in extreme dieting behaviors. One sixteen-year-old clearly associated self-discipline and control (the virtues the obese are said not to have) with extreme dieting: "That fall, I stopped eating. I associated food with weakness and decadence; my new, disciplined lifestyle would not accommodate it." Whenever she resolved to start eating again, cultural mandates for thinness confronted her at every turn: ". . . I resolved, once and for all, that I would gain 20 pounds starting at the next meal. Then two tall, slender models passed me on my way to the coffee shop. I glanced at myself in the mirror and decided I really had no reason to gain weight. I ordered coffee, black, for lunch."[33] Like the women who used Koremlu to get rid of every "unsightly" facial hair and the flat-chested women who received implants to increase their bustlines, victims of anorexia nervosa have sacrificed their health for what they believed to be beauty.

Practices intended to reshape, hide, decorate and enhance the natural human body are not unique to twentieth century American women. Body-decorating materials have been found in caves dating back to the Upper Paleolithic; for centuries, upper-class Chinese women bound the feet of their tiny daughters so tightly that their small, "beautiful" adult feet were virtually incapable of locomotion; American Indian mothers tied boards to their babies' heads to flatten foreheads and to elongate the head itself; some African women constrict their necks, arms and ankles with heavy, metal rings. Like beauty rituals in other times and places, the practices described in this essay are performed on a regular basis by many people and are endowed with magical qualities. Like the rituals of more "primitive" groups, they are sometimes painful and may be detrimental to overall health. The rituals which anthropologists describe were often undertaken in order to make clear the distinction between girls and women, women and men, the unmarried and the married, the rich and the not-so-rich. The same can be said of the beauty rituals practiced by contemporary American women.

There are, perhaps, a few differences. The beauty practices of simpler societies were taught to younger generations by their elders at the appropriate time in the life cycle, sometimes as part of public initiation ceremonies. Our beauty practices, on the other hand, are suggested to us by commercial interests in a constant stream of pictures, images, slogans and songs. The actual practice of learning and performing the rituals, however, of getting one's particular body to conform to the commercial model are often agonizing, private rituals which may not receive the approval of elders. It appears, on the surface at least, that we have more choice than did the Chinese women with bound feet. That may well be the case; the demands of popular culture may be less then the demands of culture. To put it in Erving Goffman's terms,[35] we have more flexibility in choosing which "self" to "present" to society. This also means, however, that we are held responsible for the self we choose. Thus, the "freely chosen" rituals are often performed in an atmosphere of anxiety. The rituals which on cursory glance seem trivial are actually quite serious business.

Notes

[1]Horace Miner, "Body Ritual Among the Nacirema," *American Anthropologist,* 58 (1956), 503-507.

[2]Everett G. McDonough, *Truth About Cosmetics,* (New York: The Drug and Cosmetic Industry, 1937), p. 187.

[3]"Dear Abby," *The Greenville News.*

[4]Robin Morgan, *Going Too Far: The Personal Chronicle of a Feminist* (New York: Random House, 1977), pp. 107-108.

[5]Morgan, pp. 107-8.

[6]Emily Prager, "First-Date Jitters," *Viva,* June 1977, p. 36.

[7]"Depilatories," *Consumer Reports,* January 1975, p. 61.

[8]Prager, p. 36.

[9]AMA Bureau of Investigation, "Koremlu: The Life History of a Viciously Dangerous Depilatory," *Journal of the American Medical Association* 99 (July 30, 1932), 407-408. See also

Arthur Kallet and F.J. Schlink, *100,000 Guinea Pigs: Dangers in Everyday Foods, Drugs, and Cosmetics* (New York: The Vanguard Press, 1933), pp. 80-92 and M.C. Phillips, *Skin-Deep: The Truth about Beauty Aids—Safe and Harmful* (New York: The Vanguard Press, 1934), pp. 96-103.

[10]Clifford Lee Brownell, Jesse Feiring Williams and William Leonard Hughes, *Health Problems: How to Solve Them* (New York: American Book Co., 1942).

[11]"Advice for Women Who Shave," *Today's Health,* July 1964, p. 36 and "Depilatories," 60.

[12]John Bardin, "How Free 11,307 U.S. Women Really Want to Be," *Today's Health,* January 1973, 32-35, 68.

[13]Eve Babitz, "My Life in a 36DD Bra, or the All-American Obsession," *Ms.,* April 1976, p. 15.

[14]Nora Ephron, "A Few Words About Breasts," in *Crazy Salad: Some Things About Women* (New York: Bantam Books, 1976), p. 9.

[15]Ephron, pp. 1-2.   [16]Ephron, pp. 5-6.

[17]Ephron, p. 6.

[18]Lisa Alther, *Kinflicks* (New York: Knopf, 1976), p. 45.

[19]"Dear Abby," *The Greenville News,* Nov., 19, 1979.

[20]Marjorie Nashner and Mimi White, "Beauty and the Breast—a 60% Complication Rate for an Operation You Don't Need," *Ms.,* Sept. 1977, p. 53.

[21]Nashner and White, p. 54.   [22]Babitz, p. 17.

[23]Ashton Barfield, "Biological Influences on Sex Differences in Behavior," in Michael S. Teitelbaum (ed.) *Sex Differences: Social and Biological Perspectives* (Garden City, N.Y.: Pantheon Books, 1976), p. 65.

[24]Ted Polhemus, "Introduction," *The Body Reader: Social Aspects of the Human Body* (New York: Pantheon Books, 1978) pp. 23-5.

[25]Johanna T. Dwyer, Jacob J. Feldman and Jean Mayer, "The Social Psychology of Dieting," *Journal of Health and Social Behavior,* 11 (1970), 269-87.

[26]*Harper's Bazaar,* November 1979, p. 78.

[27]Brochure from "Slender World," Anderson, South Carolina.

[28]G.L. Maddox, K. Back and V.R. Liederman, "Overweight as Social Deviance and Disability," *Journal of Health and Social Behavior,* 9 (1968), 288.

[29]Judith Thurman, "Never Too Thin to Feel Fat," *Ms.,* Sept. 1977, p. 82.

[30]Letty Cottin Pogrebin, "Barbara Cook: Fat Can Set You Free," *Ms.,* Sept. 1977, p. 82.

[31]Polhemus, p. 22.

[32]Judith Ramsey, "Anorexia Nervosia: Dying of Thinness," *Ms.,* August 1976, p. 103.

[33]Polhemus, pp. 21-22.

[34]"Shaughn Reiss", " 'Each Hunger Pain Delighted Me'," *Ms.,* August 1976, pp. 106-107.

[35]Erving Goffman, "Introduction," *The Presentation of Self in Everyday Life* (Garden City, N.Y.: Doubleday Anchor Books, 1959), pp. 1-16.

Staging the Vocational Bride
or
The Prom Queen Turns Pro

Juliette B. Woodruff

THEOLOGIANS WHO DEDICATE their lives to eccelesiastical matters have vocations. So do missionaries. So do doctors, and actors. And so, exactly, does the subject of this thesis, who dedicates herself to Staging the Wedding. This lady's vocation—the calling for which she has trained for most of her adolescent and those few adult years under her belt and for which she is particularly suited—Getting Married.

Not *marriage*, mind you. Donning the saffron robe isn't the point at all: Getting Married—The Wedding—the Actual Ceremony, the ritual (which the participants may or may not fully understand), with our girl at center, star of the show, *is*.

This female is the vocational, or professional bride because she goes about the management of this event with an efficiency and professionalism that puts to shame most businesses, with the possible exception of AT&T, General Motors and IBM. In this endeavor, usually mammoth, she invariably has the competent (and more often than not overbearing and domineering) guidance of her mother, herself oftentimes a former professional bride who seizes upon this opportunity to come out of retirement.

I have been fascinated by the concept of the professional bride ever since participating in a prodigious nuptial production several years ago. As mother of the ringbearer, I was sufficiently peripheral to see clearly, and I found myself almost speechless at being invited to 17 of the 36 parties given for the bride prior to the wedding; at 150 people at the seven-course rehearsal dinner held in the swankiest private club in town ending with brandy and cigars; at 12 bridesmaids and 20 groomsmen; at a reception featuring huge roasts of beef, hams, corned beeves, multiple champagne fountains, three bars, two bands for uninterrupted dancing that continued into the wee hours, and ending up with thousands of adorably wrapped satin and net flowers containing rice to toss at the departing bride and groom as they left for a two-week Caribbean cruise.

In addition to all this frivolity, there was a three-page set of printed instructions, and each member of the wedding party had his or her own copy. These instructions spelled out in very specific terms who did what, to whom, and where, what car each person was to ride in from wedding to reception, who was to be seated where in the church, and what sort of dress was expected at each of the functions covered in these instructions. Actually, it was extremely helpful to have everything elucidated in such explicit fashion for a wedding with so many diverse elements, and if one is contemplating a big wedding, I highly recommend such organization.

Perhaps I'd been away from the Big Wedding scene too long: my reaction to the excesses of this gigantic conjuncture was, "My word, do people *still* do things like this?" And I began to look around with more attention and I found that, yes, they indeed do.

I began to find some unvarying similarities among these Vanity Fair weddings, and while small details might change from wedding to wedding, certain criteria were *always* met, certain rituals always followed.

The girl who becomes a professional bride almost always comes from the ranks of a species of female to whom our society refers, both lovingly and scathingly as the Great American Princess. She is not the kind of princess born into the role, such as Princess Anne of England, nor even the princess who marries into the role, such as Princess Grace of Monaco. The Great American Princess we are talking about is *made,* not born.[1] She is the handiwork of modern Western society. Though we perhaps most often think of her as WASP, (white Anglo-Saxon Protestant) the Great American Princess-professional bride syndrome knows no ethnic boundaries. She can be Black, Greek, Italian, Jewish, Norwegian, or Arabic. We find her in every American ethnic group. Only the names change— all other customs and traditions and rituals correspond to each other right down the line.

Many people regard the Princess as a Jewish phenomenon, but in *New York Magazine* (22 March 1971, p. 25) Julie Baumgold makes the point that neither economic class nor religion is absolutely crucial to the development of a Princess, and cites Bette Davis, Yoko Ono, and Wendy Vanderbilt as examples of princesses whose backgrounds differ wi⌐ ⌐ly.[2]

I would interject here, though, that it *is* possible for a girl who was not raised in the pure Great American Princess tradition to step, at a moment's notice, into the role of the professional bride and to perform it admirably, such is our society's inherent attitude regarding weddings, and the nearly unchanging rituals supporting the institution. Our national feelings about weddings resemble racial memories, which enable almost any American girl to become a professional bride instantly. She...just...knows...how....

We must consider the Great American Princess as we look at the professional bride because they are closely linked. One produces the other. The Great American Princess myth begins at an early age. Through the ritual of upbringing and development, she becomes the ultimate purchaser of advanced technology and premium brands—the *best* money can buy. Although in all ethnic groups in the country there are men and women who dress and acquire in sensational fashion, our society has created a female figure as the archetype. On the one hand we envy her the possession of fine adornments we covet, but on the other we have contempt for her because we realize that unending acquisition is part of the ritual of a twisted value system.[3]

Where do we find this paragon of materiel with whom we have a love-hate relationship? Well you won't find her milking cows in a Sears $19.95 special; in fact, she rarely touches farm animals. She buys her clothes at Saks or the local equivalent, often has her own car, lunches sparingly, and the only scrubbing she does is of her face. While we have said that economic circumstances do not a Great American Princess make, her natural habitat is *usually* the upper reaches of society, and you can recognize her by the labels in her wearing apparel and the rituals of her way of life. She is, in a sense, a strategy of presentation, an exquisite package of elegant dress, exotic smells and great put-down lines.[4] She can be found at such places as museums, churches, synagogues and showings of art[5]—not, however, a Norman Rockwell unless it has been declared chic. Even Winslow Homer is marginal. To be on the safe side, look for the French Impressionists.

Such is the rarified ambiance in which the care and breeding of the Great American Princess—the rituals of her life—take place. Her mother, that staunch, dependable producer and trainer of both the Great American Princess and the professional bride, starts her off on the wonderful road to bridedom even before she becomes conscious of clothes or interested in men. She soon perceives that she is *expected* to Get Married, and further to do so in style. Frequent refrains are, "When *you* grow up and get married..." and "*You'll* have such and so in *your* wedding." She is taught to critique the various weddings to which she is witness, and her training continues as she watches the professional brides of her social circle go down the aisle to the rich strains of Wagner's "Bridal Chorus" from *Lohengrin,* for so long the very symbol of the traditional wedding.[6] She sees ecstatic brides and grooms, like so many pairs of beautifully costumed dolls[7] in ethereal, super-spectacular rituals of worship to the god Hymen, and she learns to yearn after her very own participation in same, vowing to make *her* wedding even more impressive. No man of the cloth has learned his religious service better than she, and none more determined that the service be fitting for the occasion.

The professional bride hardly ever marries immediately upon graduation from high school—after all, if she did she couldn't make her debut, and many professional brides are debutantes. The pomp and circumstance of the debut are considered part of the ritualistic training for the professional bride. (Being a debutante does have a drawback, however—she doesn't have the spotlight entirely to herself. She has to share it with the other debs, and, let's face it, sharing means you get less. Fleeting though the moment is, while she is actually a bride, she shares the limelight with *no one.*)

If she attends college at all, she may attend a small, select, all girls' school, or she may attend a big university. There seems to be no particular pattern in that regard, but whatever she chooses, you may be sure that she enjoys as many as possible of the superficial extracurricular activities that accompany academic life, such as social clubs, sororities, and, of course, fraternities.

The professional bride's age and familial connections allow her to take off six months or even a year from the "real world"—to drop out of college, which she most likely attended by her parents' grace and where she probably nibbled at higher education as though it were an olive, wondering if she could acquire a taste for it—or to resign from a job which she held as a sort of interim, stop-gap measure until she could Get Married, BE a Bride. She never really intends college to prepare her to earn a living, just as she doesn't look upon a job as a step toward a career.

The age range of the typical professional bride varies, but by and large her age can be expected to fall between 18 and 25, with a median age of 20. (I hesitate to set rigid limits because I have actually seen mature women of 35 indulge in these extravaganzas.) At 20 she is still sufficiently under mama's wing to willingly participate in this excessive celebration of epithalamion. She is also still quite naive about the relationship of value to the expenditure of money—but, again, that is characteristic of a Great American

Princess and another subject altogether.

We have said nothing thus far about the prop signaling the beginning of the action in this elaborate stage play—the diamond engagement ring. Once she "gets her ring" (that detestable phrase, so proprietary, as though, *of course,* in the words of an increasing number of television commercials which encourage snobbish narcissism, she deserves such a gift!)—anyway, once she "gets her ring," let the wild rumpus start, as Maurice Sendak says in one of his wonderful children's books.[8]

From the acquisition of the ring to the exit from the wedding reception, this nubile creature we have identified as the professional bride is in her element, playing her pre-ordained role. It is for some the high point of their lives. Never again do they achieve anything quite like it, never mind that they didn't look very far beyond the honeymoon. The Wedding is the thing. I once observed one such professional bride, at the end of her lengthy and lavish reception, run weeping into her mother's arms (where they wept together), crying, "Oh, I don't want it to be over! I don't want this to end!" Of course she didn't. She was just beginning to realize that marriage to Leonard wasn't going to be parties and stephanotis and presents and champagne.

To be perhaps painfully candid, I think the *moment* of the Wedding is something akin to the *moment* of death for the ancient culture of Orientals who practiced *hara-kiri*: for them, the entirety of life was spent preparing for death, and when it was accomplished, they were no more. When The Wedding is over, for all too many professional brides, nothing ever again approaches the glory and the splendor of that occasion.

Speaking of glory and splendor brings us to yet another element of The Wedding. All this magnificence and fanfaronade requires money. Now, money is a very important part of The Wedding, but finances *per se* aren't really germane. The financial circumstances of a family don't matter when it comes to the expenditure of money on The Wedding of its daughter. We find cross-overs in all strata, and price doesn't necessarily match income. A top debutante may choose an $85.00 dress to wear with her heirloom veil— or a bride from a family of lesser means may have 17 bridesmaids and a reception for 2,000. Of course in the latter case the father of the bride probably mortgaged everything he owned.[9]

Although there are numerous low-cost and dignified alternatives today, the professional bride usually opts for the expensive, assembly-line, catered affair, considering *it* more important than the wedding ceremony itself. In this, she is encouraged by the bridal magazines and other marriage-related enterprises. No wonder so many young people and their parents fall into the "tender trap" and go into heavy debt for the once-in-a-lifetime event![10]

(An interesting innovation that has found its way into the wedding scene with increasing popularity born of necessity is the "Catered Affair Cancellation Insurance" policy that will pay off non-refundable bills if either the bride or the groom undergoes a change of heart![11])

We find, in this image-oriented, relentlessly materialistic society of ours that *style* is a principal strategy of the professional bride. Trappings are all important: the big diamond engagement ring, engraved invitations in which are enclosed separate invitations to the reception, permission to sit "within the ribbon," and a response card to be mailed back, the wedding gown, the settings (big church or synagogue, country club), the music, flowers, food, and of course, a limousine rented for the sole purpose of transporting the happy couple from wedding to reception. (One family I know rented a 1937 black and silver Pierce-Arrow for a three-block ride.) We are talking about a part of society that produces these inordinate spectacles, a traditionally sexist society wherein the female has been reared to consume, while the male has been groomed to pay the bills and stay out of the way. The giant wedding syndrome is a natural extension of this role bifurcation.[12]

And what of the other half of the *raison d'etre* for all of this fabulous flurry, old what's-his-name, the groom?

This unfortunate man is the mark, as Samuel Butler, in *The Way of All Flesh*, says:

Papas and mamas sometimes ask young men whether their intentions are honorable towards their daughters. I think young men might occasionally ask papas and mamas whether *their* intentions are honorable before they accept invitations to houses where there are unmarried daughters.

He is usually dull and boring, since he has little time to execute practices comparable to the professional bride's. *She* is after a $3,000 diamond engagement ring, a $17,000 wedding, and a honeymoon on the leeward side of Aruba,[13] but *he* must pursue a business career for ten or twelve hours a day in order to support the Great American Princess-cum-professional bride in the style to which she is determined to remain accustomed.

However, the groom *is* absolutely essential for all of this extravagance to take place. The professional bride and her mother need him as the female black widow spider needs the male.

The importance of the mother of the bride, on the other hand, can *never* be understated. She plays the role of industrial management as distinguished from labor. She is the director of a cast of thousands! She is a Member of the Wedding! She is invincible! Her protean talents permit her to pursue her objectives with a diligence and assiduity which would put Sherlock Holmes in the shade. This lady, a powerhouse of determination and will power, is made of steel. She has previously paid her dues by entertaining lavishly for the daughters (and sons, if necessary) of her friends, and can now call in her markers and expect repayment in full.

Luci Johnson Nugent put it succinctly when she said, "Every bride has to learn it is not her wedding, but her mother's."

Why is this almost always the case? So *many* mothers raise their baby daughters to be professional brides. This girl is something of a victim of her mother, who possibly was herself a war bride with only an Army chapel as a memory.[14] Or perhaps the mother had the same sort of gigantic bash and seizes upon the opportunity, as all too many professional brides do when faced with the realities of married life, to re-live the fairy tale, make-believe quality. Or maybe she merely needs to throw a wing-ding to maintain her place in the social hierarchy.

Whatever the reason, this iron-willed lady keeps her finger on the pulse of every fact of the procedure, beginning with the purchase of one of the key props in all this panoply, the wedding gown, when she makes sure that her darling is properly pampered and fawned over. She has wedding assistants, usually of her own choosing, on hand at the church to help the bride and her attendants dress (many times in rooms built expressly for that purpose in the houses of worship where these brides are most often found). These elite helpers are armed with pins, needles, thread, smelling salts, Kleenex, cosmetics, spare stockings and all the vital equipment that could make the difference between success and catastrophe.[15]

Even though today, in certain segments of society in which tradition doesn't count as much as it used to and where weddings are much less a matter of conventional inflexibility than of what suits everybody (what would have caused a case of the vapors a decade ago is now made acceptable by social arbiters like Letitia Baldridge),[16] the days when marriage rituals were a matter of rote and rule[17] have not vanished, and indeed, still flourish in surprisingy good health and in no danger of becoming extinct.

One of the most striking changes taking place in the avant-garde wedding movement (and which our protagonist wouldn't touch on a dare) is spontaneity—or at least the appearance of it—replacing (or seeming to replace) the formality of the traditional wedding. This highly-touted and valued spontaneity may be and is expressed through various wedding media, such as clothing: the bridal gown may be in the customary white satin, but cut in a flowing, romantic "Camelot" style, or the groom may wear white satin also, with a balloon-sleeved page's shirt, or they may both wear blue jeans with wreaths of flowers on their heads; the wording of the ceremony: the reading of a Browning sonnet or part of Walt Whitman's *Song of the Open Road,* as Jenny and Oliver did in Erich Segal's highly popular *Love Story,*[18] or even a totally re-written wedding ceremony; the setting: a meadow, a seashore, CB radios, or, as happened recently in my city, in the administrative offices of the electric authority; music: folk-singing, with the congregation perhaps singing along, too, guitars, or even bird-song at dawn.

Spontaneity, which may or may not augur more awareness of the significance of the ceremony on the parts of the principals, has absolutely *no* place in the professional bride's scheme of things. Every event, every part, no matter how trivial, is determined in advance, planned in the most minute detail, and executed with precision, premeditation, and deliberation, with the kleig lights ever on the bride.

The surface details of the masterpiece are all-important. The meaning of the actual ceremony (except for the drama of the words) is not the crux of the matter at all—it is merely the *excuse,* the *vehicle,* the *catalyst* that allows this colossal rhapsody in white to be staged. Standard wedding practices include the selection of a large house of worship, where the rituals are scrupulously observed, from "Dearly beloved, we are gathered..." to "What therefore God hath joined together, let not man put asunder." None of this new-fangled nonsense like reciting poetry or quoting from *The Prophet* for *our* sweetheart!

The attendants are for the most part in the same age bracket and social milieu as the bride, and either enjoyed the same kind of immoderate bash or are avidly taking notes for their own yet to come. Flower girls and ring bearers are mandatory, and indeed I know of one wedding with not *one,* not *two,* but *three* miniature and potential professional brides, identically dressed and dripping rose petals down the aisle on which the bride delightedly trod.

Also standard for these "thick-coming fancies," as Shakespeare called them, is the elegant, catered reception after the wedding, usually at a country club, rarely if ever in the church's social hall. There is an enormous, elaborate, multi-tiered wedding cake, and often also a groom's cake of chocolate or heavy with candied fruits. Then there are imported champagne, an unobtrusive obtrusive photographer, perishable cut flowers, the official rice tossing in darling satin bags, and the inevitable, coy exit of the bride and groom[19] on their way to a pleasure dome in some posh, more or less fabled spot. This four- to six-hour blow-out costs in the thousands of dollars, money that could have made a down-payment on a house.[20] By most estimates, the kind of nuptial benediction we are talking about costs something like $6- to $15,000—just to get the bride and groom out of the church and away on their honeymoon.[21]

The wedding of the professional bride is always covered by the newspapers. Except in small communities, only the weddings of the children of the affluent are described in detail, down to the last seed pearl and out-of-town guest. The usual yardstick for connubial copy at the *Los Angeles Times,* for example, decrees that one standard is "yes" to the daughter of the owner of the International House of Pancakes chain, but "no" to the daughter of the owner of a single House of Pancakes franchise. In a small town or city, however, such as Mobile, Alabama, where everybody has lived for a hundred years, brides absolutely cannot be removed because everyone wants to read about themselves and one another. Even the *New York Times* still runs yards of wedding copy, usually on Sunday, where the brides break up acres of retail advertising.[22]

Even though it is today highly unrealistic to think that one's first wedding is also going to be one's *only* wedding, society nonetheless rarely allows a second display of this magnitude except under certain strictly enjoined circumstances. The illusion is that marriage is forever and ever.

In the past, remarriage has been an etiquette problem and couples engaging in it were well advised to keep a low profile. No one quite knew what to do or how to go about it. The wedding-related enterprises' urgings to go ahead and have a second big splash notwithstanding, most second-time-arounders among the professional bride's friends do indeed skip the hoopla and run down to City Hall at lunchtime.[23] These repeaters never wear white, no one gives the bride away, and their children generally are not the legal witnesses. In their tightly established confines, such things simply aren't allowed.

Samuel Johnson said that a second marriage represents the triumph of hope over experience. Experience is undoubtedly responsible for the interesting although hardly new phenomenon occurring in America today: lawyers, once the servants of the very rich and powerful, are advising *all* classes on a variety of financial and legal marital matters. The complications of post-divorce financial planning demand more than a notary public.[24]

More common yesterday than today, the professional bride is something of an anarchronism in this era of neo-arbitrary, do-it-yourself ceremonies and live-in partnerships, where even Walter Cronkite's daughter walked barefoot through the meadow for her wedding while her little brother played his flute. Even so, the professional bride is alive and well, living mainly in entrenched old-society bastions, where she and her mother orchestrate the rubric for something that more closely resembles a medieval pageant than a simple joining together of man and woman in holy matrimony. The Wedding of the professional bride remains a stronghold of ritualized tradition, and the professional bride of today will probably become the producer of the next generation of professional brides, thus carrying on the ritual which clearly has a tight grip on her and her associates' lives.

Notes

[1]Irving J. Rein, "The Great American Princess: a Stylistic Myth," *The Great American Communication Catalogue* (Englewood Cliffs, N.J.: Prentice-Hall, 1976), p. 135.

[2]Ibid.   [3]Ibid.   [4]Ibid.   [5]Ibid.

[6]Barbaralee Diamonstein, "Here Come the Brides!" *Good Housekeeping,* June 1971, p. 130.

[7]Ibid., p. 93.

[8]Maurice Sendak, *Where the Wild Things Are* (New York: Harper & Row, 1963).

[9]"Many Hands Slice the Wedding Cake," *Business Week,* 2 June 1962.

[10]Sidney Margolius, "Wedding Bells Need Not Leave Parents Wrung Out Financially" (Women's News Service), *Florida Times-Union* (Jacksonville, Florida), 4 Nov., 1979, sec. E, p. 8.

[11]Ibid.

[12]Rein, "The Great American Princess," p. 134.

[13]Ibid., p. 140.

[14]*Business Week,* p. 121.

[15]Ibid.

[16]"Here Come the Brides," *Florida Times-Union,* 4 March 1979, p. 13.

[17]*Florida Times-Union,* p. 13.

[18]Diamonstein, p. 130.

[19]Irving J. Rein, "The Rhetoric of the Bridal Salon," *The Great American Communication Catalogue* (Englewood Cliffs, N.J.: Prentice-Hall, 1976), p. 155.

[20]Ibid.

[21]*Business Week,* p. 120.

[22]"Flight from Fluff," *Time,* 20 March 1972.

[23]Jacqueline McCord Leo, "Marrying Again...Do It Your Way with the Help of our Etiquette," *Modern Bride,* Oct.-Nov. 1979, p. 50.

[24]Jacqueline McCord Leo, "Remarriage," *Modern Bride,* Oct.-Nov. 1979, p. 66.

Big Mac and *Caneton A L'Orange:* Eating, Icons and Rituals

Pamela Malcolm Curry & Robert M. Jiobu

WE EAT AWAY an important portion of our lives—for the traditional male, a reasonable estimate might be four out of sixteen waking hours are involved in dining and related activities; for the traditional housewife as much as eight of the sixteen hours if we count grocery shoping, cooking and cleaning up. Considering the amount of time devoted to it, eating obviously involves more than just ingesting a prescribed quantity of nutrients (after all, NASA food bricks would serve that purpose quite well). Yet, despite the broader implications, few social scientists have addressed the topic. Perhaps we have tended to ignore our own eating behavior because it is so commonplace, obvious and banal that it falls below our threshold of interests. Only under unusual circumstances does our eating become salient, and then only ephemerally.

But the human lot requires food; and as with many everyday necessities, eating is surrounded by norms and folkways, many of which are also rituals and habits. This makes life easier since day-to-day decisions, once converted to habit, require less time and effort and once ritualized provoke less anxiety. A pleasant sense of calm comes to prevail. The world appears less chaotic. Life flows more smoothly. Eating behavior, in short, becomes institutionalized.

A social institution, by definition, is a collection of norms, folkways, habits and rituals, all of which relate to an important activity—in this case, eating. Peter Berger and Thomas Luckman in a widely read sociological work say this:

> An institutional world, then, is experienced as an objective reality.... It was there before (the individual) was born, and it will be there after his death.... The

institutions are *there*, external to him, persistent in their reality, whether he likes it or not. He cannot wish them away. They resist his attempt to change or evade them. They have coercive power over him, both in themselves, by the sheer force of their facticity, and through the control mechanism that is usually attached to the most important of them.[1]

A scene from Ernest Hemingway's "The Short Happy Life of Francis Macomber" nicely illustrates the point.

Wilson, the guide, and Macomber and his wife Margot, are eating lunch served by a porter. That morning Macomber had proved himself a physical coward. He had gut shot a lion, then bolted when it charged.

> "That's eland he's offering you," Wilson said.
> "It's very good meat," Macomber said.
> "Did you shoot it, Francis?" she asked.
> "Yes."
> "They're not dangerous, are they?"
> "Only if they fall on you," Wilson told her.
> "I'm so glad."
> "Why not let up on the bitchery just a little Margot," Macomber said, cutting the eland steak and putting some mashed potato, gravy and carrot on the down-turned form that tined through the pieces of meat.
> "I suppose I could," she said, "since you put it so prettily."
> "Tonight we'll have champagne for the lion," Wilson said. "It's a bit too hot at noon."[2]

Macomber's praise of the eland meat, the way he places his food on his fork in the proper English manner, and Wilson's offhand remark on the appropriateness of drinking champagne at noon all exemplify ritualized and habitualized norms and folkways. The characters feel they must somehow play out the rituals—what we learn as etiquette and decorum—no matter how painful it might be. In other words, institutions force us to act in certain ways, yet we are unaware of it. Our behavior is thus compelled, preconscious and predictable.

Cultural anthropologist Mary Douglas points out that among the Tekopia (a Polynesian group), many ceremonies and associated rituals had to be cancelled when their crops failed—the necessary symbolic foods were not available.[3] Such behavior might strike us as a bit odd, but our culture is filled with examples not too unlike the Tekopia's.

We use a specially decorated cake to symbolize many ceremonial occasions: birthdays, christenings, weddings, anniversaries, and retirements to name a few. It's difficult to imagine a formal wedding without the traditional multitiered, white cake decorated with flowers and rosettes fashioned from sugary icing and topped off with a little plastic bride and groom. And surely the bride must ritualistically cut the cake and stuff a piece into her new husband's mouth. Similarly, a birthday party without cake and candles would seem rather empty or somehow incomplete because there wouldn't be an icon summarizing the event. And how tacky it would be if the guest of honor refused the ritual of blowing out the candles; and how odd if the candles were stuck on a dish rather than a decorated cake.

Once we begin to catalog them, other iconic foods and rituals associated with holidays and ceremonies pop into mind: Christmas cookies for carolers; chocolate rabbits and hunting decorated eggs for Easter; turkey and the gathering at Grandmother's for Thanksgiving; and champagne toasts for New Year's Eve.

Foods also symbolize life styles, whole gestalts of meanings and ritualistic behaviors. Hamburgers broiled over a charcoal grill in the backyard suggest suburbia. Even sex role behaviors are represented by specific foods: thick T-bone steaks and straight bourbon for virility and masculinity; watercress sandwiches and creme de menthe for daintiness and femininity. We could go on, but the point is clear: within an institution some (but not all) icons and rituals are linked to one another. An icon might call out a ritual, and a ritual might be meaningless without the associated icon.

Institutions emerge slowly, and in the process enfold symbols and rituals. The development of food icons and rituals can be historically traced: first, diet expanded and diversified as a result of new technology; and second, the rise of name brands, supermarkets, and fast food establishments encouraged even more diversity.

During the early days of the Republic, crude technology necessarily limited diet; but with the development of fast transportation, refrigeration and food preservation, the American diet became more varied. The increase in diversity can be indexed in the number of pages in cookbooks:

...it was not until 1796 that the first manual by an American author appeared. This volume bore the imposing title *American Cookery, or the Art of Dressing Viands, Fish, Poultry, and Vegetables, and the Best Modes of Making Pastes, Puffs, Pies, Tarts, Puddings, Custards, and Preserves, and All Kinds of Cakes, from the Imperial Plumb to Plain Cake. Adapted to This Country, and All Grades of Life. By Amelia Simmons: An Amerian Orphan....* (This) first edition was of vest-pocket size and contained only 46 pages. Its meager dimensions help to illustrate the fact that to some people the physical size of cookbooks serves to show the diversification of diet which has taken place during the past century. *The Frugal Housewife* (1829) contained 95 pages. Mrs. Putnam's *Receipt Book and Young Housekeeper's Assistant*, published in 1858, numbered 223. The 1896 edition of the Boston Cook School Cook Book contained 567 and the pages of the 1930 edition of this work numbered 831.[4]

Today, cookbooks of 600 and 700 pages are not uncommon and

the traditional ones have sales in the millions.[5] Cookbooks index a huge breadth on the one hand and specialization on the other: from the elaborate inclusive work of the renowned French chef Jaques Pepin[6] to unknowns William Shurtleff and Akiko Aoyagi, authors of a cookbook about an unknown food, *tofu.*[7] There is also great diversity as to how to cook food. There are books on quick methods (micro ranges)[8] as well as on slow methods (crock pots),[9] and everything in between. The interest goes beyond books. Cooking schools are flourishing and sales of cookware booming.[10] Technology and learning have brought us to a point where we can cook just about anything just about any way.

While technology was changing the American diet, an organizational development occurred that diversified it even more. Because they are so much a part of our everyday lives, we sometimes forget that the supermarket is a relatively new social invention. Before the supermarket, shoppers conveyed their requests to a clerk who would fetch and package the item. Many times the clerk broke bulk: repackaging items from wholesale containers to smaller ones. Specialized stores—butcher shops, produce markets and dry goods—were the rule and shoppers had to visit many different places to complete their market baskets.

But smaller, specialized stores gave way to supermarkets which were originally touted as low cost, cut rate operations. In the East they were originally called "cheapies" and were enormously successful from their inception during the Great Depression.[11] While manufacturers had already begun to distinguish their products with visual and verbal symbols, the supermarket accentuated—required in fact—that the product be symbolized. Shopping was no longer done through a clerk. Customers had to be somehow enticed to choose one brand over another as they pushed carts down aisles surrounded by competing brands and products. The role of visual and verbal symbols came into extreme prominence since without direct human contact, what better way was there to attract customers than by icon and jingle?

We can easily verify the success of advertising campaigns in creating a dependence on icons. Most adults can't identify Count Chocula, Cap'n Crunch, or Franken Berry—cartoon icons representing different brands of dry cereal. But then most adults haven't been exposed to the Saturday morning cartoon shows that saturate the TV screen with cereal icons.[12] In a supermarket all the adult sees is a shelf filled with a mass of brightly colored cartoon characters. In this situation a great asset is a child who knows the iconic language and can easily pick out those which go with each cereal.

Eating patterns have also changed. Caught in the middle of

rapid developments few families can maintain the kind of eating behavior found in the early part of this century. According to one account: "We ate at set hours: approximately 7:30, 12:30 and 6. Father sat at one end, Mother at the other; Brother on one side; I on the other. The whole family ate together, and in the dining room."[13] Today, meals are frequently catch-as-catch-can. Breakfast, if eaten at home, is often self prepared and eaten with no expectation of family interaction. A letter to Amy Vanderbilt complained:

My husband buries his head in the newspaper at breakfast and doesn't say a word to me throughout. He just hands me the second section. Shouldn't a husband be expected to carry on some conversation with his wife at breakfast?

Amy answered:

No one *should be expected* to carry on a conversation at breakfast. Many people don't really wake up until later in the day. Enjoy that second section....[14]

The forces that led to the decline of the family-centered meal—urbanization, increased labor force participation of women, increased mobility and diversification of family leisure activities—also created a complex environment that needed to be reduced to some simpler form.[15]

From its beginning, the fast food industry recognized and rushed to meet this need. The use of icons to channel behavior along predetermined lines has perhaps evolved to its highest form in the world of fast foods. Ray Kroc, the driving force behind McDonald's, describes the necessity of creating the right icons and the success that can follow:

I liked Paul Schrage's approach, because he was a "detail man" in his field, and he was on the same wave length as I was concerning the McDonald's image. For example, a great deal of study has gone into creating the appearance and personality of Ronald McDonald, right down to the color and texture of his wig. I loved Ronald. So did the kids. Even the sophisticates at *Esquire* magazine loved him. They invited Ronald to their "Party of the Decade" for top newsmakers of the sixties. McDonald's was chosen to cater the party because we had the biggest impact on the eating habits of the Americans in the decade.[16]

The right icon is important; and an industry's success in developing them is evident in that they can take on a quasi-sacred quality. For instance, they are immortal or at least never grow older. Colonel Sanders, as best the eye can tell, is as young (or old) as he ever was; and freckle faced Wendy is still the same as when introduced to the public. Even more miraculously, some character symbols become younger as they grow older. Aunt Jemima used to be mature and matronly but now is thin and young.

This quasi-sacred quality becomes salient when an icon deviates from its perceived perfection and becomes profane. An extreme example, though not a food symbol, is Marilyn Chambers who could no longer represent the purity of Ivory Snow after she starred in the porn film *Behind the Green Door*. A person who played Ronald McDonald was fired for lending out his clown costume for use at a private houseparty—clearly outside the quasi-sacred sphere.

Even though food products are meant to be eaten, the character symbols which represent them are never eaten. To do so would symbolically violate the general societal taboo against cannibalism; for the character symbols are endowed with human qualities. Star Kist constantly rejects Charlie Tuna; he will never appear in our tuna salad on rye. "Sorry, Charlie," intones the voice-over in the television commercial. The Pillsbury Doughboy supervises the baking of dinner rolls but never jumps into the oven to be heated and served. Eventually both product and icon are integrated into the overall value scheme of American culture, largely being imposed on us from above. This is nowhere more clearly seen than in the commercials sponsored by television's single largest advertiser: McDonald's. Their workers—who sing and dance a lot—are industrious, young, bouncy, attractive and smily. They alleviate any guilt we have about eating out as they sing "We're doing it all for you," because "you *deserve* a break today."

The symbols, the product, and the activity of eating at these symbolic places are thus linked with happiness, success, a job well done, and hard work. We end up being taught a curious blend of philosophies: a clown's version of a happy Puritan Ethic.[17]

The constant repetition of the icons and of the corresponding messages cause both to become completely taken for granted as part of everyday living. They disappear into the ritualistic background and we come to accept, with little challenge, that fast foods are a way to quickly eat socially approved, work-a-day meals.

The result of this acceptance by the larger society has been to polarize American eating style—schizophrenia characterizes the institution of eating. At one time we will frequent the highly symbolized yet sterile world of fast food, while at another we will leisurely partake of the ritualistic world of gourmet eating and formal dinners.

The contrast between gourmet and fast food eating is quite extreme. One is mostly ritualistic, the other is mostly instrumental. If one were to count the rituals associated with gourmet and fast food eating, surely a comparison would make the latter seem virtually ritual-less. Since few rituals exist for fast food dining, few must be learned, and few are in place to slow down the dining process. The plastic and chrome environment structures behavior and varies little from one fast food place to another: self-serve counters, plastic forks, formica tables and minimal social interaction—no waitresses, no busboys, no tips, no talk. Fast foods are fast, and dining is basically "gobble and go." So, although the rituals associated with such a spartan activity do exist, they are scarcely noticeable and only barely inhibit the flow of traffic in everyday life.

Such is not the case, obviously, when dining in a gourmet or more conventional restaurant. There certain rituals have to be engaged. For instance, we must first choose the restaurant itself, and this can take much time: a whole litany of questions and answers, feelings and biases must be considered in finally choosing which restaurant one will "dine" in on any certain occasion. Once there, a person must choose a wine from an elaborate list of brands and types, the names of which we might hesitate to pronounce in our high school French. And when the waiter serves the wine, we must examine the cork and, if satisfactory, delicately try the first sip. But what are we looking for when examining the cork, and how should the wine taste? That we know the technically correct answers to the questions is far less important than that we correctly go through these rituals, and all the other rituals of etiquette and deportment, including how many times and to what extent to be displeased with the preparation of the food itself, up through eventually knowing when to tip the person who brings the car around.

None of these rituals (and others) are really "rational." We could eat just as well without them. They do not directly contribute to the taste of the food. Nevertheless we must learn and observe them if we are to engage in gourmet eating, for stripped of ritual gourmet does not exist.

While the symbols remain relatively fixed over time, one can expect the links with American values and popular culture to modify with the changing environment.

The American diet is becoming a national political issue. The Senate Select Committee on Nutrition and Human Needs, chaired by George McGovern, published a report the purpose of which was "to point out that the eating patterns of this century represent as critical a public health concern as any now before us."[18] The report advocates that Americans substantially decrease their consumption of meats, fats, high cholesterol foods, sugar and salt while increasing consumption of fruits, vegetables, whole grains, poultry and fish. A minor brouhaha followed the release of the report. It was condemned for not going far enough—chemical additives were not mentioned. And, to no one's surprise, it was condemned for going too far, notably by the affected food industries.[19]

The condemnation of the American diet may be gaining even more momentum, this loud cry against the fast food industry becoming itself a ritualized litany of the woes that will affect the nation if the trend is not reversed. The Junk Food Hall of Shame recently opened in the nation's capitol city. Its goal is to educate the public to the sorry state of the American diet. While we expect sugared cereals and soft drinks to be center displays, it shocks us to see such stand-bys as Shake 'n Bake, Jello and Dream Whip also nominated to the infamous Hall.

Still, the alarms of the McGovern report, the Hall of Shame, and other media warnings have not significantly altered the American diet. Though several inchoate counter trends can be observed, none seems on the verge of taking off and encompassing the bulk of the population. The fast food rituals are too deep seated to be easily brought to the surface and purged.

People who practice alternative diets—vegetarian, lactovegetarian, ovolactovegetarian, and opponents of chemical additives, for example—must learn a different set of behaviors. At first everything is problematic for them. Only slowly, and by trial and error, do they find their own routines, establish their own rituals and learn a different set of icons.[20]

Under these circumstances, rather than switching diets, it seems more likely that an ever increasing dominance of fast food will lead to a new set of standards and rituals. This may be occurring already in regard to home cooking. Recently a brand of "heat-and-serve" fried chicken was introduced via advertisement on our local television. The mother is harried and tired and obviously "deserves a break today"; but she feels guilty about eating out again. Her family should have a home cooked meal. What to do? Aha! The solution! Out of the freezer and into the radar range with heat-and-serve fried chicken that the announcer claims is "as good as the kind you go out for!"

The inevitable conclusion? Over time, technological and social changes have slowly brought eating behavior under the firm control of icons and the rituals that go with them. As consumers this works well for us. Our daily lives are rendered more orderly and our decision making more efficient. It also works well for entrepreneurs, helping them to capture specific segments of the commercial market.

Fast food restaurants have made particularly heavy use of icons to attract customers and rituals to keep people buying once they have learned; but at the same time, have divorced their icons from eating rituals. Fast food dining is pretty much instrumental and pragmatic.

By way of contrast, gourmet dining—the highest form of restaurant eating—is virtually all ritual but calls few icons to mind. Indeed a problem that such restaurants have is advertising the notion of gourmet without seeming crass. The announcement of stars, which are symbols of rare quality, is perhaps as iconic as gourmet establishments become.

In a broad sense, social science maintains—doomsday prophecies and changing technology notwithstanding—that we go through our daily lives in a highly structured, unthinking, organized, routinized and ritualized way. Eating as a social institution and as part of popular culture is yet another confirmation of this valid generalization.

Notes

[1]Peter L. Berger and Thomas Luckman, *The Social Construction of Reality* (New York: Doubleday Anchor books, 1966), p. 60. Our discussion of institutions relies heavily on this work. Sociologists and anthropologists almost always connect ritual to religion in some way. We do not. Our use of the term ritual is simply as a ceremonial act in accordance with custom; it may or may not be religious. George A. Theodorsen and A.G. Theodorsen, *A Modern Dictionary of Sociology* (New York: Thomas Y. Crowell, 1969), p. 351.

[2]Ernest Hemingway, "The Short Happy Life of Francis Macomber."

[3]Mary Douglas, "Account for Taste," *Psychology Today* 13 (July 1979), pp. 44-51. The Tikopia were described by Raymond Firth, *Social Change in Tikopia* (London: Allen and Unwin, 1960).

[4]Richard Osborn Cummings, *The American and His Food* (New York: Arno Press, 1970), p. 42.

[5]In the last 80 years almost 19 million copies of *Better Homes and Gardens Cookbook* were sold, and 13 million copies of *Betty Crocker's Cookbook*.

[6]Jacques Pepin, *La Technique* (New York: Pocket Books, 1976).

[7]William Shurtleff and Akiko Aoyagi, *The Book of Tofu: Food for Mankind* (New York: Ballantine Books, 1979).

[8]For example, Luisa Scott and Jack Denton Scott, *Mastering Microwave Cooking* (New York: Bantam Books, 1976).

[9]For example, Rose Cantrell and Ruth Kershner, *Crockery* (New York: Crown Publishers, Inc., 1979).

[10]"The Kitchen: America's Playroom," *Forbes* 117 (March 15), pp. 24-38; "Food: The New Wave," *Newsweek* (August 11, 1975), pp. 50-57; "In Ohio: Sauteing Together," *Time* 112 (May 21, 1979), not paginated.

[11]Rom J. Markin, *The Supermarket: An Analysis of Growth, Development and Change,* revised edition (Pullman, Washington: Washington State University, Bureau of Economic and Business Research, 1968).

[12]A monitoring of 5 Boston TV stations revealed that 25% of childrens' advertisements were for cereals. In total, children see about 20,000 TV commercials a year. See *Consumer Reports* 43 (August 1978), p. 432.

[13]James H. Bossard and Eleanor S. Boll, *Ritual in Family Living* (Philadelphia: Univ. of Pennsylvania Press, 1950).

[14]Amy Vanderbilt, *Everyday Etiquette* (New York: Bantam Books, 1979), p. 13. (Italics added.)

[15]See, for example, Robert S. Lynd and Helen M. Lynd, *Middletown in Transition: A Study of Cultural Conflicts* (New York: Harcourt Brace Jovanovich, 1937).

[16]Ray Kroc and Robert Anderson, *Grinding it Out: The Making of McDonald's* (Chicago:

Henry Regnery Co., 1977), p. 152.

[17]For several discussions of McDonald's see Marshall Fishwick (ed.) "Focus on the World of Ronald McDonald," *Journal of American Culture* 1 (Summer 1978), pp. 336-474.

[18]Select Committee on Nutrition and Human Needs, *Dietary Goals for the United States* (Washington, D.C.: U.S. Government Printing Office, 1977), p. v.

[19]"The Pure, the Impure, and the Paranoid," *Psychology Today* 12 (October 1978), pp. 67-77, 123.

[20]See, for example, "A True Believer Who Gave Up the Faith," *Psychology Today*, 12 (October 1978), p. 85.

[21]Marshal Sahlins, *Culture and Practical Reason* (Chicago and London: Univ. of Chicago Press, 1975), pp. 170-176. Not everyone agrees with Sahlin's argument. See Marvin Harris and Eric B. Ross, "How Beef Became King," *Psychology Today*, 12 (October 1978), pp. 88-94.

World War II as Southern Entertainment: The Confederate Air Force and Warfare Re-Enactment Ritual

C.R. Chandler

ALEXIS DE TOCQUEVILLE observed in the nineteenth century that the great mass of Americans resisted militarism and war as being opposed to their "own little undertakings" aimed at accumulating material goods.[1] Later commentators have generally agreed with this assessment.[2] And yet it seems also to be true that, until the last few years of the Vietnam conflict, many Americans have also taken pride in their country's military accomplishments and bestowed honor upon war veterans and heroes. W. Lloyd Warner went even further; when, speaking primarily of non-combatants, he wrote that "most Americans had more real satisfaction out of the Second World War ... than they had at any other period of their lives."[3] War attracts and concentrates people's attention to a degree hardly equaled by any other event. It calls for extreme qualities, whether those be conceived as heroic and virtuous or sadistic and immoral. Afterwards, the question, "What did you do in the war?" becomes more than a cliche to many individuals. Its answer takes on personal significance to those who were alive during the war period. People compare themselves with those cultural models of heroism which emerge from warfare. From before the time of Achilles these ideals have been blazoned forth and have left many of those who failed to serve with a feeling of guilty inadequacy and belated resentment that they missed the one big event of their lifetime. And over time, some of those who did serve romanticize their experience and wish to re-live it vicariously for their own amusement, and they think, often mistakenly, the entertainment of others.

It may be protested that this is no longer true; that the age of the anti-hero is firmly established. But observe the adulation of the actor John Wayne who continually portrayed one-dimensional heroes so successfully during a moving picture career that spanned several decades, including the period of Vietnam; and notice how the mass media are currently leading a great quest for new heroes. Even with regard to Vietnam I have recently talked with several

258

young men who were openly apologetic and remorseful that they were not involved in that conflict now that it is over. Apparently the recent anti-war movies may have the effect of making some people dream of what heroes, or what sensitive anti-heroes, they might have been.

That warfare at a distance or in retrospect also has entertainment value hardly needs to be documented. Accounts of great battles and heroic deeds are found among the earliest folklore and literature—the Iliad may qualify as both—and have been the subject of poems, novels, radio dramatizations, films and every medium for art, exhortation and amusement. Sex and violence, it is said, sell everything from comic books to sociology courses, and warfare must qualify as an extreme form of violance; one which can easily incorporate sexual subplots.

I am saying that war is both positively and negatively valued in American society. As such it has been the basis for ritual devoted to sacred objects, the subject of myth, and a source of temporary revitalization—all of which bring it very near to being a minor religion. Indeed, if America has a civil religion as Bellah has claimed,[4] martial glory is at least a small part of it.

Reverting to the other side of the debate, Klapp has maintained that industrial societies display a poverty of ritual, and indeed with respect to those observances associated with war, Americans hardly qualify as zealots in the civil religion.[5] Warner described Memorial Day as involving ritual and myth.[6] But his description comes from small town America shortly after World War II. Americans do not enthusiastically celebrate anniversaries of important military events and seem not even to be aware of them until reminded by the news media.

But, while official holidays and traditional ceremonies appear meaningless, a significant number of people have begun establishing commemorative rituals and games of warfare, and even larger numbers are drawn to these events as spectators. The Confederate Air Force (CAF) is an important case in point. Starting as a tiny recreational flying club in a small South Texas town, it has grown to international proportions in terms of membership (with Wings as far away as New Zealand) and impact (most notoriously when the Japanese government protested a 1976 re-enactment of the bombing of Hiroshima). A description and interpretation of the social meaning of this group and its activities form the substance of this essay.[7]

Sacred Toy: The Warplane

The first attraction of the Confederate Air Force to members and spectators is not warfare but warplanes. And not just any warplanes, but those built between 1939 and 1945. These machines, to pursue the religious analogy, are the sacred objects of a technological religion which Albanese has defined as a "life orientation centered around the machine, its products, its values, the modes of consciousness and unconsciousness it encourages, and the forms of action it applauds."[8]

In the beginning was the warplane and an ex-Army Air Corps flight instructor who had wanted to fly fighters but instead had been assigned training duties throughout World War II. Lloyd Nolen, founder and still unofficial leader of the CAF, was a Mercedes, Texas, crop duster in 1951 when he purchased his first war surplus fighter plane. This was a P-40, best known as the plane flown in China by the Flying Tigers and by Dennis Morgan and John Wayne in the movies.

Six years later Nolen had sold the P-40 and he and four other men—all either cropduster pilots or farmers—purchased a P-51. This was a fighter which had extraordinary performance capabilities and was of great military importance in the closing years of the war.

Other aircraft were bought because it was discovered that you couldn't run a race or have a dogfight with just one plane.[9] Soon the pilots were calling themselves the Confederate Air Force, with all members holding the rank of Colonel.

The element of play, sometimes organized into a contest, was at this stage more prominent than was ritualistic re-enactment of historic air battles. There would seem to be a strain between this recreational motivation and the serious patriotic and educational purposes which the organization proclaims to the public. The CAF itself appears to recognize such a contradiction since it makes officer candidates swear never to look upon the organization as a "pleasure group."[10] If one agrees with Durkheim's analysis of commemorative rites, however, there is no necessary conflict between the serious and the comic or recreational aspects of ritual.[11] Durkheim claimed that "representative rites and collective recreations are even so close to one another that men pass from one sort to the other without any break of continuity." The CAF Colonels appear not to have read *The Elementary Forms of the Religious Life*, but, in any event, their slight unease over reconciling what they call "high seriousness" with what Durkheim termed "simple public merrymaking" has not inhibited their enjoyment of the latter.

The aesthetic and recreational aspect of flying the airplanes of the 1940s is lost on most Americans who are not pilots, have grown accustomed to being encapsulated in jet airliners, and are more frightened than pleasurably thrilled when any aircraft within which they are riding deviates from smooth, stready routine. Airline captains may be fired, reprimanded, or, if lucky, made into public heroes when they loop or roll their planes, or "fly like cowboys" in aviation argot. But flying as sport is still popular and the idea of flying as spiritual and aesthetic experience is occasionally encountered, the foremost exponent of the latter view being Richard Bach, author of *Jonathan Livingston Seagull* and several other popular books.[12]

As might be expected, psychoanalysts have interpreted the attraction which grown men feel for sport and military aircraft. Douglas Bond, a psychiatrist, has commented that flying, like sex, has a "climactic quality," and brings "relief," and includes the following statement as part of his analysis:

Unconsciously, the combat aircraft, most purely the fighter, fulfills childhood desires for an exaggerated phallic power. Fighter pilots commonly speak of the plane as an extension of their own bodies. "It's part of me and I'm part of it." The shape of many aircraft is strikingly phallic.[13]

One can guess with confidence what Douglas Bond would have said had he considered the motivations of women who operate such machines.

The men who started the CAF would not have talked of mystical experiences or sexual sublimation, but claimed only to be pilots having a lot of weekend fun, flying high performance aircraft. As propeller-driven warplanes became scarcer, however, they became more valuable and precious in several ways. (Most fighters are currently worth a minimum of $100,000, and one P-51 is named "Precious Metal.") Besides the astronomical increase in monetary value, the machines took on status as historically important artifacts. Their aesthetic qualities came to be better appreciated. And, as World War II receded into the past and simultaneously expanded in the public consciousness as the "last just war" in which good—and the United States of America—triumphed over evil, the warplanes of that era became to many the symbols of heroic struggle and victory. These trends, taken together, transformed the warplanes into something resembling icons, sacred objects, at least to many enthusiasts.

In the early 1960s the small group of South Texas fighter pilots began to be invited to put on aerial demonstrations at military bases. The Rebels, as they termed themselves, seemed simultaneously to note the monetary advantages and the patriotic and educational value to be gained from expansion and the production of larger and more numerous airshows.[14] Thus began the process of growth, eventually establishing and almost achieving the goal of obtaining one each of every American military plane from the Second World War and keeping them flying. More elaborate organization was required, and simple airshow routines were developed until they became re-enactments of major battles.

But the key to their enthusiasm and public acceptance was the emotional and aesthetic appeal of the airplanes they so enjoyed flying. To the devotee they are indeed sacred objects in accordance with Durkheim's criterion that they inspire respect "without regard for any consideration relative to their useful or injurious effects."[16]

The Airshow

The Confederate Air Force puts on several demonstrations in widely separated parts of the United States each year. In 1979 they also staged a large and successful show in Mexico. But it is in October of each year that the scattered members of the CAF assemble in Harlingen, Texas, for their consummate re-enactment of the more felicitous aspects of World War II. Some description of this event is necessary.

The setting involved in any airshow is a broad expanse of flat land, usually windswept and sunscorched, with large hangars in the background, expanses of grass or concrete and the sky in the foreground.

In Harlingen, terrestrial space is organized in such a way as to allow the public selected views of back-stage areas, sometimes at an additional fee. These include hangar interiors, the flight line, and the Officer's Club. Some areas remain back stage, for instance flight briefings. For a discussion of a front and back continuum, developed from Goffman's writings, see MacCannell.[16] MacCannell argues that selected glimpses of back regions heighten authenticity, and this would seem to be true of CAF shows since close-up views of rare airplanes, including those undergoing maintenance, spare engines, etc., reinforce the impression that this is a real, working air force, as in many ways it is.

Celestial space is "organized" through the direction of air show announcers, the location of bleachers, and the "set" which airshow enthusiasts develop, i.e., to look up over the center of the airfield into the three-dimensional "stage." There are off-stage areas in the sky where planes circle waiting to "go-on."

Time involved depends on the activity being considered and the viewer's imagination. A snap roll by an airplane may require less than a second. The annual CAF airshow, including social events and official functions, lasts for four days and nights. Maintenance, flying and paper work go on continually. And the main part of the airshow tries to take the spectators back several decades to the period 1936-1945, compressing those nine years into two hours.

During the four show days, large numbers of people drive down blocks of streets lined with American flags—one of the streets is named Iwo Jima Boulevard—and file through the main gate of the forty acre CAF compound. How many attend can only be estimated. In 1977 an aviation periodical stated that "over 90,000 spectators" had been present.[17]Of the approximately 3,600 CAF Colonels, at least several hundred, and possibly over a thousand, attend the October corroboree.

At the start of the show, most of the more than seventy warplanes are out of sight. Then the announcer asks the audience to imagine that the year is 1936, and the dramatization begins with authentic German planes and counterfeit German paratroopers launching an "attack" on "Spain." Most of the acts are in themselves very simple. Aircraft types that were in a certain battle make low passes over the field. One airplane "shoots down" another when the victim switches on a smoke generator and dives toward the horizon. Aircraft simulate bomb runs as explosives are set off in an area just beyond the nearest runway to the audience. All the time the announcer is narrating the events being staged as if he were telling the entire story of the war and, in the background, a tape player is providing sound effects, parts of speeches by Hitler, Churchill and Roosevelt, and martial music.

Thus described, the program may sound unimpressive. Its success depends upon the powerful effect of more than fifty antique mechanical monsters charging and swirling at low altitude in a confined airspace and doing so with an ear-shattering roar. The most enthusiastically received act is the attack on Pearl Harbor. This is not, presumably, because the audience sides with the Japanese, but because this is the most complex and realistic performance. (Ironically, it is usually the only act which includes replica rather than actual warplanes: the Japanese planes are movie rather than war surplus.) Attacking the field are dozens of "Zeroes," "Kates," and "Vals," as explosives are set off with abandon and an errant American B-17, pursued by a "Zero," simulates a one-wheel landing with an engine pouring smoke. The act is choreographed precisely, perhaps because most of the "Tora, Tora, Tora" pilots come from one CAF wing and spend much time rehearsing.

The most controversial act is the final one, in which the CAF's giant B-29 "Superfortress" participates in the "bombing of Japan." In 1976, the B-29 was described as dropping the atomic bomb on Hiroshima and a large charge of explosives, set off on the airfield, represented the detonation of the bomb. Because of governmental pressure, the airshow narrative no longer states that the B-29 bomb run represents the attack on Hiroshima. The same aircraft is still used in the act, however, and in recent years its pilot was still Paul Tibbets, the actual pilot for the Hiroshima mission.

I shall postpone to a later section discussion of arguments concerning the propriety of this simulation. It is mentioned here because it is part of the re-enactment, just as it was part of the war, and because the reaction to it by many people who have no interest in aviation demonstrates the impact of symbolic acts re-creating significant historical events.

The term ritual has been used to describe these re-enactments, and they are ritualized to the extent that performances have followed the same format for several years. The entire script, including narration and stage directions, has been printed in a booklet.[18]

Glimpses back stage reveal that the show sometimes becomes ragged and confusing, however, as Rebel Control exhorts pilots to hurry ("Come on you dive bombers, you're on stage!"), pilots cannot locate their fellow actors ("B-25, where you at?" "I'm right here with you."), and a plane gets into the wrong scene.

Exceptionally good performances also occur as a result of impromptu maneuvers, directing skill and chance. Rebel Control gets excited as a Wildcat attacks "Japanese" planes, yelling, "Come on, Gerald, whip it around . . . . Smoke that Val right in front of you . . . . Beautiful, now roll right around on that Kate." As P-38s, P-47s and P-51s make high-speed strafing runs with American "parachute troops" dropping in the background, Rebel Control exults, "Ah , what a beautiful D-Day!" (Quotations in the last two paragraphs are from taped radio transmissions not broadcast to the audience.) War kills, but even simulated it may bring people to life. And this makes it attractive in a society where "moments are to be lived through, not lived."[19]

Southern Symbolism and Humor

There are individuals and groups other than the Confederate Air Force who collect memorabilia of war, including airplanes, and who re-enact historic battles. No one does these things on the enormous scale of the CAF, and it is likely that none combines such incongruous symbolism and humor with their ritualistic and patriotic activites. The strange symbolism, along with the buffoonery and wit, add to the showmanship and popular appeal of the group's performance. The very name of the organization arouses interest (and criticism), especially when one considers that the CAF's goal is to maintain and fly World War II aircraft, not hot air observational balloons from the American Civil War.

The Confederacy motif was originated in 1957, developed

throughout the sixties, and persists despite a campaign by CAF leadership to minimize it. In early days, Rebel flags were painted on the airplanes, sewn on uniforms and otherwise included in insignia. As late as 1977, dozens of Confederate banners were flying from the CAF "PX" at a regional airshow in which a new Wing was participating. The mythical commander of the CAF is Colonel Jethro E. Culpeper. Like Commander Culpeper, members are expected to wear a pearl gray Rebel hat and a string tie with first-class uniforms. Airshow events in the nineteen-sixties included "Yankee Attack," "Culpeper's Raiders," "The Yankee Polecat," etc.[20]

Early airshow programs also included encomiums of the Old South. They praised "Southern cookin', leisurely drinkin', catfishin', pocket knife whittlin', rockin' chair rockin', and plain ole shade tree settin'."[21]

At recent airshows in Harlingen, such literary effusions in tribute to the Old South had disappeared from programs and only American flags were flown. (In 1979 one aircraft crew flew a Confederate flag despite requests by a high CAF official that they not do so.) An order has gone out that no more Rebel flags are to be affixed to uniforms. CAF literature now repeats an argument that the CAF never intended to memorialize the Confederacy but was only rebelling against the destruction of historically significant aircraft.[22]

Generational and regional factors appear to account for the Confederacy theme. Most early members of the CAF were from the South and had grown up at a time when the "War between the States" was still a matter of emotional importance and symbolic identification. Indeed, it had occurred to an earlier group of Southern pilots to call themselves the Confederate Air Force.[23]

The Confederacy theme was often associated with humor, sometimes centering upon opposition between Rebel and Yankee. It was the Yankees who had issued the orders to destroy the warplanes; and Union troops were carrying out those orders.[24] One of the official objectives of the CAF—since abandoned—was "to use all our political influence to have the Capitol building in Washington turned to face the SOUTH."[25]

Much CAF humor has involved feigned self-depreciation. The Rebel aviator is pictured as a bumbling, obtuse, drunken sex maniac who navigates using a Texaco road map ("Missouri is brown; Illinois is yellow"), and reports that major cities have been moved to new locations. When he lands, totally lost, he is cunning enough not to admit it and merely asks for directions to the men's room. He can read his location painted on the hangar. He flies a "great circle route" because his rudder is bent. He defines a stewardess as "a gal who asks you what you want, then straps you in so you can't get it."[26] Perhaps it should be noted that, however much fun he may have, the CAF pilot is actually a very competent aviator.

The CAF's love of what they consider to be Southern Rebel humor suggests a possible function of the Confederacy motif, viz., to establish role distance. Does it seem a bit absurd that a middle-aged man spends his time flying a war surplus fighter or bomber? Maybe so, but it's all in fun. And to let everybody know that he doesn't take it too seriously he paints "Confederate Air Force" on the side of the plane and makes jokes about Rebels and Yankees. But as the organization takes on more serious goals and becomes recognized by the government for its educational and patriotic services, the old mechanism for achieving role distance becomes embarrassing and distance must be established between it—the Old South fun and games—and the new character of the group.

As symbols of the Confederacy fade, representations of another great war become predominant. World War II, and particularly the flying of World War II aircraft, is the main concern of the CAF. The airplaines have now been painted in authentic Second World War colors and markings. The most common CAF uniform is, except for being gray, basically derived from World War II military apparel. Confederate flags have been officially banned from uniforms, although some may still be seen; and an American flag is now sewn onto the right sleeve. The CAF organizational chart follows modern terminology, listing a Fighter Wing, Bomber Wing, Army Air Corps Group, Navy-Marine Group, etc. Social events and awards ceremonies, while retaining a modicum of Rebel allusions, are more often based on World War II themes. A USO dance would be an example.

Symbols of the two wars and later periods are intermingled. CAF "intelligence officers" are said to make up the OSS, but the initials stand for "Office of Southern Security." The women's support group has been known as the SBI (Southern Bureau of Investigation) and also as "Culpeper's Angels" after a popular television program. (Women have been denied membership as Colonels, but the CAF regulations were changed in October, 1979, to allow women full rights of admission.)

Most of the Colonels seem unconcerned about such changes as admission of women and reduction of the Confederacy symbolism. They do not expect many women to become active CAF pilots and have great respect for those who have already been flying unofficially with the organization. And judging from actual behavior of the members, those who wish to stress the Confederacy theme will go on doing so.

Perhaps an organization like the CAF could have originated

outside the South and outside of Texas, but none has; and although there are new CAF Wings as far distant as New Zealand, the center of activity remains in the Southwestern United States.

Conclusion: The Controversy over Social Consequences

One does not see the blood and suffering of war in the CAF's dramatizations, and this omission, combined with the fact that a deadly war is the basis for an entertainment in which the performers are having the most fun, strikes some observers as indicative of a certain insensitivity. The Japanese government adopted this view of the CAF's re-enactment of Hiroshima in 1976. So did a group of protesters who threw red paint on the B-29 when it was at Selfridge Air Force Base the following year. One editorialist condemned the CAF for claiming to have education as one of its purposes when it was actually misleading the public by emphasizing the glorious aspects of war.[27]

CAF defenders have replied to these criticism by stating that the Japanese are inconsistent since they have not protested the CAF staging of the attack on Pearl Harbor, and that since the dropping of the atomic bomb on Hiroshima did actually occur, it would be a distortion of history to omit it from the show. In addition, they point out that negative statements about war are included in their narrations and literature and that, indeed, one of their purposes is to educate Americans about the necessity to remain militarily strong in order to deter aggressive acts against this country.

The debate, thus, takes on a familiar form, pitting those who believe peaceful solutions to international disputes can be promoted by reduction of military forces and a submerging of martial values, against those who believe the threat of effective military reprisal is necessary if foreign domination is to be avoided.

Most CAF Colonels would be surprised to find that they were participants in such a debate. It is not so much a debate between factions as it is a conflict between two propensities within individuals. Many of us are ambiguous in our attitudes toward war, martial values and the artifacts of warfare, finding them both repulsive and yet somehow attractive and even—what we do not wish to admit—entertaining. The CAF brings this ambiguity out into the open, thus inviting condemnation.

It is impossible to determine, at present, whether warfare re-enactments make people want to go to war. And if such dramatizations are to occur, it is equally impossible to decide the effect which more emphasis upon the sufferings of war might have. In a famous essay, William James, while proposing substitutes for war, noted that "...modern man inherits all the love of glory of his ancestors" and went on to say it was useless to protest war's "irrationality and horror" for "the horrors make the fascination."[28] James may have been wrong about the futility of protest, but if he was right about the horrors making the fascination, then the CAF might be commended for *not* showing the blood and pain of combat.

Finally, it seems to me the Rebel aviators are involved in a revival of patriotism among those Americans nostalgic for the glory days of the Second World War. Their activities, especially their more elaborate airshows, provide a unique form of entertainment which has become part of Southern, national and even international popular culture. In addition, it may be ventured that the CAF's commemorative rituals serve, for a considerable number of people, the solidifying functions delineated by Parsons in his discussion of expressive symbolism,[29] and most dramatically stated by Durkheim when he spoke of rites which "revivify the . . . collective conscience." The Confederate Air Force Colonels might feel that Durkheim was referring specifically to them when he wrote:

> The glorious souvenirs which are made to live again before their eyes, and with which they feel that they have a kinship, give them a feeling of strength and confidence; a man is surer of his faith when he sees to how distant a past it goes back and what great things it has inspired.[30]

Perhaps such reassurance is all the more necessary to those who retain the faith when many around them have rejected it.

Notes

[1]Alexis de Tocqueville, *Democracy in America* (1835, 1840; rpt. New York: Harper & Row, 1966), p. 623.

[2]Merle Curti, *The Growth of American Thought*, 2nd ed. (New York: Harper & Row, 1964), p. 654.

[3]W. Lloyd Warner, *American Life* (Chicago: Univ. of Chicago Press, 1962), p. 27.

[4]Robert N. Bellah, "Civil Religion in America," *Daedalus*, 96 (Winter 1967), 1-21.

[5]Orrin E. Klapp, *Collective Search for Identity* (New York: Hold, Rinehart & Winston, 1969), pp. 126-8.

[6]Warner, pp. 1-34.

[7]The information upon which this study is based comes from 58 hours of participant, and 27 hours of non-participant observation, plus 12 interviews and a collection of letters, printed materials, photographs and tape recordings. CAF personnel were notified as often as was feasible, under the circumstances, of the purpose of my study.

[8]Catherine Albanese, "Technological Religion: Life Orientation and the Mechanical Bride," *Journal of Popular Culture* 10 (Summer 1976), 14-27.

[9]Confederate Air Force, *History of the Ghost Squadron* (n.p.: Taylor, 1975), p. 17.

[10]Field notes, October 8, 1977.

[11]Emile Durkheim, *The Elementary Forms of the Religious Life* (1912; rpt. New York: Free Press, 1915), pp. 417, 424-25.

[12]Richard Bach, *Jonathan Livingston Seagull* (New York: Macmillan, 1970).

[13]Douglas A. Bond, *The Love and Fear of Flying* (New York: International University Press, 1952), pp. 23-25.

[14]Since mention has been made of monetary incentives, it should be noted that all monies received by the CAF apparently go into meeting the heavy expenses of maintaining and flying very old, mechanically complicated airplanes which were hardly designed to conserve fuel. In the

July-August, 1979, issue of the *CAF Dispatch*, it was noted that in a recent twelve month period the organization had spent, without reimbursement, $52,000 supporting military open-house programs.

[15]Durkheim, p. 237. The aircraft are certainly useless in the sense of being impractical. They are valuable because they are collectors' items, but if this were the only reason for the respect in which they are held they would be put on static display and never flown. It is doubtful if anyone makes a profit flying these planes in shows, and certainly any gain would not be worth the risk of possible destruction of the rarer machines.

[16]Dean MacCannell, "Staged Authenticity: Arrangements of Social Space in a Tourist Setting," *American Journal of Sociology*, 79 (November 1973), 589-603.

[17]Jo Ann Aduddell, "Airshow '77 Thrills Crowd," *Texas Aviation News*, October, 1977, p. 3.

[18]Confederate Air Force, "Narration of the World War II Air Power Demonstration by the Confederate Air Force," n.d., n.p.

[19]Erving Goffman, *The Presentation of Self in Everyday Life* (Garden City: Doubleday Anchor, 1959), p. 260.

[20]Confederate Air Force, *The Fourth Annual Air Show* (n.p.: 1966), pp. 70-71.

[21]Ibid., p. 106.

[22]*Texas Aviation News*, October, 1977, p. 3.

[23]*Flying*, June, 1948, p. 42.

[24]Confederate Air Force, *Second Annual Rio Grande Valley Air Show* (n.p.: 1964), pp. 5-6.

[25]Ibid., p. 7.

[26]Ibid., p. 73.

[27]Russell Munson, "Two Sides to Glory: Another Point of View," *Flying*, Feb. 1978, p. 48.

[28]William James, "The Moral Equivalent of War," in *Memories and Studies* (London: Longmans, Green, 1911).

[29]Talcott Parsons, *The Social System* (Glencoe: The Free Press, 1951), pp. 397-98.

[30]Durkheim, p. 420.

Dancing and Cockfighting
At Jay's Lounge and Cockpit:
The Preservation of Folk Practices
in Cajun Louisiana

Steven L. Del Sesto

JAY'S LOUNGE AND Cockpit: The Last of the Honky-Tonks," reads a ubiquitous bumper sticker in and around southwestern Louisiana. Owned and operated by native Cajuns Jay and Marie Saucier, Jay's Lounge is a familiar landmark and rural social institution down among the swamps and bayou country known to many as "Acadiana."[1] At present, the oil boom in the Gulf of Mexico is rendering a veritable cultural transformation in Acadiana, often euphemistically called "development," and rural honky-tonks like Jay's are giving way to clubs which sport canned entertainment in the form of all the lastest dance crazes and "that damned disco music," as many old-time Cajuns complain. Indeed, the huge influx of new money, people and values has served notice to many traditional customs and lifeways that the time for change has come. Yet places like Jay's, living on the rituals and ceremonies of past times, remain intact, and you can still dance to traditional Cajun folk music in an oldtime dancehall atmosphere. Or, if you prefer, you might enjoy a quiet game of bourré in the backroom with friends, or witness cockfights in the pit out behind the lounge on Saturday nights. Jay's is unique in that part of the country and in our time: it has something for everyone.

Jay's Lounge and Cockpit is more than a place for eating, dancing, drinking and socializing. It specializes in *traditional* Cajun customs and entertainment; there is no "bump" or disco dancing on the dance floor, but Cajun waltzes, two-steps and other

270

traditional dances. Similarly many old-timers and a growing number of young people are caught up in the rooster fights—a "sport" practiced in Acadiana for more than 200 years. And with the card games and gumbo suppers after the dance, Jay's seems more like a holdover of a rapidly disappearing past than a viable social institution that has resisted the forces of growth and urbanization in the Louisiana-Texas Gulf Coast area. Honky-tonks such as Jay's offer some of the few remaining bulwarks against the steady decline and erosion of many traditional customs and lifeways of the Louisiana Cajuns. Indeed, such places and the largely ceremonial and ritualized activities that occur there provide a great deal of cohesiveness for the maintenance and continuation of the Cajun sub-culture as such.

*   *   *

It's Saturday night in the little town of Cankton, a village about six or seven miles west of Lafayette off Interstate 10. About halfway to the community of Sunset, Cankton is first marked by a giant Schlitz beer mug sign that rises high in the quiet country air in front of the sagging patchwork building that is Jay's Lounge and Cockpit. Even by 9 p.m. the parking lot is filled to the brim as usual and cars and trucks are scattered up and down the highway. The Saturday night ritual has begun. Several dozen people are milling around outside drinking beer; some are waiting for accordionist Clifton Chenier and His Redhot Louisiana Band to get the dance started, while others are simply observing the impressive variety of cockers from all over the South, who are bringing their roosters out back to the cockpit entrance where they prepare them for a long evening of fighting.

The people are a varied group, but a core of "regulars" seem to come by every Saturday night without fail; they would not miss the ceremony and ritual of attending these weekly get togethers. There are young farmers present, with longish hair and overalls, some sporting cowboy boots and new "International Harvester" caps. The ritual is always the same. As one walks through the door the attendant gazes at him or her from beneath his usual enormous straw hat such as the kind the farmers wear in the fields in this part of the country, as he takes the modest $2.00 cover charge and stamps on the wrist "First Class Mail" in indelible ink. There is an interesting variety of people inside, from senior citizens dressed in their Sunday best to young children kibitzing around the large hardwood dance floor and generally observing the band setting up their equipment. Meanwhile several people are already bopping to the sound of the well-worn jukebox and having a good time.

The rooster fights generally begin well in advance of the dance, in the dimly lit backroom and the cockpit. A modest 50¢ fee (women get in free) enables a man to get a ticket stapled to his shirt collar, enabling him to come and go as he pleases for the rest of the night to watch or bet on the carefully staged ritual of the cockfights. On one side of the 15 foot-square cockpit, which was ringed by four tiers of wooden bleachers painted a dull robin's egg blue, stands an old mustachoed Cajun wearing lizard skin cowboy boots, a pearl button cowboy shirt and a Stetson hat. He places his rooster on a tiny scale, gently cradling the bird and making soft, reassuring clicking noises as he completes the weigh-in. This ritual is the first step and a prerequisite for obtaining a match. On this particular night, a short rugged man wearing a Yankees baseball cap was standing on the other side of the pit, shouting a barely understandable streak of Cajun-French to his friend only a few feet away who was engaged in the careful task of shaving a bird's natural spurs so that hand-made inch-and-one-half long fighting spurs could be affixed to the rooster's legs with several strands of high quality adhesive tape. These spurs often take several days of painstaking work to fashion, or they may be purchased from various "specialists" who make a lucrative living by crafting these lethal weapons full-time.[2]

The fight is nearly ready to begin, and "poolers" for each side are busily going through the usual ritual of collecting the bets from the spectators, offering even money to all comers. People line up and place their bets on their favorite roosters, as the poolers record the names and amounts on a sheet of paper. When the two pools are even, two men bring their birds to the "score" lines in the center of the pit for "billing," or preliminary pecking that is meant to arouse the birds' fighting instincts. After this intricate ceremony, the fight commences in a surprisingly spectacular and exciting display of feathers, flapping wings and shouts from the frenzied crowd.

Throughout the fight there are always three men in the pit with the roosters: an "umpire" and two "handlers." The umpire watches the match closely and is responsible for handling the technicalities of the match—"counts" between the "rounds," interpretations of the rules, deciding outcomes in questionable cases, and so on—for the rooster fights are hardly *ad hoc* affairs, but are carefully prepared and staged events based on a complete set of roles, rules and procedures which govern the sport.[3] Meanwhile, the two handlers handle their roosters in a fashion similar to trainers handling professional boxers. Their duties include untangling the birds when a spur has lodged so deep that the birds cannot free themselves, bathing and stroking the roosters between rounds, and coaxing and cajoling the birds to fight when the next round begins.

Most of these hack fights last anywhere from 20 to 30 minutes, depending on the skill, speed and respective strength of the cocks. Throughout, the match is marked by periodic, often fierce, side-betting between spectators—all a part of the cockfight ritual. The level and extent of the side-betting is always a function of the birds in the pit, with the betting activities depending upon the closeness of the contest. The spectators yell out various odds and money they are willing to give a prospective taker. A wave of the hand or a simple nod of the head usually is enough to accept a bet. All the while people are cheering and rooting for their favorite cock, as the old folks seem to watch with incredible indifference to the whole thing.[4]

Meanwhile another aspect of the ritual at Jay's has begun with the arrival of Clifton on the stage. He steps into the crowd carrying his 40-pound Hohner piano accordion on his shoulders, greeting them with *"Attencion, attencion,* we're gonna have a good time tonight because I feel gooood!" The crowd respond with Cajun and rebel yells: "Aaaaaaiiii, aaaaaaiiiiii." Clifton was joined on the bandstand by his brother Cleveland, who uses a handful of metal bottle openers to play a corregated stainless steel rub-board which hung loosely from his shoulders, Buc Sengal on rhythm and lead guitars, John Hart on tenor saxophone, and Robert St. Judy on drums—no doubt one of the hottest and most lively acclaimed back-up groups in all of Cajun country.[5]

Clifton is the master at staging a live performance, and after a few blistering French tunes played in his usual way, the wild, dancing throng is worked to a fever pitch. The dancing and carrying-on is so intense that the walls of Jay's old broken down building seem bound to collapse. The beer is cold and numbs the throat as it goes down, while the straight shots of Wild Turkey whiskey warm the stomach for several seconds. Between the intense heat, the cheap prices (beer is 50¢, whiskey 65¢) and the madness, the alcohol flows freely and people dance until they are weary and their feet ache. Meanwhile Clifton and the band play and work on for four straight hours with neither breaks nor repeated songs.

By the time Clifton begins to wind down, empty beer cans litter every inch of every table, and the place is generally topsy-turvy. Everyone is exhausted but manages just enough energy for one more encore before the band shuts down for the night and people spread out for their trips home laughing and joking about the "hot time on the bayou tonight." And, if you muster enough stamina to be around later when Jay and the crew finally start cleaning things up they might ask you to join some of the regulars and the band in the backroom for steaming bowls of Jay's famous homemade gumbo and ice cold beer. This too is all part of the weekly custom and ceremony at Jay's.

*   *   *   *

By this time you may ask what is the significance of this curious mixture of cockfighting, wild dancing and Cajun-country music found at Jay's Lounge and Cockpit in the backwoods of rural Louisiana. It would be easy to simply dismiss such Cajun customs, and particularly the cockfighting, as "backward" or "primitive" customs and practices. Yet to view honky-tonks like Jay's and the activities and people who congregate there in such terms would miss the essential point: Jay's and similar places are viable institutions attempting to withstand the lure of mass culture, economic development and other forces of "modernization." They offer an alternative of traditional activities, and their various rituals and ceremonious character have real meaning and purpose for the people engaged in them.[6]

It is significant that such activities contribute importantly to the maintenance of a larger sub-cultural web of social relations between people and institutions. Considering that the existence of social units depends on what Parsons has called functional requisites—adaption, goal attainment, integration and latency or cultural pattern maintenance—dancing and cockfighting at Jay's help fulfill one or several of these functional requisites concurrently.[7]

The functions of dancing and cockfighting may be manifest or latent. That is, they may be intended or recognized by the individuals in a given social system, or they may be neither intended nor recognized and emerge largely out of the theoretical analysis of the social scientist.[8] Consequently we must *deduce* certain latent aspects of dancing and cockfighting from sociocultural settings such as Jay's Lounge and Cockpit because the actors themselves do not always know the functions of the activities in which they are engaged, and this isn't merely the case for members of the Cajun sub-culture, but tends to characterize individuals in most societies. Hence a particular cockfight or dance almost always has both manifest and latent functions that we may suggest by way of theoretical analysis.[9]

Adaption is a key societal requisite concerned with the vital link between the social system and the surrounding environment. It is often seen largely in terms of providing goods and services from the environment to the society. Although dancing and cockfighting appear to contribute little to adaption functions, a closer look reveals that they have important latent functions.

First, the dance obviously contributes to adaption primarily in an economic sense. The dance offers a salary and a modest living for many local musicians, the owners and operators of Jay's and other local honky-tonks, for the employees and others. Moreover, the dance helps support food, liquor and other related businesses which supply goods and products to bars and honky-tonks. However, the economic contribution to adaption is insignificant compared to the more important symbolic and identificational elements of the dance. It is a *traditional* Cajun celebration, or nearly so, and those who participate in the activities become identified with cultural values which bind the Cajun sub-culture.

As for the cockfight, it is less important as a means of livelihood, since hardly anyone expects to earn a living from the fleeting whims of Lady Luck. Most of the individuals engaged in cockfighting have other jobs and occupations; cockfighting is an avocation that is never considered a primary occupation.[9]

Yet the cockfight does have important adaptive functions when seen as a symbolic representation of man's continual struggle for survival, as displays of courage and bravado in the face of adversity, and as attempts to understand the meaning and suffering of death. This function of the cockfight is nothing new; Caesar required his legionnaires to see cocks in battle, hoping the gamecock's gallantry and bravery would inspire them. Similarly the Persian kings required their soldiers to engage in the sport, for the gamecock provided a good example of the vitality and courage possible in the face of conflict, an example they might emulate in their own struggles in life.[10] For all practical purposes, this aspect of the cockfight in practice and ritual has not changed. The Cajuns who engage in the practice appear to use it in symbolic fashion to deal with timeless existential questions much like other peoples have throughout the ages.[11]

Goal attainment is the second requisite of all societies. This function involves not only the nature of the goals themselves, but also the mobilization of resources, both physical and human, to attain them.[12] Traditional Cajun dancing apparently has contributed to motivating hard work, courtship, marriage and eventually procreation. Dancing and celebration are intimately associated with many forms of work, especially during the major harvest seasons, as in the case of the *boucherie* or hog butchering.[13] It is more than coincidental that ceremonies and festivals are connected to nearly every major crop in southern Louisiana, as well as to the trapping and fishing industries which provide a substantial livelihood to many Cajuns. For example, the community of Crowley, which relies heavily on rice as a major form of economic sustenance, sponsors the Internal Rice Festival every October. This festival includes beauty contests, pageants, parades, cooking bees, and above all, wild and gala dancing in the streets (and elsewhere). Dancing is also an intricate part of the annual Sugar Cane Festival in New Iberia, the Crawfish Festival in Breaux Bridge, and the Cotton Festival in Ville Platte.[14] Dancing at places like Jay's provide diversion, distraction and generally makes the week's work less of a chore.

Dancing also has neglected, though important, latent functions with respect to courtship and marriage.[15] Before the turn of the century (and later in some of the isolated rural communities), it is said that the weekly dance, or *fais do-do* as it was called, was an important community gathering place. Several early sources suggest that major features of the dance were structured around courtship functions, and encouraged an amicable atmosphere in which young people could mix under the watchful eyes of parents and relatives.[16] Dancehalls like Jay's obviously lack most of the trappings of the traditional *fais do-do,* but it is not too much to say that the weekly dance still performs many latent courtship functions in much the same fashion.

The contribution of the cockfight to goal attainment is less clear. However, one of its latent functions concerns the acquisition of a great deal of significant information about the nature and habits of the chicken—one of man's most important domesticated animals. Cockfighting ordinarily involves a long "training period" in which the cocks are given specially prepared feeds and tonics, are subjected to muscle building and exercise programs and are studied and experimented with in terms of developing new and more hardy breeds.[17] Jay and other Louisiana cockers claim that the knowledge gained while preparing roosters for battle results in improved feeding programs that add to the longevity and survival of all the birds. According to Jay, who has been fighting roosters for more than thirty years, learning how to train a cock for battle yields many practical advantages which go far beyond whether a chicken wins or loses in the pit.

Yet cockfighting contributes to goal attainment in another important way. Most of the folks who fight chickens are "regulars," generally farmers and ranchers whose families have been fighting roosters in rural Louisiana for many generations. Consequently they don't fight chickens and simply let it go at that; traditionally, the rooster fights are also a place where business deals among friends are discussed, farming and ranching information exchanged, and other types of community business conducted. In short, the cockfight facilitates contact and communication regarding the business of allocating certain community resources. This is less significant in the more urbanized areas like Lafayette, but such functions are still important in the outlying rural areas.[18]

Integration's primary purpose is to link, through interaction, emotion and shared value perspectives, otherwise autonomous groups and individuals, so that a goal attaining unit is formed. Within the Cajun sub-culture, the dance and cockfight contribute to this function in several ways. Perhaps most important is that the medium of dance may help insure sufficient courtship opportunities for young men and women—a critical prelude to creating a nuclear family. This is among the reasons why many men and women in Acadiana take dancing so seriously: the dance still brings together youth for acquaintance and possible marriage, and certain dance movements may attract a potential partner.[19]

Second, there is little question that social dancing as ritual almost always promotes solidarity between people and groups. Hence in Acadiana, the weekly dance is a socially unifying factor in which people come together to participate, converse, interact, spread news and gossip, and meet with friends. In this way, the dance actually becomes a microcosm of society, particularly in the case of large *bals* and festivals such as Mardi Gras and the Sugar Cane Festival, where the solidarity aspects of dancing are pronounced.[20]

Finally, the Cajun sub-culture resembles other societies which have specialized social units with multiple tasks to perform; to a considerable extent societal effectiveness depends, at least in part, on each member's knowledge of, and commitment to, these specialized roles, statuses and groups. Dance often contributes to the realization of social units and their functioning, especially in terms of the duties and privileges that accompany them. While probably less true of dancing at Jay's Lounge, this fact is conspicuous at various Mardi Gras *bals* and the selection of the royal courts, where certain kinds of "elite dancing" are required.[21] The same is true for other more or less "formalized" dance occasions such as the *bal de maison* (house dance), whose function is to help maintain close family ties and distinguish family identities, and the *bal de noce* (wedding dance), which cements inter-family and general community relations.[22] Although the functions of honky-tonk dancing may not serve social integration in a conscious and demonstrable way at these specific levels, there is little question that it promotes solidarity of friendship and peer group relations among the middle and working class groups who frequent dancehalls like Jay's.

The integration functions performed by the cockfight, on the other hand, contribute chiefly to social solidarity among specific primary groups mostly within rural communities. Typically an evening of cockfighting at Jay's and other Louisiana cockpits reveals that members of various friendship and primary groups support and "sponsor" each other's roosters. Generally, a half-dozen or so key people heavily involved with the rooster fights breed, raise, and own the roosters; they are the leaders in their primary groups. Other group members rally around these people and support their roosters during the course of an evening of fighting. A person, for example, always bets with his group rather than trying to pick the winning rooster; quality of the birds makes no difference—one supports his friends' roosters in all matches. If he does not, he suffers possible ridicule and humiliation from his friends, who become angered by the lack of support. Thus, the rooster fights contribute much to primary group solidarity and loyalty, and, therefore, are important elements in promoting overall community solidarity as well.[23]

Finally, the cockfight functions much like the weekly dance in another way: it is a good place where members of the community may socialize at specified times during the week, irrespective of whether they are intimately involved with the technical aspects of cockfighting as such. Again, news is spread, information communicated, and social solidarity promoted. In this way the Saturday night cockfights contribute a great deal to social integration within rural communities.

Latency or cultural pattern maintenance is concerned with the importance of social institutions, in this case through stylized and ritualized practices, in transmitting key cultural values and generating and coping with societal tensions.[24] The functions can be either conservative or change-oriented: the transmission of cultural values may imbue societal members with "appropriate" motivations and values in order to guide actors' behavior and sustain their support, or they may induce significant change. By the same token, tensions may be either generated or decreased by the dance and cockfight. In some cases generating tensions may have overall stabilizing or destabilizing effects on society, but destabilization actually may have some positive effects. [25]

Dance is often part of the larger socialization process and contributes to an individual's ability to learn his culture and his role in the group. Most Cajuns learn to dance at an early age, and there are positive sanctions for executing dances which most effectively portray Cajun ethnic values, dances such as traditional Cajun waltzes and two-steps. Dance helps socialize individuals to a variety of social behaviors, including family obligations, and political and occupational norms.[26] Again, this appears especially true with respect to dance that accompanies the festivals of the harvest season.

Dance is also related to psychic tension management. Many cultures use music and dancing to help ease periods of critical strain, emotional readjustment, changes in life status or sexual frustration.[27] Cajuns use dancing as a catharsis; it helps reduce anxiety or emotional stress by acting out frustrations and releasing tensions. Dancing has powerful social-psychological functions in terms of preventing depression and other forms of psychic stress.

The cockfight has similar tension-management functions. It is a mechanism whereby hostility and pent-up emotions can be vented with few or no deleterious consequences for the individuals involved. Although the participants and spectators may shout and jeer at one another in the heated competition of the cockfight—as well as vent other emotions that people rarely express openly in the course of everyday life—no one "really" suffers but the cocks. Death and destruction is confined to the wire surrounding the pit; it crosses this line and enters the community only symbolically. In this way, the cockfight provides a mechanism for dealing with hostility, emotion, aggression and competition.[28]

Finally, both cockfighting and dancing at Jay's appear to have a strong hand in maintaining traditional Cajun values. After all, even though the weekly dance is no longer the same as the traditional *fais-do-do,* and the cockfight certainly not as prevalent as it once was, both have come to hold significant symbolic value: they are signs and reminders of certain time-honored Cajun traditions and folkways; they are elements of the Cajuns' cultural heritage—part of what it means to be "Cajun." In short, they act as ways in which individuals may symbolically reaffirm, through participation, their cultural heritage.[29]

In sum it is clear that dancing and cockfighting at Jay's and similar places play significant roles through the rituals in aiding the preservation of many elements of the Cajun sub-culture as a whole. The existence of traditional folkways, like most other things, requires both ecological areas where they might be practiced, and a defined group of people who regularly participate and support them. In this regard these rural honky-tonks are more than simple bars or dancehalls; they are bonafide social institutions that help maintain the marvelous cultural diversity and uniqueness found in south Louisiana to this day. They provide a rich source of material for the social scientist interested in the preservation and continued vitality of folk and ethnic sub-cultures throughout America, and for people interested in the rituals and ceremonies which help provide the muscle and spirit of this continued vitality.

Notes

[1]A general overview of the Cajun sub-culture may be found in Steven L. Del Sesto and Jon L. Gibson (eds.), *The Culture of Acadiana: Tradition and Change in South Louisiana* (Lafayette, La.: University of Southwestern Louisiana, 1975.)

[2]Much of this discussion is drawn from Steven L. Del Sesto, "Roles, Rules, and Organization: A Descriptive Account of Cockfighting in Rural Louisiana," *Southern Folklore Quarterly* 39 (March 1975), 1-14.

[3]Ibid. For a discussion of the rules and procedures of cockfighting, the most authoritative source is still William H. Nugent, "Cockfighting Today," *American Mercury* 17 (May 1929), 80-81.

[4]Del Sesto, "Roles, Rules and Organization."

[5]For a brief discussion of Cajun music see Steven L. Del Sesto, "Cajun Social Institutions and Cultural Configurations," in Del Sesto and Gibson (eds.), *The Culture of Acadiana,* pp. 121-142.

[6]On the significance of cockfighting in Bali, see Clifford Geertz, "Deep Play: Notes on the Balinese Cockfight," *Daedalus* 101 (Winter 1972), 18-25.

[7]A summary of Parsons' work in this respect may be found in Talcott Parsons, *Social Systems and the Evolutionary Theory of Action* (New York: Free Press, 1977).

[8]A discussion of manifest and latent functions is found in Robert K. Merton, *Social Theory and Social Structure* (New York: Free Press, 1968), Chapter 3.

[9]See Del Sesto, "Roles, Rules and Organization."

[10]G.R. Scott, *The History of Cockfighting* (London: Charles Skilton, Ltd., 1957). See also Lawrence Fitz-Barnard, *Fighting Sports* (London: Odhams Press, 1921).

[11]Del Sesto, "Cajun Social Institutions," pp. 133-134.

[12]Parsons, *Social Systems,* pp. 262-269.

[13]Del Sesto, "Cajun Social Institutions," pp. 136-138.

[14]Ibid., pp. 131-133.

[15]Many of these points draw on the discussion of Judith Lynne Hanna, "Dance, Odyssey and Theory," in Tamara Comstock (ed.) *New Dimensions in Dance Research: Anthropology and Dance—The American Indian* (New York: Committee on Research in Dance, 1974), pp. 85-97.

[16]*Viz.* the early account given by an unidentified traveller about 1870:

The neighborhood ball is orderly and well-conducted, with whole families attending. A section known as the *parc aux petites* is provided for the babies so the mothers can keep a careful watch on their older daughters, while the fathers enjoy a quiet game of cards in an adjoining room. The older women also come to play cards, each carrying with her a bag of coins. Some of the mothers are quite young to be relegated to places along the wall; and as they follow the dance with sparkling eyes, they perhaps hum under their breath, half humorously, half sadly, snatches from an old Acadian ditty:

Dance my children while you are young
Soon my daughter will make me a grandmother
Instead of dancing the gavotte, one gossips idly in a big armchair!

Cited in American Guide Series, *Louisiana: A Guide to the State* (New York: Hastings House, 1941), pp. 193 ff. See also Roy V. Hoffpauir, "Courtship and Marriage in Acadiana," unpublished field notes, Univ. of Southwestern Louisiana, 1968.

[17]Del Sesto, "Roles, Rules and Organization." See also Tim Pridgen, *Courage: The Story of Modern Cockfighting* (Boston: Little, Brown, 1938).

[18]Del Sesto, "Cajun Social Institutions," pp. 133-134.

[19]Hanna, "Dance, Odyssey and Theory," p. 95.

[20]This point is discussed in Tom Ireland, "Mardi Gras Balls as a Microcosm of Society." Paper presented at the Louisiana Folklore Society Meetings, April 19-20, 1974, Lafayette, Louisiana.

[21]Ibid. See also Thomas J. Cottle, "Social Class and Social Dancing," *Sociological Quarterly* 7 (Spring 1966), 179-196 for related materials.

[22]See Revon Reed, Paul Tate and Cathy Bihm, "The Voice in the Soul of Cajun Music," *Louisiana Heritage* 1 (April 1969), 14-15 and Del Sesto, "Cajun Social Institutions," pp. 127-128.

[23]Del Sesto, "Roles, Rules and Organization."

[24]Parsons, *Social Systems and the Evolutionary Theory of Action,* pp. 45-46.

[25]Hanna, "Dance, Odyssey, and Theory," pp. 89-90.

[26]See Judith Lynne Hanna and John Hanna, "The Dance-Plays of Biafra's Ubakala Clan," *Anthropologica* 11 (1969), 243-273. See also C.B. de Courtencey Jedrzejewicz, "Folk Dance Wedding Customs in Poland," *Journal of the English Folkdance and Song Society,* 2 (1935), 24-30.

[27]See Anya Peterson Royce, *The Anthropology of Dance* (Bloomington, In.: Indiana Univ. Press, 1977). See also Franz Boas, *The Function of Dance in Human Society* (New York: Dance Horizons, 1972).

[28]Del Sesto, "Cajun Social Institutions," p. 135.

[29]Materials on this point may be found in Royce, *The Anthropology of Dance,* pp. 22, 25, 79, 110, 112, 155-156, 163-164. Relevant materials may also be found in T.O. Ranger, *Dance and Society in East Africa* (Berkeley: Univ. of Calif. Press, 1975), James L. Peacock, *Rites of Modernization: Symbolic and Social Aspects of Indonesian Proletarian Drama* (Chicago: Univ. of Chicago Press, 1968), and Robert Bocock, *Ritual in Industrial Society* (London: George Allen and Unwin, 1974).

Ritual, Process & Definition: Hawthorne's *The Artist of the Beautiful* and the Creative Dilemma

C.T. Walters

Upward unto the living light
Intensely thou dost gaze,
As if thy very soul would seek
In that far distant maze
Communion with those heavenly forms
That, lifting to the sight
Their golden wings and snowy robes,
Float on a sea of light.

*   *   *

Such are the thoughts that rise
In him, who 'neath thy upturned brow,
Behold thy searching eyes.

Edward Augustus Bracket,
"Lines Suggested on Finishing a
Bust of Allston," *My House, Chips*
the Builder Threw Away.

FOR THE STUDENT of the often misunderstood world of 19th century American painting and sculpture, Nathaniel Hawthorne's "The Artist of the Beautiful" has special meaning. With the skill of professional critic Hawthorne crafts a fictional treatise that is infinite in its suggestive possibilities. As an epitaph, the story commemorates the plight of America's first romantic painter, Washington Allston. As a commentary, it criticizes the practices of artists like Asher B. Durand who practiced the imitative doctrines championed by John Ruskin. It is also a study in the ambiguities of language. Virtually every word has a latent meaning that requires both analysis and adaption of contemporary artistic nomenclature. Using a rhetoric that is naive, sometimes sentimental and often archaic, Hawthorne devises a verbal portrait of his hero—Owen Warland—that leaves fundamental issues purposely unresolved. This calculated ambiguity transforms the tale from a simple story of failure and disillusionment into a cultural document commemorating the creative dilemma that all American artists faced at the time. That dilemma was the creation of an object of Beauty that still demonstrated practical use.

The rituals that Owen Warland used to reach this goal were as important as the goal itself. The creative ceremony involved in constructing an insect that would fly gave Hawthorne's story much of its intellectual shape. Indeed throughout the essay, Hawthorne makes surreptitious allusions to the creative process, a method circumscribed by accommodation and compromise. To succeed, Owen was forced to tread a middle ground between the realism provided by nature and the idealism of his own imagination. He could enforce his will upon nature; he could choose his subject, but only at the risk of alienating the pragmatic tasks of his audience.

The organizational principle that sustains Hawthorne's story lies in its title. Hidden beneath the intricacies of an allegorical format, the author fashions a descriptive criticism of the most evasive of ideal visions, the concept of moral, intellectual and physical beauty. This initial theme determines an important part of Warland's creative predicament. Adapted to meet the individual needs of specific artists, the interpretations bestowed upon the ideal of tangible beauty were as pluralistic as American society. When Hawthorne wrote his story, the concept of Beauty had as many meanings as there were painters and sculptors. Appropriately, the sculptor Anne Whitney eulogized Beauty as a mysterious woman, both bride and mistress of artistic impulse.[1] For Asher B. Durand it was an ideal sustained by a meticulous elaboration of detail; for Erastus Dow Palmer, it was the perfection of realism; for William Wetmore Story, the celebration of process. Despite its variety, this "eternal fugitive," to borrow an appropriate phrase from Ralph Waldo Emerson's poetry, was usually given one or two interpretations.[2] It waivered beneath the dictates of deductive and inductive reason; each set of circumstances providing its own technical and intellectual rituals; each variation its own set of liabilities and contradictions.

Beneath the surface of anecdotal incident, Hawthorne conceals both accounts. Beauty, Hawthorne first informs us, was circumscribed within the "ample verge."[3] Measured by the broad gesture of the rainbow, it was subjected, with equivocal consequences, to the appropriate creative ceremony. Warland submitted his idealistic vision to the demands of classic abstraction. He selected his butterfly; he chose his ideal and then forced naturalistic detail to conform to his own assumptions. He could be creative, but his creativity, as Hawthorne implies, was rewarded by a sense of personal frustration. Since he made nature subservient to his own imagination, rather than to the pragmatic demands of his audience, his butterfly degenerated into prettiness and artificiality. Hawthorne intimated an alternative to Warland's predicament: the option of Ideal Beauty characterized according to the stipulations of inductive reason. Accordingly, the artist copied the minute, the diminutive, and the fragmentary, and thereby expressed an artistic thesis, in the case of 19th century landscape painting the attributes of Divine Intervention. To borrow from contemporary jargon, the smallest vein of the smallest leaf acknowledged the omnipotence of God, a presence that demanded from the artist a particular technique.[4] To such counsel, Warland partially acquiesced. He crafted an artifact that was microscopic in detail; yet his butterfly was so tediously overworked that it never became anything more than a mere compendium of morbid facts.

The conflict that Warland faced between the minute and the ample—the tension between the real and the ideal—characterizes much of the American art of the mid-19th century. This dualistic impulse, this constant arrangement and rearrangement of surface, transfigures American art into a series of mechanical butterflies, for indeed neither a Thomas Cole painting nor a Hiram Powers' sculpture were ever defined according to their own sense of reality. Painting was not simply painting, sculpture never simply sculpture: both were oftentimes something less. Manifestations of both compromise and ambition, they were expressions of a specific cultural heritage, strongly influenced by the intellectual rituals of the time. Hiram Powers, Hawthorne's mentor and friend, for example, sculpted not nude women, but rather illustrations of sentimental literature. Thomas Cole and Washington Allston constructed landscapes whose supposedly realistic surfaces conceal an intricately reasoned aesthetic in which each naturalistic element assumes a double life. Allston transformed his own romantic vision into canvases that reveberate with a mysterious glow. Cole translated his didactic heroisms into Arcadian landscapes in which the gesture of individual trees assume anthropomorphic proportions.

One of the most important keys to unravelling the aesthetic puzzle of Hawthorne's tale lies in the historic identity of Owen Warland, who the author informs us was carefully modeled after the quintessential *poet maudit*, Washington Allston. Warland's life, therefore, parallels that of his artistic surrogate. While Warland dissipated both energy and talent in a futile attempt to reconstruct an artificial butterfly, Allston struggled with the infamous *Belshazzar's Feast,* a project that literally consumed energy and ambition for the last twenty-five years of his life. Both men lacked discipline; neither could sustain his ideas. When confronted with difficulty, Allston played the role of stylish dilettante. Allston squandered his talent not in quaffing Warland's cup of oblivion but in an equally enervating pursuit, smoking cigars, charming his friends with his skill as raconteur when he should have been chartering his next artistic performance.[5] The two artists of the beautiful also shared their method of working. While Warland toiled under a flickering lamp, Allston usually painted at night.[6] Assuming the pose of a romantic fop, Allston sat up all day in his bed, affecting an air of carelessness, indulgence and insouciance, a role that Warland mimicked when he wasted the sunshine. He wandered in the fields when he should have been hard at work.

Despite their faults both Allston and his fictional proxy attempted, as artists of the beautiful, to give tangible definition to the most evanescent of aesthetic abstractions. Allston did so by painting, by writing and by living a life that was soon to be poeticized into myth.[7] Warland, on the other hand, attempted to encapsulate Beauty within the fragile contours of his butterfly. Hawthorne sustains Warland's quest by dividing his fictional essay into a series of events that depict the formation of Ideal Beauty. He refers to its origins, its visual manifestation, and the actual process used to convert what was "earthly" into "spiritual gold" (p. 472). The ultimate source of this Ideal vision, Hawthorne suggests, resided in the hues of heaven; its visible expression in the rhythms, colors and shapes of nature. Hawthorne, however, devotes most of his attention to specific techniques of expression; it was the making of the object that established the stature of the artist. Although part of the creative process was attributable to sheer impulse, Hawthorne discloses that Warland drew his own methodology from a combination of two sources—the reality of nature supplemented by his own internal vision. To convert thought into fact, Warland imitated what he saw, taking particular care to temper his observations with the veil of memory. The ritual of putting the spirit of beauty into form endowed the artist with certain powers. Manufacturing the butterfly exerted its toll in effort and anxiety, but its construction did provide specific rewards. Because Warland possessed the strength to spiritualize matter, he was annointed. He stood apart, an ethereal being among more prosaic contemporaries.

Based on the artistic theories of the decade, Hawthorne's story rivals the intellectual organization of Allston's *Lectures on Art*.[8] Allston described the source of Ideal Beauty as being omnipresent. It could be unearthed beneath the cadences of nature in "the woods, the fields, in plants, and animals."[9] This same impulse, complemented to be sure by microscopic incident, furnished Warland with his artistic incentive. The beautiful movements of nature, matched by the expansiveness of the rainbow, enveloped Warland and provided him a protective canopy. The development of these resources was less rational. Its evolution Hawthorne compares to a burst of light, which after having illuminated the artist's subconscious enigmatically vanishes (p. 458). This sense of mystery again unites Hawthorne with Allston, who seemingly felt that the inspiration motivated by Beauty was presented to artists' minds by means of a nebulous cloud, what he labelled a "mysterious *condition.*"[10]

The process used to convert these ideas into tangible form was more precise. Allston, for one, outlined a ritual based on the artistic tool of imitation, the exact means that Warland employed.[11] When Hawthorne selected the term, he fully understood its implicit dangers. Taken to its logical conclusion, imitation could and often did prove to be obsessive, inflexible and impersonal—a total detriment to the creative spirit of the artist.

When Hawthorne adapted this instrument of expression to his story, therefore, he carefully cushioned its impact by concealing the word itself beneath a number of artistic euphemisms. Warland did not copy. He labored "upon a reality;" he put "Beauty into form;" he "converted the reality of nature into spiritual gold" (pp. 449, 452). For Hawthorne, as for Washington Allston, imitation did not imply photographic duplication. Instead, it was a first step, a means to an end. The artist began by ritualistically imitating nature, but then he was given the liberty to abridge, to modify and to combine—to make realism, the servant of his own idealistic intentions.

Although carefully reasoned, the methodology that sustained Ideal Beauty was subject to important qualifications that neither Allston nor Hawthorne could deny. Allston conceded that his theoretical expertise was based on a fallibility. For all his erudition, he admitted that the attainment of this vision extended beyond the grasp of even the most skillful technician. The artist, he believed, possessed the knowledge that his finished work never fulfilled its original conception. The attainment of Ideal Beauty, Allston maintained, was impossible because its ultimate truth was determined by the perfectibility of God's mind, a plateau that no artist could reach.[12] These inescapable flaws Hawthorne incorporates in his narrative. Warland experienced the same disappointment that Allston suggested when his butterfly was released from his hands. With furrowed brow Warland observed that he had lost sight of his inspiration: that his butterfly was not as he had conceived it in the days of his youth. Warland's predicament was more profound. The butterfly, Hawthorne laments, could only be finished in the "hues of heaven" (p. 467). For all his ingenuity, Warland's butterfly was left unfinished, defective, incomplete because God and not the artist had the moral strength to realize the absolute truth of perfection.

Battling against not only the practical hand of his audience but also against the forces of artistic evolution, Warland faced still another quandary. A survivor of the past, a reluctant participant of the future, he held a tenuous position in history. He was an anachronism, forced to exist between the strategies of Allston and the pronouncements of younger artists who now championed the minute and the miscroscopic. By the 1840s, when Hawthorne wrote the story, the creative latitude that Allston advocated was becoming obsolete. The expansive breadth so much a part of Allston's romanticism was replaced by an innovation that reversed priorities, changing them from the ideal sustained by the real to the real sustained by the ideal. The minute, as Hawthorne carefully stated, now superseded the ample. Following the theories of John Ruskin, American artists constructed Ideal Beauty from the inside out, from the realistic fragment to the idealistic whole. Painters like Asher B. Durand and Frederic Edwin Church presented faithful presentation of naturalistic forms and phenomena, because it was believed that even the most prosaic wildflower mirrored the existence of a preordained ideal.

To preserve the sequence of God, Beauty, Nature and Man, Hawthorne provided his hero with the appropriate scenario. Warland placed himself with the rhythms of nature—the flights of birds, the patterns created by small animals—and then imitated what he saw. Though elliptical, this brief sequence puts Warland partially in the camp representing the new realism, the artists of the Hudson River School. Writing in *The Crayon* Durand, the school's leading spokesman, codified a specific ritual that helps to illuminate Warland's problems. In terms that paraphrase Hawthorne, Durand advises that the artist go directly to what was designated as "The Studio of Nature."[13] Then, using the tool of imitation, he should reflect through the minute sensorium provided by nature, the attributes of the "Great Designer."[14] Durand's advice is deceiving in its simplicity. On the level of studio practice, Durand meant that the artist, with his easel and box of paints strapped to his back, should go to specific locations, primarily in the Catskills, and approach nature but still maintain an objective distance. Durand was afraid that the artist might become entangled in the intricate web of nature and never be able to extricate himself. As Durand feared, Warland lacked the equilibrium for realism. He looked so closely at butterflies and water insects that he became inebriated. Hawthorne realized that Warland's temptation was not an isolated phenomenon. Thomas Cole, who like Warland bridged an historic gap between the romanticism of Allston and the pragmatism of Durand, virtually fell in love with Nature, her rhythms and rituals. In words that would make any self-respecting landscapist of the 1850s wince, Cole asked the following of his supreme mistress, nature:

> Ye mountains, woods and rocks, impetuous streams.
> Ye wide-spread heavens, speak out, O speak for me!
> Have I not held communion deep with you,
> And like to one who is enamoured gazed
> Intensely on your every-varying charms?[15]

With the ambiguities endangered by nature in mind, Hawthorne created Warland's environment from a collage of time and space. When we first encounter Owen, he is struggling indoors over his work. His self-imposed isolation, however, is far from complete. When he was a schoolboy, he played outdoors. What Hawthorne implies is that Owen's present existence was substantiated not by nature, but by the memory of nature. Warland was virtually a prisoner of his environment. So much so that when he ventured from the dusty confines of his studio, his exuberance threatened to destroy the fine line between reality and illusion.

For Hawthorne, Warland violated the carefully prescribed sequence that underscored the realism of the Hudson River School. Rather than being constantly rejuvenated by the salutary effects of environment, he purposely isolated himself, resisting the temptation provided by nature. Toiling day after day on an object cultivated not by the rays of the sun but by the luster of an artificial lamp, his focus was so intimate that he was oblivious to anything else. Tempted by his own ingenuity, to borrow Durand's language, Warland supplanted his Creator.[16] He had not transcribed from the scripture of nature; he had copied from the richness of his own vision. Repeatedly, Hawthorne makes the point that Owen attempted to put Beauty into form; he tried to create it. Both Peter Hovenden and Robert Danforth asked Owen the same question. Hovenden inquired of Owen Warland, "Have you created it [Beauty] at last?" (p.468) "How comes on the Beautiful" Have you succeeded in creating the Beautiful,?" demanded Owen's nemesis Danforth

(p. 469). The query that Hawthorne placed on the lips of these antagonists was vital, because the artist who subscribed to the doctrine of imitative representation never created beauty. The painter instead became, in a sense, "a transparent eyeball" whose canvases reflected the structural functions of nature put before him by the hand of the Great Designer, by God himself.[17]

Warland's predicament was further compounded by the fact that he misapplied one of the stock tools of the trade, the ritual of imitation. He spent his life and labor on a reality but in doing so overstepped his mandate as artist. He became obsessed with process. According to contemporary practice, imitation was a means to an end. Durand argued that an artist had to have the skills to imitate because imitation provoked characteristic truths. Imitation produced not more imitation but instead led to "representation"; the specific to the general, the minute to the parenthesis of the rainbow. Each step of the ritual was irrevocable, since any aberration compromised the divine eloquence of nature.[8]

Warland violated this premise for a very important reason. He transcribed his own visions in an attempt to establish his creative identity, something that was missing from the impassive topography of realistic landscape. Hawthorne, a romantic who cherished the aesthetic suggestiveness of the sketch, felt that imitation was a faulty instrument of expression. Not only did it defy the idiomatic language of art but it also made the artist a slave and not a master of his professional fate. Painting based on mimickry, as even Durand admitted, diminished the creative options available to the artist. The most that an artist could do was to select "the time and the place" where nature displayed her image of "perfection," her contours of "repose" and "action."[19] He no longer possessed what Allston called the "divine prerogative." This impassivity played an important part in Warland's creative dilemma. It made the painter a mere reporter of contemporary fact. He could not furnish dreams of the past or predictions for the future. He was explicitly rooted in the present. Hawthorne was saying, in effect, that anyone who followed this imitative dictum to its logical conclusion faced the risk of being reduced to at best the status of a craftsman, at the worst to the importance of a scientific machine.

Warland's ambitions constantly eluded him. The nearer he approached his goal the more illusive it became. Neither timeless enough to exist on its own merits nor didactic enough to teach a moral lesson, part of nature yet still isolated from it, Warland's butterly fluttered between the real and the ideal, an example of handicraft that Emerson would have termed "effeminate," "imprudent" and "sickly."[21]

The product of Warland's ambition was carefully sustained by a series of purposefully drawn contradictions. Though his butterfly possessed form and color, it was neither a painting nor a sculpture; yet it had both a frame and a pedestal. Its scale was contradictory: the butterfly was neither monumental nor microscopic. Nor was the butterfly complete. The suggestive surfaces of Warland's artifact match the contours of Allston's paintings, many of which survive as sketches, diagrams of a mind that was undisciplined, records of an artist disappointed with his own performance and unsure of the demands of his public. His *Belshazzar's Feast* was left incomplete, because as Gilbert Stuart pointed out, Allston had already moved on to newer problems.[22] He had reached another level of achievement. He had followed the path that Hawthorne had placed before Owen Warland, the path of a small boy whose image decorated the ebony box protecting the butterfly. Allston had progressed from cloud to cloud, from idea to idea, from one unresolved problem to another.

The one consistent element in Owen's work of art was color. The butterfly emitted a supernatural glow more real than reality itself. Beneath the radiance of its wings, an entire system existed that expressed the intellect, the imagination—the essence of Owen Warland's soul. This emphasis on color and the substructure beneath again aligns Warland with Washington Allston. Allston's *Moonlit Landscape,* painted in 1819 shortly after his return from Europe, is also characterized by a supernal lustre. This glow represents not only specific emotional experiences, but also exemplified Allston's carefully planned ambitions for American painting. His work contains naturalistic objects, the sea, the moon, the sky. Beneath this surface, however, Allston, like Hawthorne, suggests an intricate series of metaphors. Not merely an arrangement of space, form and color, Allston's canvas evokes his own feelings as he stood looking out over the prow of his ship toward Boston harbor. In Allston's mind, the sea is transformed into a "prairie of amber," the moon into a "living thing" both partners in a glittering dance of light and color.[23] Allston completes his palette with allusions to historic precedent.

The painting represents Allston's attempt to infuse a simple landscape with the lessons he learned while traveling in Europe. When he saw Rembrandt's picture of *Jacob's Dream,* he noted the quality of color. When he viewed a Raphael painting in the Vatican he noted its harmonious, its bouldness, and intensity. When he examined Michelangelo's *Last Judgment,* he noted its interminable space.[24] We find all of these qualities in Allston's deceptively simple landscape. Like a Rembrandt painting the color in Allston's *Moonlit Landscape* is mysterious; like a Raphael the composition is carefully planned: like a Michelangelo the space is breathtakingly sublime.

Like the surface of an Allston painting the skin of Owen's butterfly concealed many secrets. Its exterior camouflaged a sense of mystery, a feeling of vision, nostalgia and romantic tragedy. For all its beauty, however, Owen's butterfly was of little use. Durand's transcriptions of nature, on the other hand, were more utilitarian. Durand invited his public to look over his shoulders to view not the process of his own heavenly flight, but to partake of the realistic scriptures revealed by nature. Durand employed technical devices— repoussoir trees, ground planes and country roads—calculated to draw the viewer into a participatory drama. Paul Akers, whose *Dead Pearl River* Hawthorne incorporated in the *Marble Faun*, believed that an object like Durand's painting, based on the perfection of reality lead the viewer "God-ward."[25] Durand's landscapes expressed the inevitable cycle of life, death and rebirth; the rhythms of the old gliding into the new; the Christian ideals of redemption and salvation.

These careful records made from nature included built-in disadvantages. Durand's paintings were so totally rooted in the pantheistic belief of a specific time that they survive only as archaeological remnants. Stripped of their external paraphernalia, they have the drama of documentary photographs. Yet his success with his own contemporaries was undeniable. While Owen Warland starved, Durand enjoyed a style of living that any entrepreneur would have envied. More important, perhaps, the Artist of the Beautiful who mirrored the presence of God was given a Beautiful Soul.[26] While the process that Owen employed enslaved him— making him as delicate as the artifacts he produced, those who adhered to the doctrine of imitation were considered to be priests of the Beautiful whose vocation was as important as that of a blacksmith.[27]

Warland was a sculptor who carved images as a child, a method of training he shared with his contemporaries. Hiram Powers began his career modeling wax figures; Thomas Crawford carved tombstones.[28] Throughout the 19th century sculpture was assembled according to a very efficient method that included three separate steps. The artist made a clay model; the model was cast in plaster; the cast was enlarged and then carved in marble, not by the artist himself but by a studio of trained craftsmen.[29] The product that resulted was a carefully restricted form of expression. W.W. Story stated the problem in his *Conversations in a Studio*. He wrote that "sculpture while in nature must also be above nature." Sculpture could be imitative, he continued, but only partially so. A mere copy of nature produced an effigy not a noble "treatment of form."[30] These contradictions were attributable to the ambivalence of nature. For indeed, the naturalistic affinities of sculpture challenged the most inventive minds to be found in 19th century America. Power's *Greek Slave* demonstrated its affinity to nature because it existed within the realm of sentimental literature. The texts that accompanied Power's sculpture were filled with allusions to Arcadian settings.[31] This inclination was maintained by the description given to the materials used in the construction of sculpture. W.W. Story suggested that marble resembled crystals that had fallen to earth, while H.T. Tuckerman equated the whiteness of marble to snow and the pallor manifested by *rigor mortis*.[32] Contemporary authors also took pains to establish the naturalistic inclinations of the format attributable to sculpture. Gulian Verplanck felt that sculpture sprang from nature, a venerable plant, so to speak, an evaluation he shared with Justin Windsor, who equated the silhouette of sculpture to the form of trees.[33]

If Owen Warland had followed the advice of one of his contemporaries, Erastus Dow Palmer, his dilemma would have been partially resolved. He did what Warland could not do when he labored over *his* butterfly. In an article, "The Philosophy of the Ideal," Palmer described the mechanical ritual whereby the real could be converted into the ideal. Palmer drew two human profiles that were identical except for the fact that the ideal head had its hair drawn back to reveal a very high forehead. Palmer was saying that the ideal and the real were so closely related to each other that the differences were imperceptible. The real was the ideal, the ideal mirrored the real.[34] To achieve these results Palmer advised the tool of imitation. For sculpture the word had a particularly problematic definition. It could mean one of two things. It implied the exact duplication of the three-dimensional form. Thanks to the use of mechanical aids like the life mask and the caliper, this was a literal possibility. The sculptor could reproduce in marble the exact likeness of any sitter. For Palmer, however, imitation meant something more than copying. It implied a spiritual modification of three-dimensional form. Representing the effects of nature rather than nature itself, the sculptor transposed his realistic observations, modifying them to complement the technical limitations of his material.

Where Warland failed, Palmer succeeded. His work had use. His sculpture suggested a series of abstract virtues, paradigms of conduct that his Victorian audience cherished. His bust of *Resignation* was beautiful because it extolled the consummate beauty of trust and hope. His famous statue of *The Dawn of Christianity* intimated spiritual beauty; his bust of *Morning* suggested the beauty of a future filled with promise.[35] But despite his achievements, Palmer's success was still equivocal. He was forced to tread the same path that Hawthorne constructed for Warland. His sculpture, according to his detractors, was too closely identified with nature.[36] His statues were so naturalistic that they were embarrassing. They were not nude; they were naked. To make his art more accessible, Palmer removed sculpture from its idealized pedestal. He had imitated the surfaces provided by nature, but had not improved upon them, the point being that he could not without violating his own philosophy of the ideal: a realistic portrait modified in an all but invisible way.

Rooted in the past, Hawthorne's tale is so carefully conceived that it becomes a prophecy for the future. Critics writing throughout the rest of the century expressed exactly the same concerns stated in "The Artist of the Beautiful."[37] Art in America decayed for the reasons that Hawthorne feared. The ritualistic devotion to naturalism, so much a part of Warland's dilemma, virtually killed art. It was revived only when the painter exerted his own individuality by using nature to serve his purpose and not that of a pseudo-religious dogma. By the end of the 19th century the two surfaces of American art would merge so that form became form; content form. Painting developed into an expressive mechanism that existed according to its own internal laws. The value of a painting resided not in what it looked like, but in its expressive potential. W.W. Story put it succinctly when he stated that the artist's victory was attributable "not to [the] product, but to the producing."[38] This struggle redeemed Warland's otherwise tragic career. Because he had risen high enough to attempt the Beautiful, he succeeded even as he failed. The application of paint to the surface of the canvas, the mark of the chisel on the surface of marble block, each of these rituals helped to resolve Warland's creative dilemma.

Living his life in obscurity, Owen Warland emerged as a survivor, an enlightened cynic who possessed a knowledge that his audience did not. Smiling the smile of a late Rembrandt self-portrait, an expression of dillusion mingled with self-confidence, Owen was the perfect hero. With his eye focused somewhere in the heavens, Owen Warland emerged as a triumphant figure who left his own best epitaph. "His spirit possessed itself in the enjoyment of its [own] reality."

Notes

[1] Anne Whitney, "Five Sonnets Relating to Beauty," *Poems* (New York: 1859), pp. 22-26.

[2] Ralph Waldo Emerson, "Ode to Beauty," *Poems* (Boston and New York: Centennial Edition 1904), p. 89.

[3] Nathaniel Hawthorne, "The Artist of the Beautiful" (Columbus: Ohio State Univ. Press, 1974), p. 450. Subsequent references are from this edition and incorporated in the text.

[4] The most eloquent expression of this Ideal can be found in Asher B. Durand's series of "Letters on Landscape Painting," published in *The Crayon*, Vol. 1, 1855, pp. 1-2; 34-35, 66-67, 97-98, 145-146, 209-210, 273-274, 354-355. Vol. II, 1855, pp. 16-17.

[5] William Dunlap, *The History of the Rise and Progress of the Arts of Design in the United States*, Vol. II (Boston: 1918, first pub. 1834), p. 333.

[6] John Neal, *Observations on American Art: Selections from the Writings of John Neal* (1793-1876), ed. with notes by Harold Edward Dickinson (State College, Pa.: 1943), pp. 17-18.

[7] See for example, William Ware's *Lectures on the Works and Genius of Washington Allston* (Boston: 1852).

[8] According to information provided by Roger Welchans in his unpublished dissertation, *The Art Theories of Washington Allston and William Morris Hunt* (Case Western Reserve Univ., 1970), Allston prepared his final project for his *Lectures* during the winter of 1842-43. Following Allston's death in 1843, his nephew, Richard Henry Dana, prepared the draft for final publication in 1850.

[9] Washington Allston, *Lectures on Art, Poems and Monaldi* (Scholarly Facsimiles and Reprints, 1967), p. 20.

[10] *Ibid.*, p. 64.   [11] *Ibid.*, p. 75.   [12] *Ibid.*, p. 7.

[13] Asher B. Durand, "Letters on Landscape Painting," *The Crayon*, Vol 1, No. 1, Jan. 3, 1855, p. 2.

[14] *Ibid.*, Vol 1, No. 1, Jan. 17, 1855, p. 34.

[15] Rev. Louis L. Noble, *The Course of Empire, Voyage of Life and Other Paintings of Thomas Cole, N.A.* (New York: 1853), p. 119.

[16] Durand, *op. cit.*, Vol. 1, No. 5, Jan. 31, 1855, p. 66.

[17] Quoted in Barbara Novak's, *American Painting of the Nineteenth Century* (New York: 1969), p. 110.

[18] Durand, Vol. 1, No. 10, March 7, 1855, p. 145.

[19] *Ibid.*, Vol. 1, No. 18, May 2, 1855, p. 275.

[20] Allston, p. 13.

[21] Ralph W. Emerson, "Art," *Essays* (Boston and New York: AMS Edition, 1968), p. 366.

[22] W.G. Simms, "The Writings of Washington Allston," *Southern Library Review*, Vol. IV. Oct. 1843, pp. 392-93.

[23] Dunlap, Vol. II. pp. 327-28.

[24] *op. cit.* "Sonnets," pp. 274-76.

[25] Paul Akers, "Art Expression," *The Crayon*, Vol. II, No. L, July 4, 1855, p. 5. For Hawthorne's mention of Akers, see p. 14 of his Preface to *The Marble Faun*.

[26] "Duty in Art," *The Crayon*, Vol I, No. 4, Jan. 24, 1885, p. 49.

[27] See "The Revelation of Art," *The Crayon*, Vol. II, No. 22, Nov. 28, 1855, pp. 335-36.

[28] According to Dunlap, Vol. II, p. 297. Warland. Allston drew landscapes in the ground; he made small cottages from sticks; he made little men and women from "forked stalks of wild ferns."

[29] For Hawthorne's treatment of this ritual, see Chap. XIII, "A Sculptor's Studio," *The Marble Faun*.

[30] William Wetmore Story, *Conversations in a Studio* (Boston and New York: 1890), Vol. II, p. 332.

[31] For his *Eve Tempted* (1839-1842), Powers selected for his poetic text; *The Death of Abel*, written by the Swiss-German Sulomon Gessner (1730-1788). For his Ginerva, (1838), he chose a poem by the same name written by the English poet Samuel Rogers (1763-1855). Both selections are filled with references to the Arcadian environment.

[32] W.W. Story, *Nature and Art, A Poem*, (Boston: 1844), p.11, Henry Theodore Tuckerman, *The Collector*, (London: 1868), p.308.

[33] Gulian C. Verplanck, *Discourses and Addresses on Subjects of American History, Arts and*

Literature, (New York: 1833), pp.142-143. Justin Winsor, "The Humanity of Nature," *The Crayon,* Vol. II, No. 17, October 24, 1855, p.255.

[34]Erastus Dow Palmer, "Philosophy of the Ideal," *The Crayon,* Vol. III, Part I, January 1856, pp.18-20.

[35]*Catalogue of the Palmer Marbles,* (Albany: 1856), p.7, 10, 11, 18.

[36]See "Palmer, The Sculptor," *The New Path,* No. 3, July 1863, pp.25-30.

[37]See for Example J.E. Cabot, "On the Relation of Art to Nature," Part One. *Atlantic Monthly,* February 1864, Vol. XIII, pp. 183-196. Part II, March 1864, pp.313-329. See also W.J. Stillman, "The Decay of Art" and "The Revival of Art," *The Old Rome and the New and Other Studies,* (Boston and New York, 1889, pp.169-197; 198-231.

[38]Story, *Conversations in a Studio,* Vol. II, p.310.

In Memory Of:
Artifacts Relating to Mourning
in Nineteenth Century America

Martha Pike

'I have always thought,' he said reflectively, 'the system of mourning, of immuring women in crepe for the rest of their lives and forbidding them normal enjoyment is just as barbarous as the Hindu suttee.'[1]

RHETT BUTLER'S COMMENT to Scarlett O'Hara about mourning is probably the twentieth-century's best-known and most succinct damnation of nineteenth century mourning practices. But mourning customs of the nineteenth century, although they may appear bizarre, even morbid, to people of the twentieth century, served both societal and personal needs. Modern readers should be encouraged to view with some sympathy the ways in which the nineteenth century dealt with the universal incomprehensibility of death, and tried to make it meaningful.

Many objects related to these mourning customs are now in museum collections: clothing, costume accessories, jewelry, embroideries, paper ephemera, coffins and coffin plates, hearses, paintings, drawings and prints. Study of these artifacts in conjunction with the literature of the period shows that these mourning customs accurately reflected the society of the period, and provided a socially functional workable mechanism for dealing with the inevitable grief of death.

Artifacts of mourning in the nineteenth century may be grouped into at least three main categories: memorial[2] (items which perpetuate the memory of the loved one); ritualistic (objects prescribed for use in the ritualized etiquette of mourning); and funereal (artifacts actually used in the funeral services).

296

Memorial Mourning Pieces

The memorial aspect of mourning is seen in a plethora of objects which still exist today. One of the most fascinating of these objects is the memorial picture, painted or embroidered, usually on silk, or painted with watercolors on paper. This was a form of schoolgirl art which flourished in the first decades of the nineteenth century. Most studies of this type of art have focused on the art historically.[3] A fine example of this combination of painting and embroidery is seen in Fig. 1.

Such embroidered and/or painted memorial pictures were done primarily by an educated elite, young women whose families could afford to send them to select seminaries where such genteel arts as painting and needlework* were taught. In the late 1830s or early 1840s, however, Nathaniel Currier and other print-makers began to publish low-priced prints of similar subjects. It is difficult to determine exactly when these began to be published, as the earlier prints are undated, but the dress styles in these prints are generally of the period 1838-1842. The earliest dated print located so far was entered in the Clerk's Office of a New York District Court in 1845. This print, similar to that in Fig. 2, is a mourning scene set in New York's St. Paul's churchyard. Nathaniel Currier published this particular print in several variations, possibly to afford the purchaser the appropriate selection of mourners for his or her personal situation. Almost all of these memorial prints have a blank space on the side of the tombstone with a printed inscription, usually "In Memory Of"; The purchaser filled in the blank with the name of the deceased, and frequently the date of his or her death. Memorial prints continued to be published throughout the 1840s and 1850s, though later less frequently, at least few new print designs were entered in the record according to act of Congress. During the Civil War, several prints were published for use as memorials to soldiers slain in the conflict.

Most of the mourning prints portrayed traditional churchyard burying places rather than rural cemeteries, which flourished in many urban centers in the United States during much of the nineteenth century. This raises a question as to the audience or purchasers of these prints: were they primarily rural people, and thus more used to the traditional churchyard than to the newer rural cemetery, or were they more sophisticated urbanites? Or did these prints reflect a nineteenth century mind steeped in nostalgia for the pre-industrial age, whose own art often selectively omitted the most modern and dynamic images—factories, mills, wars, strikes—in favor of a bucolic "nature" genre, and revealed a deep ambivalence

*Editor's Note: Most women learned utilitarian needlework at home or at school.

Fig. 1. Memorial Picture, silk and watercolor on silk, made by Lucretia Carew, Norwich, Connecticut. Dated 1800 on the glass, but probably made a decade later. Collection of The

Fig. 2. Lithograph, Nathaniel Currier. No date. Courtesy of Greenfield Village and Henry Ford Museum.

toward change?

In addition to the popular taste for mourning prints, there was also a vogue for memorializing the dead in photographs and paintings taken after death. The taking of photographs of dead infants was particularly widespread; Fig. 3 is of a Rhode Island child. William Sidney Mount, one of the major American painters of the nineteenth century, did many portraits after death. Fortunately, he also kept copious journals, in which he made frequent references to the practice, which he found distasteful, of taking portraits of the dead. In an autobiographical sketch, Mount wrote: "I pass over several portraits, a few taken after death. I had rather paint the living but death is a patron to some painters."[4] Since most of Mount's portraits look perfectly lifelike, it is only by cross-referencing the paintings to the notes made by the artist that one is able to identify portraits of the dead. Fig. 4 is of young Jedediah Williamson, son of a neighbor of the Mounts: "I made a sketch of Col. Williamson's Son after he was killed by a loaded waggon passing over his body. A portrait. $15.00."[5]

William Sidney Mount's brother, Shepard Alonzo Mount, an able portraitist, left a poignant visual and written record of the death of his granddaughter Camille in 1868. The painting of the child is seen in Fig. 5; a letter to his son discusses Camille's death and his painting of her:

Telling you of Joshua and Edna—I am obliged to sadden your heart—They have lost their little Camille—she is dead—the sweet beautiful babe is dead. She died from the effects of teathing [sic]. It so happened—providentially I thought—that I was at Glen Cove—and for two or three days before she died, I made several drawings of her, which enabled me, as soon as she was buried to commence a portrait of her and in 7 days I succeeded in finishing one of the best portraits of a child that I ever painted. All the family seem'd surprised, and delighted with it and to me it was real joy to have been the instrument of affording so much comfort to all—Joshua and Edna would sit before it for an hour together and Mr. and Mrs. Searing are in raptures with it. I have framed it and hung it up for all to see and love—for next to the dear babe herself—it is now the idol of the family. Alas! how everything fades from us—Joshua arrived home the day after she was buried. How sad the shock. She was laid out in a beautiful casket and she looked like an angel— Her eyes were bright and heavenly 'till the last. I painted her with Mr. Searings watch lying open in the foreground. the hands pointing to the hour of her birth. while she is seen moving up on a light cloud—the image of the lost Camille—[6]

In addition to prints, paintings, and photographs, memorial jewelry was quite common. Most historical collections include jewelry made of human hair. Although hair jewelry is commonly called mourning jewelry today, most pieces were mementoes of the living rather than of the dead: In Alcott's *Little Women* we see the common use of hair jewelry as a token of sentiment. " 'How can I be otherwise?' said Mrs. March gratefully, as her eyes went from her

Fig. 3. Photograph of Amos C. Barstow III, died June 29, 1879, aged 2 years and 22 days; Manchester Brothers; Providence, Rhode Island. Collection of The Museums at Stony Brook.

Fig. 4. William Sidney Mount, "Portrait of Jedediah Williamson," not dated, oil on panel. Collection of The Museums at Stony Brook; bequest of Ward Melville, 1977.

Fig. 5. Shepard Alonzo Mount, "Small Girl with Watch (Portrait of Camille)," not dated, oil on canvas. Collection of The Museums at Stony Brook; bequest of Dorothy DeBevoise Mount, 1959.

husband's letter to Beth's smiling face and her hand caressed the brooch made of gray and golden, chestnut and dark-brown hair, which the girls had just fastened on her breast."[7] Elaborate confections of hair, usually in the form of wreaths or floral arrangements, were also quite popular; these were ordinarily used for parlor ornaments. Instructions on how to make such jewelry or ornaments of hair appeared in many ladies' magazines. Unless there is a memorial inscription on a piece of hair jewelry or on an ornament, or there is an impeccable provenance as to its use as a memorial piece, such an item should be considered a sentimental piece rather than a mourning memorial.

Memorials to the dead often took more literal form than the personalized prints, paintings and jewelry. The burial place also began to take on a new configuration. The rural cemetery movement began in 1831 with the opening of Mount Auburn Cemetery in Cambridge, Massachusetts. Cities throughout the eastern and midwestern United States followed suit in the ensuing decades, for example, Laurel Hill, Philadelphia, in 1836; Green-Wood, Brooklyn, in 1838; Cave-Hill, Louisville, in 1848; and Oakland, Atlanta, in 1850.[8] These cemeteries can be considered artifacts in themselves. They reflect the hopeful, heavenward-looking religion of the nineteenth century, one markedly different from that more fearful and more starkly realistic religion evident in the crowded churchyard burying grounds of the seventeenth and eighteenth centuries. The rural cemeteries were consciously designed as new kinds of burying places:

A voice from 'the Green-Wood! A voice! and it said,
Ye have chosen me out as a home for your dead;
From the bustle of life ye have render'd me free;
My earth ye have hallowed; henceforth I shall be
A garden of graves, where your loved ones shall rest![9]

Guide books were published to some of the better-known cemeteries such as Mount Auburn and Green-Wood. These were often illustrated with engravings depicting the beauties of the cemeteries and demonstrating that mourners and sightseers were visiting the cemeteries. Individual prints of these cemeteries were published by print-makers, an example of which is the Nathaniel Currier print in Fig. 6. Many of these cemeteries were major sightseeing attractions during much of the nineteenth century.

The tombstones and tomb sculptures of these rural cemeteries reflect nineteenth century Christian beliefs—homeward bound was the major theme: angels transporting the dead toward heaven, children sleeping peacefully, angels pointing heavenward. All is confident expression of the hopeful belief in a happy afterlife.

Fig. 6. Lithograph, Green-Wood Cemetery, Nathaniel Currier, 1855. Courtesy of Greenfield Village and Henry Ford Museum.

Curiously, the mourning family or individual is seldom portrayed in Victorian cemetery sculpture, although a few such monuments exist.

Ritualistic Mourning Objects

The second group of artifacts relates to the ritualistic practices of mourning, rather than to the memorializing of the dead. There were rigid guidelines for the behavior of the widow; the widower had much less restrictive guidelines to follow. Etiquette books and ladies' magazines are good sources of information about mourning rituals. The rigidity and complexity of mourning rituals described in etiquette books increased substantially during the latter half of the nineteenth century. Concurrently, however, there were increasingly frequent references to people's right to choose whether or not to go into mourning. Perhaps detailed guidelines of socially acceptable behavior only became necessary when there were increasing numbers of people wishing to do the proper thing, but not knowing the rules.

Etiquette books of the period 1830 to 1870 mentioned mourning in passing; perhaps it was assumed that appropriate behavior was known. A brief entry from *Godey's Lady's Magazine* (May 1844) editorializes:

We have always advocated the custom, old as the records of social life, of expressing by outward token the sorrow which every truly affectionate heart must endure under the bereavement of death. The custom of wearing mourning apparel will, we hope, never be discontinued.[10]

There are, however, no detailed descriptions of what was considered proper mourning apparel. Another brief mention of mourning appears in an etiquette book of the same year: "Do not wear *black* or colored gloves, lest your partners look sulky; even should you be in *mourning*, wear *white* gloves, *not black*. People in DEEP mourning have no business in a ballroom at all."[11]

Although etiquette books of the 1840s do not dwell on detailed descriptions of appropriate mourning behavior or dress, mourning prints of the period show women and children in deep black mourning. Comparison of the garments in such prints with descriptions and prints of mourning garb later in the century demonstrates that there was less rigid codification of proper dress in the earlier period. For example, lace and embroidery appear in some early garments, but they were frowned upon later in the century. An 1856 periodical included the following mention of mourning apparel:

At JACKSON'S we admired several long cashmere *bournous*, trimmed with crape, graceful yet grave, from the deepest to the slightest mourning. Bugles and velvet are very much used, as are also embroideries on crape for collars and sleeves.[12]

Etiquette books of the last three decades of the nineteenth century frequently devoted at least a chapter to the etiquette of mourning, giving procedural details about how long mourning should be worn, how funeral invitations should be issued, how appropriate dress should be chosen and to what degree behavior should be restricted. Descriptions of acceptable fabrics, dress ornaments, and jewelry fill the pages of etiquette books, for example, in 1884:

> The deepest mourning worn is that of a widow, which consists of crape and bombazine. The present fashion is to cover everything with crape. The widow's dress is made without ruffles or flounces, but heavily overlaid with crape. The veil reached to the feet, and is nearly wide enough to meet at the back. The hem is half a yard deep.
>
> There is now in all large dry-goods stores a mourning department, where new goods for all grades of mourning are shown.[13]

Many of the objects mentioned in etiquette books and periodicals of the nineteenth century have survived, and are in private or museum collections. Full costumes of deep mourning are relatively rare, although some do exist in museum collections.[14] Some costumes of second or partial mourning also survive. Mourning dress was carefully graded: the deepest mourning was usually worn for at least a year by a widow, then it was gradually lightened, changing from solid black to black and white, gray, or lavender, before changing to colors. Mourning in its various states usually lasted a minimum of two years. Some widows, however, remained in heavy mourning until their own death. There appears to have been no general agreement on exactly how long each phase of mourning should last, although most writers on etiquette agreed on a total mourning period of at least two years.

Nineteenth century periodicals such as *Godey's Lady's Book, Peterson's,* and *Harper's Bazar* included not only hints on mourning etiquette, but also illustrations of proper and fashionable mourning dress; Figs. 7 and 8 are fashion plates from an 1895 *Harper's Bazar.*

Many black dresses covered with jet beads, usually from the 1880s, are sometimes called mourning dresses today simply because they are black. This is not necessarily true. The assumption that a dress was used as mourning apparel should be made only for those garments made of or trimmed with crape, or for those with reliable documentation of mourning use. These bead-decorated dresses *may* have been mourning, but it is not safe to assume that they were: "For lighter mourning jet is used on silk and there is no doubt that it makes a very handsome dress."[15]

The relative scarcity of full mourning costumes surviving today

Fig. 7. Mourning Costume with Cape, *Harper's Bazar*, New York, August 31, 1895, p. 708.

Fig. 8. Mourning Bonnets and Parasol, *Harper's Bazar*, New York, August 31, 1895, p. 709.

leads one to question whether or not the full panoply of mourning dress was often worn. Full mourning was undoubtedly expensive: "Mourning is very expensive, and often costs a family more than they can well afford."[16] This raises the question of artifact survival. Unlike wedding and christening dress, mourning dress was not symbolic of a happy event. This may explain why relatively few complete costumes have survived. On the other hand, more modest mourning accessories such as black crape veils and black-bordered handkerchiefs have survived in large numbers. Because these items were small and did not go out of style quickly, they were probably saved for later use. Other small artifacts relating to mourning have survived. For example, to assure that no glint would relieve the sombreness of black, mourning pins, straight pins for fastening one's mourning veil, had black glass heads and shafts of blued steel.

Stationery and calling cards were black-bordered, and many examples have survived:

Cards and notepaper are now put into mourning by those who desire to express conventionally their regret for the dead; but very broad borders of black look like ostentation, and are in undoubted bad taste. No doubt all these things are proper in their way, but a narrow border of black tells the story of loss as well as an inch of coal-black doom.[17]

Fig. 9 shows some of the accessories associated with mourning.

The large number of surviving mourning accessories leads one to suspect that mourning rituals were more widely practiced than one might think from the number of garments that have survived. Women of limited means could have bought a widow's veil and bonnet and worn them with a dress dyed black to mourn, rather than going to the expense of full mourning. Additional research is yet to be done on the question of who carried out the mourning rituals dictated by etiquette books and ladies' magazines, and how widely spread in society these rituals were.

Jewelry considered appropriate for mourning was as strictly prescribed as the dress itself: jet or onyx were the preferred materials; occasionally pearls or brilliants were set into the jet or onyx. There was no consensus but some writers of etiquette books proscribed the wearing of any gold jewelry.

The question of men and how they mourned is little mentioned in the literature of the period. At most, the widower wore black or dark grey clothes, a crape band on his hat, black gloves and tie: "They knew of my affliction, they noticed the weed on my hat...."[18] Judging from surviving artifacts and from the literature, the burden of mourning fell primarily on women. Mourning was yet another sphere in which woman figured as the pillar of home and society. She was the one who came "from the *carbon* of *man's* flesh and bones, the pure diamond of purity and beauty, and light of moral perfectness, which he enshrined in the form of *woman.*[19] As late as 1888 Mrs. M.F. Armstrong, in an etiquette book originally written for the students of the Hampton Institute, wrote, "The principal power in general society undoubtedly lies in the hands of its female members—that is, it is to them that Society looks for a careful standard of refinement."[20] Women's lives, especially widows', were truly circumscribed.

Many of the mourning rituals in the United States derived from English customs.* Passages and even entire chapters of English

---

*Editor's Note: Italians, Poles and others of Catholic background had different mourning customs, as did those of Jewish tradition.

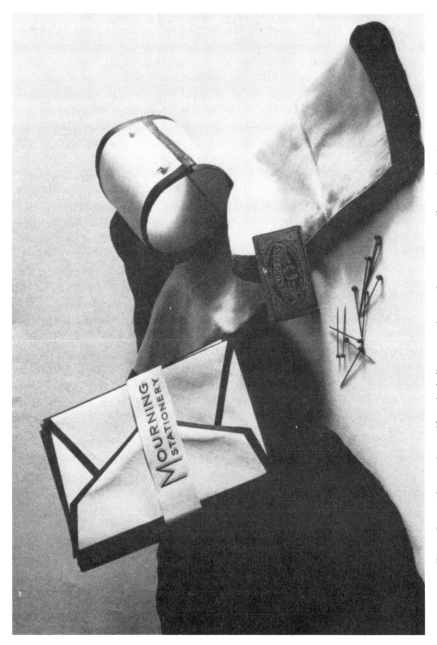

Fig. 9. Group of mourning artifacts including mourning stationery, crape veil, mourning pins, black bordered handkerchief and cuff. All late 19th century. Collection of The Museums at Stony Brook.

etiquette books were published in American etiquette books, often without mention of the original source. But, as frequently occurred in America's borrowing of customs, mourning customs were somewhat changed to coincide with American tastes. Nineteenth century writings, especially etiquette books, show that there was considerable awareness of this: "We have shown the good taste of America in abolishing the hired mutes, the emblazement of the emblematic horrors of death, the skull and crossbones on the panels of the hearse, and all that 'luxury of woe' so remarkable in the English funeral.--[21]

Victorians of mainstream Protestant faiths professed belief in a blissful afterlife; evidenced in their grave sculptures, and in the optimism of their popular writings, and yet they, certainly the women, draped themselves in black.[22] Occasionally they noted the contradiction:

Therefore we have a difficulty to contend with in the wearing of black, which is in itself, to begin with, negatory of our professed belief in the resurrection. We confess the logic of despair when we drape ourselves in its gloomy folds.[23]

There are several possible explanations for this contradiction, none mutually exclusively: the drive for propriety was so strong that it overpowered the religious origin of behavior; the mourning rituals were symbolic of woman's place in the world, and became, possibly, a source of her feminine power;[24] the bereaved were mourning for themselves rather than for the deceased, mourning because they were left behind while the loved one had gone on to a better world.

Funereal Items

The third category of artifacts is funereal, relating to the funeral itself. One of the most interesting artifacts in this category is the coffin, which underwent a curious change of both style and nomenclature during the nineteenth century. During the latter half of the century the "coffin," usually hexagonal and vaguely body-shaped, became the "casket," which was rectangular in shape. The use of the term "casket" was euphemistic:

It is known, and some of you to whom I speak have had painful opportunity to know, that there has been, of late years, an improvement in the little depositories in which we convey the forms of infants and young children to their last resting-place.
Their shape is not in seeming mockery of the rigid, swathed body; the broken lines and angles of the old coffin are drawn into continuous lines; they look like other things, and not like that which looks like nothing else, a coffin; you would be willing to have such a shape for the depository of any household article. Within, they are prepared with a pearly white lining; the inside of the lid is draped in the same way; the name is on the inside; and a lock and key supplant the remorseless screws and screw-driver.[25]

The change in the shape and name* of the repository for the body of the dead from coffin to casket paralleled the growing rigidification of mourning customs, and perhaps presaged the twentieth century avoidance of death, what Philippe Aries calls "forbidden death."[26] Concurrent with the change in the coffin was the gradual rise of the profession of funeral direction; the funeral director assumed the duties previously performed by a variety of people: providing the coffin (handmade by the local cabinet-maker in the first half of the nineteenth century, but often patented and mass-produced in the latter half of the century); preparing the deceased for burial (previously done by family members and friends); and counseling and consoling (previously done by friends and ministers). This intermediation of the funeral director between the immediate fact of death and the bereaved probably contributed to the avoidance of the concept of death which exists today.

The expression of private grief so acceptable, even required, in the nineteenth century, is forbidden today. As Aries wrote,

Too evident sorrow does not inspire pity, but repugnance, it is the sign of mental instability or of bad manners: it is morbid.... One only has the right to cry if no one else can see or hear. Solitary and shameful mourning is the only recourse, like a sort of masturbation. (The comparison is Gorer's.)[27]

This standard of behavior leaves both the bereaved and his or her friends in anguished isolation. There are no guidelines for their behavior. Although nineteenth century attitudes and customs regarding death and mourning may appear to us to have been excessive, people of that time did have social mechanisms to deal with the inevitable grief of death.

Studies of past mourning customs may not only help us to evolve more useful patterns of behavior to cope with the grief of death, they should also lead to our greater understanding of earlier societies. The mourning customs of nineteenth century America, especially those of the period frequently called Victorian, accurately reflect that society; these customs comprehend the changes in religious thought, the uniquely idealized status of women, the relationship between the sexes and their relative positions in society, and the growing rigidification of social systems of the latter half of the nineteenth century.[28] That social entrenchment probably occurred in response to the increasing turbulence in society characterized by accelerated urbanization, industrialization and immigration.

The rigid guidelines for appropriate mourning behavior

*Editor's Note: the change in linguistic meaning from "coffin" (the repository of a dead body) to "casket" (the repository of any treasured item to be preserved) signifies a perhaps subtle but powerful change from the connotation of death to that of "preservation" and treasuring.

314 Rituals and Ceremonies in Popular Culture

deteriorated toward the end of the nineteenth century; etiquette books mentioned ever more frequently the right of people to decide not to go into mourning. Rules for mourning procedures and dress appeared less and less often. By the turn of the century trade catalogues and periodicals devoted much less space to the accoutrements of mourning. The practice of mourning rituals continued, albeit less frequently, until the shattering cataclysm of World War I. Today, the remnants of Victorian mourning practices are seen in an abundance of collected nineteenth century artifacts, and in national public mourning for departed leaders.

Notes

[1]Margaret Mitchell, *Gone With The Wind* (New York: Macmillan, 1936), 122.

[2]See Phillippe Aries, *Western Attitudes Toward Death: From the Middle Ages to the Present* (Baltimore: Johns Hopkins Press, 1974), Chapter III, "Thy Death," 55-82.

[3]Anita Schorsch, *Mourning Becomes America: Mourning Art in the New Nation* (exhibition catalogue, William Penn Memorial Museum, Harrisburg, Pennsylvania, 1976); Betty Ring, "Memorial Embroideries by American Schoolgirls," *The Magazine Antiques* (October, 1971), 570-575; Beatrix T. Rumford, "Memorial Watercolors," *The Magazine Antiques* (October, 1973), 688-695.

[4]William Sidney Mount, autobiographical sketch (The Museums at Stony Brook, Stony Brook, New York).

[5]Mount, catalogue of portraits and paintings (The Museums at Stony Brook, Stony Brook, New York).

[6]Shepard Alonzo Mount, letter to his son William Shepard Mount, May 15, 1868 (The Museums at Stony Brook, Stony Brook, New York).

[7]Louisa May Alcott, *Little Women* (Boston: Little, Brown, 1968), 107.

[8]Stanley French, "The Cemetery as Cultural Institution: The Establishment of Mount Auburn and the 'Rural Cemetery' Movement," in David E. Stannard, ed., *Death In America* (Philadelphia: Univ. of Pennsylvania Press, 1974), 69-91.

[9]Nehemiah Cleaveland, *Green-Wood Illustrated* (New York: R. Martin, 1847), 10.

[10]*Godey's Lady's Magazine* (May, 1844), 244.

[11]Charles William Day, *Hints on Etiquette and the Usages of Society with a Glance at Bad Habits* (New York: A.V. Black, 1844), 76.

[12]*Frank Leslie's Gazette of Fashion and the Beau Monde* (December, 1856), 102.

[13]Mrs. M.S. Rayne, *Gems of Deportment and Hints of Etiquette* (Chicago: Tyler and Co., 1881), 410.

[14]See Barbara Dodd Hillerman, "The Evolution of American 'Widow's Weeds' 1865-1965, A Study in Social History," unpublished master's thesis (Univ. of Maryland, 1972).

[15]Mrs. John Sherwood, *Manners and Social Usage* (New York: Harper & Bros., 1884), 130.

[16]Sherwood, 128.

[17]Sherwood, 130.

[18]Nehemiah Adams, *Agnes and the Key to her Little Coffin* (Boston: S.K. Whipple & Co., 1857), 135.

[19]Sarah Josepha Hale, *Manners, or, Happy Homes and Good Society All the Year Round* (Boston: J.E. Tilton and Co., 1868), 19-20.

[20]Mrs. M.F. Armstrong, *On Habits and Manners* (Hampton, Va.: Normal School Press, 1888), 53.

[21]Robert Tomes, *The Bazar Book of Decorum* (New York: Harper & Bros., 1870), 268-269.

[22]See Ann Douglas, "Heaven Our Home: Consolation Literature in the Northern United States, 1830-1880," in David Stannard, ed. *Death in America* (Philadelphia: Univ. of Pennsylvania Press, 1974), 49-68.

[23]Sherwood, 125.

[24]See Ann Douglas, *The Feminization of American Culture* (New York: Knopf, 1977).

[25]Adams, 15.

[26]Aries, Chapter IV, "Forbidden Death," 85-107.

[27]Aries, 90.

[28]An exhibition, *"A TIME TO MOURN: Expressions of Grief in Nineteenth Century America",* accompanied by a comprehensive catalogue, was held at The Museums at Stony Brook, Stony Brook, New York, May 24, 1980—November 16, 1980. The exhibition then travelled to the Brandywine River Museum of the Brandywine Conservancy, Chadds Ford, Pennsylvania, where it was exhibited January 17, 1981—May 17, 1981. This article was written when very preliminary research had been carried out on the subject of nineteenth century mourning practices. Exhibition and catalogue were made possible by a generous grant from the National Endowment for the Humanities. The catalogue is available from The Museum Store, The Museums at Stony Brook, Stony Brook, New York 11790.

This essay will appear in *Journal of American Culture,* 3:4, Winter, 1980.

The Contemporary
American Funeral Ritual

Walter W. Whitaker III

WHEN SPEAKING OF the "Last Rite," we often compare it to the game of roulette: "round and round she goes and where she stops, nobody knows!" Death is that way, but the mores of the funeral ritual are apparent to all, even to the inane ethnic in the joke when he reads his first obituary column: "My gosh, they all died in alphabetical order!"

The organized ritual centering around death symbolically marks the end of another's time on the "living" plane, but more importantly it helps those of us who remain to organize our relationship with the deceased, to remember the deceased within a framework (both in time to come and during the bereavement period) which is representative for the time that we are aware, and also to celebrate the death with decorum. The unification of these factors within the ritual leads to a more subtle importance. Whenever a person dies, the survivors experience a vast amount of frustration, and as Freud suggests, that frustration will quite naturally lead to aggression, whether directed toward a higher god-like power which the bereaved suspects has let him or her down, or toward the people or earthly powers with which you must deal daily, or most prevalently aggression (in the form of guilt or withdrawal) directed toward oneself. Through brevity and propriety the funeral ritual becomes a basic way to channel this aggression effectively into an attitude which is both productive and supportive.

In dealing with what the funeral ritual does, it is first necessary to decide whether it is a ritual or merely an event of culmination. There is a number of criteria which a ritual must entail: it must be symbolic, repetitive, stereotypical and a complexly patterned event. Symbolically, the event celebrates the loss of an individual to his

316

community. The funeral is repetitive in that it is nearly identical wherever you may travel in the United States. In a survey of 8,227 American funeral directors, it was found that 94% of the funerals had both the viewing of the body and a graveside service.[1] The ritual specialists (the doctor, the funeral director and the spiritual leader) enhance the ritual stereotypically. The funeral ritual is also a complexly patterned event in that it has both secular and sacred aspects. For this study I have broken the pattern down into five distinct areas: the post death activities, the viewing of the body (the wake, for some ethnic groups), the religious ceremony,the graveside disposition and the post funeral socialization. These five segments do something that no one person can achieve for the survivors: they lend dignity to the deceased and help to reorganize the surivivors' existence.[2] This ultimate rite of passage for the deceased is also a rite of passage for the survivors and it culminates in a rite of unity for them.

Post Death Activities

The post death activities begin with the declaration by a responsible individual (pathologist, doctor or coroner) that a person has fulfilled the legal qualifications for being pronounced dead. The qualifications may vary from state to state, but it is at this point that the ritual specialists begin their task of helping the survivors.

The ritual specialists come from many professional areas in the community. They could be the doctor who was treating the patient (because of Americans' attempts to achieve immortality, approximately 40% of them die in the hospital[3]), the nurse who helps to fill out the forms, the coroner or the policeman who was at the scene of death (the second most popular way to make the transition, with approximately 23%, is by the way of accidents[4]), and most importantly, that American small businessman, the funeral director. These people have two things in common as ritual specialists: 1) they have had some sort of professional training in dealing with the survivors and 2) they must objectify the deceased for their own mental health.

The ritual is initiated by one of the ritual specialists in locating and notifying a responsible survivor. Unless other arrangements have been made (donation of the body to a medical center or the deceased is a member of a funeral society), the responsible survivor will contact a funeral director. The funeral director is selected in a number of ways. The director could have dealt with the family on a previous occasion, could have been recommended by a friend to the responsible survivor or he may have a monopoly in the community (25% of the 8,227 funeral directors surveyed in 1971 stated that they had the only funeral home in the community[5]). Because of the psychological factor of wanting to get over this initial hurdle of the ritual as quickly as possible, the responsible survivor will select the funeral director with little shopping around. Leroy Bowman suggests that "the family doesn't hire a funeral director to weep with it; it hires and wants a normal mind to guide and advise its abnormal minds in every . . . manner that it may show proper respect to its deceased according to customs and caste."[6]

The number of things which must be done in preparation of the viewing of the body does require a normal mind. At the initial contact with the funeral director, the responsible survivor must do a number of things. The first is to give the funeral director permission to obtain the body. After this permission is granted, the director and the survivor must prepare the death notice which will appear in the obituary column of the newspaper or elsewhere. The next step is most important and probably causes the most controversy concerning the funeral director: the responsible survivor must select a casket.

In the economic aspect of the funeral, it should be pointed out that the price of pick-up, embalming, cosmetics and the rental of the home and vehicles for the funeral is included in the purchase price of the casket. The reasoning behind this package is that the buyer does not see the preparation of the body but does see something tangible in the casket. For the buyer most of the funeral director's services are pretty intangible (maintenance of the vehicles and the funeral home, twenty-four hour availability, buying and stocking a wide economic range of caskets and, most importantly, his emotional support) and therefore the buyer does appreciate it when he or she receives something definitive, such as the casket or other tangible "extras." For instance, a funeral home in Pittsburgh supplies a briefcase which will hold the guest register, the documents which certify the individual's death and a large exterior pocket designed to hold the letters of condolence. Another relatively new practice has been initiated by one of the casket companies—they are presently offering to plant a memorial tree for anyone purchasing their casket.

After the selection of the casket, the funeral director must begin his work. He must retrieve the body and transport it to the preparation room of the funeral home. This room is reminiscent of the operating theatre in the hospital and it is here that the embalming process takes place. After washing the exterior of the body, the funeral director must "clean" the interior. The first step is Arterial Embalming. By a gentle, systematic pressure, a diluted embalming fluid and tint are forced into the veins and arteries to replace the blood. The embalming fluid partially restores a natural color to the body and will preserve the body long enough for it to be viewed. Therefore this portion of the process is primarily for cosmetic purposes. The body is not embalmed for preservation, as it was in ancient times; it is embalmed to give a representation of the person as he or she existed in life and for sanitation and disinfection. A study by Snell Laboratories concluded that microbial flora was reduced 99% within two hours of completion of the embalming process.[7]

The second part of the process has an exceptionally violent nature. In cavity embalming the Trocar is "stabbed" into each of the organs and through the conjunction of a vacuum apparatus the gases and fluids trapped in the organs are reduced and/or removed. These gases and fluids contain colon bacilli which are the primary source of decomposition. The fluids and gases are replaced by vaporous formaldehyde which enhances preservation and sanitation. The violence of the process helps the funeral director emotionally create an object from the once living body. By thus creating an object out of a former living human being he can remove himself from the human involvement and be less subjective. Therefore he can go on to be professionally supportive of the survivors.

Upon completion of the embalming process, the body is once again washed, and while the funeral director is waiting for the tissues to firm (firm tissues being a sign of preservation) he will cap the eyes so that they will not accidentally open. It is also necessary to close the mouth. There are several ways this can be accomplished but the end result for the funeral director is an image of restful repose. Before dressing the body the cosmetics will be applied and the hair done as required. Quite often the funeral director will not have known the deceased and will require a photograph to make the corpse look like himself/herself while alive.

After being dressed the body is placed in the casket and taken to the funeral home's viewing area. The director must then display the appropriate religious symbols for the deceased. He is also responsible for receiving the floral displays and their arrangement. This can quite often be a problem because the director does not know the true hierarchy within the family and could unintentionally slight someone by misplacing a floral arrangement.

At this point the funeral director's handiwork is ready for display.

The Viewing of the Deceased
The body is first seen by the responsible survivor before normal

viewing hours. This ritual has a two-fold purpose. The funeral director gets a final approval in case he has made a minor error (by parting the hair on the wrong side or neglecting to put a piece of jewelry on the body). It is also to lessen the shock of death. This initial viewing is the worst for the spouse, or someone else very close, because at this point it is impossible to deny the death. One of the widows interviewed by Robert Weiss stated that this initial viewing created a realization that the "loss suddenly became almost unbearable." Weiss found that 52% of the widows he talked to felt that this viewing of the body was a negative experience.[8] There is an anomalous reaction which funeral directors dread. The spouse sometimes will attempt to crawl into the casket to be close to the loved one. The funeral director has no way to anticipate this action because it is quite common for the spouse (and other close family members) to approach the coffin and touch the deceased or even give the corpse a kiss. This touching and kissing is also a way for the bereaved to realize that the body is dead because the temperature of the corpse will be at that of the room rather than the normal 98.6 degrees. This viewing also helps the spouse, or other close persons, to prepare to deal with the visitors.

These series of shocks and realizations quite often lead to the return of that other ritual specialist, the family doctor. He is the source of medication and pertinent information. At this time the widow[9] develops an almost morbid interest in the why of her husband's death, while the widower will not ask such questions of the doctor.[10]

After the proper explanations and medications have been given, the responsible survivor is faced with the viewing hours during which the friends and family will come to the funeral home to pay their last respects. This tradition is historically based and serves a useful purpose. For example, invariably a new king could not take the throne until he had displayed the late king to the subjects. This was proof that he was actually dead and the next in line to the throne was not trying to usurp authority. Two separate studies[11] have demonstrated that the survivors generally do not approve of closed casket funerals and they are uncomfortable when the body of the deceased is not available for any of several reasons; undoubtedly this accounts for the great efforts expended in trying to recover the bodies of people in unusual accidents.

The practice is, further, an American political statement. In our striving for equality (even though individual funerals are by no means equal) and our rejection of even the faintest hint of any kind of caste system, Americans feel that every one of us, from president to pauper, has the right to a *proper* burial. This democratic urge is undoubtedly one of the reasons that the funeral ritual is relatively standard across the United States.

One of the standards of this common funeral ritual is the brief viewing hours. They are normally for a couple of hours in the afternoon and couple of hours in the evening for two days (Jewish tradition is an exception in that it has only one day for viewing the body). These short viewing times are beneficial to all the survivors.

The viewings are normally quite solemn and the visitors dress up out of respect for the deceased. They are there for three reasons. They want to share their love for the deceased with the responsible survivor. They wish to display the importance of the survivor to the community (Weiss suggests that the visitor's status reflects the status of the deceased and the more important the visitor, the better the widow will feel[12]). And most importantly, they wish to express a continuation of affection for the responsible survivor.

This continued affection is normally expressed in the action of reorganizing the memories of the deceased. This organization is probably the most important facet of this portion of the ritual. Each survivor in attendance will probably have many memories of the deceased, and there is something of a compulsion to share them with the other survivors. The survivors are justifying their presence and also channeling the aggression into a supportive and positive reaction to the death. This compulsion usually proceeds to a point where, even in their grief, the survivors will begin to tell humorous anecdotes. This is not a negative reaction but actually a comfort to the other survivors because the levity is an attempt to balance the grief.[13]

It can be seen that viewing the body accomplishes two things: it establishes the reality of death and brings the mourners together.

The Religious Ceremony
The religious ceremony in the funeral ritual entails the most variety because man has attempted to make his peace with God in many various ways. It can vary in type (Catholic, Protestant, Jewish, or other), place (the funeral home, the cemetery chapel or any church) and spiritual leader (priest, clergyman, rabbi, or other religious leader, or layman). Even with all the different options there are many similarities to the ceremony itself. It would seem to follow that the decrease in religious commitment would also be reflected in a changed funeral ritual too. But in actuality fewer than 2% of the funerals conducted in the United States have neither a public nor a private religious service.[14]

The major differences lie basically in performance and organization. The Catholic Church has laid down specific rules which the priest must and will follow explicitly. The Protestant clergyman or the layman is free to follow the procedure of his or her choice (I was told by one funeral director that once you know a clergyman's routine it will not vary unless the family specifically requests it). Judaism requires that a *minyan* (ten adult Jewish males) say the *Kaddish* (the mourning prayer) during *shivah* (the seven days of mourning following a person's death); other religious creeds have their own particularities. The particularities do not have as much importance in the American funeral as the similarities.

The basic factors for any of the morning services is that they follow a formal and solemn format which is a relatively short time period of approximately thirty minutes. The sacredness which is involved is obvious. The meeting place is most usually somewhere reserved for reverence (even when the funeral home is used for the chapel, it has the trappings of the church, such as pulpit, font or other sacred icons) and the officiating spiritual leader has somehow gained the respect of his community in being capable of representing some higher power. The formally attired survivors are arranged backward from the closed casket which dominates the front of the meeting place. Their seating order, radiating from front to back, reflects their closeness to the deceased when he was alive.

This same order will be reflected in the funeral procession whether it leaves from the funeral home or the church. By following this procedure the survivors have done their best to insure the deceased a place with the higher power which they have agreed to revere for the time being. In ranking themselves behind the casket, they have also agreed, symbolically, that they too will follow the deceased in their good time.

The Graveside Disposition

The graveside disposition actually begins with the funeral procession beginning at the church or the funeral home. This last ride for the deceased marks the beginning of the end of the formal portion of the funeral ritual. It is the final step in which the deceased is the central figure. The ride is slow, somber and dignified as befits respect for the dead. The cars arrive at the cemetery with their little flags fluttering, marking that they are part of the procession (actually the flags are for the police escort so that no one will get lost) which honors the deceased.

Upon arrival at the gravesite, everyone gathers around in the same order that was held at the church and in the procession to witness the pall bearers bringing the casket to the gravesite. When the casket has been positioned among the flowers, if there are any, a short prayer is said by the spiritual leader and a eulogy by him or by a close friend or family member is intoned followed by the benediction by the spiritual leader.

Almost without warning the formalities are over and each survivor is thrown back into the chaos of having to live his or her life without the deceased. Grief is not complete and many survivors are not satisfied with the outcome but the formal portion of the funeral ritual is complete. It is easy to parallel the graveside brevity to the brevity of the whole process.[15] The bereaved are now on their own and are no longer attended to by any of the ritual specialists.

The Post Funeral Socialization

The formal funeral is complete but the survivors, wary of being alone with their grief, must have one last step to make the ritual complete: the post funeral socialization. This portion of the funeral ritual is for the survivors and their return to the reality of *living* life. It is a throwback to the days before the science of embalming restricted the care of the dead to the funeral home. The home of the deceased was the focal point of the funeral ritual. This socialization permitted then, and still permits, the survivors to restore "life" to the home of the deceased and it also was a deliberately relaxed period as distinguished to the formal structure of the early parts of the ritual. The activity of re-organization that was found in the earlier portion of the ritual when the body was being viewed continues here within a different sort of framework.

The ritual and its welcome disorganization begins in the cemetery when the survivors disband and go to their cars to separate and then later draw back together at the post-funeral socialization for self and community. The survivors will generally return home momentarily to change from their formal attire and to get their contribution for the communal feeding that will be served at the home of the deceased. There might be a second socialization by the peers of a young deceased. This is normally done because they are not as close to the family as they are to the deceased. Of course many people attend both socializations, therefore uniting the two groups of mourners. The necessity of the two inheres in the necessity of the socialization requiring a sense of comfort for all attendees.

Some of these implements of comfort are the relaxed attire, the freedom to go to the place of socialization at one's own choice of time, the permissiveness of eating as much as one chooses, and, most important, generally the presence of alcohol. Even in households which do not maintain a liquor cabinet or permit drinking under normal circumstances, one will find an abundance of liquor, which will be used for both its positive and negative aspects. It will be a relaxant and will symbolically celebrate life, as is found in communion. It is also used in its capacity as a depressant. Alcohol, by its very nature, can help to bring a true grief and a moribund nature to the surface. The combination of these two effects helps the survivors to release tension which has been suppressed over the events of the last few days.

This suppression is also released through humor. For some reason the release of anguish surfaces as hilarity,[16] though this hilarity is probably closer to hysteria.

Between the condiments and the place of socialization two things happen: the survivors achieve a renewed sense of community and a personal re-organization of their memories and a sense of how they can go on living without the deceased.

Conclusion

It is easy to see that the funeral ritual is structured for use in a number of aspects. The first and foremost is, of course, its capacity for enabling us to handle our grief. Norman Linzer breaks grief down to four major areas: need, value, structure and role.[17] The funeral ritual satisfies all these aspects. The need is in that it rechannels our psychological aggressions and frustrations. The value lies in the fact that the funeral ritual is successful in what it does. The structure is in the idea that the whole community understands and accepts the ritual. The roles are fulfilled by the ritual specialists and the mourners, each "knows the duties which they are to perform. Therefore the funeral ritual explores *and* satisfies our own personal fear of death."

Another aspect is that it brings us back to our popular, daily entertainments, making them very familiar and therefore comforting and satisfying. Consider the common formula that entertainment (television drama and comedy and most films) shares. The situation is set up; a conflict occurs; there is a climax and a resolution. The portions of the funeral ritual follow this "formulaic" pattern. The post-death activities set the situation; the viewing of the body is the secular conflict which parallels the sacred conflict of the religious ceremony; the graveside disposition can be considered the climax of the event, and the post-funeral socialization forces the individual to resolve the death for himself or herself and the community.

If we combine the psychological aspects of grief and the sociological familiarities it is found that the funeral ritual serves two purposes. It provides a comfort for the deceased (who wants to die "alone") and it resolves a portion of the guilt of the survivors. This resolution is for the individual and the community.

This generalization of the ritual does not deny the individuality of any funeral, but its purpose is to provide a systematic framework which is both recognizable and comforting as a sum total.

Notes

[1]Vanderlyn Pine, *Caretaker of the Dead: The American Funeral Director* (New York: Irvington, Inc. 1975), pp. 201-03.

[2]It should be noted that my concentration is on the individual rather than the equally important economic and theological aspects.

[3]Herman Feifel, ed., *New Meanings of Death* (New York: McGraw-Hill, 1977), p. 234.

[4]Ibid., p. 236.

[5]Pine, p. 192.

[6]Leroy Bowman, *The American Funeral: A Study in Guilt, Extravagance and Sublimity* (Washington: Public Affairs Press, 1959), p. 32.

[7]*Embalming: Ancient Art/Modern Science* (U.S.A.: The Embalming Chemical Manufacturers Assoc. n.d.) p. 12.

[8]Robert S. Weiss, Ira O. Glick and C. Murray, *The First Year of Bereavement* (New York: John Wiley, 1974), pp. 108-11.

[9]Ibid., p. 112.   [10]Ibid., pp. 204-06.

[11]Richard A. Kalish and David K. Reynolds, *Death and Ethnicity: A Psychocultural Study* (Los Angeles: Univ. of Southern Calif. Press, 1976). Paul C. Rosenblatt, R. Patricia Walsh and Douglas A. Jackson, *Grief and Mourning in Cross Cultural Perspective* (U.S.A.: H.R.A.F. Press, 1976).

[12]Weiss, p. 115.

[13]Elizabeth Kubler-Ross, *Questions and Answers on Death and Dying* (New York: MacMillan Co., 1974), pp. 154-163.

[14]Pine, p. 205.

[15]It may be interesting to note that weather will dictate how quickly the survivors disperse. In cold or wet weather they will be out of the cemetery within fifteen minutes. On a balmy summer day they will take up to forty-five minutes.

[16]Bowman, p. 6.

[17]Norman Linzer, ed. *Understanding Grief and Bereavement* (USA: Yeshiva Univ. Press, 1977), pp. 245-46.

Consumption as Ritual
in the High Technology Society

David E. Wright and Robert E. Snow

VISITORS TO THE United States, especially those from Third World and Eastern Block countries, are struck by the ubiquity of advertising in America. In 1980 the U.S. will spend about fifty billion advertising dollars on print, radio, and television insuring that each of us experiences through the media a virtually continuous exhortation to consume. Particularly on television, these advertisements appear as ritual microdramas of American life. For example, one current commercial depicts a young family on a tour of a cave. Suddenly, the guide turns her flashlight on the husband and decries his "ring around the collar." The wife is mortified. There follows a quick transition from this public humiliation to a laundry room scene where the reassured wife examines a clean shirt and endorses the detergent which has restored her self-esteem.

Another commercial depicts a monk being admonished by his superior to copy a huge number of manuscripts in an impossibly short time. Using a photocopying machine, however, the brother completes his task and satisfies his superior who proclaims, "it's a miracle." In yet another commercial the viewer witnesses a young businesswoman emerging from a large office building. As she approaches the camera, the narrator says, "you know you're strong, you know you're independent, but [the product] will make him remember you're a woman." She applies the perfume then hugs the handsome man who awaits her.

These commercial dramas are the most widely shared experience in our culture spanning differences in geography, social status, age, educational background, and political ideology to bind us together in a giant "consumption community."[1] They keep constantly before us images of the good life and the proper behavior to achieve it. In fact, as one studies these commercials singly and collectively, one begins to see that they portray nothing less than the transformation of the individual through consumption. The use of the product instantly allays personal fears and gratifies fantasies. For example, in the first commercial the wife's deepest fears, symbolized by the cave and by dirt, are resolved by a detergent. The monk is freed from slavish toil and wins respect through his photocopier. And the businesswoman can resolve her anxiety about success through perfume which makes her sexy as well as powerful.

The ritual quest of the everyconsumer reveals the metaphysics of our high technological society. We believe that progress and individual completion—long the twin goals of Western civilization—are achieved through the consumption of goods and services. Many of us would deny that we, personally, hold such a belief, but most of us behave as if we do. We labor to consume, and we consume in excess of need in order to feel successful, powerful, sexual, or just adequate. Our culture requires that we feel and act this way. As Vance Packard has written:[2]

Our enormously productive economy demands that we make consumption our way of life, that we convert the buying and use of goods into rituals, that we seek spiritual satisfactions, our ego satisfactions, in consumption.

To make explicit what Packard implies: there are synergystic bonds between the metaphysics, ritual, social structure, and technology of a viable society.[3] As they interact, these elements create a "cultural style," or, in Western society what should be called a "technological style"—"technological" because technology *and* our faith in its effectiveness have shaped our civilization more than any other factors.[4] Each component of a "technological style" is important, but rituals of consumption are critical to the maintenance of the high technology consumer society which emerged early in the twentieth century. It was born when growth and even stability could only be achieved through extranecessitous consumption, that is, with consumption that was no longer equated with personal survival, or even comfort, but with fantasy. From then on consumption had to be mystified and made obligatory. Modern advertising appeared at that historical juncture.

Since then progress and consumption have been paired as the metaphysics and essential ritual of high technology society.[5,6] Consumption is the *essential* ritual because it is the major avenue through which metaphysical and techno-economic commitments are joined and made manifest in social life.[7] Ritual does this by providing metaphorical codes which, like dramatic scripts, direct both psychic and social acts and therein unite belief and practice.[8]

On a personal level these metaphorical codes direct the transformation of the participant from an extant to a hoped-for condition.[9] To achieve such a transformation, the participant must accept as literally true the metaphysics embodied in the code. With rituals of consumption, as with other rituals, these transformations metaphorically move the everyconsumer along the dominant axes of human experience—from outsider to insider, from bondage to extrication, and from defilement to cleansing.[10] The final goal of the consumer's quest is, of course, to achieve that state of grace which Tom Wolfe has called "The Life."[11] If cultures run on alternating rhythms of commitment and release (e.g. work/leisure), then "The Life" is vicarious and effortless commitment paired with ecstatic and perpetual release.[12] Of course, we never achieve "The Life," or at most, achieve it only momentarily before even more consumption is needed to keep it from slipping away from us. So the ritual repeats itself endlessly as it must to support high technology society. And we consumers in pursuit of "The Life" must say with Jay Gatsby, "It eluded us then, but that's no matter—tomorrow we will run faster, stretch out our arms farther...And one fine morning"[13]

The power of a ritual to effect belief and practice depends in large measure on how thoroughly the participants have internalized its central or root metaphors, the transforming agents (or "active ingredients") of rituals. In short, metaphor translates metaphysics into action through ritual, transforming through perceptual and social control. This raises two questions which we want to discuss before returning to the examination of television commercials as rituals of consumption. These are: How do metaphors accomplish perceptual and social control? And, what are the root metaphors of high technology society embodied in rituals of consumption?

Put briefly, metaphor may be understood as the product of the psycholinguistic process of equating the apparently dissimilar This occurs through the identification of the metaphor's two components, the tenor and the vehicle, both of which are images. "To use a metaphor is to overlap [these] images" so that "our sense of both is subtly altered, by a sort of elision."[14] When a successful metaphor acts on us, we come quickly to take it literally, and it changes from "figurative language" to myth.[15] That is, we internalize the metaphorical identifications as literally true. Root metaphors (i.e. the Aristotelian "the world is organism" versus the Cartesian "the world is mechanism") are the foundations of world views and determine the kinds of problems we will notice and the kinds of answers that will suggest themselves to us. In this way, metaphors filter, transform, and organize our perception of reality.[16]

Metaphor also functions as a social control. Rituals involve metaphorical strategies which, through the process of identification and internalization, transform the individual from a weak outsider to an accepted, often powerful, member of the community.[17] He achieves this transformation only by submitting to the beliefs and behaviors stipulated by the ritual.

The root metaphor on which our rituals of consumption are based is the same one that undergirds technological civilization as a whole. It is the Promethean, "man becomes god through technology." This complex metaphor became compelling when two subsidiary metaphors merged: one bonding machines and god, and the other bonding man and machine.

The machine-god part of the metaphor originates at least in nascent form in Aeschylus.[18] The instrument by which man may ultimately achieve divinity must be perceived as awesome in its own right. This idea has gained ground steadily in our times. For instance, in the eight decades since Henry Adams stood awed in the "great hall of dynamos" at the Paris Exposition, his intuition that technology has become a "symbol of infinity...a moral force, much as the early Christians felt the Cross..." has seemed increasingly compelling for many.[19] In contrast with the conventional historical analysis that the centuries since the scientific and industrial revolutions have witnessed a process of inexorable secularization, the work of Mumford, Ellul, Harvey Cox, Peter Berger and others has focused attention on what we call the metaphysics of the technological society.[20] Rather than losing faith, we have reinvested our religious energies in a reified and deified technology. As Adams concluded:

Before the end, one began to pray to it; inherited instinct taught the natural expressions of man before silent and infinite force. Among the thousand symbols of ultimate energy, the dynamo was not so human as some, but it was the most expressive.

The ubiquity of the god-machine metaphor today is visible in a sampling of science fiction films. Whether benevolent, demonic, or ambivalent, the gods depicted in *Close Encounters of the Third Kind, Star Trek (the Movie), The Black Hole,* and *Collossus: The Forbin Project* are all machines.

The man-machine part of the metaphor seems to have begun with the scientific revolution of the 16th and 17th centuries. In the latter there developed "a lively interest in comparing men and machines and in making life-sized mechanical replicas of people."[21] The mechanical metaphor found initial exposition with Descartes and was refined by Hobbes, Voltaire, d'Alembert, Spinoza, and La Mettrie.[22] It is ubiquitous in modern culture. The universe, society, the human body, and nearly all human functions are frequently described in mechanistic terms—the universe as clock, the pendulum of history, the frontier as safety valve, the heart as pump, the knee as hinge, intercourse as screwing. More recently and subtly, and probably more powerfully, the cybernetic system has replaced the simple machine in the man-machine metaphor. The power of this metaphor, which subsumes both organism and mechanism, is evident in the way we think and speak of ourselves as giving "input" and "feedback," of working in different "modalities," producing "units of service," and being measured in fractions of "full-time equivalents." Manfred Stanley considers the social control implicit in the cybernetic metaphor in his provocative book, *The Technological Conscience*.[23] In a chapter titled "Social Cybernetics: Subjugation by Metaphor?" he observes:

We find in a wide diversity of specific institutional settings certain tendencies converging toward a common, cybernetically relevant mode of policy and decision vocabulary. These tendencies include the reduction of decision strategies to cost-accounting systems; the transformation of values into quantifiable social indicators; the codification of ends into legislated and measurable accountability criteria; the computerization of centrally stored information banks; and the encapsulation of social life into simulated models of experience...we must examine the implications of whatever superordinate vision gives [these tendencies] their teleological coherence. That vision is the pantechnicist model of cybernetics. The concept of realtiy as consisting of cybernetically self-regulating natural systems, adaptive (or calibrated to be adaptive) to their environment, generates a vision of policy design as a potential branch of natural law. In an atmosphere of anxiety and crisis, cybernetics could become the metaphysics of a precarious society driven by the need for total societal regulation.

Not only are people and society conceived in terms of technology, but increasingly technologies of all kinds are anthropomorphized. A robot declared itself a candidate for president in 1980 claiming that "since many of the most famous politicians are robots" his campaign was not unusual.[24] And in fact, with popular heroes like the Bionic Man and the Incredible Hulk (created by technical miracle and laboratory accident respectively), with the controversy over the potentials of genetic engineering, and with the promise of creative computer intelligence, images of men and machines increasingly merge in our society.

The psychological process which gave birth and power to man-machine-god metaphors is analogous to the one Joseph Campbell describes as operating in primitive peoples:[25]

For the primitive hunting peoples of those remotest human milleniums when the sabertooth tiger, the mammoth and the lesser presences of the animal kingdom were the primary manifestation of the alien—the source at once of danger and of sustenance—the great human problem was to become linked psychologically to the task of sharing the wilderness with these beings. An unconscious identification took place, and this was finally rendered conscious in the half-human, half-animal figures of the totem-ancestors.... Through acts of literal imitation...an effective annihilation of the human ego was accomplished and society achieved a cohesive organization.

Marshall McLuhan, David Edge, and others argue that something like this process continues today. Now, however, we identify with technology rather than animals in our attempts to master the "industrial ecosystem."[26]

The complementary cultural traditions that have joined the man-machine and machine-god metaphors in the Promethean, "man becomes god through technology," are discussed by Edward Ballard in his recent *Man and Technology*. Western culture has always seen the self as potential, he argues.[27] While the Greeks saw self-completion as humanly achievable through rational discipline, the Christian view is that man's incompleteness can only be salvaged by "the other." In a curious combination of the two traditions technology has become the emblem of both rational self-completion and of the mystical "other."

The godhood we have achieved in our high technology society is, of course, paradoxical. We have powers and wealth the Greek gods would have envied. But we seem to have achieved these powers through a narrowing and rigidifying of human belief and practice. We must think and act in ways that keep the consumer society going. As workers, we must be ever more productive and efficient; as consumers we must be perpetually dissatisfied with what we have, but perpetually hopeful that with the purchase of our next car, home, or pair of shoes, we will achieve "The Life."

In the light of increasing amounts of leisure time for contemporary workers, judged by historical standards, and of the blossoming of so many diverse subcultures and lifestyles in America, one might argue that we are hardly being narrowed and rigidified. Anything seems to go. But the wonder of high technology capitalism is the chameleon illusion of cultural pluralism created around its rigid dictum: be productive and buy. It has no ideology save its own maintenance. Therefore, it can be eclectic, even omnivorous. It engorges any ideology, any social movement, and excretes it as a consumer product. The sexual revolution and the counterculture of the 1960s, the feminist and environmental movements of the late '60s and '70s, growing interest in voluntary simplicity, the current alternative technology movement, and many others have been co-opted. That many of these are highly critical of the high technology society makes no difference. Sex, anti-authoritarianism, the new woman, pollution reform, and solar energy have all found their way into commercials as saleable commodities.

After years of development, the thirty-second television commercial has become a remarkably sophisticated form of entertainment and persuasion, usually more carefully written and produced than any television special. Each second of commercial air-time may represent literally thousands of dollars of production effort. Of course commercials vary greatly in strategy, content, and quality. But if they are analyzed from the perspective of the ways in which they reflect the metaphysical commitments of our high technology society, most television commercials fall into one of four major genres: cornucopian display, celebrity sales, persuasion by authority, and microdramas of consumption.

The simplest of these genres, cornucopian display, is the straight forward presentation of a product or service. Little more than an animated newspaper ad, these advertisements dominate the media efforts of local businesses, but they are also used by national and international corporations to advertise sales at their local stores or franchises. Often the goods offered for sale are piled up or brought together in great profusion. Beneath the appeal to buy a certain product or to shop at a particular store, the underlying message is that the way to a good life is through the retail cornucopia of material things.

The next two genres, celebrity sales and persuasion by authority, are closely related. More complex metaphorically than cornucopian display, one relies upon our desire to gain access to "The Life," while the other trades on the prestige of science and technology. Celebrities are highly visible symbols who seem to demonstrate that, at least for some, "The Life" has been attained. When Joe Dimaggio—showcased in a luxury apartment—demonstrates with quiet dignity the virtues of a Mr. Coffee brand coffee maker, the connections linking Joe Dimaggio's good life, our striving to achieve "The Life," and ownership of a "Mr. Coffee" seem to hover just beneath the level of conscious awareness. If it works for Joe, it should work for me! The possession of such a product provides tangible evidence for all to see that the owner has a piece of "The Life"—however modest that piece may be.

Commercials utilizing a strategy of persuasion by authority attempt to capitalize upon the diffuse sense of awe which, until recently, surrounded anyone who invoked the prestige of science and technology. Typically they present an authority figure—usually male and anonymous and sometimes dressed in a white laboratory coat—who urges us to buy a product on the basis of a logically specious assertion or a simplistic demonstration. A recent example is the commercial which claims "only Comet has chlorinal, so nothing cleans and disinfects bathroooms better." Despite the very tenuous connection of such commericals to genuine science and technology, this genre draws its power from an appeal to a fundamental conviction of the high technology society—the good life is founded upon the discoveries of science and technology. Even pseudo-scientific evidence, especially when it is presented in commercials where there is little opportunity to think carefully about the claims, provides strong support for a product.

But, by far the most important of these genres is ritual microdrama. Deftly interweaving plot, narration, and theme, microdramas create a special kind of fiction which often literally depicts the transformations which the other three only imply. By repeatedly portraying consumption in action, they invite us to internalize the metaphors which structure both a sense of self and social reality appropriate to the high technology consumption society. To illustrate more clearly how this occurs, two of the many microdramas which might have been examined will be described and analyzed in some detail.

Microdrama One: A couple is spending a quiet evening at home on a stormy night. In the center foreground the husband relaxes in a reclining chair watching television. In the background over to one side his wife is quietly reading a book. Suddenly the television picture breaks up and the husband, mumbling incoherently, struggles to his feet in frustration. Then the action freezes as the narrator interjects, "Before you go out in that storm to get it fixed—wait—make your first step with your fingers in the Yellow Pages." The picture shifts to a hand and finger moving across Yellow Page ads for dry cleaners, a florist, pizza, and T.V. repair. The scene shifts again focusing on the hands of a repairman making the final adjustments to the television picture as the man of the house exclaims enthusiastically, "Now that's what I call service." As the repairman turns toward the husband, once again relaxing in his recliner, the front door bursts open and in come three delivery men bringing pizza, flowers for the wife, and dry-cleaned garments. In the climactic, final scene, the excited and animated wife with her flowers and four gesturing "servants" summoned by the phone are grouped around the "master."

A service (Yellow Pages) and a machine (telephone) have transformed a frustrated, incoherent, and seemingly powerless male into the center of admiring attention. Virtually in an instant a cheerful repairman summoned out of the night has finished his work, a necessary errand has been completed (the dry-cleaning), and with the arrival of pizza and flowers the stage has been set for a party. The simple and seemingly magical act of walking through the Yellow Pages relieves stress, brings husband and wife together for celebration, and allows the wielder of that great power to regain control of his small universe.

Microdrama Two: An attractive and energetic young woman is coaching what appears to be a Little League baseball team. Animated, assertive, warm, and enthusiastic, she is shown leading the boys in calesthenics, instructing a batter, encouraging a base runner, arguing with a middle aged and overweight male umpire, and sharing with the kids the excitement of victory when the deciding run crosses home plate. She is an ideal woman who is rightfully prideful and confident. As the fast-packed action unfolds (19 different scenes in 30 seconds), first a chorus presents the theme of the story... "You're feeling good about yourself... and it shows." Then an association between feeling good and drinking diet Pepsi Cola is made. A male announcer claims,

You're feeling good about yourself. You're drinking Diet Pepsi Cola with just one calorie and the great Pepsi taste. And it shows in the way you look, the way you feel, and in everything you do. Diet Pepsi, one small calorie—one great taste.

Somehow the ideal woman of the '80s—competent, confident, challenging male authority, succeeding in a traditional male role, yet still supporting and encouraging and helping children—seems to owe not only the way she looks and feels, but also her performance in every aspect of life to drinking Diet Pepsi. The commercial ends with a split-screen picture. On the left is a can of Pepsi next to a full glass while on the right is a close-up of the young woman—triumphant in victory with her head thrown back and her arm raised in celebration. At the same time the chorus is singing the last emphatic note of,

> And you're drinking
> (one calorie)
> Diet Pepsi...
> And it shows!

A perfect example of "The Life" achieved—effortless commitment joined with estatic release.

We are convinced that these rituals of consumption are the essential rituals of the high technology society and that they impose perceptual and social controls in the same way that more thoroughly studied rituals do in traditional and primitive societies. Ours is a culture committed to the secular religion of progress. We believe that progress is achieved through perpetual economic and technological growth. To achieve this growth we absolutely must consume and aspire to consume ever increasing levels of goods and services. As Edwin Newman said in a 1978 television documentary, "I want It All Now," consumption is a patriotic duty for Americans.[28]

The rituals of consumption we have been discussing mystify this obligation. That is, through their metaphorical codes they promise that economic and technological growth will lead to the even more highly prized "human growth" which has become the holy grail of our times. They demonstrate this by depicting the everyconsumer being moved by consumption along the axes of human existence, achieving power, love, sexual gratification, and prestige. These rituals have been perfected through the years until they are by far the most refined and professionally produced information carried by our media. And we are subjected to them with a regularity and intensity that visitors from other cultures find awe-inspiring. No big-brother totalitarian state ever purveyed its propaganda with anything like the sophistication and frequency of commercial advertising.

From its birth at the beginning of the century until today our high technology society, undergirded by its essential rituals of consumption, has been remarkably successful. We have capitalized on our abundant natural resources and the opportunities that history has cast before us to create an incredibly wealthy society. If our society is "me"-oriented, it's because we have the leisure to contemplate the self—not just a few aristocrats, but most of us. Further, our wealth has allowed us to achieve some measure of social progress, bringing many people into the mainstream of American life in a manner that would be much more difficult in a poorer society. In this light some of the paradoxical promises embodied in rituals of consumption have been kept.

Other paradoxes of the high technology consumption society are more problematical and perhaps threaten its destruction. On a personal level, for example, rituals of consumption offer us freedom of all kinds, yet they impose rigid behaviors and beliefs. Most cruel is that we are forbidden to be satisfied with our lot. For the society to work, we must want more. On a social level, the creed of growth where everyone is promised at least a little more is often a substitute for social responsibility. It invites us to ignore huge disparities in the distribution of wealth that would stand out in high relief and perhaps be redressed in another kind of society. Moreover, we have been so successful in exporting the images associated with our rituals of consumption, that we have created a revolution of expectations all over the world. Since we have built much of our wealth on the economic exploitation of less developed countries whose resources we need for continued growth, this revolution is a threatening development. On the level of energy, natural resources, and pollution there may be real limits to growth. If and when we reach those limits, our society will be in for a painful adjustment since it has been dedicated to the proposition that there are no limits. Finally, the high technology consumer society's omnivorous ideology and rituals of consumption make it very difficult to consider alternative futures. Critical movements of all kinds have been co-opted, defused, and transformed into saleable products. On occasion they have effected substantial changes in some areas of society, but they have never successfully challenged the basic commitments to growth and consumption. If we come hard up against any of these potential psychological, social, or environmental problems with our basic commitments yet unchanged, our society will not prove very flexible. Either technological fixes will be found so that our primary cultural business can proceed as usual, or we will experience a radical restructuring of American life.

Notes

[1]The phrase is Daniel Boorstin's in *The Americans: The Democratic Experience* (New York, 1973), pp. 89-166.

[2]Vance Packard, *The Wastemakers* (New York, 1960), p. 25.

[3]On the complex question of the relation of ritual to mythic or religious belief (i.e. metaphysics) see G.S. Kirk, *Myth: Its Meaning and Functions in Ancient and Other Cultures* (Berkeley, 1970), pp. 12-31.

[4]See D. Wright and R. Snow, "The Battle of Technological Styles in America: A Brief History and Analysis, *Journal of American Culture,* 3:3 (Fall 1980), forthcoming; and R. Snow and D. Wright, "Analyzing Symbolic Dimensions of Technological Disputes (Pt. II, Methodological Techniques for the Study of Science, Technology and Human Values," *Science, Technology, and Human Values,* 5:29 (Fall 1979), 15-19.

[5]"Metaphysics" is used throughout to indicate the fundamental ontology and teleology of a culture.

[6]For the purpose of this essay ritual is defined as "rule-governed activity of a symbolic character which draws the attention of its participants to [and molds their behavior in accordance with] objects of thought and feeling which they hold to be of special significance." This definition is Steven Lukes in "Political Ritual and Social Integration," *Sociology,* 9:2 (May 1975), 289-308, save for the clause in brackets which we have added. Lukes points out that his definition is consistent with Turner's view of ritual in *The Ritual Process* (London, 1969) and in *Dramas, Fields, and Metaphors* (Ithaca, 1974).

[7]By "essential ritual" we mean those that are crucial to the functioning of a cultural or technological style. There are other treatments of the term, for instance, Robert E. Knittel's "Essential and Nonessential Ritual in Programs of Planned Chance," *Human Organization,* 33:4 (Winter 1974), 394-397.

[8]The idea of ritual code as a dramatic script is taken from Frederick Bird, "The Contemporary Ritual Milieu," elsewhere in this volume.

[9]Writing from an anthropological perspective, James W. Fernandez provides a stimulating discussion of the function of metaphorical codes in "Persuasions and Performances: Of the Beast in Every Body . . . and the Metaphors of Everyman," *Daedalus,* 101:1 (Winter 1972), 39-60. See also Levi-Straus, *The Savage Mind* (London, 1962) on ritualistic mediation of the extant and hoped-for.

[10]See Harvey Cox, "The Virgin and The Dynamo Revisited," *Soundings,* 44:2 (Summer 1971), 125-146. Cox credits Paul Ricoeur for the idea of axes.

[11]See Wolfe's *The Pump-House Gang* (New York, 1968).

[12]The commitment/release rhythm of culture is discussed by Phillip Rieff, *The Triumph of the Therapeutic: The Uses of Faith After Freud* (New York, 1966).

[13]F. Scott Fitzgerald, *The Great Gatsby* (New York, 1925), p. 182.

[14]David O. Edge, "Technological Metaphor," in *Meaning and Control,* ed. D.O. Edge and J.O. Wolfe, (London, 1973), p. 33.

[15]The significance of the transformation of metaphor from figurative language to literal truth is discussed in David O. Edge, "Technological Metaphor and Social Control," *New Literary History,* 6:1 (Autumn 1974), 135-147.

[16]Max Black, *Models and Metaphors* (Ithaca, 1962) provides a seminal discussion of the epistemological role of metaphor in science.

[17]This is a major theme in the article by Fernandez cited in note 9.

[18]Aeschylus, *Prometheus Bound* (470 B.C.). See Robert Nisbet's *The History of The Idea of Progress* (New York, 1980) for a discussion of Aeschylus as an early expositor of faith in human progress.

[19]Henry Adams, *The Education of Henry Adams* (New York, 1931), p. 380.

[20]Lewis Mumford, *The Myth of The Machine* (New York, Vol. 1, 1967; Vol. 2, 1970); Jacques Ellul, *The Technological Society*, trans. of *La Technique* (New York, 1964); Harvey Cox, op. cit.; Peter Berger, *Pyramids of Sacrifice* (New York, 1975).

[21]Cox, 138.

[22]Floyd Matson, *The Broken Image* (New York, 1964), Chap. 1, "The Mechanization of Man," pp. 3-29.

[23]Manfred Stanley, *The Technological Conscience* (New York, 1978), pp. 136-137.

[24]The robot was interviewed on National Public Radio's *All Things Considered*, early December, 1979.

[25]Joseph Campbell's *Hero With a Thousand Faces*, quoted in Marshall McLuhan's *The Mechanical Bride* (Boston, 1951), p. 33.

[26]This phrase is Sheldon Novik's. See "The Electric Power Industry," *Environment*, 17:8.

[27]Edward G. Ballard, *Man and Technology: Toward The Measurement of a Culture* (Pittsburgh, 1978), pp.36-40.

[28]Edwin Newman, "I Want It All Now," NBC, 20 July 1978.

Ritual and the Humanities "Intellectual"

or

Reclassifying the Classics

Ray B. Browne

IN THINKING ABOUT the classics the 20th century "intellectual" is faced with a basic contradiction. We are pushed and pulled by rituals and our reactions against them, by an acknowledged need to participate in rituals but with a strong desire to discount their power over us in our secular age. We tend to insist that even if rituals—which are often equated with folk beliefs and practices, with the unsophisticated mass society—are important to most people, we as intellectuals are above such practices and strong enough to resist the resulting behavior. Ralph Waldo Emerson's *The American Scholar* is one of our touchstones, but unlike Emerson, who had the courage of his seeming or real inconsistencies, most of us would rather be suspected of harboring hobgoblins, in Emerson's term, than of being inconsistent or false to our teaching.

In our compulsion to be intellectually consistent, everyday we constantly perform the basic rituals of our vocation and what is to a large degree our self-delusion. We assert that we are the most openminded of all individuals—we are the cream of society—always ready for new ideas, eager to seek new points of view and new evidence, always examining the subjects to discover if we are properly reading the "truth" (our avowed goal) and are teaching it in the most effective ways; our curricula committees in colleges and universities burn thousands of hours every year seeking the proper study of their fields. Usually they find that there is not much wrong with what they have been doing and the way they have been doing it. Perhaps a slight change in subject matter is needed here and there—a slight updating—and a somewhat different emphasis in spots but nothing radically wrong.

This ritual of self-examination and self-congratulation if not recognized for what it is can be restricting and destructive. Many so-called "intellectuals," to be sure, do experiment and seize new ideas and methods. Perhaps most often the people most willing to change are those in the sciences rather than in the arts, and probably because they have fewer vested interests to protect than do those of us in the humanities; they have fewer "classics" which by definition to most of us demand unquestionable loyalty.

Many of us who profess the classics—the "great" works in themselves or in a survey—have a rigid frame of reference and fixed interests. We often think that the arts are so rich in "elite" and valuable materials, in those that have been handed down to us traditionally, that the canon has been pretty much formalized, with the classics, however we define the term, taking up most of our time. We rationalize our search for the esthetically satisfying, for the "profound" works by saying that one does not have time to deal with everything so why bother with the less consequential, with those that have not yet been "proven" to be of merit. We rely on the sieve method of evaluation. We wait until time has tested the product, has sifted out the chaff, and then we assume that what is left is valuable and constitutes the "classic."

In sticking with these classics we are assisted by a whole bureaucracy of timidity and inertia. We rationalize our attitude by thinking that we inherit the greatness of the past—that we are somehow the vestal virgins keeping the sacred flames of the humanities alive.

But this is a real and potentially dangerous point of view. For example there seems to be something inherently mistaken in the attitude stated by Joel Connaroe, Executive Director of the Modern Language Association in the March, 1980, Editor's column of the *Publication of the Modern Language Association*: "In humanistic scholarship [which I assume would include the classics], as in any cultural tradition worth preserving, the inheritors of the past—today's leading teachers and critics—seek the satisfaction of knowing that their work will be carried on and improved upon by a younger generation they themselves have nurtured. The mission of educators deserving the name, Coleridge said, is 'keeping alive the past in the present for the future'." Obviously Prof. Connaroe thinks he is writing for his constituency. The Modern Language Association has in fact made great strides in modernizing members' thinking in the last two decades. But apparently it is difficult to teach an old academic a whole repertoire of new tricks, for Connaroe's is a peculiar statement for one of the avant-garde.

There are countless other quotes one could use to back up Coleridge and Cannoroe. For example, one noted 19th century writer said "The true University of these days is a collection of books."[1] And another averred that "A good book is the best of friends, the same today and forever."[2] No doubt such attitudes are useful as far as they go. But a much more useful statement is Emerson's "'Tis the good reader that makes the good book." In using historical quotes to "prove" something one must be careful to remember the time and context in which they were uttered; and then for them to be of value to us they must be updated. Thus the first of the two quotes above should be modernized to read, "The true University of these days is a Collection of Books which is supplemented by practice and experience." The second quote should then read, "A properly inquisitive mind is the best of friends and tools, useful today and even more useful tomorrow." Coleridge should be modified to indicate that we are more interested in creating the new, in training the *mind* for the present and the future than merely reliving the past. Even Emerson's words would be more reassuring if he had said "'Tis the critical mind that makes the good book."

In truth we must ask ourselves and face the answer no matter how it goes against our grain: How many classics would be read today—and *are* read today—if they were not forcefed? The answer is very few. Heretical as it sounds to many, the loss of the classics might not be an unmitigated evil. To paraphrase the historian George Santayana's dictum: If we forget the classics we will be obligated to remake them! In the making we would be forced to exert our greatest efforts, and the resulting intellectual and artistic stretch would be helpful to us and to society.

Such an attitude in fact would be very useful in blowing the cobwebs from the mind of many academics. We frequently are taught and insist on learning the wrong things. We do not learn an openmindedness, a searching attitude toward new discoveries, not just confirmation of the already-discovered. Instead we learn a set of attitudes and methodologies—and a corpus of material—which we are most reluctant to change. Taking a metaphor from the development of this country, we are much more likely to be settlers than pioneers, second generation people on the land rather than Daniel Boones. Often we assume that all the frontiers have been discovered and pacified, that our role then is to develop the areas already settled. Unlike Boone, we love to smell the smoke of similar opinions arising around us. We throw up all kinds of intellectual dust with seemingly potential rich fall-out to result, but as that dust settles it is often more arid than fruitful. In our feeling of security in the familiar, there are too few of us like the late Associate Justice of the Supreme Court William O. Douglas, who prided himself on not searching for precedents—the usual attitude of the legal mind—but in *creating* them. Most of us in fact hide behind precedents as though they were military tanks insuring us safety as we push old ideas against a new world.

We thus become the latest generation in a long line of "intellectuals" who overly limit our interests and fields of inquiry. We learn the classics, and we tend to teach them, spending our time bringing more light on the old subject. The concept of the classic to the average intellectual means those books and objects which have generally been accepted through time as those which tell us about the generalities of life, about the humanities, about human nature, that will humanize us. We thus have a ten-foot shelf of these worthies: Homer, Virgil, Dante, Shakespeare, Mozart, Raphael, Michelangelo, Beethoven, etc., etc. The conventional wisdom is that these works teach us about ourselves. We therefore go through the ritual of self perpetuation in a kind of Catch 22 situation. These are the classics which teach us about ourselves, and they teach us about ourselves because they are the classics. Generally, they constitute the needed canon. We make the motion of examining that canon regularly but we usually come back to the conclusion that those that have always been accepted are the worthiest.

But even those seem to be failing us, or fooling us these days. According to William Arrowsmith, professor of classics at Johns Hopkins University, "We still don't possess a first-rate translation" of Plato. If this is correct, the fact boggles the imagination. Even if we do not agree with Arrowsmith on this point we might well concur that American scholarship is "suffering from an arrogant provincialism," as he feels, by neglecting the literature of other countries and other times. At least some of us would insist that our greatest arrogance comes from our neglecting the literature that is right at our own front door—our own popular classics. If as Arrowsmith believes, "Translation is the foreign policy of literature,"[3] then broadening the base of the classics is the heartbeat of democracy.

Yet everyone knows how difficult it is for new material to be admitted into the academic and "intellectual" inner sanctum. We "intellectuals" have limited peripheral vision in the business of christening new classics. One trouble is chronology. Everyone is acquainted with the Old English scholar who will say, with half a smile but with obvious conviction, that there has been nothing written since Beowulf that is worth studying; the Shakespearean who says with a straight face that after the Elizabethan age all drama and literature has gone downhill. In the first decades of this century American literature was bitterly resisted at Harvard and other schools, American Studies was belittled in the 1930s and still is in many schools (Berkeley, for example). Folklore has lived a borderline existence for well over a hundred years. Ethnic and women's studies—often following political winds—are approved or disapproved depending on local enthusiasms. Cambridge University appointed its first sociologist to the faculty in 1969, with the skeptical understanding that if he did not prove his worth the position would be eliminated. If you ask the Chairs of many schools of art and music why modern art and music are not being taught in their colleges and universities, you will be burned with the classic put-down: "Is there such a thing?"

One area that is pushing hard for what the participants call the "New Humanities" and the "New Classics" is Popular Culture. In the last ten years academic study of popular culture has grown from perhaps a hundred thousand students a year to something more than a million, from almost blind and rampaging opposition on several counts to all degrees of acceptance.[4] In the study of popular culture all scholars try to take the wide and democratic approach, believing that the intellectual should be interested in all aspects of the culture around him or her.

With Dr. Johnson we believe that no aspect of life is too insignificant to be accorded its time before the bar of evaluation. With us not all deserve the same length or intensity of scrutiny; some are obviously meritorious and some ephemeral. But we believe in the openminded approach. We do not want to automatically condescend to Martin Tupper as being a poetaster beneath contempt, just as we feel we must read and understand Tennyson though he may not appeal to us. We do not despise Queen Victoria's literary efforts in *Leaves From a Journal of Our Life in the Highlands, 1848-61* (1867-68), to cite merely one more example, but rather treat the book as a revealing statement of the mind and attitude of a most influential English queen. Every item has its potential service. In discovering the *new* classics and reclassifying the old, nobody wants to do away with any that are still useful. But we are interested in supplementing the conventional classics and in seeing that they pull their own live—not dead—weight. This means that the notion of what constitutes the classics should be reexamined and modified.

Although surely some intellectuals still hold to the notion that a classic must be ancient or old, nearly all of us open the doors to modernity to a certain extent by defining the classic somewhat in Matthew Arnold's terms as the greatest "universal" thoughts which have been most powerfully expressed, preferably of somewhat long standing, and presumably "elite." Those who advocate the Reclassified Classics would modify those criteria somewhat. They believe that the winds of democracy are blowing so strongly that such criteria, exposed and perhaps anachronistic as they are, cannot long withstand those winds, nor should. To such minds a more realistic definition is limited to something like *outstanding, strong, unusual, memorable, the strongest* in the class, in a kind of *consensus favorite.*

Under such criteria the ten-foot shelf housing the consensus classics must be stretched a hundred-fold. Thus Cotton Mather's sermons become classics of religious bigotry and intensity. The stocks that were used to punish and humiliate the Puritans in old New England were classic forms of punishment. The widow walks that topped the houses of sailors' wives were classic statements of loneliness and resignation. The magnificent horses that pulled the wagons from Philadelphia to Pittsburgh along the original Pennsylvania Turnpike were classics, as were the wagons they pulled, especially after they got to the wide open West and became Prairie Schooners. The 19th century China Clipper was a classic, as was the magnificent Mississippi River boat, as was the Buffalo Bill Circus that entertained people of all kinds.

We have the classic political statements: Marie Antoinette's "Let 'em eat cake," surely one of the most unforgettable, and Thomas Paine's "These are the times that try men's souls," a classic of somewhat different nature. We have the classic photograph of the classic egg-head politician—Adlai Stevenson with the hole in the sole of his shoe. The classic Camelot—Jack Kennedy and family in the White House. The classic political faux pas—George Romney admitting that he had been "brainwashed."

There are classics in comics—as well as Classic Comics: Senator Claghorn, Li'l Abner and Daisy Mae; Little Orphan Annie and Daddy Warbucks; Krazy Kat; Thimble Theatre; Donald Duck; Flash Gordon and *Doonesbury*, which many people regard as the current political microcosm of America.

We have the classic television shows—The Mary Tyler Moore Show and M*A*S*H—and many classics of less strength and value—*Dallas* and *Vegas*, for example.

In the classic statement of questionable taste in statuary we have the electric lamp in the form of a nude female with a clock in her belly button.

We have the greatest classic of all times in fashion—jeans; classic race horses and horse races; automobile races and drivers; classic statements of man's fortitude and courage in solo acts (Lindbergh's flight over the Atlantic); the classic statement of power and mobility in the old railroad engines and trains; the classic automobiles (Duesenberg, Model-T, Edsel and Volkswagen Beatle); the classic nose (Durante's, Hope's, Cyrano de Bergerac's and Pinocchio's)

We have the classic pornographic movie (*Deep Throat*), and scores or hundreds of other classics (Chaplin's, Bogart's, Dietrich's, Monroe's, *The Birth of a Nation, The Wizard of Oz, Shane*). We have the classic singing cowboy (Gene Autry), the classic gunfighter (Palance in *Shane* and Peck in *The Gun Fighter*), the classic dancer (Astaire and Kelly), the classic dances—in *Swan Lake* and *Oklahoma.*

American culture has the classic contest between man and machine in the songs about John Henry the black "steel-drivin' man" who broke his heart trying to beat technology; and the classic error in the logging business in Paul Bunyan's Round River Drive, in which Paul and his loggers made the mistake of trying to float their logs out of the woods and down to the mill only to find that they were not advancing because the river was round and only brought them back where they had been before; and the classic folksong about the westering spirit in this country in "Sweet Betsy From Pike," who "crossed the wide desert with her lover, Ike."

We have the classic athlete in Jesse Owens, who won four gold medals in the 1936 Olympics in Berlin, flying in the very face of Hitler and his philosophy of the superior Aryan race.

We have the classic poster, featuring the nude body of Marilyn Monroe, and the classic movie poster advertising Howard Hughes' movie *The Outlaw* (1943) featuring Jane Russell's low-cut blouse and the provocative and unforgettable question, "How would you like to tussle with Russell?" Both pictures were of course sexist. But most classics are sexist and racist into the bargain.

Contrary to the usual definition, classics do not have to be universal or even appealing to or understood by large groups, but only to a segment—sometimes a very small segment—of a population, for a small in-group, even a family. For example, we have the classic buffalo jump in the West (the sharp cliff over which Indians drove buffalo in order to kill them for food and hides), the classic lover's leap (the local romantic spot imbued with the legends that heartsick Indian maidens threw themselves off when they became despondent about the absence of their lovers off at war), the classic baseball card (some of which because of their scarcity or featuring of some particular individual or characteristic are worth up to $1000. in 1980). And post cards and stamps among collectors. For example, a postcard with a stamp called the Running Chicken dated 1870 sold in 1979 for a quarter million dollars.

On the more general scale, classic self-help books and heroes abound. Dale Carnegie's *How to Stop Worrying and Start Living* (1944), and Norman Vincent Peale's *Power of Positive Thinking* are both excellent examples. Another is the 97 pound weakling Charles Atlas, who had perhaps more classic impact on the self-help movement than anybody else in developing into the prototypical he-man.

In music and among musicians we have hundreds or thousands of classics. Country music's *Great Speckled Bird* and *Wabash Cannon Ball*, to cite only two. Vincent Youmans' *Tea for Two*, Hoagy Carmichael's *Stardust*, Irving Berlin's *Over There* and *White Christmas*, John Philip Sousa's *Stars and Stripes Forever*, Elvis Presley's *Hound Dog* and *Love Me Tender*, the Beatles' *Hey Jude, Sgt. Pepper* and *Yesterday,* the first million copy record to shatter the standard format of 8-bar unit repeated with variations are excellent examples. Among singers there are hundreds—Bing Crosby, Frank Sinatra, Peggy Lee, Ethel Merman, Judy Garland. Among swing bands, country bands, rock bands there are scores.

In the printed word, there are many examples: most of the issues of *Black Mask* magazine and the 1912 *All-Story* containing the first appearance of Edgar Rice Burroughs' Tarzan, which has become perhaps one of the half dozen most pervasive creations of all times throughout the world.

In literature many works have become classics, sometimes through the front door and sometimes through the back. There are, for example, the classic detective authors: Agatha Christie, Dorothy Sayers, and the improved classics, the so-called "hard-boiled school": Raymond Chandler, Dashiell Hammett, Ross Macdonald,

John D. MacDonald. There are also the classic Westerns, of Zane Grey and *Shane*. And there are those that are far superior to Grey's—those of Louis L'Amour which in the summer of 1980 will reach the 100 millionth sales.

And there are dozens of other kinds of best sellers that grow out of all kinds of traditions, new and old. Suppose, for example, that you wanted a story that would put puny man against the monsters of the sea and at the same time develop a primordial theme about women and the basic selfishness of mankind. What kind of monster would you choose as your antagonist. Whales and marlins have been used; in fact the whale has been used several times. Then why not a giant squid or manta ray? Neither really looks or behaves the part. Then why not a giant shark, which has all the physical characteristics needed? And why not call the book *Jaws* instead of the name of the leading male character or the generic classification of the leading protagonist? Peter Benchley developed such a story and created a classic.

Suppose you wanted to take a group of southern business men in the 1970s and show how the male menopause affects them? How they had to get away from it all for a time, and what the ultimate result was? Would you choose the canyons of Atlanta's business district and would you name the book *Bartleby Revisited*? Or would you use the setting of the white water on a southern river and the towering walls bordering it, and call the book *Deliverance*? James Dickey's novel by that name has already been read by far more people than will ever read Herman Melville's story about Bartleby the Scrivener.

Many books get into the classic category whether they teach high-minded ideals, detestable social philosophy, or none at all. *Uncle Tom's Cabin* (1852) may or may not have started the Civil War (as Lincoln once said) and it may or may not have spoken out sufficiently against slavery, but it is a never-dying classic. So is *Gone With the Wind*, no matter how it overbeautifies the antebellum South. So, too, is Kyle Onstott's *Mandingo* (1957), with its glorification of slavery and miscegenation and its deplorable effect of setting the pattern for dozens of racist books that might, in fact, have fueled the fires of the Ku Klux Klan burning ever more brightly at the dawn of the 1980s.

Leslie Fiedler likes to tell about his being asked to explain the movie *Birth of a Nation* to a group of hardline leftwing communists and his surprise when they applauded the wrong sections, when the Klansmen ride in to attack the debased blacks who were raping the pure white maidens of the South. This was not a testimony to the propaganda, but to the art, a masterpiece of movie production despite the message it so powerfully presented.

One of the reasons for the conventional definition and use of the classic has been, of course, its stability. In a world of rapidly changing major works, especially when everything new has been hyped as colossal, the ultimate, the final when in fact it may be blown away the next day, it is understandable when the staid and conservative academic "intellectual" is somewhat bewildered and afraid he will get his hands burned if he touches the new. But the classical aspects are present in contemporary popular culture, and there are so many present-day classics that there is not room to accommodate them all and some must be replaced. But are these conditions peculiar to present-day America? Had there been our rapid way of life and communications in earlier times how many of those ancient classics would have burned out also? Who knows how many did not survive? How many Epics of Gilgamesh were there in the 2nd millenium B.C. that did not make it to the present time? How many Homers were there that could not get sung and published and dropped into the oblivion of history? We are constantly amazed at the quality of materials that in one way or another and for one reason or another get found these days. Examine the recent recordings of early English music, for example, which are more and more being discovered and reintroduced. How many songs like the unmatched English folksong *Greensleeves* remain to be discovered between the 15th century and today?

The number of "discoveries" constantly being made in all fields is legion. A recent one is that of German photographer August Sander, who spent the years 1910-1933 "documenting" the entire range of German people—from the "lowest" to the "highest"—and thus trying to describe an entire nation, the people's bodies as well as their souls. Lost in Hitler's Germany, his works have now been rediscovered and are being exhibited at the Philadelphia Museum of Art, before being taken on tour, and in a book named *August Sander: Photographs of an Epoch.* According to *Newsweek*'s critic Douglas Davis (March 24, 1980, p. 63), Sander "composed his images with the eye of a Renaissance painter, striving after an arrangement of face, limb and body bordering on the classical. This is what makes his jut-jawed painter, his umbrella-sporting parliamentarian 'universal' in the best sense: they are trapped in the finality of high art."

In Davis' remarks we perhaps see the crux of the whole problem of the "intellectual" and the classic, the paradox that bends him or her into unusual and unflattering shapes of inconsistencies and of a contradiction of the Renaissance attitude that we claim we admire most in our artists and in ourselves but which we evidence so rarely. We want the "universal" so that the mirror we look into tells us about the whole world of existence. Yet we realize that the universal is found in the particular and the unglamorous and unbeautiful. The drop of water is a sea in everything but magnitude. Worst of all we insist that these universals of the classics be "trapped in the finality of *high* art." Why not just *art*? We err in assuming that there are two kinds of art with a great and unbridgeable chasm separating them. All art exists on a continuum, a flattened ellipsis. At one end are the greatest accomplishments, at the other the weakest. But the scale is horizontal, not vertical. And most of the works of classical proportions cluster toward the left quarter of their particular segment, with frequent overlaps. Sometimes there are worlds of difference in intent, in technique, in accomplishment in all kinds of art, even in the elite. The differences must be kept in mind. One cannot, for example, contend with any reason that Mozart's music is superior to Cole Porter's, Tchaikovski's to Jerome Kern's, that Shakespeare's plays are more appreciated in God's eyes than Neil Simon's, that Robert Frost's poem "Birches" is to be more appreciated than Joyce Kilmer's "Trees." Comparing the two sets is comparing apples and oranges, and are more matters of taste than of intrinsic value. There are fresh and firm apples, and there are rotten ones. There are the juiciest oranges, and there are many past their prime. It is a serious error in judgment not to keep the types separate and their own intentions in mind.

As long as the "intellectual" believes that there are forms of *high* and *low* art, of valuable and valueless classics we obviously need a reclassification not only of what constitutes a classic but also of what constitutes an "intellectual" and his or her role in present-day living.

Thomas Carlyle once said that "The great law of culture is: Let each become all that he was created capable of becoming." He might as well have extended the generalization to society and its creations. A culture needs to be invited and encouraged to produce its finest expressions, and all should be given the respect due them, free from any bias and stigma attached because of point of origin or medium of dissemination.

We "intellectuals" need to free ourselves from the knee-jerk ritualistic reaction to the overtones of bias and prejudice and more freely bend to the natural rhythm of a free and unencumbered mind and body. Until we do we are doing a disservice to the conventional classics as well as to all those which exist with the power and appeal natural to them as they strive to reach their proper place in the sun. It little becomes the "intellectual" to be victimized by his own process of thinking about ritual while unable to liberate himself from one of its most obvious manifestations.

Notes

[1]The author is of course Thomas Carlyle.

[2]The author is English poet Martin Tupper (1810-1889), author of innumerable poems and ballads on such topics as the Crimean War, emigration and public affairs, including *Proverbial Philosophy*.

[3]*Chronicle of Higher Education*, March 24, 1980.

[4]*Journal of Popular Culture*, XII:2, Fall, 1978, p. 202.